Songwriting For Dummies

Cheat Sheet

Music Industry Contacts

- The American Society of Composers, Authors, and Publishers (ASCAP): (212) 724-9064, www.ascap.com
- Broadcast Music, Inc. (BMI): (212) 586-2000, www.bmi.com
- National Academy of Recording Arts and Sciences (NARAS): (310) 392-3777, www.grammy.com
- Nashville Songwriters Association International: (615) 373-7872, www.nashvillesongwriters.com
- The Recording Industry Association of America (RIAA): (202) 775-0101, www.riaa.org
- SESAC (a performing rights organization): (615) 320-0055, www.sesac.com
- The Songwriters Guild of America (SGA): (201) 867-7603, www.songwriters.org
- U.S. Copyright Office: (202) 707-3000, www.loc.gov/copyright

Magazines to Check Out

- *Billboard Magazine:* www.billboard.com
- *R & R:* www.rronline.com
- *American Songwriter Magazine:* www.americansongwriter.com
- *The Gavin Report:* www.gavin.com
- *Rolling Stone Magazine:* www.rollingstone.com
- *Performing Songwriter Magazine:* www.performingsongwriter.com

For Dummies: Bestselling Book Series for Beginners

Songwriting For Dummies®

Useful Web Sites

- **101 Music Business Contracts:** www.order-yours-now.com
- **Association for Independent Music (AFIM):** www.afim.org
- **American Federation of Musicians (AFM):** www.afm.org
- **All Songwriters Network (ASN):** www.tiac.net/users/asn/index.htm
- **Billboard Musician's Guide to Touring and Promotion:** www.musiciansguide.com
- **Blues Foundation:** www.blues.org
- **Century Music Group:** www.centurymusicgroup.com
- **Country Music Association (CMA):** www.cmaworld.com
- **Gospel Music Association (GMA):** www.gospelmusic.org
- **International Bluegrass Music Association (IBMA):** www.ibma.org
- **It's Only Words:** http://itsonlywords.com
- **Jingle University:** www.jingleuniversity.com
- **Muse's Muse:** www.musesmuse.com
- **Musician's Atlas 2002:** www.musiciansatlas.com
- **Rhythm and Blues Foundation:** www.rhythm-n-blues.org
- **Singer Songwriters:** www.singersongwriter.ws
- **Songwriter's Market:** www.writersmarket.com
- **Songwriters Resource Network:** www.songwritersresourcenetwork.com
- **TAXI:** www.taxi.com
- **TONOS:** http://aol.tonos.com

For Dummies: Bestselling Book Series for Beginners

Songwriting FOR DUMMIES®

by Jim Peterik, Dave Austin, Mary Ellen Bickford

Foreword by Kenny Loggins

Wiley Publishing, Inc.

Songwriting For Dummies®

Published by
Wiley Publishing, Inc.
909 Third Avenue
New York, NY 10022
www.wiley.com

Copyright © 2002 by Wiley Publishing, Inc., Indianapolis, Indiana

Published simultaneously in Canada

For general information on our other products and services or to obtain technical support, please contact our Customer Care Department within the U.S. at 800-762-2974, outside the U.S. at 317-572-3993, or fax 317-572-4002.

Wiley also publishes its books in a variety of electronic formats. Some content that appears in print may not be available in electronic books.

Library of Congress Cataloging-in-Publication Data:

Library of Congress Control Number: 2002108102

ISBN: 0-7645-5404-2

Manufactured in the United States of America

10 9 8 7

1B/SQ/QY/QS/IN

Ⓦ Wiley Publishing, Inc. is a trademark of Wiley Publishing, Inc.

About the Authors

Jim Peterik has enjoyed a 35-year love affair with music, and it seems as though his journey is just beginning. He has written or co-written a memorable array of top-40 hits such as "Hold On Loosely," "Caught Up In You," and "Rocking Into The Night" with Southern-rock legends, 38 Special, "Heavy Metal" (theme to the award-winning animation of the same name), with Sammy Hagar, and with group co-founder Frankie Sullivan, wrote the entire catalogue for the group Survivor (of which Jim was a founding member) including smash hits like "High on You," "I Can't Hold Back," "Is This Love," "Burning Heart" (theme from *Rocky IV*), the #1 single "The Search Is Over," and the timeless ode to the fighting spirit — the triple-platinum, Grammy-winning, Oscar-nominated theme from *Rocky III* — "Eye of the Tiger." Other credits include songs with Henry Paul and Blackhawk, Marzette Griffith, Lynyrd Skynyrd, Anthony Gomes, Rick Ferrell, Cathy Richardson, Cook n Miller, Dennis DeYoung of Styx, Kevin Cronin and REO Speedwagon, Tony Orlando, The Doobie Brothers, Cheap Trick, Kelly Keagy of Night Ranger, Cinderella, Mecca, Van Zant, John Wetton, Kevin Chalfant, Brian Anders, Leslie Hunt, Kelly Moulik, Brooke Allison, Two Fold, and many others. Today, when not spending time with his wife of 30 years, Karen, and 12-year-old son, Colin, Jim is busy discovering and producing new talent and collaborating with a vast array of some of the world's best song-writers. He still plays regularly with The Ides Of March and performs with his World Stage superstar lineup for special events. In his solo "Storytellers" style concerts, he gets to tell the stories behind the songs he's written throughout the years. You can visit Jim at www.jimpeterik.com.

Dave Austin has written the critically acclaimed book, *The Unfinished Cross — Listen to the Voice Within,* published by Hampton Roads Publishing Company. He is also CEO of Transcension Music Group, a record company with a mission to bring positive music to the forefront of today's listening audience and bring together well-respected veterans in the music industry for a common cause of taking quality music to a higher level. Over the past 20 years, Dave, along with his good friend Phil Ehart (founding member of Kansas), has produced and promoted a series of all-star concerts with some of the greatest talent in the industry including: Carlos Santana, Melissa Etheridge, David Foster, The Commodores, Rush, REO Speedwagon, Kansas, Alan Parsons Project, Mr. Big, Survivor, Eddie Money, Queen, Loverboy, Peabo Bryson, Michael McDonald, James Ingram, Pablo Cruise, Ambrosia, Danger Danger, Micky Dolenz, Stephen Bishop, Paul Davis, Lou Graham, Micky Thomas, and America. His life's experiences include playing professional tennis and traveling the world while competing on the pro tour; acting in films, television and commercials; guest lecturing and speaking engagements on an international basis; as well as providing workshops and motivational coaching for professional and Olympic athletes. Dave lives in Camarillo, California, with his wife Cathy and four sons, Jason, Shane, Chase, and Daniel. You can visit Dave at www.daveaustin.org.

Mary Ellen Bickford has been involved in writing, film production, and music for over 20 years. As a writer, she has authored two books, *The Language of Light* (co-authored with Norman B. Miller), and *Eloquence,* a book of poetry. She has also written and co-written film scripts, treatments, and corporate publications. Her work in film production includes co-writing and producing a television show for UNICEF's International Day of Broadcasting and coordinating the filming of *Hands Across America* and the unveiling of the *Statue of Liberty Celebration* for Imax producer Greg MacGillivray. She also was the Director of Education for the noted Imax movie *The Living Sea.* Her work in music includes the co-production of seminars that use music, light, and color as mediums for healing and inspiration. Currently, Mary Ellen serves as an officer and board member for two nonprofit organizations: The DoveSong Foundation (providing education about positive music) and The Kids X-Pressions, Inc. (providing opportunities for the young at heart to express themselves freely through the media). Mary Ellen currently lives in Northern Georgia where she is developing a film script for an animated motion picture and co-writes songs with her husband, composer/musician Don Robertson. You may find out more about their work by visiting www.dovesong.com.

Dedication

We dedicate this book to the legacy of great songwriters through the years who have shared their inspirations and continue to enrich our lives, and to the songwriters of the future — may they inspire and motivate us all to make this world a better place.

This book is also dedicated to the late, great Cub Koda — rocker extraordinaire and co-writer of *Blues For Dummies*. You were taken from us much too soon, but your spirit and music will always live on. We know you're still smokin' in the boy's room.

Author's Acknowledgments

The authors would like to give their heartfelt thanks to the many, many people who made this book possible. First and foremost a special thank you goes to Cathy Austin, Chris Horn, and Don Robertson who gave their unending love and support to this project and who spent countless hours and incredible dedication to helping take this book to a higher note. Words cannot fully express our great appreciation to Kenny Loggins for the wisdom and insights he's brought to this book and for the gifts he continues to bring to this world. With special gratitude, we'd also like to acknowledge the special efforts of our acquisitions editor, Tracy Boggier, and our project editor, Linda Brandon, as well as Elizabeth Kuball, and P.J. Birosik, and music attorney, Lannie J. Cates for his wonderful expertise. Appreciation and gratitude also goes out to all of the songwriters and industry people who lent their words and wisdom to this project — we're especially glad to have you a part of this team effort, and to music attorney, Lannie Cetas for his words of expertise. Lastly, but certainly not least of all, we'd like to give a big thank you to Bill Gladstone and everyone at Waterside Productions for bringing this project to life in the first place.

From Jim: Personal thanks goes to my amazing family — Karen and Colin Peterik for sticking with me through the long process of writing this book — I truly could not have done it without your love and support; to my extended family, Alice Anne and all the McCabes, the Mouliks, the Verres the Kuras, and Tom and Diane Soares, for their support and constant inspiration. Thanks also to my late mother and dad — Alice and Jim who put the song in my heart and always seemed to put me and my music first. Accolades to my dear sister Janice who always brought me roses. Thanks also to Wiley publishing, especially Linda Brandon and Tracy Boggier for their belief in us. Thanks to my wonderful collaborators, Dave Austin and Mary Ellen Bickford, and to Don Robertson (your music comforts me). Also to Cathy Austin — thanks for your good taste and diligence. Special thanks to Bill Gladstone for helping to create this opportunity and putting this team together. I'd also like to acknowledge all the great songwriters who were nice enough to give me quotes and permissions. Extra special thanks to my brothers in The Ides Of March — you are the gift that keeps on giving. I'd like to thank my buddy Steve Salzman for his last-minute research as well as Mike Aquino for his invaluable input. Finally I'd like to thank that higher power that is always there inspiring me and giving me the perspective and accepting love I need. You are truly my favorite collaborator.

From Dave: Personal thanks goes to my hard-working wife Cathy, and to my four boys for putting up with us during this very hectic schedule — and to my entire extended family for allowing me the time and freedom to get it completed. Deep gratitude goes out to my fellow co-writers, Jim and Mary Ellen — without you this book would not have taken flight. Heartfelt gratitude goes to all those at TMG Music for carrying the extra load during my frequent absences, while meeting these publishing deadlines,to Brian Anders and Amy Isnor, our new artists who were understanding and patient while meeting these publishing deadlines, and to John Bigalow, who' has had to wait patiently for me to finish this project in order to continue our work together. And, as always, a very special and loving thank you goes directly to the higher sourceGod from which comes all inspiration — together we make a great team and I look forward to many more "works" to come.

From Mary Ellen: Personal thanks goes to goes to all the peopleeveryone who have that believed in me throughout the years: thank you mom, blessings to all of my brothers and sisters, especially my sister Cathy, my cousin Michael Perry, and to my loving and supportive husband Don. who stands beside me and guides me and supports my freedom and independence. Big hugs go to my faithful kids Paul (and his wife Elizabeth), Lorene, and Teresa (and her husband Mark) — who joyfully contributed priceless hours of secretarial assistance in sending out the letters for permission and organizing all the paperwork for the book. Thank youI am grateful for the endless support from my friends Don Roper, Wave, Geela, and John Maschino. Thanks for introducing me to Bill Gladstone, and to Jim, Dave, and Cathy for all that you have taught me. I thank all of the great songwriters of past and present whose songs have melted my heart and moved my emotions. Most importantly to our heavenly father above — otherwise I wouldn't be writing this thank you.

Publisher's Acknowledgments

We're proud of this book; please send us your comments through our Dummies online registration form located at www.dummies.com/register/.

Some of the people who helped bring this book to market include the following:

Acquisitions, Editorial, and Media Development

Project Editor: Linda Brandon

Acquisitions Editor: Tracy Boggier

Technical Editor: P.J. Birosik

Senior Permissions Editor: Carmen Krikorian

Editorial Manager: Christine Beck

Media Development Manager: Laura VanWinkle

Editorial Assistant: Carol Strickland

Cover Photos: © Getty Images

Production

Project Coordinator: Maridee Ennis

Layout and Graphics: Scott M. Bristol, Melanie DesJardins, LeAndra Johnson, Kristin McMullan, Jackie Nicholas, Brent Savage, Betty Schulte, Jeremey Unger, Mary J. Virgin

Proofreaders: Laura Albert, Andy Hollandbeck, Susan Moritz, Carl Pierce, TECHBOOKS Production Services

Indexer: TECHBOOKS Production Services

Special Help
Michelle Hacker

Publishing and Editorial for Consumer Dummies

Diane Graves Steele, Vice President and Publisher, Consumer Dummies

Joyce Pepple, Acquisitions Director, Consumer Dummies

Kristin A. Cocks, Product Development Director, Consumer Dummies

Michael Spring, Vice President and Publisher, Travel

Brice Gosnell, Publishing Director, Travel

Suzanne Jannetta, Editorial Director, Travel

Publishing for Technology Dummies

Andy Cummings, Acquisitions Director

Composition Services

Gerry Fahey, Executive Director of Production Services

Debbie Stailey, Director of Composition Services

Contents at a Glance

Cartoons at a Glance

By Rich Tennant

"Get me the ant spray, honey. My B-flat just became an F-sharp!"

page 311

"Hey George, give it a rest. Let's have lunch. I picked up some bluefish. Man, I love bluefish. Do you love bluefish, George?"

page 5

"I know every love song needs a hook, but couldn't it be something other than a duck-call?"

page 51

page 295

"Okay, one more time past the music publishers house, and then I resume the route, and you've back to 'Pop Goes the Weasel.'"

page 197

page 119

"Denise is a natural at helping me with the lyrics. She's been finishing my sentences for over 20 years anyway."

page 163

Cartoon Information:
Fax: 978-546-7747
E-Mail: richtennant@the5thwave.com
World Wide Web: www.the5thwave.com

Table of Contents

Foreword

*H*ow do you know if you are a songwriter? When does a person actually decide to be one? Looking back, my first clue was when I was only eight years old watching a movie called "Yankee Doodle Dandy." I still remember when George Cohan wrote a song to impress the musical star of the era, Mary. She was quite impressed, but more importantly, so was I. Actually, I couldn't sit still and remember saying to myself excitedly, "I can do that!" Before that moment, I'd never even thought of being a musician. It was as if some part of me was remembering itself, as if my soul was speaking to me.

A few years later, my brother decided that he'd write songs. I watched him struggle for weeks and couldn't help thinking to myself, "I can do that — and it's got to be *simpler* than that." I truly can't say where that inner message came from, or why one person feels he can write music and another thinks he can't. Songwriting is a way of expressing what's in the heart, mind, and soul. Some of us are just more inclined towards taking this road than others as a creative path. I assume that's why you're reading this book.

One of the first songs I learned on the guitar was the anti-war ballad, "Blowin' in the Wind," by a little-known, young songwriter named Bob Dylan. I was blown away. Learning his song that night literally changed my life. The first song I wrote was "Bringing It All Back Home," in honor of this writer that had started the creative juices flowing in me. Right behind Dylan came Lennon and McCartney onto my radar screen. Like so many songwriters of that era, my sense of harmony, melody, and lyric was hugely influenced by their work. Gradually, the more I wrote, the more refined my style became, and the more "me" showed up in my music. To this day, my songwriting continues to lean not only on my early influences, but on everything I've heard since. I think that's truly the nature of songwriting. One song leads to another. Music, just naturally, *influences itself.* We all "borrow" from each other, whether we know it or not. And yet, these influences create new music that become touchstones for the next generation.

When asked which one of my songs is my favorite, I always reply that it's like being asked to pick a favorite child. Yet I have to admit my early songs have an innocence about them that I find endearing. In those days, songs came from a less "crafted place" and more from the spontaneous "soul place." I didn't really know what I was doing technically, so I simply wrote what I felt. My "inner critic" was practically nonexistent, so I was free to create un-self-consciously, loving every note as a new gift. It was always a rush to stand back from a fresh creation and say to myself in surprise, "Did I just do THAT?"

Two of my best-known tunes, "Danny's Song" and "House at Pooh Corner," came from those innocent days as a senior in high school. And I still strive to write from that "feeling place" — where the music REALLY comes from — and shy away from the "thinking place" as best I can. My most effective stuff happens when my head gets out of my way and my heart takes over. As songwriters, we've found a way to spontaneously express ourselves from our hearts. We then learn the craft to become better at expressing that seemingly simple task. As such, it is a metaphor for how to live.

A couple of years back I was seriously considering retiring. One night before putting Luke to bed, I told my seven-year-old son that "Daddy has decided to retire." He asked, "What does that mean?" I said that means "I'm not going to sing for people anymore. I'm just going to stay home and we're going to play a lot more." To my surprise, instead of being happy, Luke started to cry and nothing I said would ease his tears. Finally, I had to leave the room so that my wife, Julia, could just hold him and calm him down. Luke at last whispered through his sobs, "If Daddy stops singing, he'll die." That was the most important wake-up call I've ever received. It felt as though God was talking right to me. I soon pulled the old notebook back out. Slowly, but unsurely, I got back in touch with my muse and onto solid emotional ground. I discovered that with the decision to write again came the biggest blessing of all: the awareness that I do what I do because I was born to, because I love it, because it keeps me alive and fills me with a sense of purpose. Songwriting is my survival.

If you are an aspiring songwriter reading this book for some cagey words of advice that might set you on the path to fame and fortune, I would smile and say one thing: be wary of following trends too closely. Do your best to write music that expresses who you are and what you feel at this exact moment of your life. Write with your heart. Remember, your goal is to be someone that people imitate, not one of the many who imitates. The authentic "you" is the reward you truly seek, and writing is your path home. It is the obstacle course you run to get to yourself. Enjoy.

Kenny Loggins

Multi-platinum singer/songwriter, winner of two Grammy Awards — Song of the Year for "What a Fool Believes" and Best Pop Vocal with "This Is It" — and recipient of an Academy Award Nomination for his first #1 single, "Footloose."

Introduction

Welcome to *Songwriting For Dummies*. If you're merely dog-earing through the pages right now at the local bookstore (looking for the fast track to writing a sure-fire hit), do yourself a favor and buy it. You'll thank us later! There's simply too much information packed into this baby to get a hold of in one sitting. If you've already purchased this book and are sitting down ready to discover the ins and outs of songwriting, congratulations! It's going to be a great ride. We think we're on the verge of a great songwriting revolution. What better time to be a part of this business? The record labels are once again looking for memorable, meaningful, and long-lasting songs for their artists — songs that make a difference — not disposable ditties (at least this is our reverent prayer). What you'll find in this book is a practical and lighthearted look at that impractical and unnecessarily serious subject of writing a song. We hope you get some encouragement and inspiration from our labor of love. We know that with a little work and dedication you can unleash the creativity inside you. Feel free to share it with a friend — who knows, he may be your own Bernie Taupin!

About This Book

This book was written to give you a hands-on, behind-the-scenes look at the noble pursuit of songwriting. It offers basic songwriting concepts, as well as shortcuts and slightly unconventional methods not necessarily found in other books. It's coming from authors who have "been there" and "done that" in all areas of the music business. This isn't for people who dream about writing a song, this is for those who are ready to dig in and try it. The book is also meant to be useful to the already up-and-running or successful writer who'd like to refocus his creativity or gain a little validation on what he's been doing right all along. The text of the book covers all aspects of the business and the pleasure of songwriting from the collection of ideas to the creation of a song, from creating a demo of your song to assembling a team for its marketing. It includes not only the nuts and bolts of constructing a song, but the spiritual or mystical side that gives it wings. It includes a Practice Makes Perfect section at the ends of Chapters 2-12 geared toward honing your songwriting skills that helps you take the first step in that area of songwriting. It includes the latest resources to go beyond the bindings of this book and explore the outer reaches of cyberspace and the inner reaches of your limitless imagination. Above all, it debunks the idea that you have to be a virtuoso on a particular instrument or that you need years of music theory and schoolin' to write a song. All you really need are ears, a good imagination, a lot of determination, and a (reasonably) organized procedure in order to make your bid at enhancing the world through music.

Foolish Assumptions

We're assuming that you are in some way curious about how a song gets written. Maybe you're wondering if you have what it takes to write a song. Perhaps you're looking for the next step in getting your song from your bookshelf to the shelves of the record stores. In any case, we don't assume that you're a musical genius or that you have astounding technique or any technique, for that matter, on a particular instrument. Our whole premise is that anyone can write a song with the right inspiration, methods, and collaborators. The genius in writing a song is your ability to bring all your skills into a common focus to create a verse and chorus that the world wants to hear.

How This Book Is Organized

This book is organized into six parts, which cover everything from writing lyrics to selling your songs.

Part I: So You Want to Write a Song

The first section of this book asks you to identify and assess your ambitions, prior experience, expectations, and preconceptions regarding songwriting. You'll take an inventory of the talents and skills you can bring to your own songwriting experience. This part also shows you how to capture song ideas so they can't escape and gives an introduction to song structure with a discussion on song forms.

Part II: Unleashing the Lyricist in You

This part is dedicated to channeling the "word power" and expressiveness within you into the lyrics of your next song. We give you some concrete tips for writing lyrics, including the definition of a hook and where to put it and how to use rhyme in your lyrics. We also show you the successful lyrics of many popular songs, telling you exactly what they did to achieve greatness.

Part III: Creating the Music

This part addresses how rhythm, chords, and melody come together to make a great song. All these ingredients are critical to a song's success — and we make sure you don't neglect any of them.

Part IV: Writing Songs in Different Styles

This part explores the vast smorgasbord of styles to choose from when writing and arranging your songs. You can write the next pop hit or try your hand at country or R&B. You can also write for many different types of arenas, such as the stage, screen, and television. The possibilities are virtually endless.

Part V: Getting Down to Business

In this part, we examine how the words *music* and *business* can shake hands and be friends. From finding out just who the business players are to filling out paperwork and from making a demo to networking, it's the part you must force yourself to read to assure your song is being properly looked after once it's created.

Part VI: The Part of Tens

In this section we review some of the great songs, songwriters, and songwriting teams, through history to the present.

Part VII: Appendixes

This part showcases three useful appendixes. We get you started in locating contracts, people, and companies in the music industry, and we also provide a glossary of terms you should be aware of.

Icons Used in This Book

For Dummies books are nothing if not user-friendly and fun. To this end, we have included various graphic icons in the left-hand margins of the pages. These clever little cartoons give you an immediate "heads up" to nuggets of truth you need right away, plus snacks you can choose to save for later.

This is a lesson we've learned in our decades of experience. It can be as crass as a shortcut to success, or as heady as a gateway to your soul.

This icon is the "Mother" of all icons. This is the reminder of what you should already know through reading this book. Fight the temptation to slam down the book and cry, "Give me some credit for brains, ma!"

This needlessly ominous icon is reserved mainly for blatant no-no's in either the creation of a song or with the business and legalities of songwriting.

This icon indicates yet another "pearl of wisdom" from our resident expert, Jim Peterik, of Ides Of March and Survivor fame. It's usually a practical and anecdotal inside look at the passion that has been fueling Jim for over 35 years of songwriting.

This icon, usually attached to the "Practice Makes Perfect" sections, indicates the motivational words and hands-on concepts of *For Dummies* team quarterback, Dave Austin.

This icon indicates a quotation from one of the top experts in the various areas of the music business that we have corralled just for you.

This icon indicates the "under our breath," down-and-dirty truth that you now have the dubious privilege of knowing. With whom you share these boardroom secrets is entirely up to you, but please, act responsibly!

Where to Go from Here

Please note that it's okay to skip around in this book. Although we had some crazy notion about a logical unfolding of information, truth be told, it works even if you throw all the chapters into a blender and hit "frappé."

Part I
So You Want to Write a Song

The 5th Wave   By Rich Tennant

"Hey George, give it a rest. Let's have lunch. I picked up some bluefish. Man, I love bluefish. Do you love bluefish, George?"

In this part . . .

We all have songs inside us just waiting to come out. The real key to songwriting is not only figuring out the combination to what unlocks that music within you, but also developing methods to capture these little gems of inspiration before they fly away. And like most gifts, there is some assembly required so it's vital to discover the what-goes-where of a song. This part of the book gives you everything needed to get started in your songwriting journey.

Chapter 1

Everything You Need to Write a Song

▶ ▶ ▶ ▶ ▶ ▶ ▶ ▶ ▶ ▶ ▶ ▶ ▶ ▶ ▶ ▶ ▶

In This Chapter

▶ Looking at what motivates people to write songs

▶ Examining the role of music in your life

▶ Finding out what it takes to write a song

▶ Taking your first six steps in songwriting

▶ ▶ ▶ ▶ ▶ ▶ ▶ ▶ ▶ ▶ ▶ ▶ ▶ ▶ ▶ ▶ ▶

Songs — the combination of music and words (or *lyrics*) — have the power to make people laugh, cry, or even scream out in protest. They cause people to pound on their steering wheels as they're driving down the road — button-down businesspeople are transformed into their favorite rockers during morning commutes. And thousands become pop divas in the privacy of their own shower stalls. Songs can transport you to a moment 30 years in the past, and some of the songs you enjoy today will stay with you for years to come.

Given the way songs can move and inspire people, you're not alone if you're interested in writing a few of your own. Maybe you've even come up with some lyrics, or thought of a melody, but you're just not sure where to take it from there. In this chapter, we guide you through all the facets of songwriting that you need to be aware of. Whether you're just starting out or you already have a few songs (or portions of songs) under your belt, you're at this book's beginning, and as Julie Andrews sang, that's "a very good place to start."

Understanding Why People Write Songs

People write songs for many reasons: to express their feelings, spark debate, inform their audience, push others to act. . . . There are probably as many reasons for writing songs as there are people who write them. Songs are often written by people who have a hard time verbalizing what's in their hearts — sometimes, pairing their feelings with music helps people say what they really feel. Others may write songs because they have a message to get across — a message that much of the world may not be quite ready to hear — and putting that message to music can help penetrate even the most shielded of ears.

You may want to write a song to:

- ✔ Express your true self in a song.
- ✔ Release the music inside of you that's just waiting to get out.
- ✔ Give back to your songwriting heroes some of the joy and inspiration they have given you.
- ✔ Develop the gift of expression you may have born with.
- ✔ Gain acceptance and make new friends.
- ✔ Earn a living at something you truly love!

Whatever your motive, the goal is the same:

- ✔ To come up with words and music from the inner reaches of your imagination.
- ✔ To connect with others through a song.
- ✔ To create something of lasting value.

Finding the Songwriter in You

Fortunately, the main requirements for writing a song are exactly the same, whether it's strictly for yourself and for your loved ones or for the music-buying public. The main ingredients are a passion for music, a need to express yourself in song, a mind receptive to the ideas that come floating your way, and a willingness to find and network with other talented individuals that can help you realize your musical vision. Ironically, many songwriters say that some of their biggest hits were never intended for mass exposure or written with success in mind. They were a personal expression of something in their hearts as a gift to themselves or for family, friends, and loved ones.

This book is for everyone that shares the dream of harnessing the songwriting power we all have within. You've come to the right place if your heart keeps tugging at you to write a song — but you're uncertain as to the process of the craft or what's required to create a really good one. You bought the right book if you're wondering how to collect and organize your ideas. You bought the right book if you have pieces of songs lying in notebooks and on countless cassettes but can't seem to put the pieces together. This book is for you if you have racks of finished song demos but don't know what to do next to get them heard. If you know the elements that make up a great song and how the pros go about writing one, you can get on the right path to creating one of your own. Our mission statement throughout this book is simple: Writing a song isn't rocket science, no matter what the music theory books would have you believe. Not that a little book learning isn't a great thing; it's just that complicated notions can stop you before you get started. Songwriting is about 80 percent inspiration, 10 percent perspiration, and 10 percent implementation. So let's not get it backwards. Hopefully we can take down some of the roadblocks to writing a song and get to the heart of the matter — cause that's where a song is born.

Being aware of your personal connection to songs

If you are compelled to be a songwriter, you've probably gotten a great deal of enjoyment from listening to songs over the years. When you think back on your life (whether you've lived 18 years or 80), how many songs come to mind when you think of important moments? Do certain songs bring to mind sights, sounds, smells, and emotions from the places you were when you first heard them? Have certain songs become your favorites because they express exactly what you hadn't been able to put into words yourself?

If you could easily compile a soundtrack to your life, full of all the songs you've loved over the years, you're off to a good start. If you would have trouble fitting that soundtrack onto one tape or CD, that's even better! Why? Because if your life has been greatly affected by the power of music, you're in the right position to affect others through the songs *you* write. (The rest of Part I starts you on the path to gathering ideas for lyrics and music and getting to know common song forms to put those pieces together.)

Taking a look at your instincts

If you feel a deep connection with certain special songs throughout your life, you can be pretty sure that you have the emotional capacity to express yourself in the context of a song. Besides having that appreciation for other people's songs, check out the following list to roughly determine your S.Q. (yeah, you guessed it, your "song quotient").

You just may be a songwriter if:

- You've ever sung a melody into your shower mic and started gyrating wildly when you realized it was a song that didn't yet exist.

- You often find yourself lost in the industrial section of an unfamiliar town when you realize that the great lyric ideas you've been jotting down have totally obscured that little road map your friend had scribbled down for you to get to her house.

✔ You create a gaper's block in the freezer section of the supermarket when you take your cassette player out of your bag and start chanting the hook of the new rap song you've created that documents the multiplicity of brands of frozen vegetables.

✔ You create a new angry lyric and shouted melody over the chord changes of "Muskrat Love" while performing Karaoke at the local club.

✔ You bring a flashlight to the cinema to jot down snippets of the latest movie's dialogue onto your popcorn box. (And pray that no other songwriters heard the same line.)

✔ On an airplane you check first for the barf bag, not because you're afraid you'll get airsick, but so you have something to write on when inspiration strikes.

✔ You visit friends and rudely spend most of the time in their 8-year-old son's bedroom, strumming some new chord changes on his toy ukulele.

✔ You start haunting every club for musicians to put your latest poem to music.

✔ On the street, you stop everyone in a black turtleneck sweater to see if they're a poet who could supply words for your music.

✔ Your hands are rubbed raw from pounding out rhythms on your desktop, laptop, dashboard, dog, or garbage can.

✔ You've just purchased your fourth copy of *Songwriting For Dummies* since you left the other copies at various round tables and writers' nights for three weeks running!

If you can identify any aspect of yourself in this inventory list, you may be on your way to writing a song. If you haven't already done any of these things, don't despair. You can still develop your instincts and try your hand at songwriting. Who knows? You just may unlock a part of you that you never even knew existed. (Parts II and III reveal the mysteries of writing lyrics and creating music.)

Starting at the Beginning —
Before You Write a Song

After you figure out why you want to write songs, and after you discover that you have what it takes to give it a shot, you're ready to dive in. But writing a song can be an intimidating process. After all, where do you begin?

Is formal music training a must?

Music training is not a prerequisite for songwriting. However, if you don't at least have some ability on the piano or guitar to help put the ideas in your head into some tangible form, you *may* be at a disadvantage. (Notice we said "may." Funnyman Mel Brooks composed the musical score to his hit Broadway show *The Producers* by humming the melodies into a tape recorder and having someone translate that into musical notes on a page.) Even if you're solely a lyricist (the one who puts the words to the music), it may be helpful to your collaborator (the person writing the music to go with your words) if you have a working knowledge of an instrument. Musical ability could also help you with the rhythm of your words and the structure of your songs. All of this musical expertise is advantageous, but not required.

Although songwriting is more than just an assembly line of components to be bolted together, it doesn't hurt to know what's available in the "parts bin." A song is made up of chords (a combination of two or more tones sounded together in harmony), melody (the arrangement of single tones in sequence — the part you sing), rhythm (the beat or pulse of the song), and words (often called *lyrics* in the context of a song). Many successful songwriters excel in one area or another. Rare individuals can do it all. Even the ones who are a songwriting "one stop" often choose to collaborate with others to come up with that magical song that comes from a blend of styles and personalities. It's your task at hand, if you are challenged in a given area, to find writers to complete your vision and supply the expertise you lack.

Most of what I know about songwriting, I learned by being a fan of music. Truly the best teacher is listening. I emulated the styles of songs that inspired me, and gradually, over the course of many years, integrated these influences into a style of my own. The Beatle's songwriting, to cite a notable example, was heavily influenced by the American rock 'n' roll of Chuck Berry, Carl Perkins, The Everly Brothers, and Little Richard. The Beatles created songs by absorbing those influences and adding their own unique personalities. The fact that they could barely read music hardly mattered. They had ears! Studying music theory, history, and arrangement can only enhance your abilities as a writer, but it would be a mistake to infer that formal training is a necessity to write a great song. Music appreciation classes can open your eyes and ears to what you should be listening for in songs, but you really don't need anyone to tell your foot when to start tapping or your lips to break out into a big smile when the chorus hits — that's just the power of great music. Start with your love for the songs you hear and then tap into all you have to express in your soul.

If you're still not convinced that you don't need training, consider the fact that some of the greatest songs ever written were composed by people with virtually no formal music training. Folk music, chants, delta blues, country, and rock 'n' roll all got their start with people who had the raw talent to create songs. On the other hand, many legendary composers have extensive musical training in all forms of music, including classical composition. Just don't let the so-called "rules" hold you back or keep you frozen.

In college, my harmony teacher told me at the end of the semester, "You know all that stuff I taught you about avoiding parallel fifths? Forget about it! If it sounds good, just do it!" By the way, that was the only formal music training I ever got, other than two years of piano and a few years of saxophone lessons. I earned a C+ in that class. It is my belief that life is the best teacher, and listening to and enjoying a good song are perhaps the best ways to learn to do it yourself.

Although some songwriters do well with the trial-and-error method, the more you know about music, the better your chances are to write a great song. The more adept you can become at an instrument, the easier it will be to create and demonstrate the ideas in your head. You do not need to enroll in a college course to study music. Instructions in music theory, composition, instrument performance, and voice are available at a per-session rate. Qualified, reasonably priced private teachers can be located through your local music shop or record store or in the back pages of the local "freebie" entertainment newspaper. Finding someone who inspires you will make songwriting a lot easier.

Being prepared when inspiration strikes

Ideas will come into your brain while you're in the strangest of places, at any time of the day or night. You've probably heard stories about how some of the greatest hits were born. Paul McCartney has said some of his best songs came to him in his dreams. Billy Joel got the song "River of Dreams" from — you guessed it — a dream. And Sting, former lead singer of the group The Police, awakened in the middle of the night, wrote a song in ten minutes, and went back to sleep. The song? "Every Breath You Take." (Makes you want to get plenty of shut-eye, doesn't it?)

Capturing that loving feeling

In a survey based on performances, sheet music, and record sales, *Variety,* the entertainment trade paper, once named the 100 most popular songs of all time. An analysis of the themes of those 100 titles showed that about 85 percent of them were love songs. Many of those blockbuster golden oldies are still generating new recordings after 50 years.

When a melody or a lyrical idea pops into your head, make sure you have a way of freezing it in time. Try to carry with you, at all times, a notebook to jot down ideas and a cassette recorder to capture your musical phrases. Never fool yourself into thinking you'll remember the ideas when you get home. And don't think that "If it's really so great of an idea, I won't forget it." Some great songs will never be heard because the songwriter couldn't reconstruct some once-in-a-lifetime moment of inspiration.

A flash of inspiration may hit you when you least expect it. Be ready to catch it — then be prepared to work hard at turning the initial idea into a finished song.

Finding inspiration within yourself

So you aren't being awakened in the middle of the night by divine inspiration? Not to worry. You can find inspiration even if it doesn't seem to find you. The unique way you look at the world and feel about things, the mood you project in life and all your emotions are unmistakably projected in your song. In other words, write about what you know and feel, and you're sure to come up with something unique (because even though you thought your mother was lame when she said it, there's only one you).

Some writers, through their melodies, chord progressions, and lyrics, project a powerful optimism. Others project wonder, a bittersweet sadness, or pure anger. But few songwriters can project all emotions within a single song or even on one CD — so don't pressure yourself to cram in every possible emotion all at once.

Whatever the mood, all great songs have the ability to move people, to make them *feel* something.

Psychologists say that songs can put us in touch with our feelings. We all know what it feels like to be happy, sad, afraid, or in love. Often, a song is what puts us in touch with emotions.

Expressing your authentic feelings in a song is not only therapeutic to you as a person, but it can also be the clay from which a lasting song can be sculpted. If your audience can see a little bit of themselves in your song, if they can identify directly with what you are saying, your song just may stay in their hearts and minds (and CD players) long after it has dropped off the *Billboard* charts. When there is an issue you feel passionate about, when you are swept away by some new fad or idea, whether you are moved to tears by a movie or the passing of a loved one, or when you've recently fallen in or out of love —

these are the subjects and feelings that will resonate in your song. Of all the songs I've written or co-written, the ones based on personal experience, like "Eye of the Tiger" (co-written with Frankie Sullivan; hasn't everyone felt at one time or another like the underdog trying to beat the odds), "Hold on Loosely" (co-written with Don Barnes and Jeff Carlisi; I based the lyric behind Don's title on some advice my future wife once gave me), and "The Search Is Over" (co-written with Frankie Sullivan; the idea of taking for granted what's most precious to you) became some of the most lasting hits. Our own experience is perhaps more universal than one thinks.

"Whatever moves me to write a song is usually a pretty good reason. I can really only write about what I feel in my heart. On September 11, 2001, I received a call from a good friend of mine who works on the rooftops in Manhattan. He was just witness to one of the great tragedies of our or any time, as he heard a huge explosion and watched helplessly as the first of two jet aircrafts crashed into the World Trade Center. He called me and said that when he looked around, all of his co-workers had tears streaming down their faces. I said to him, "This has got to be the day America cried." As I watched the images of destruction all that day, I started to sing a melody that seemed to mirror my emotions at the time. The next day I called up my good buddy Jim Peterik and told him that there was a song to be written here that could possibly do some good. I sang him a piece of the melody I had in my head. The first words out of Jim's mouth were, "In the shadow of the Statue of Liberty" to which I added, "In the torchlight of the land of the free." From there, with the help of ma bell, digital recording, and the grace of God, a song was born. We are proud to say that the fruits from our labor of love became the title song to The Day America Cried *album, helped raised some money, and hopefully expressed a few emotions locked in so many hearts. That's the power of a song."*

—Johnny Van Zant, lead singer of Lynyrd Skynyrd and Van Zant

Creating the mood

As the chapters of this book unfold you'll see the elements that come together to make a great song. But it all starts with you — who you are and what feeling or mood you're able to project. The number of people who will be able to connect with and relate to the mood you're creating will determine just how successful your song will be.

In some great songs, the mood of the music matches perfectly to the lyric. Minor chords often become the basis for sadder, deeper, and more introspective songs. Listen to "New York State of Mind" (written and sung by Billy Joel), "New York Minute" (written by Don Henley, Daniel Kortchmar and Jai Winding; sung by Don Henley) or "Paint It Black" (written by Mick Jagger and Keith Richards; performed by The Rolling Stones). Major chords generally result in happier and more optimistic songs like "You Are the Sunshine of My Life" (written and sung by Stevie Wonder) or Survivor's "High on You" (written by

Jim Peterik and Frankie Sullivan). In other songs, the mood of the lyric is in direct contrast to the vibe of the music, such as in Elton John's deceptively happy ditty "I Think I'm Going to Kill Myself" (written by Elton John and Bernie Taupin) and "I'll Never Fall In Love Again" (written by Burt Bacharach and Hal David; sung by Dionne Warwick). That bittersweet contrast between the words and the music is often what gives a song its potency.

I've always felt that the greatest intimacy we share with our audience as songwriters (and our greatest responsibility) is the transference of the mood we have created in a song. Taking that idea a bit farther, we're also sharing with our audience the mood we happened to be in as we were creating the song. It's a thought-provoking notion that when we respond emotionally to one of the great classics, we're actually feeling a little bit of what the composer was feeling at the moment of creation, even if it was many years ago. Such is the transcendent, timeless nature of songwriting.

Ready, Set — Begin

Well now you have your notebook at your side, a gross of freshly sharpened pencils, your cassette recorder in your bag, and you're just waiting for the next drip of inspiration to hit you on the head. First off, don't expect miracles right off the bat. Your first ideas might not be ready for prime time. But there is really no such thing as a bad idea, only ones that need to be refined, clarified, or made more unique and clever — and real. You've got to start somewhere. Try to find some time each day to write. Before long, those moments you set aside will become an oasis in the often dry climate of a typical day. The more you practice your craft, the better your odds of coming up with that one special song that the world wants to hear.

"When writing a song, if you're afraid to suck, you'll never write a note."

—Jeff Boyle, singer-songwriter of "Cubs Win" and hundreds of TV commercials including Coors Light and McDonald's

Songwriting takes an enormous amount of patience and hard work. Fortunately, there's a lot of fun to be had along the way. In that spirit, we have compiled for you — the six steps to writing your first song:

1. **Find a message you feel passionate about.** Choose a cause that resonates with you. Write about the girl you've been too insecure to ask out or that guy that you wish would take notice of you. Write about what interests you. Write about what you know. Keep it simple. If a subject is vital to you, it just might be vital to others as well. Similarly, if you don't care about a subject, don't expect others to either.

2. **Find a simple melody.** So many new songwriters get in over their heads trying to be complex to win friends and influence publishers. Songwriters

are not paid by the note — we're rewarded by the connections we make in the synapses of our audiences' brains. Often the easiest melodies are the longest lasting.

3. **Find a simple set of chord changes.** Search your piano keyboard or your guitar for this needed element of your song, or search the Internet or local clubs for the musicians that can furnish your words and melodies with a comfortable music bed.

4. **Find a place to write.** Find a quiet, pastoral setting to clear your mind, light some incense, and let the melodies and emotions flow. If this is not possible, any chaotic subway station will do. Other key areas to write: supermarkets, flea markets, soccer matches, P.T.A. meetings, in the car and anywhere else where the distractions merge to zero.

5. **Find a 9-foot Bosendorfer concert grand piano in an ancient cathedral and let your fingers land sensuously on the keys as you compose your masterpiece.** If this is not possible pick up any old instrument that's lying around the house and see if you can coax some sound out of it. It's really all about what you're hearing *in your head.* If you can imagine what the finished song will sound like, you can write it on your late Uncle Louie's banjo.

6. **Find the confidence within yourself to put your heart and soul on the line and share your song with others.** It's through this loop of constant feedback that we'll learn how to improve our songs. Resist the urge to discount everything but positive reaction. Resist the urge to devalue the positive reactions. Breathe in the accolades and weigh the brickbats. Take it all in, but before making any changes, always check it against your heart for the truth.

Chapter 2

Coming Up with That Solid-Gold Idea

In This Chapter

▶ Gathering song ideas from the world around you

▶ Keeping track and organizing your ideas and inspirations

▶ Documenting your thoughts

*U*nless you're lucky enough to have songs come to you fully finished in your deepest dreams, or to somehow take dictation from the ghosts of Tin Pan Alley (the publishing area located in New York City in the 1930s and 1940s), most of us need to summon the forces, sources, reasons, seasons, events, causes, passions, hobbies, and relationships that give us the necessary motivation to draw a song from our heart of hearts. Given that initial spark, we then need the best means of gathering those ideas, organizing them, putting them into form, and documenting them as they roll in, before they roll right out again.

Have you ever noticed how you can remember a powerful dream just after you've awakened only for it to vanish into thin air in the cold light of day? Song ideas can be just as illusive. Songwriting is all about capturing the moment of musical inspiration at its source. This is perhaps the single most important element of songwriting because, like the moment that rain turns to snow, at the instant of inspiration, your mind grows wings and an idea becomes a song.

In this chapter, we'll explore the various places to mine for inspiration for your songs, ways to gather information, and methods of documenting your ideas. We'll also demonstrate the importance of brainstorming ideas with others and provide simple exercises to show you the way.

Paying Attention: Stop, Look, and Listen

Living life actively everyday is as good a place to start as any when writing a song: being observant to all that is swirling around you, making note of your own reactions to situations, taking notice of other people's reaction in similar situations, and trying to put yourself in the other guy's shoes to better empathize with what he might be feeling. Like they say in all those contests, "You must be present to win!" By keeping your feelings close to the surface and refusing to disown even one, you are opening up a panorama of emotions that can be channeled into a song. The melodies that enter our consciousness when our guard is down and our inner antennas are up are perhaps the most authentic of all.

The melodies and ideas are out there somewhere in the cosmos; it's just a matter of us being receptive to what's coming in. I'm constantly amazed when I hear a melodic phrase I'd been working on suddenly on the radio in someone else's song. He got there first and tapped into something in a more efficient way than I could. It's happened the other way around too, where a writer will tell me that I beat him to the punch on a melody or lyrical concept.

As a writer, don't get discouraged if you hear echoes of a song you've been slaving over in a new song that just came on the radio. They just happened to access the ideas before you could. At least it shows that you're paying attention to the right inspiration.

Coming up with concepts for songs

Before you set your pen to paper to write the words (also known as lyrics) to your song, it's good to have a concept (a sort of idea roadmap) that points the way to your final destination — a finished song. If you can write out one sentence that explains what your song is about (this sentence is called a "thesis"), you're on the right track to the kind of clarity and focus needed in a good song. Refer back to your thesis sentence often to make sure the words you're coming up with still support your initial concept. If your words start taking you in a different direction, it could be a sign you need to change your thesis. There might be two separate songs to be written.

Make sure each song that you write has one cohesive idea that flows through the song and that all of the lines support that idea. If there is more than one concept fighting for life, no one concept will win.

One of the first things I ask someone that I am co-writing a song with is, "What matters to you right now in your life? What are you feeling passionate about?" We sit and talk for as long as it takes to find a concept that resonates and feels real to both of us. At least then we stand a fighting chance of writing a decent song.

Here are just a few of the subjects that have provided concepts for songwriters since the day the very first song was written — the headings are general, but the emotions you harness and the situations you create around these subjects is what will set your song apart from the others:

- **Love:** The most universal of all feelings is surely the gold standard when it comes to subject matter for your song. Refer to "Love Is the Answer" (written by Todd Rundgren, John Wilcox, and Roger Powell; performed by Utopia), "Love Me Two Times" (written and performed by The Doors), "Love Is a Battlefield" (written by Mike Chapman and Holly Knight; sung by Pat Benetar), and "I'm Not in Love" (written by Graham Gouldman and Eric Stewart; performed by 10 cc). Take a week off from work and make a list of the couple of thousand more you can think of on your own!

- **Friendship:** As a sub-genre of love, the bonds of friendship can bring out some of the strongest, sweetest emotions known to man. Refer to "You've Got a Friend" (written and sung by Carole King), "He Was a Friend of Mine" (written by Roger McGuinn; performed by The Byrds), "Friends" (written by Mark Klingman and William Charles Linhart; sung by Bette Midler), and "Can We Still Be Friends" (written and sung by Todd Rundgren).

- **Family:** The family unit and its members has been the springboard for countless great songs. It's easy to see why. Your family most likely supplied you with some of your first memories. The nature of those memories will probably determine whether your song will be filled with joy, sorrow, regret, love, hurt, admiration, disdain, the desire to distance yourself from them, or your commitment to get closer. Refer to "Mother" (written and sung by John Lennon), "Ghost Story" (written and sung by Sting), and "Butterfly Kisses" (written by Bob Carlisle and Randy Thomas; sung by Bob Carlisle).

- **Conflict:** Songs of war, strife, struggle, and broken hearts have helped countless generations deal with and heal the wounds of conflict. Verbalizing the feelings common to the heart of mankind is one the songwriter's most sacred privileges and responsibilities. Refer to "War" (written by Norman Whitfield and Barrett Strong; sung by Edwin Starr), "Building the Bridge" (written by Kevin Cronin; performed by REO Speedwagon), "Separate Ways" (written by Steve Perry and Jonathan Cain; performed by Journey), "Lost Horizon" (written and performed by Burt Bacharach and Hal David), and "We Just Disagree" (written by Jim Krueger; sung by Dave Mason).

- **Winning:** The winning spirit has long provided inspiration to countless songwriters. Refer to "Eye of the Tiger" (written by Jim Peterik and Frankie Sullivan; performed by Survivor), "While You See a Chance" (written by Steve Winwood and Will Jennings; sung by Steve Winwood), and "We Are the Champions" (written by Freddie Mercury; performed by Queen).

✔ **Loss:** When the pain and sometimes devastation of loss and the deep disappointment of losing can be put into a great song, you have a very effective delivery system for an all-natural cure. Your song will become as popular as the number of people who can see themselves in your song and the ones that can draw healing from the sentiments you've expressed. Refer to "The Day America Cried" (written and performed by Johnny Van Zant and Jim Peterik), "I'm Losing You" (written by Cornelius Grant, Eddie Holland, and Norman Whitfield; performed by The Temptations), and "The End of the Innocence" (written by Don Henley and Bruce Hornsby; sung by Don Henley).

✔ **Music and song:** Because of every songwriter's inherent love for what he does, writing about the object of his affection has been very popular since time immemorial. Refer to "I Write the Songs" (written by Bruce Johnston; sung by Barry Manilow), "Let There Be Music" (written by John Hall and Larry Hoppen; performed by Orleans), "I've a Strange New Rhythm in My Heart" (written and sung by Cole Porter), and "Piano in the Dark" (written by Brenda Russell, Scott Cutler, and Jeffrey Hall; sung by Brenda Russell).

✔ **Geography and travel:** All of the world's natural wonders are always good stepping off points for a songwriter. Trekking, hiking, biking, flying, and driving can supply you with endless reasons to write. Refer to "Route 66" (written and sung by Bobby Troup), "Rocky Mountain High" (written by John Denver and Michael Taylor; sung by John Denver), "Rocky Mountain Way" (written by Joe Walsh, Joey Vitale, Ken Passarelli, and Rocke Grace; sung by Joe Walsh), and "Wichita Lineman" (written by Jimmy Webb; sung by Glen Campbell).

✔ **Faith, hope, belief, God, and spirituality:** Although all very different subjects, we have put them together because they tend to intersect in some key areas. Looking for meaning outside of ourselves, believing in something greater than us all, searching for feelings beyond that which our five senses can validate, and looking for strength when you seem to have none have been the impetus for some of the world's greatest songs. Refer to "The Greatest Love of All" (written by Linda Creed and Michael Masser; sung by Whitney Houston), "How Great Thou Art" (written and sung by Stuart Hine), and "Climb Every Mountain" (written by Richard Rodgers and Oscar Hammerstein II; sung by Kate Smith).

✔ **Sports:** Whether you're writing about a specific sport or about the feeling you get from it or the formula you've come up with to do well at it, if sports is your passion, there are countless ways of harnessing your enthusiasm into a song. Refer to "Take Me Out to the Ball Game" (written and performed by Jack Norworth and Albert Von Tilzer), "Center Field" (written and sung by John Fogerty), and "Surfin' Safari" (written Brain Wilson and Mike Love; performed by The Beach Boys).

✔ **The afterlife and past lives:** These subjects have been the source of speculation, inspiration, and intrigue since time began. Heaven and hell as concepts fill the pages of songbooks and now, more than ever, there is a tendency for many of us to check out our lineage through the centuries. Refer to "We May Never Pass This Way Again" (written and performed by Seals And Crofts), "Ever Since the World Began" (written by Jim Peterik and Frankie Sullivan; performed by Survivor), "I Knew I Loved You Before I Met You" (written by Darren Hayes and Daniel Jones; performed by Savage Garden), and "From Here to Hereafter" (written by Jim Peterik and Mathew Thornton; performed by World Stage).

✔ **Protest:** To register their feelings of disagreement with something; some people picket; some cause destruction; and some participate in parades, bed-ins, be-ins, marches, demonstrations, and strikes. We as songwriters usually grab a pen, run to a piano, and attempt to express our frustration through song. Refer to "Where Have All the Flowers Gone" (written and sung by Pete Seeger), "Blowin' in the Wind" (written and sung by Bob Dylan), "Change the World" (written by Gordon Kennedy, Tommy Simms, and Wayne Kirkpatrick; sung by Eric Clapton), and "What's Going On" (written by Marvin Gaye, Al Cleveland, and Renaldo Benson; sung by Marvin Gaye).

✔ **The future, the past, and the present:** Some songs look back upon a bygone day or even just yesterday. Some look hopefully, pessimistically, or presciently into the future and some are rooted in the good old here and now. Whatever your vantage point, a lot of material can be stitched together from the fabric of time. Refer to "Time in a Bottle" (written and sung by Jim Croce), "Night Moves" (written and sung by Bob Seger), "Yesterday" (written by John Lennon and Paul McCartney; performed by The Beatles), "Right Now" (written and performed by Van Halen), "When My Ship Comes In" (written by Gus Kahn and Walter Donaldson; performed by George Hall Orchestra with Allen Church vocal), and "Space Oddity" (written and sung by David Bowie).

✔ **Fads, crazes, and passing fancies:** Who could forget all those timeless songs about Power Rangers, Pokemon characters, dance steps, Ninja Turtles, and skateboards? The fact is they have made an indelible impression in our memory banks. Start with writing the ones you have a true affinity for, and then move to the ones that you're commissioned to write for big bucks by a major motion picture company. Refer to "The Twist" (written by Henry Ballard; sung by Chubby Checker), "The Locomotion" (written by Carole King and Gerry Goffin; sung by Little Eva), "Macarena" (written by Monge Antonio Romero and Rafael Ruiz; performed by Los Del Rio), and "Sidewalk Surfin" (written by Brian Wilson and Roger Christian; performed by Jan & Dean).

✔ **States of mind:** This ever-popular subject, which ranges from sanity to insanity, elation to depression, and all stops in between has always provided some good therapy for writer and audience alike. Refer to "Sorry Seems to Be the Hardest Word" (written by Elton John and Bernie Taupin; sung by Elton John), "Soak Up the Sun" (written by Sheryl Crow and Jeff Trott; sung by Sheryl Crow), "Crazy" (written by Willie Nelson; sung by Patsy Cline), and "Walking On Sunshine" (written by Kimberley Rew; performed by Katrina and the Waves).

We have, of course, only touched the surface of the subjects that may inspire you to create a song. Anything in life is fair game to write about. It's up to you to find unique and compelling ways of presenting these ideas and concepts through your words and music. Finding the subjects you're most passionate about, the ones that "strike a chord" in you will make it easier to write a song you're satisfied with and that'll connect with others.

I always felt that the better the source of inspiration, the better the song would be. If I came across a very compelling cause that moved me, I would be motivated to write a compelling song. If I met a girl that knocked me out, I tried to make sure that the song I wrote about her would knock *her* out. The better the movie script was from which I was basing a song, the better the song tended to be. Always look for the highest form of inspiration that you can find when writing a song.

"Your best songs will come from true life experiences!"

> — Joe Isaacs, singer-songwriter in the Bluegrass and Gospel genres; many artists have recorded his songs including Ralph Stanley, who recorded Isaacs' "Man From Galilee."

Listening for lyrics

There are song titles, song concepts, catchy phrases, rhymes, rhythms, and reasons all around us — you just need to keep your eyes and ears open and audition practically everything as a potential candidate for your song.

Sometimes I'll think of a phrase such as "You might like it too much" and put it on a page in my notebook labeled "Potential Titles." (That particular title became a song I wrote with Blackhawk.) Other times, a phrase will be inappropriate such as the title "champaign Eldorado" but will be okay to put it on a list of "Intriguing Phrases" to be used in the context of a future song. (That particular phrase ended up in "Wild Eyed Southern Boys," which I wrote for 38 Special.)

Take a look at some of the places a songwriter might find lyrical stepping off points, story ideas and concepts, and catch phrases:

- ✔ **Overheard conversations:** Next time you're at a restaurant, tune in to the conversation at the table next to you. (Usually, they're talking so loudly you won't have to strain.) You may catch a glimpse of a conversation that could spark a song.

One day while on a writing trip in Nashville, I was at a local eatery with a fellow writer. In the booth behind us we couldn't help overhearing two young ladies discussing their love lives. As the blond girl was listening to the brunette recount the wonders of her current beau, the other one sighed and said, "Now that's true love." My friend and I looked at each other, quickly paid the bill and repaired to his piano room to write, "Now That's True Love" in about an hour and a half.

✔ **Situations you or your friends may be involved in:** There is nothing more real to write about than actual situations. The dynamics of people's lives can provide thousands of stories. Obviously it's okay to enhance or modify a real-life story (after all we're usually writing fiction here), but many writers at least base their song on the interactions of real people.

✔ **Items in the news:** You'll find an endless supply of song ideas just by reading the daily newspaper and watching the news on television. Of course it's important to watch actively not only taking in and comprehending the events, but also taking the implications of the events to the next stage and searching for the motivation behind them. As you're doing all this — you are auditioning different situations for the emotional impact they could have in the context of a song, and just how deeply the event impacts you.

Thinking "outside the box" is a songwriting goal. It's vital to look at every implication of a situation to find the perfect theme for your song.

✔ **Items in magazines:** Magazines can be a great stepping off point for a song. Well-written articles can inspire an idea, colorful ads can transfer a feeling of what's considered current in the world of pop consciousness. Magazines are basically just another way for a writer to keep his "ear to the street."

✔ **Television and movies:** This is a big and vibrant category when it comes to shaking loose some great ideas from that head of yours. Just the feeling that a certain movie evokes can be enough to write a song. The message contained in so many series and shows can sometimes be harnessed into a song. In good drama and comedy, the interactions between people can serve as a template for relationships in your song. Often, there is a particular character that you're drawn to or can identify with. Write about him or her or from *their* perspective.

A great movie or a music biography episode on television has to be one of my favorite inspiration points for a song. After watching a VH-1 special on Bruce Springsteen (showing him in the studio recording his latest masterpiece), I was suddenly able to walk over to the piano and finish the song that previously alluded me, based on the determination and musical genius I saw from Bruce in that show. Many years ago, after being incredibly moved by my first viewing of Capra's classic, *It's a Wonderful Life,* I came up with the beginnings of "Ever Since the World Began" (co-written with Frankie Sullivan). This song, which ended up on Survivor's *Eye of the Tiger* album, is based on the realization that each life is just a piece of the puzzle of this "wonderful life," and how one life touches the other in ways people may never realize.

The song title "The Search Is Over" (written by Jim Peterik and Frankie Sullivan; performed by Survivor) was a phrase that Jim Peterik jotted down in his notebook after he heard a newsman say it one day on the evening news program.

Making up music

Everyone has a melody inside of them. The simplest three notes put together just right can be a melody that lasts for ages. That song you whistle while doing the laundry, walking the dog, mowing the lawn, driving, or taking a shower could be "Jingle Bells," the latest Elton John smash, or just as likely something you've pulled out of thin air.

To avoid a potential copyright infringement suit, it's critical to know the difference between a song you've heard somewhere before and one you've come up with on your own. If you think you've heard it before, screen the charts, your memory banks, and your record collection to make sure it's original. It's well documented that soon after Paul McCartney began writing "Yesterday" he went around singing it for friends to make sure he had not stolen its melody from an old song. He was finally convinced that he'd just written a new and original classic.

A working ability on guitar or keyboard can also help you experiment with and eventually find melodies for your song. When you finally put the music together, you can create a suitable bed against which you can road test your lyrics and eventually perform your finished song. Although certain people can write entire songs "in their head," most of us need an instrument at our disposal to help coax the ideas from our cranium.

Although I am far from a virtuoso on the keyboard, I use a process I call "creative noodling" to help create ideas. I'll simply dial up an interesting sound on my keyboard synthesizer (generally a reassuring combination of piano and strings, although for edgier ideas perhaps a distorted electric piano setting or clavinet), and let my fingers find their way across the keys. (Let's call it "The Columbus Method" — just finding a "key" and landing on it!) Often the sound itself will dictate the type of musical idea I come up with. (I wonder if John Lennon would have come up with that haunting pattern of notes for "Lucy in the Sky with Diamonds" if not for that cool harpsichord sound he stumbled upon.) I try to keep a cassette recorder close by to catch anything close-to-good. One truism I have learned is — that if I don't have my recorder handy, I most certainly *will* come up with a good idea that I *won't* quite remember later.

"The better you can become on your instrument of choice, the easier it will be for you to consistently come up with good song ideas. It is also helpful when you can demonstrate to others how your song goes. Facility is not a prerequisite for writing a song, but it sure can help the process along."

—Jeff Jacobs, songwriter, arranger and keyboardist with Foreigner

Recording and Organizing Your Ideas

Practically anyone can write or co-write a song. Ideas, concepts, and melodies can come from anywhere, but documentation and organization of those special moments of illumination are a necessary, although often tedious, part of the process.

Have you ever had an original melody in your head all day long, only to lose it by the evening? This is why the notebook and the cassette recorder were invented! I learned the hard way many years ago to disregard the statement, "If it's really a great idea, don't worry . . . I'll remember it." Many good melodies and ideas have fluttered away because I didn't have a net to catch them. And some of these rare butterflies only come around once in a lifetime.

Using a cassette recorder

Any songwriter — whether aspiring or accomplished — should at all times — carry an inexpensive, hand-held cassette recorder (the kind with the microphone built in). Quality of sound is not nearly as important as merely documenting the idea. Extra batteries are always a must.

When you're driving down the road or waking up from a profound dream and think of a great line or words for a song, grab your recorder, press the record button, and do the following:

1. **State the date, time, your location, and anything else to help identify the moment of creation.**

2. **Identify the working title of the song you're creating — or, if it's something new, give it a working title.**

3. **Start saying or singing the words or melodies that come to mind. If you're recording lyrical ideas, say them slowly and intelligibly.** With musical ideas, make sure that if you don't have an instrument handy, you give your melody a count off (as in 1, 2, 3, 4, start) so you can tell later where your musical phrase starts. It's also essential to hum the "root note" (the tonic or base note of any chord) of the key you are in, if you possibly can, so that your melody has a musical reference point when you review it later. (See Chapter 8 for more on music and notes.)

Recording your ideas is one thing, but without a system for organizing and labeling all the tapes you record, your ideas can be lost or extremely hard to find again. A month from now, you probably won't remember that the song you just thought of is on the 90-minute cassette tape about two-thirds of the way into the first side. With all the time you'll be spend searching for the song in question, it's probably easier to start a new song.

You can create any organization system that works for you, but a basic system is to date a particular cassette (month, day, and year), and then label each idea on the *J-card* (the official term for that flimsy cardboard insert inside the plastic tape cases) immediately after you record the idea. If you start accumulating numerous tapes, you may even want to create a list of the contents of each tape on your computer (something simple in a word-processing spreadsheet program will work just fine — plus, it's searchable, so you won't have to waste a lot of time scanning through a notebook). If you document your ideas on mini-disk system or a Smart Media device like the Zoom Ps 02, you can, with great ease, access your ideas without all the fast forward and rewind time.

On a recent biking tour in Europe, I labeled the idea-catching cassette I carried with me in my shoulder bag "July 6, '01 — Vienna to Prague." At least I'd be ready to write a few polkas and maybe even a waltz! Entry one was marked "Melodic hard rock thing in Austria." As I was winding through the streets of some quaint Austria town, I heard the sound of American rock-and-roll emanating from a boom box in someone's living room. The music was like hearing from an old friend. I stopped my bike and sang a new idea into my recorder that was inspired by the mood of that moment. I always try to classify the idea as to genre and include any detail that may help bring to mind the genesis of the idea. I also use a star-rating system (one through four), indicating my level of excitement about the idea. The next entry was "work on possible Skynyrd seed" — perhaps a stepping off point for my upcoming writing session with them. After that I entered "Boy-band type rock." When I got home, I filed this tape with hundreds of other cassettes arranged by month and year. When I'm having a creative dry spell I'll spend a lot of time going through these tapes. Take a look at Figure 2-1 for an example of my J-card.

Jotting down ideas in a notebook

As a songwriter, at any stage of success or experience, it's always a good idea (in addition to your portable recording device), to carry along a traditional notebook, and, if you happened to be versed in notating music (this process is defined and described in Chapter 8), a notebook that contains staff paper — pages that are pre-lined with the five lines of the musical staff. This would be for jotting down melodies in note form and their accompanying chords. As for your standard notebook, we would recommend one of the spiral ones divided into three or more sections, with pockets lining each divider panel. This notebook configuration can help you organize your creative output in the following way. If you have purchased a three-section book, here's how your notebook could be organized:

(Back Home) 6. Forgive Me   work on.

4. Dream Song moody. ***5. Wild in America!!

3. Good Alternative piece in plane from Prague.

Side II

July 6, 2001 Vienna to Prague
Jim Peterik

July 6, 2001 Vienna to Prague Bike Ride Tape

Side A
**1. Melodic Hard Rock thing in Austria. 2. Work on
poss. Skynyrd seed   "American English" in Trebón.

Side B
***1. Boy Band type Rock (Layla style modulation).
In Cerviche   "You Took the Music With Me"
new chor.

Figure 2-1:
A sample
J-card.

- ✔ **Section one:** The first section could be for the miscellaneous ideas, phrases, titles, concepts, observations, rhymes, and pieces of lyrics that you're likely to collect as you go about your day.

- ✔ **Section two:** This section could be "songs in progress" — the ones that you may have a verse but no chorus, a chorus only or verse, a rhyme with no reason or reason with no rhyme. It'd be wise to notate on these pages the current date and a cross-reference to the exact cassette where the corresponding musical tidbit can be found. This section might include songs with a few permanent or "keeper" lines (you know, the ones you're really satisfied with), and the rest of the song comprised of dummy lyrics.

The *dummy lyrics* are lines that serve to fill up the correct amount of space that the line should occupy, but it's usually made up of temporary words off the top of your head or substandard stuff that you fully intend on replacing at a later date. That being said, about half of the words that end up in my finished song started life as a dummy lyric. That may be because when you take the pressure off yourself to be "brilliant" it often opens up creativity you didn't even know you had.

✔ **Section three:** This section is reserved for finished lyrics. We suggest you leave a few pages between songs to allow for the inevitable rewrites.

✔ **Section four:** If you've purchased a notebook with five sections, you could make section four a list section — songs to be finished, songs already finished, projects in progress, ideas on who to pitch your tunes to. (Refer to Chapter 17 on marketing your song.)

✔ **Section five:** In this section, you can just doodle your brains out until inspiration strikes, or make lists of songs already written and ideas of which artists might be appropriate for each song. If you have an upcoming writing appointment, you may want to write down some *seed ideas* (starter ideas that could spark creativity in you and your collaborator). If you're writing with a specific artist in mind or will be collaborating with a band or artist, you may want to put together lists of prospective titles and concepts that seem in keeping with your target artist.

In the pockets of your notebooks, keep the scraps of paper that you originally scribbled down ideas contained in the notebook. It's great to have these crude representations when your song hits number one. Also keep in these pockets anything connected to the song's creation, such as the paragraph in the magazine that triggered a song, the photo of the girl who broke your heart and triggered a song, and so on.

"I generally write my lyrics in progress on the right-hand page of my notebook. I keep the left side reserved for what I call "spare parts" — phrases that occur to me that relate to the song I'm working on, alternate lines, alternate titles, trial phrases, and ideas I'd rather not forget. These "left page words" as I like to call them, can be worth their weight in gold, especially a few days later when you need some fresh inspiration."

—Don Barnes, singer, guitarist and songwriter with 38 Special

Always put your name, address and contact number somewhere near the front of the notebook (perhaps on the first page or on the cover) with the words, "If found, please return to. . . ." Also, make note of the date the book was started and the date of your last entry.

Practice Makes Perfect

As you go about your daily routine today (or any day for that matter), try to notice everything that enters your consciousness. In that receptive state, be sure to have a cassette recorder or a notebook close by — ready to catch your inspirations. Write down all observations, feelings and realizations that you have that day, even if they seem trivial at the time. If you think of a catchy phrase or see an intriguing headline in the newspaper or notice a slogan on a bus as it's going by, or incorrectly hear something your child says to you, jot those things down too. When you get home, try to find a little "quiet time" and look over your "crop" of ideas from the day. Audition them all as potential candidates for future songs. If the mood hits you, set your notebook on your piano, if you happen to play, open it up to today's bounty, and informed by your own words, see where your fingers take you. Try the various phrases and ideas against the music of your mind. Who knows, before you know it — you might have a good start on a new, original, and genuine song.

Take the phrase that strikes you the most and start building a song around it. Have some fun with it. Now start your file of song ideas. Your writing sessions will become much more productive if you have a decent way of filing your thoughts and concepts on paper or on tapes. You might have a thought one day that you believe can be really good material, but you're not sure where it may take you. Now, if you've been disciplined enough to store away these thoughts for future use, when the moment comes that you can now take it further, you'll be able to recapture that original thought and let it inspire a new whole song when the time is right.

REMEMBER

If you let your mind go and let your imagination take flight, writing songs can be easy. But being able to do this takes practice and discipline. Be ready for that moment of inspiration, and always be prepared to catch those thoughts before they float on by. Even though they seem so simple at the time and so easy to remember, they'll haunt you forever if you decide you're too busy or lazy to write them down!

COACH DAVE SAYS

Saying hello to a good idea

It's always fun to be around Jim, because you never know when something said or seen is going to become the new title for a song or part of its lyrics. Just being around such a prolific songwriter has truly raised my own antenna without much effort on my part. Once, in a meeting we had at the record company I previously worked for, Jim (who had just written the title track for the debut CD of our new artist) needed to get going to another meeting across town. Everyone excused themselves and left the room, but before we knew it, Jim and I got to talking about something else and time slipped away from us. A while later, the CEO of the record company came back into the room and told Jim, "Boy, you're bad at goodbyes."

Jim took out his pocket notebook and wrote down the words, "Bad at Goodbyes," saying what a great song idea that was. I agreed — so much so that I couldn't get it out of my head. That night I awoke in the middle of the night filled with the words to that song. Thank goodness I had listened earlier to Jim's advice and had a pad of paper and pen available by my bedside. Quickly, I wrote down the words floating around in my mind.

Chapter 3

Getting Your Song Into Shape: Song Forms

In This Chapter

▶ Understanding songwriters' terminology

▶ Knowing the basic fundamentals of the verse

▶ Getting a handle on AABA forms

▶ Expanding into the verse-chorus forms of songwriting

▶ Picking apart your favorite songs

*W*hen you hear a new song on the radio, the average listener will probably not turn to his friend and say, "Wow, awesome pre-chorus — I love how it sets up the hook!" Nonetheless, every song has a structure that it's built upon. The framework can follow any of several tried-and-true patterns or it can break the mold and go where no song has gone before. Knowing basic song forms, also referred to as "formats," will help guide you as you're constructing a song. It'll also help identify what you are doing instinctively. It's important to understand the basics of song structure even if you choose to stray from it in certain instances. There is, however, something reassuring to the ear about the use of familiar song organization that can help a songwriter sound immediately more professional and commercial.

In this chapter we'll look at many of the most commonly used and successful song forms. We'll break down a song to its basic modular components and show how the various sections can be organized to create a synergy that is greater than the sum of its parts.

Talking the Talk

Before we start looking at song forms, it's important to understand the terminology songwriters use when they're talking shop. Here are the main terms for the various sections of a song:

✔ **Intro:** This section, which starts out the song, is typically an abbreviated instrumental form of the chorus or sometimes the verse. Its purpose is to get the ear ready and introduce all that is to come. Listen to any radio station. The majority of the songs you hear will have some form of intro, and your "tune-out factor" will be directly affected by how effective the writers and arrangers are at catching your attention right off the bat.

✔ **Verse:** The purpose of the verse is to reveal the storyline of the tune. It helps propel the listener to the chorus while conveying the song's basic mood and message. The words, or lyrics, of the verse, tend to expand from verse to verse with new information added to move the story along. The melody and chord pattern of the verse is usually the same from verse to verse except for minor variations in melody usually to make a lyric fit.

✔ **Pre-Chorus:** This section, also known as the "B" section and the set-up, among other nicknames, is the optional section preceding the chorus that provides a little fresh terrain both lyrically and chordally before pressing on to the chorus. It's usually no more than 8 bars in length and sometimes contains the identical lyric each time it comes around. The decision to use a pre-chorus is strictly on a "need-to-use" basis. If a song is propelled sufficiently to the chorus without it, then you don't really need the extra baggage.

✔ **Chorus:** The chorus is the "money section" of a song — which is to say that if you've done your job well, this is the part that people will go around singing as they plunk their hard-earned money down to own a copy for themselves. This section usually contains the title or "hook" of the song either at the beginning or end of the chorus. The chorus features a signature phrase or musical figure that's repeated throughout the song and serves as the main identifying portion of the song. Musically and lyrically, choruses tend to be identical except for minor variations. (One exception to this generality is the song, often a country song that saves the surprise lyrical payoff for the last chorus and is therefore very different.) In most cases, songwriters like to keep their choruses identical so it's harder for the audience to muff a line in the big sing-along.

✔ **Bridge:** The bridge, sometimes called the *release* or *middle eight* (referring to the eight musical measures that the bridge tends to occupy), comes after the second chorus in the majority of pop songs. It's not a necessity in all songs. It can either contain lyrics or be instrumental in nature. Whether the bridge contains words or not, its main function is to give the ear some fresh real estate to land on.

✔ **Coda:** A special ending section, also called an *outro* or a *tag* that can be added to the end of a song. It's typically a kind of grand finale.

Now that you see the various components that make up a song, take a look at the various ways of organizing them. Again, there's no right or wrong way, only what *sounds* right or wrong to the ear. The sections of the song are each designated by a letter, the first melodic section you hear (generally the verse) is "A." The second melodic section we hear is designated "B," and the third section is called "C." The fourth section (usually the bridge) is then called "D." If you repeat a melodic section, even if the words are different, it's still assigned the same letter. We'll now take a look at some of the most frequently used sequences of those sections.

As you read this chapter (and the rest of this book), don't hesitate to flip back to this list of terms so that you know for sure what we're referring to.

Dealing with Verses

The basic fundamental section for any song is the verse. We'll start out by talking about songs that consist of nothing else but verses.

The AAA or the verse form

The *verse form* is often referred to as the *AAA form*. This is when different lyrics are place over the same music and are repeated in close succession. Since the chorus and bridge are often eliminated in this form, the title will often appear in the first or last line of the verse. This form is often used when a story is being told, using each verse to propel the action forward. Church hymns usually fall into the AAA category, as do many folk songs. Many of the songs of Joni Mitchell, Joan Baez, and Judy Collins use the AAA form as well.

It's especially important for your melody to be interesting in this form, so that it can withstand the repetition of identical sections. Often a musical section can come between verse sections to add interest. Sometimes a writer can throw in a sort of *faux chorus* (that's a section that is chorus-like, but doesn't contain the title hook of the song). Songs like this are generally considered a variation of the AAA in form.

The number of verses in a song written in the AAA, or verse form, varies widely. Jimmy Webb's song "By the Time I Get to Phoenix" (Glen Campbell's breakthrough hit) only takes three verses to tell the story.

There are three well-crafted verses and that each presents a location that the singer is thinking about as he embarks upon his journey away from his former girlfriend in California. The song is about what she'll be doing when the singer arrives at each of three destinations: Phoenix, Albuquerque, and Oklahoma.

The title of the song is only mentioned once, in the first line of the first verse. That's because each verse describes a different location, which Webb has cleverly shown in his first lines. Webb also has a clever use of lyric elsewhere in the song — for example, "She'll just hear that phone keep on ringin' off the wall" is followed by a simple "That's all." True to the verse form, the song tells a story that progresses from verse to verse.

For another example, check out "All Along the Watchtower" by Bob Dylan and made famous by Jimi Hendrix. It consists of three verses and is a good example of the style of lyric writing that Bob Dylan introduced during the 1960s.

If you listen carefully to these well-crafted words, you'll hear that there's no hook (see Chapter 4 for more on hooks) in the song at all: The title, "All Along the Watchtower," is introduced in one place only, as the first line of Verse 3. Notice, however, that it's probably the best candidate in the song for a title. Dylan could have called the song "Two Riders Were Approaching" or "There Must Be Some Way Out of Here," but neither of these phrases comes close to "Along the Watchtower" as its great title. Look up some (or all) of the songs in Table 3-1 for more help with this form.

Table 3-1	AAA Song Examples	
Song title	*Songwriter(s)*	*Singers/Performers*
"Amazing Grace"	John Newton	Judy Collins and many others
"Turn, Turn, Turn"	Pete Seeger	The Byrds, Pete Seeger
"Subterranean Homesick Blues"	Bob Dylan	Bob Dylan, Red Hot Chili Peppers
"Born in the U.S.A."	Bruce Springsteen	Bruce Springsteen
"On Broadway"	Barry Mann, Cynthia Weil, Mike Stoller, Jerry Leiber	The Drifters

The two-verse form or AA form

In the classic songs that were written by American composers for film and Broadway, a type of form called the *two-verse form,* or *AA form,* arose and became very popular. This form was very common from the 1940s through the 1960s and is the form of choice for many standards. Because of its lack of chorus, it has not been used much in the pop music of the 1970s and beyond, but songwriter Lionel Ritchie did use an extended two-verse form for his hit 1980s song "Hello."

This form consists of, as its name implies, only two verses, but in these two verses, a complete and tidy story is told. Each verse is traditionally 16 bars long (check out Chapter 8 for more on bars). The second verse is usually a musical repeat of the first, but in some songs the second verse resembles the first, beginning the same way, but wraps up differently musically.

If you want to study the AA form in more detail, take a look at the list of other songs to pick from in Table 3-2.

Table 3-2	AA Song Examples	
Song title	*Songwriter(s)*	*Singers/Performers*
"Moon River"	Johnny Mercer, Henry Mancini	Henry Mancini, Stevie Wonder, over 1,000 recordings by various artists
"In My Life"	John Lennon, Paul McCartney	The Beatles
"White Christmas"	Irving Berlin	most of us, made popular by Bing Crosby
"Stardust"	Hoagie Carmichael, Mitchell Parish	Willie Nelson, and many others
"Walk On By"	Burt Bacharach, Hal David	Dionne Warwick

The AABA Form

The form known as AABA was *the* form of choice in the first half of the twentieth century. It's still used today in songwriting, but has fallen off in popularity. However, it's good to know this form because you never know when it'll be the perfect fit for the song you are writing.

Learning about the AABA form

In the *AABA form,* the A sections are the verse sections, and the B section is a *bridge*. In other forms, B represents whatever section comes second in the song. The title is usually placed either in the first or the last line of each verse and is in the same place each time it comes around.

The bridge is a section that provides a contrast to the verse sections by using different chords, a different melody, and sometimes a shift in the focus in the lyrics. It provides an interlude between verses, which can be very effective if it's done well.

In the classic AABA song, the A sections are usually 8 bars in length and constitute the main melody of the song. Each of the three A sections has a different set of words, although the last verse section can be a repeat of the first, as is the case in the song "Monday, Monday" performed by The Mamas and The Papas (written by John Phillips). In fact, all three verses can be the same, as in John Lennon and Paul McCartney's "Do You Want to Know a Secret?" But these are exceptions to the rule and you won't find many songs that repeat verses like that. Songwriters usually compose three separate sets of lyrics for the verse sections of the AABA form.

The AABA form continues to be used today in many styles of music — country, gospel, Christian, pop, jazz, theatre, and film — but not as often as it once was. The form can be used to provide a very effective emotional satisfaction: The first two verses establish the main melody of the song, and then when the bridge is sung, it provides a different feeling because of its contrasting quality. Thus, the return to the last verse provides an emotionally satisfying return to what was presented before.

There are always exceptions to every rule — that's what makes life (and songs) interesting. Some AABA songs don't introduce the title in the first or last line of each verse. "The Christmas Song" (written by Mel Torme and Robert Wells) is an example of this. Everyone knows this song ("Chestnuts roasting on an open fire. . . ."), but the title, "The Christmas Song," does not appear in the lyrics at all (because the title describes what the song is about and it's not a phrase that would sound good in the song itself.

Another example of a different placement for the title is George Gershwin and Ira Gershwin's famous song "I Got Rhythm." The title appears at the beginning of the first verse, and then gets transformed in the next two verses. In the second verse it becomes "I got daisies," and in the third verse, it's "I got starlight." This is a great trick, the same one used by songwriter Jimmy Webb in "By The Time I Get to Phoenix." Take note of it — you may want to do the same thing in a song of your own someday.

In the following sections, we steer you toward a couple AABA songs that illustrate what the form is about.

A real classic, "Over the Rainbow," was sung by Judy Garland in the film *The Wizard of Oz.*

This is a great example of an AABA song with an added section at the end called a *coda.* The verses have a flowing feeling to them with the expansive quality of the words ("Somewhere over the rainbow, bluebirds fly"). This is perfectly contrasted by the quick movement of words in the bridge ("Where troubles melt like lemon drops away above the chimney tops"). The bridge provides a perfect interlude between the second and third verses.

The following list includes songs written in the AABA song format. Table 3-3 shows some great songs for you to explore in order to discover more about the form.

Table 3-3	AABA Song Examples	
Song title	*Songwriter(s)*	*Singers/Performers*
"Something"	George Harrison	The Beatles
"Blue Moon"	Richard Rodgers, Lorenz Hart	Chris Isaak, Willie Nelson, and many artists
"Save the Last Dance for Me"	Doc Pomus, Mort Shuman	The Drifters
"Just the Way You Are"	Billy Joel	Billy Joel
"Will You Still Love Me Tomorrow?"	Carole King, Gerry Goffin	The Shirelles

The extended AABA form

Beginning in the 1960s, some songwriters began using an extended version of the AABA form, called the *AABABA*. This is merely the AABA form with an additional bridge and a final verse. This final verse may be a repeat of a previous verse or even just a part of one of the previous verses.

John Lennon and Paul McCartney's song "Yesterday" uses an extended AABA form. The title appears as the first line in each verse except for Verse 2, where the word *suddenly* is used instead. The title also appears in the last line of each verse, and in the last line of the bridge, and the final verse is just a repeat of Verse 3.

This AABABA form is also used in other Beatles songs (written by John Lennon and Paul McCartney), including the following:

- ✔ "I'll Follow the Sun"
- ✔ "I Want to Hold Your Hand"
- ✔ "Hey Jude"
- ✔ "Hard Day's Night"
- ✔ "Long and Winding Road"
- ✔ "I Call Your Name"

Things get a little more complicated in a few of McCartney's songs. "Michelle," for example, has a form of AABABABA. The fourth verse is not sung but is instead played as an instrumental. The words in the second verse are repeated in the third and fifth verses, so all these verses are the same. All three bridges have different words, however. This is a very unusual and innovative formal structure. Because the formal structures in *many* of the songs written by McCartney and Lennon are very advanced, you can get a lot out of studying them. (Don't you wish your studies in school were this much fun?)

The Verse-Chorus Form or ABAB Form

The verse-chorus form is the most common in today's pop, rock, gospel, R&B, and country music. In the *verse-chorus form,* or *ABAB form,* verses alternate with a chorus section. The chorus is always the same except, perhaps, at the end, where you can extend it to make a really great ending for the song.

The story that the song unfolds is contained within the verses. When the chorus is sung, it usually proclaims the title as the hook. Pop or rock songs that work well usually start out right away with a line that people relate to; then the words of the verse pull the listeners in, get them hooked. But the power comes when the chorus is sung. A good chorus is something that listeners really take notice of; and because it is repeated over and over, if it's a great chorus, the song will imprint itself in listeners' minds.

Throughout this section, we take a closer look at the verse-chorus form, starting with "Yellow Brick Road" by Elton John and Bernie Taupin.

This song has two verses that tell the story about a person who is tired of the high life and wants to return to his life on the farm. The chorus emphasizes his feelings, bidding farewell to the "yellow brick road" and stating that he's going back to his former life on the farm. No matter how many verses there are in the song, the chorus will always apply because it describes the main topic of the song. Notice that it starts and ends with the title, which helps it stick in the listener's mind as the song's hook.

The best place to put a title in a verse-chorus song is in the first line of the chorus. Some songwriters place the title in both the first line and the last line (as in "Yellow Brick Road").

Another great verse-chorus song comes from Alicia Keys, the very first artist to be released on legendary producer and Arista Records founder Clive Davis's new label, J Records. Her song "Fallin'" is a great example of a very simple verse-chorus song elevated to high art by a smoldering vocal and a brilliant arrangement. Two chords make up the entire song — the basic blues progression that you've heard in the classic song "I Put a Spell on You" by Screamin' Jay Hawkins (covered by The Animals in the '60s). The progression that toggles between

E-minor and B-minor has never sounded more elegant. The structure is the verse-chorus form with a very simple chorus. The song gains its momentum through repetition and the swelling of strings and background vocals in the arrangement. The song begins with a gospel-drenched *a cappella* (group or solo singing without musical accompaniment) opening line: "I keep on falling in and out of love with you" and then continues with the verse supported by piano:

"Fallin'" written and sung by Alicia Keys

Verse 1 (A)

I keep on falling in and out with you
Sometimes I love ya, sometimes you make me blue
Sometimes I feel good, at times I feel used
Lovin' you, darlin', makes me so confused

Chorus (B)

I keep on falling in and out of love with you
I never loved someone the way that I love you

Verse 2 (A)

Oh I never felt this way
How do you give me so much pleasure
Cause me so much pain
Just when I think I'm takin' more than would a fool
I start fallin' back in love with you

Chorus (B)

I keep on falling in and out of love with you
I never loved someone the way that I love you

Coda

I'm, I'm, I'm, I'm fallin'
I, I, I, I'm fallin'
Fallin', Fallin'
I keep on fallin' in and out of love with you
I never loved someone the way that I love you
I'm fallin' in and out of love with you
I never loved someone the way that I love you
I'm fallin' in and out of love with you
I never loved someone the way that I love you

Words and Music by Alicia Keys ©2000 EMI April Music, Inc., and Lellow Productions (ASCAP)

"Yellow Brick Road" and "Fallin'" stick to the verse-chorus form exactly. Sometimes, however, a verse-chorus song will present two verses before the first chorus is sung. This form variation would be described as AABAB, and you can look up the lyrics to some (or all) of the songs listed in Table 3-4 to help learn about two verses before the chorus. This approach is sometimes an effective way to get into the feel of the song before the chorus arrives.

Table 3-4	AABAB Song Examples	
Song title	*Songwriter(s)*	*Singers/Performers*
"Daniel"	Elton John, Bernie Taupin	Elton John
"Helpless"	Neil Young	Crosby, Stills, Nash & Young
"Did You Ever Have to Make Up Your Mind"	John Sebastian	The Loving Spoonful

If you want more examples of verse-chorus songs in ABAB form, you may want to study songs from the following list in Table 3-5. As you're reading the lyrics and/or listening to these songs, pay close attention to the placement of the titles and ask yourself what title placement accomplishes.

Table 3-5	ABAB Song Examples	
Song title	*Songwriter(s)*	*Singers/Performers*
"American Pie"	Don McLean	Don McLean, Madonna
"The Wind Beneath My Wings"	Larry Henley, Jeff Silbar	Bette Midler
"Foolish Games"	Jewel	Jewel
"Amazed"	Marv Green, Aimee Mayo, Chris Lindsey	Lonestar
"If You Ever Have Forever in Mind"	Vince Gill	Vince Gill
"I'll Never Break Your Heart"	Albert Manno, Ronnie Broomfield	Backstreet Boys

The verse-chorus form using a pre-chorus or the ABC form

A *pre-chorus* — a short section that leads up to the chorus — is a great device that you can use when writing a verse-chorus song.

JIM SAYS

Your vehicle to success

My first number one song, "Vehicle," performed by The Ides of March, is probably the simplest song I've ever written. The verse just kind of merges seamlessly with the chorus as opposed to being set up by a pre-chorus:

Verse

I'm the friendly stranger in the black sedan
Won't you hop inside my car
I got picture, got candy, I'm a lovable man
And I can take you to the nearest star

Chorus

I'm your Vehicle, baby
I'll take you anywhere you wanna go
I'm your Vehicle, baby
By now I'm sure you'll know
That I love you (love you), need you (need you)
Want you, got to have you, child
Great God in heaven you know I love you

*Words and music by Jim Peterik © 1970/1999, Bald Medusa
Music (ASCAP)*

I have to write another one like that! As a songwriter, I tend to devalue the simple songs I write, but those seem to always be the ones that turn out to be the biggest hits. In this example, every section has a hook, climaxing with "Great God in heaven you know I love you." It took me years to figure out what I was doing right in my more successful songs, but it usually boils down to simplicity, relatability, and a great beat.

The Beatles' "Lucy in the Sky with Diamonds" is an excellent example of a song that uses a pre-chorus with great success. If you don't know the song well, listen to it while reading the words so you can get a good idea of what the pre-chorus sounds like and what it accomplishes.

You'll notice that Lennon and McCartney create a pre-chorus (each with different words) before the first two times that the chorus is sung, but not before the last time it is sung.

Think of the pre-chorus as a mini bridge, because like the actual bridge of a song, it's taking your listeners' ears and minds into some new territory. It also allows the lyricist to build the story before hitting the chorus.

The next time you're writing a song, ask yourself whether your chorus would have more impact if it were set up by a pre-chorus. Often a good pre-chorus will have some fresh chord changes that haven't been used in the verse, especially if the chorus is in the same key as the verse.

Songwriter Chad Kroeger and the band Nickelback have created a very powerful hit song, using the verse-chorus with pre-chorus. What's innovative about the song "How You Remind Me" is the placement of the title in the pre-chorus instead of the chorus. The pre-chorus leads to a powerful sing-a-long chorus that's very effective.

In the second verse, the singer tells about how he has failed in the past. The pre-chorus is restated with the title and thesis of the song, then the chorus.

The final verse is simply the first verse, but this time a completely stripped-down version using only the vocal and electric guitar, using just the first two lines. The pre-chorus is then repeated and it leads into a full-stride version of the final chorus accentuated by dramatic breaks from the entire band. In this song, the pre-chorus, like the chorus, uses the same words each time.

The verse-chorus form using a bridge or ABABC form

The purpose of a bridge is to provide an interlude between other sections. Verse-chorus songs with bridges are very much a part of today's world.

In this section, we look more closely at a verse-chorus song that makes use of bridges.

Vertical Horizon is one of those bands that took many years and multiple albums to become an overnight sensation. Released in 2000, "Everything You Want" became their big breakthrough. In a mere 4 minutes and 17 seconds, it defined what modern rock would sound like — intelligent, concise, catchy, cryptic, and extremely well crafted. The song is basically written in a verse-chorus form with the writer using two verses before hitting the chorus. Starting with a telegraphic electric guitar figure and soon joined by acoustic guitar and bass, the very "in-your-face" vocal starts the verse and immediately pulls you in.

After the first two verses, the song now hits the very catchy and repetitive chorus. This is really the part you remember most when you first hear the song. Next comes the third verse, which treads some of the same emotional ground already covered but in a slightly different way. The chorus is now repeated. Following is the bridge — and it's everything a bridge should be: It blazes new ground chordally and thematically, and it raises the stakes as the singer strains for higher notes. Finally, the song enters the fourth verse — the kind of nostalgic looking back that's a perfect wrap-up for this song. Following this is a double chorus — the first a clone of the other two choruses. The repeat chorus changes into the first person, however. Weaving in and out of the song is a magical, moody guitar motif. It's probably as important an element as anything else in the song.

If you like bridges and want to know them better, check out the songs in Table 3-6 and see how they were used to create some pretty big hits.

Table 3-6	ABABC Song Examples	
Song Title	*Songwriter(s)*	*Singers/Performers*
"Here Comes the Sun"	George Harrison	The Beatles
"As Long As You Love Me"	Max Martin	Backstreet Boys
"I Turn to You"	Diane Warren	Christina Aguilera
"I Want It That Way"	Max Martin, Andreas Carlsson	Backstreet Boys
"Hands"	Jewel	Jewel
"Un-break My Heart"	Diane Warren	Toni Braxton

The verse-chorus form using both a pre-chorus and a bridge or ABCABCD form

This very popular song form, sometimes referred to as *ABCABCD,* pulls out all the stops to convince the listener a song means business. This form includes not only a pre-chorus before every chorus, but also a formal bridge at the center of the song, usually after the second chorus, before the *out chorus* (as the final chorus is sometimes called). The truly daring can further test the audiences' attention span by adding a third verse after the bridge, before the out chorus.

This form expands the author's chances of getting his lyrical point across, gives him the opportunity to make additional musical statements, and challenges the programming directors at radio stations across the country with songs longer than their formats allow. When using this form, make sure that it doesn't collapse under the weight of too many sections.

"Hold on Loosely," the top-ten hit by 38 Special (written by Jim Peterik, Don Barnes, and Jeff Carlisi), is an example of a song that just flat out works in this form, as validated by its continued airplay. Take a look at how the song builds as you sing along and you'll see why it has become a staple at classic rock radio:

"Hold on Loosely" written by Jim Peterik, Don Barnes, and Jeff Carlisi

Verse 1 (A)

You see it all around you
Good lovin' gone bad
And usually it's too late when you
Realize what you had

Pre-chorus (B)

My mind goes back to the girl I met
Long years ago, who told me

Chorus (C)

Just Hold On Loosely
But don't let go
If you cling too tightly
You're gonna lose control
Your baby needs someone to believe in
And a whole lotta space to breathe in

Verse 2 (A)

It's so damn easy
When your feelings are such
That you overprotect her
That you love her too much

Pre- chorus (B)

My mind goes back to the girl I met
Long years ago, who told me

Chorus (C)

Just Hold On Loosely
But don't let go
If you cling too tightly
You're gonna lose control

Your baby needs someone to believe in
And a whole lotta space to breathe in

Bridge (D)

Don't let her slip away
Sentimental fool
Don't let your heart get in the way
Yeah, yeah, yeah

Verse (A)

You see it all around you
Good lovin' gone bad
And usually it's too late when you
Realize what you had

Chorus (C)

So Hold On Loosely
But don't let go
If you cling too tightly
You're gonna lose control
Your baby needs someone to believe in
And a whole lot of space to breathe in

© 1981 WB Music Corp. (ASCAP), Easy Action Music (ASCAP) and Rocknocker Music Company. All Rights o/b/o Easy Action Music administered by WB Music Corp. All Rights Reserved. Used by permission. Warner Bros. Publications U.S. Inc. Miami, FL 33014

As you may have noticed, the last verse bypasses the pre-chorus and heads right to the final chorus. By this time in the song, the writers felt it was no longer necessary and more important to get to the main hook.

One of my favorite songs that I've ever co-written is "I Can't Hold Back," a hit for my band, Survivor, back in 1985. It starts with an intricately picked guitar intro figure, then hits the first verse, "There's a story in my eyes. . . ." then into the pre-chorus, "I can feel you tremble when we touch. . . ." into the chorus, "I can't hold back — I'm on the edge. . . ." From there it goes unexpectedly into an instrumental version of the pre-chorus, then slides into a spacey bridge, "Another shooting star goes by. . . ." then glides straight into the pre-chorus. Next, instead of going into a chorus, the song returns to a reprise of the verse, "There's a story in my eyes. . . ." then it skips the pre-chorus and goes directly to the out-chorus. Whew-boy! When my writing partner, Frankie Sullivan, and I were sitting at the piano at the Record Plant recording studio in Los Angeles with our producer, Ron Nevison, throwing around ideas, I wasn't sure this unorthodox structure was going to work, but the next day when we recorded it, it was magic! The experience taught me not to be afraid to play around with song structure. Take a look:

"I Can't Hold Back" written by Jim Peterik and Frankie Sullivan

Verse 1 (A)

There's a story in my eyes
Turn the pages of desire
Now it's time to trade those dreams
For the rush of passion's fire

Pre-Chorus 1 (B)

I can feel you tremble when we touch
And I feel the hand of fate
Reaching out to both of us

Verse 2 (A)

I've been holding back the night
I've been searching for a clue from you
I'm gonna try with all my might
To make this story line come true

Pre-Chorus 2 (B)

Can ya feel me tremble when we touch
Can you feel the hands of fate
Reaching out to both of us
This love affair can't wait

Chorus (C)

I can't hold back, I'm on the edge (I can't hold back)
Your voice explodes inside my head
I can't hold back, I won't back down
Girl it's too late to turn back now

Bridge (D)

Another shooting star goes by
And in the night the silence speaks to you and I
And now the time has come at last
Don't let the moment come too fast

Pre-Chorus 3 (B)

I can feel you tremble when we touch
And I feel the hand of fate reaching out to both of us

Verse 3 (A)

There's a story in my eyes, turn the pages of desire
Now it's time to trade those dreams
For the rush of passion's fire

Chorus (C)

I can't hold back, I'm on the edge (I can't hold back)
Your voice explodes inside my head
I can't hold back, I won't back down
Girl it's too late to turn back now

Pre-Chorus 4 (B)

I can see you tremble when we touch
Oooh, And I feel the hand of fate reaching out to both of us
This love affair can't wait

I can't hold back, I can't hold back
I can't hold back, I can't hold back

Words and music by Jim Peterik and Frankie Sullivan III

Listen to the songs of Lennon and McCartney and the various Motown writers. It's a great way to learn about the variations of song structure.

Even though the songs in Table 3-7 are older, they set the template for much of the new music you currently hear every day and demonstrate some non-standard song forms.

Table 3-7	Structure Variations	
Song Title	*Songwriter(s)*	*Singers/Performers*
"Standing in the Shadows of Love"	Holland/Dozier/Holland	The Four Tops
"My Girl"	Smokey Robinson, Ronald White	The Temptations
"I'm Looking Through You"	John Lennon, Paul McCartney	The Beatles
"We Can Work It Out"	John Lennon, Paul McCartney	The Beatles

"Drops of Jupiter" (written and performed by Train) is one of those songs that makes an immediate impression. Usually with brilliant songs like this, you remember where you were and what you were feeling when it first hit your ears. It's an example of a song that takes a standard tried-and-true song form and twists it here and there to make it sound unusual and fresh — a pop/rock masterpiece. The song starts with the piano figure of the verse. The first verse contains the only reference to the song's title. So much for the traditional wisdom of driving the hook into the ground — but that didn't seem to hurt sales at all.

By the way, the music charts, such as *Billboard, Radio and Records*, and so on, have taken to putting the words ("Tell Me") after the song's title for those of us who can't identify it by its cryptic title, "Drops of Jupiter."

The chorus comes next, although it's not a traditional type of chorus in that the title is never stated. After the chorus, a significant instrumental signature is created by a string section. We now hit the second verse. It follows the same structure of the first verse, except that the last line before the second chorus is extended for extra impact. The song cleverly uses modern-day references such as "*tae-bo*" and later on, "*soy latte.*" What's unusual in the second chorus is that although the rhythm of the words and melody stay the same, practically all the words are different. The hook "*Tell me*" is about all that stays the same. Moving the action along in a chorus as opposed to marking time is unique.

A bridge follows the second chorus, although not in the traditional sense in changing keys and mood. It's more chant-like and modifies the action by changing up the rhythm of the words. The arrangement then breaks down to just piano and voice again, and the song enters the final chorus. Again, the writers break form by combining elements of both earlier choruses into one. The song ends with the infectious "*Na, na, na*" refrain with alternating vocal ad libs lifted from various sections of the song. The last line is a brand-new variation on an earlier passage. The lyrics in this song, are very open to interpretation. The majestic tone of the music matches perfectly the broad scope of the lyric.

There are some great songs out there that don't play by the rules. The writers have ignored the standard forms to create something truly unique. "Drops of Jupiter" by Train can be corralled, kicking and screaming, into some kind of traditional form but it's really a maverick. As an experiment, try challenging the listener by shifting your sections around to make your song stand out from the pack of cookie-cutter tracks. If your song becomes confusing and unfocused when playing it for others, it's time to go back to the drawing board!

Practice Makes Perfect

Often the best way of learning a craft is taking the best examples you can find and start tearing them apart to see what makes them tick. Pick five of your favorite songs (could be anything from a '40s standard to the latest by Radiohead!). Listen to the song and analyze its structure by writing out the lyric in its entirety (you can find accurate transcripts of lyrics on many music sites on the Internet and printed on the actual CD label). It should then be easy to note the song's various sections by verse, pre-chorus, chorus, bridge, out chorus, and whatever other spare parts you may encounter. See if the songs you like the most follow any particular pattern — if so, you may want to pattern your song after that form.

When analyzing the structure of your favorite songs, notice the various ways in which the great ones push the boundaries of song craft to the max. As you are listening and making notes, take an especially close look in the following areas:

- ✔ **What is it about each section that sets it apart from the rest of the song?** For instance, notice how the story builds verse to verse as the song unfolds, how the chorus lifts the song to new heights, how the bridge does its job by giving the listener some fresh chord changes and some new emotional ammunition.

- ✔ **What is truly unusual or original in the songs you love the most?** Most songs you encounter that have survived to make a difference in this world have one or more elements that elevate it above the pack. "We Built This City," (written by Bernie Taupin, Peter Wolf, Martin Page, and Dennis Lambert) the 80s hit for Jefferson Starship, starts right out with the sing-a-long chorus. Certain songs defy logic by shifting their key signature down on the last chorus instead of up. Find those special elements in the songs that really get your attention.

- ✔ **Where do the titles appear in your favorite songs?** The traditional practice of placing the title at the beginning of the chorus is often disregarded by daring writers. Notice songs that position their title at the end of the chorus, in the verse or pre-chorus, or that dispense with it altogether.

Part II
Unleashing the Lyricist in You

The 5th Wave   By Rich Tennant

"I know every love song needs a hook,
but couldn't it be something other
than a duck-call?"

In this part . . .

One of the first elements people notice when they hear a song are the words. Without effective words, also known as *lyrics,* it's hard for someone to care about the music underneath it. In this part, we look at the art of writing a catchy, yet meaningful, lyric. (Yes, the two *can* co-exist!) We examine some of the great songs of our time to see how lyrical devices helped these songs scale the charts and stay in people's memory banks. We then show you ways to develop your own lyrical power.

Chapter 4

Snagging Your Listeners with a Hook

In This Chapter

▶ Identifying the various hooks used in songs

▶ Using hooks without overusing them

▶ Trying your hand at hooks, titles, and ideas

*W*hen a fisherman casts his lure, he waits — sometimes all day — for some unsuspecting fish to find the hook. As a songwriter, you don't have the luxury of having a listener wait that long for the *hook* — the catchy part that sticks in the listeners' head. You have to hook them in right away so that they'll want to hear the rest of the song and keep listening to the song time and time again. In this chapter, we look at that very important element of a song (the hook), see what types of hooks are in the musical tackle box, and show you how to use them in your song to win fans and reel people in.

Stocking Your Tackle Box with Hooks

The types of hooks you'll find in your favorite songs are:

✔ Melodic hook

✔ Lyrical hook

✔ Musical hook

✔ Rhythmic hook

✔ Sound-effect hook

Sometimes you'll find more than one type of hook in a single song. In fact, most successful songs combine several different types of hooks. However, there's usually one that takes precedence over the others to command your attention. In the following sections, we cover each of these types of hooks and show you how they work.

Too many hooks in one song is not a good thing. If every phrase is vying for the listener's attention, remembering the one or two key phrases may be difficult. Some lines in your song should move the action along and help tell the story, but they shouldn't call attention to themselves. In the same vein, make sure you don't have too many melodic hooks competing with each other in one song. Too many melodic hooks may obscure the main hook and leave the listener confused about which part is the really important part. As they say, "Too many hooks spoil the broth" (well, at least songwriters say it!).

The melodic hook

The melodic hook is perhaps the most persuasive element in a songwriter's tackle box. If you choose a melodic hook, your challenge is to have at least one section of your song instantly hummable, regardless of the words that accompany it. That section is the *melodic hook*. It should stick in your listeners' heads long after the song is over. It should be the part of the song that people listen for each time the song comes around, sort of like finding an oasis in a desert.

In the following sections, we take a look at a few songs that have made millions, in no small part, because of their infectious melodic hooks.

Beethoven's Fifth

No, not the fifth of whiskey Beethoven may have carried around with him, but his famous fifth symphony written early in the nineteenth century. This piece contains perhaps the most famous series of four notes ever connected. These three short notes and one long one (dum-dum-dum dhaaa) have spanned generations with their timeless power. Some have called it the ultimate riff, because it needs no lyrics to convey the feeling of urgent emotion.

In World War II, the rally cry was the letter *V*, for victory. And the legendary status of Beethoven's Fifth was only enhanced by this. Why? Because in Morse code, the letter V is "short-short-short-long," which just happens to be the melodic hook of Beethoven's Fifth.

"The Way"

Though hundreds of years and musical light years away from Beethoven, this 1999 pop gem performed by Fastball (written by Anthony Scalzo) is defined by a super-infectious melody that greets its listeners at the chorus. The words that accompany this musical feast, "Don't you know the road that we walked on was paved with gold" are nice, but what you really remember is the exuberant mood of that particular series of notes. The song, which lacks a strong title or musical hook, really relies on the chorus melody to make it stand out in high relief from the hundreds of other songs in the pop genre.

"Land of a Thousand Dances"

This trashy '60s gem performed by Cannibal and the Headhunters (written by Chris Kenner) defined the term *garage band*. Over one droning chord, the honorable Sir Cannibal enumerated the many cool dances in this mythical teen paradise. But the real hook didn't rely on words. It was a primitive, wordless chant: na, na na na na, na na na na, na na na, na na na — na na na na! This is when the tough guys at school would tie their bandanas around their heads at the dance and really get down and dirty.

The lyrical hook

Nothing can endear a person to a song more than a strong lyrical hook. When two people fall in love and ordain one song as "their song," they usually do so because of the strength of the song's message. And the *lyrical hook* is the part of the song that summarizes that message.

Often, the title is a key part of the lyrical hook. A title is how people identify a song. Finding a particular piece of music is fairly difficult if you don't know the title. We once saw a woman go into a store and start performing the song she was searching for — the store clerk had no idea which song she was singing, and she left empty-handed! And that's part of why titles are so important.

Songwriters often refer to the title of a song as its lyrical hook because they can use the title in particular ways that'll hook the listener and imprint the song's title in the listener's mind.

It took me a while to get used to referring to the title as the hook of the songs. To me, there are potentially so many different kinds of hooks in a song that you can't just give the title alone that distinction. Suffice it to say, you'll run into this terminology in the music business, so be prepared.

Hooking your listeners with the title

Titles become hooks when they're repeated throughout the song. Titles, just like concepts and ideas, can come from anywhere — daily headlines, popular expressions, movie dialogues, book titles. Titles are practically everywhere and since, except in rare cases, they can't be copyrighted, they can be a popular source of inspiration.

The title of a song is often carefully placed and repeated in the song. This is how a title is used to hook the listener. Titles can appear at the beginning or end of the chorus (and sometimes in both places) or at the end of each verse. Sometimes titles are repeated over and over. It's this placement and repetition that drives the title home to the listeners, so they can tell their friends, "did you hear such-and-such on the radio?" But don't think that a title has to be unique or clever to be valid. A name may be the quickest way to identify a person, but it's only the entrance to what a person is all about. If a song title is like a person's name, then the song

itself is like the soul and being of a person. Many times a common song title can be infused with new meaning through the insights of the song itself. Common words can suddenly seem profound, and clichés can be twisted and reinvented. In most cases, it's what you make of a title that separates an average song from a great one.

Sometimes, the title isn't used as a hook at all. In fact, the title may never even be used in the song, though the song may be nonetheless memorable: "For What It's Worth" (written by Steven Stills; performed by Buffalo Springfield), "Positively Fourth Street" (written and sung by Bob Dylan), and "Badge" (written by Eric Clapton and George Harrison; performed by Cream) are all examples of songs in which the titles never appear. (The song "Badge" got its name when George Harrison, who played guitar on the song, was reading the lyric sheet upside down and mistook Clapton's notation of *bridge* as *badge*.)

 Try setting up a groove on your rhythm machine. You can make one up from scratch simply through experimentation or use one of the preprogrammed settings. Try your hand at creating a simple chord progression that goes with the beat. Now try creating a melody on top of that, and then find a lyrical hook to go with the melody.

Often, there is one word in a lyrical hook that just leaps out at you and becomes a permanent file in your cranium. In the following sections, we take a look at some great lyrical hooks — both in the title and in the song.

"I Heard It Through the Grapevine"

This Motown classic (written by Barrett Strong and Norman Whitfield) made famous by the late, great Marvin Gaye (predated by a version by Motown labelmates Gladys Knight and the Pips) encapsulates its powerful lyrical premise in the title itself. When you hear the title, you pretty much know what the song is about — the rumor mill of careless whispers that can sink a love relationship. The word *grapevine* in and of itself is a descriptive and colorful word that's unusual without being too obscure for the average listener.

Try to make your title a kind of condensed version of the song itself. When someone can read the title and have a clue as to what the song is about, it'll only pique his interest to see how the idea is developed. Avoid generic titles that are too frequently used, unless you can truly pump new life into it in the context of the song. For example, if you title a song "I Love You," it had better be a whole lot different from the thousands of other songs with the same title. Make your title intriguing enough so the listener wants to hear it and experience more of the song that follows.

"She Loves You"

This classic from the early days of The Beatles (written by John Lennon and Paul McCartney) proves that oftentimes the main lyrical hook of a song is not always the title. In this case, the three little words "Yeah, Yeah, Yeah" became the rally cry for the Baby Boom generation and those words are now crossing all boundaries to future generations. If you're hung up on making your hook profound, all you have to do is look at "She Loves You" to find proof that it isn't a necessity when it comes to writing lyrical hooks.

I first saw the phenomenon called The Beatles on some grainy footage Jack Paar brought back from England with him for his *Jack Paar Show* audience, a full three months before The Beatles appeared on *The Ed Sullivan Show*. I heard the future of rock 'n' roll, and woke up the next day singing "Yeah, Yeah, Yeah." I ran to the record shop and sang these words to the stunned lady behind the counter, even though I didn't know the title of the song — proving the power of an infectious lyrical hook within a song.

"Just the Way You Are"

This classic by singer/songwriter Billy Joel proves again that the strongest lyrical hook is not always the title. It probably drives Billy to distraction that so many people refer to this song as "Don't Go Changing." When a phrase that unique opens a song, there is a great likelihood that it'll take over the actual title when listeners identify it.

"Oops, I Did It Again"

This song (written by Martin Sandberg and Rami Yacoub) performed by Britney Spears found itself at the top of the charts with this suggestive confection. The title immediately makes the listener want to know just what it is that Britney did, how often she did it, and with whom.

The musical hook

Oftentimes, the musical hook, or *money hook* — the one that sells the song — is not technically an element of the songwriting itself, but a part of the song's arrangement. A musical hook can be a riff, like the guitar figure in the intro of "Daytripper" (written by John Lennon and Paul McCartney, performed by The

Beatles), or anything instrumental that cries for the ears attention. Many disagreements have occurred through the years between musicians and songwriters about where songwriting ends and where arranging starts. If a musical hook helps identify a song so well that it's used as an indispensable part in countless versions, many in the songwriting profession would consider it an element of the song itself. Other terms that fall into the category of the musical hook include the following:

- ✔ **Riff:** A series of repeated notes often played on guitar, keyboard, or brass section that's positioned throughout the song.

- ✔ **Lick:** A throwback term from the old be-bop days, a lick is like a riff, only shorter.

- ✔ **Figure:** A catchall phrase that refers to any repeated series of notes, generally identical throughout the song.

In the following sections, we use these terms as we look at some prime examples of musical hooks within tunes.

"Satisfaction"

If Keith Richards's only contribution to this Rolling Stones classic from 1965 was to create the fuzz tone riff at the opening of this song, he'd easily have earned his keep as a songwriter. The fact that he was far more helpful than that (appropriating the memorable title from a line in an old Chuck Berry tune) was icing on the cake. This riff, which Keith always heard as a horn figure (and was done that way in subsequent versions — most notably Otis Redding's 1966 cover), was inspired by the great Motown hooks of the '60s, specifically "Dancing in the Streets" (written by Marvin Gaye, Ivy Hunter, and William Stevenson; performed by Martha and the Vandellas). You hear that riff and know exactly which song you're listening to.

"Vehicle"

The five-note horn riff that starts off this classic performed by Chicago's Ides of March (written by Jim Peterik) has to be one of the most recognizable phrases in horn-rock history. Setting up the lyrical hook "I'm the friendly stranger in the black sedan, won't you hop inside my car," the figure involves the listener with its urgency and power.

"Someone to Call My Lover"

This 2001 smash by the resilient Janet Jackson (written by Dewey Bunnell, James Harris, Janet Jackson, and Terry Lewis), *samples* (uses pieces of previously recorded snippets of music) the musical riff from the group America's 1972 hit "Ventura Highway" (written by Dewey Bunnell) and adds it to a brand-new tune. The result is a cutting-edge song with the added depth of musicianship that the guitarist from the group America was famous for.

It's important to note that the practice of sampling is prevalent in modern recording. However, please be aware that it requires the permission of the writer and publisher of the original work and commands a fee called a mechanical royalty or licensing fee to be paid for the privilege of *lifting* (the current term for using) such a sample.

JIM SAYS

Frankie Sullivan and I received a request from Busta Rhymes, the multi-platinum rapper, to sample our song "Eye of The Tiger." His version used much of the music we'd written but substituted our lyrics with off-color language that fit the rap genre but didn't fit the spirit of the song we'd written. We independently decided to decline his request and forfeit a potentially lucrative payday to uphold the uplifting message of the song. On the other hand, when an enterprising rap group, Strata III, asked for permission to sample my song "Vehicle" for a good-natured interpretation called "Hop Dis," I gave it my full blessing!

The rhythmic hook

As Bob Dylan said in the '60s, "The times, they are a-changin'." Songwriting used to be rigidly defined as words and music. Nowadays, rhythmic elements often form the basis of a song, especially in the urban, hip-hop, and rap categories, and can be as integral to the song as any other element. Of course, the use of the rhythmic hook is nothing new — songs from the '50s and '60s were the predecessors of today's trends. The following sections show how different rhythms add memorable punch to songs.

"Hey, Bo Diddley"

The jungle rhythms of Bo Diddley set the stage for many artists to follow. Punctuated by Bo's distorted electric guitar, this song and many of his others played one chord into the ground and built momentum with the intensity of the rhythm. Many of the early Rolling Stones songs, such as their fierce reworking of Buddy Holly's "Not Fade Away," used Bo Diddley's work as a stepping-off point. Also showing this influence was "I Want Candy" (written by Bertram Berns, Bob Feldman, Gerald Goldstein, and Richard Gottehrer; performed by The Strangeloves) and "Bad to the Bone" (written by George Thorogood; performed by George Thorogood and The Destroyers).

"Wipe Out"

The surfer's classic by The Surfaris (written by Robert Berryhill, Patrick Connolly, James Fuller, and Robert Wilson) owes its success in a large part to the manic tom-tom sticking of their young drummer. The crazed laugh at the intro was nice, the guitar work tasty, but everything else existed to set up the rhythm hook.

JIM SAYS

As my high school band director used to say, "First there was rhythm." He was right. What was the first thing the contestants on *Dick Clark's American Bandstand* would say when they were rating a new record? "It's got a great beat. You can dance to it. I give it a 97!"

"Stayin' Alive"

This song is a first-class example of a rhythmic hook — showcased in the timing of the Bee Gees' "Stayin' Alive" (written by the Bee Gees) from the *Saturday Night Fever* soundtrack to the actual rhythm of John Travolta's steps as his character Tony struts down the streets of New York. The brothers' use of rhythmic breath ("hah-hah-hah-hah, stayin' alive, stayin' alive") is one of the most recognizable hooks of the entire '70s — whether you loved or hated disco.

The sound-effect hook

Though not technically a part of the song, sound effects have become an indispensable component in certain hit songs. When constructing your song demo, weigh the possibility of adding certain sounds, whether they're sampled real effects (CDs full of sampled effects — everything from church bells to explosions — are available for sale in the back pages of countless musician and recording magazines) or sound effects generated on your synthesizer. Sound effects can add atmosphere and, at times, even become a hook in your song. In the following sections, we provide a few examples of hits that use the sound-effect hook to their advantage.

"Let's Roll"

This song (written and sung by Neil Young) was sent out to radio in a plain brown wrapper soon after the tragic events of September 11, 2001. There was nothing plain about the response to this song that addressed the heroic passengers aboard Flight 93, who overthrew would-be suicide terrorists and crashed their plane into a field in Pennsylvania before it could reach its intended target. Neil uses the words that one of the passengers spoke before taking the plane down, "Let's Roll," as the song's title, as well as the chilling sound effect of three rings of a cell phone in the song's introduction to denote the passengers' last communication. In this case, the use of sound design enhanced an already effective and poignant song.

"Reflections"

Motown producers like Holland-Dozier-Holland and Smokey Robinson were no strangers to the use of certain sound effects on their records. This song (written by Lamont Dozier, Brian Holland, and Edward Holland; performed by Diana Ross and the Supremes) uses the new technology (for the time) of the Moog Synthesizer to emphasize the emotion of the title. The ethereal sound of the Moog becomes like another voice filling the song with bittersweet feelings.

Although the electronic sounds of the Moog have been elevated to high art since then; in "Reflections," the sound was used more to create an ethereal mood. Next time you hear the song, try to imagine it without the effects created by the Moog.

"Barbara Ann"

This Beach Boys cover of the hit (written by Fred Fassert; performed by The Regents) became a very big hit on its own as a part of the Beach Boys *Party* album. What most people don't know, however, is that the party was added later! They call this *post-production* nowadays, which means effects are added after the song has been recorded. The sound effects of a crowd having an absolute ball added an element of fun to an already exuberant track.

"The Kiss Off (Good-Bye)"

This song, for young dance pop diva Brooke Allison (written by Jim Peterik and Jeff Jacobs), uses the well-known America Online (AOL) sign off, "good-bye," as its sound effect hook. At the end of each chorus, Brooke sings, "I got just one thing to say to you," after which the voice of AOL Elwood Edwards intones "good-bye."

"Leader of the Pack," "Last Kiss," and "Teen Angel"

"Leader of the Pack" (written by Jeff Barry, Ellie Greenwich, and George Morton; performed by the Shangri-Las), "Last Kiss" (written by Wayne Cochran; performed by J. Frank Wilson), and "Teen Angel" (written by Jean Surrey; performed by Dion and the Belmonts) all use the sound of automotive crashes to help tell their stories of teen tragedy. Next time you hear J. Frank Wilson's weeper "Last Kiss," listen for the background-singing angel who seems to expire on the high note along with the hero.

The songs of The Beatles

There's not enough room to mention all the songs by The Beatles that have used sound effects to add atmosphere and hooks to their music, starting with their album *Revolver* and reaching a climax on *Sergeant Pepper*. Listen to the great circus sound effects on "For the Benefit of Mr. Kite" or the cacophony of sound created by the orchestra at the end of the first section of "Day in the Life." The Beatles, especially Paul McCartney (who was enamored by the sonic experimentation of Karlheinz Stockhausen), took every opportunity to include avant-garde sound samples in the mix. Their producer, George Martin, made available to them the vast sound effects library of the BBC (British Broadcasting Corporation) and its array of electronic devices for their experimentation and taught them techniques of slowing down and speeding up the tape machines to warp the tonality (or timbre) of the sound, and actually reversing the tape for even more other-worldly effects (like the backwards guitar solo in "Taxman" by The Beatles).

The use of different types of hooks in one song

There are, of course many examples where different types of hooks are used in one song. When you team them all together you get a pretty compelling package. Although using too many hooks of the same type is not a good idea, a variety of different kinds of hooks constantly persuades the listener to hang in there until the end of the song. Here are good examples of songs with an extremely well-stocked tackle box.

"Turn Out the Lights"

This 2001 hit for the Canadian Nelly Furtado (written by Nelly Furtado) combines many different types of hooks to excellent advantage. The intro starts right off with what sounds like a Gregorian chant (a melodic hook) building into a backward cymbal (a sound-effect hook), then launches into the sparse hip-hop groove, (a rhythmic hook), then into the hypnotic electric piano figure (a musical hook), and Nelly hasn't even opened her mouth yet! Accompanying the intro elements is the subtle disharmony of birds and crickets and some indecipherable filtered voices. Nelly sings the verse and pre-chorus with understated charm — the perfect setup for the chorus, which contains the big melodic/lyrical hook of, "They say that girl ya know she act too tough, tough, tough — well it's till I turn off the light, turn off the light." Everything about that line is a hook, from its sing-along melody to its rhythmic repetition of the word *tough,* rhyming with the thrice-repeated *rough* in the next line. She then ups the ante with the machine gun repetition of the words "follow me" and "down." Nelly's bridge is what could be considered a rap section with melody. The final chorus closes out with the return of the nighttime choir of crickets and birds.

"Music"

Madonna's multi-platinum hit from the year 2000 (written by Miruais Amhadzai and Madonna) is one of those songs from which every last ounce of fat has been trimmed, exposing nothing but the hooks. It opens with the main lyrical hook (even though it's not the title), "Hey Mr. D.J., put a record on, I wanna dance with my baby" spoken by a male in a cool, dry delivery. The song then hits the underlying musical hook (reminiscent of the organ riff in The Animals' '60s hit, "It's My Life" written by Roger Atkins and Carl Derrico) combined with an unstoppable groove created by Miruais Ahmadzai. The song then hits the main musical hook performed on a synthesizer using the four notes D, B-flat, and C with the last note repeated (the sound seems to be run through a voice simulator making what sounds like the words "Do You Like It?") Madonna then takes center stage with the sung version of the earlier spoken words, "Hey, Mr. D.J. . . ." This lyrical hook is now combined with the secondary melodic hook (the main melodic hook will hit in the chorus) to create a double-whopper. The setup to the haunting chorus is a filtered vocal (sound-effect hook) of the words to come. Now it's time for the main hook: "Music makes the people come together. . . ." It's a vaguely Eastern melodic motif combined with the powerful main message of the song. After the second verse and chorus, the song starts an instrumental section emphasizing electronic effects and sweeps leading into a severely *filtered* version of the song's verse (filtering is the practice of limiting the frequency response of a sound — the telephone effect is a good example). Now a third melodic hook enters for the very first time, a couple of minutes into the tune (hey, when you're Madonna you can get away with anything!), and is soon counter-pointed by the four-note hook introduced earlier in the song. As complex as this all sounds, like most smash hits it comes across as elegantly simple — the real proof of a great song and arrangement. This is one song that tests the theory that too many hooks spoil the broth!

Having the Right Mindset When Working with Hooks

There's no such thing as the universal hook — one hook that always works with every listener. (If there were, it would be included in every song.) Each person is receptive to slightly different stimuli. Songwriters have the tendency to get discouraged if everyone isn't absolutely captivated by every hook they throw into the pond, but it's important to remember that *no* song is loved by everyone.

I used to be devastated if someone didn't respond to one of my songs. I remember sending four songs that I had just co-written with an emerging young artist to the president of a well-known record company. After waiting the customary week for a reply, I called him instead. He told me straight-faced that he "must have his tin ears on this week because he just doesn't hear a hook!" Even though I got the artist signed to another deal (with the same songs), that "tin ear" comment will forever live in my memory banks.

The amount of times you use a hook and the different ways you use it can effect the shelf life of your song. Everyone has heard songs that they love right away but that they're totally sick of after hearing it 50 or 60 times. This could be a result of what is known in the hushed corridors of publishing empires as *hook dysfunction*. To prevent hook dysfunction from happening to you (although it happens to us all from time to time), be careful that you don't drive the main hook into the ground (with too many repetitions) or that the melodic hook isn't so insipid (refer to "Chewy, Chewy" written by Joey Levine and Kris Resnick; performed by the Ohio Express) that it haunts your nightmares.

Strive instead for a song that hooks you subtly at first, then takes hold and won't let go. If the lyrics have enough to say, they'll build in power with repeated listening and give your song staying power.

Not everyone will listen to every word of your lyrics the first few times they hear them, so make sure there are a couple of easy-to-digest, hook-like phrases that sum up the *premise* (or idea) of the song.

Practice Makes Perfect

Check out the top ten songs on *Billboard's* Top 100 Chart and pick three songs you like. Listen to each song and figure out how many hooks are in each song. *Remember:* You're looking for melodic, lyrical, musical, and rhythmical hooks, as well as the use of any sound effects or other qualities that make the song memorable. By dissecting current hits, you'll really get a flavor for writing your own hooks. After you've picked out what different types of hooks are used in these songs, make a note of how many times each is repeated within the songs.

If you have a song already written or have one started, go through it and analyze the types of hooks you use, how effective they are and how they can be sharpened and improved. If you haven't yet written your first song, come up with what you feel is a good hook. It could be a potential title, a musical riff, an intriguing sound, a hypnotic rhythm, or a catchy series of chords. Hold on to it as you discover more about the mechanics of writing a song.

Choose five of your closest friends or relatives — or those who will still love you in the morning — then ask them each to write down what they remember the most about your song after playing it for them. If you find, after reading the secret ballots that you're not voted off the island, and that one element of the song seems to have been mentioned on all five sheets, then you may just be on your way to having a good hook. If they call you in three days slightly irritated that they can't get that song out of their heads, then you know you've developed that special quality that gives a song staying power.

Chapter 5

Getting Acquainted with the Different Kinds of Lyrics

. . . .

In This Chapter

▶ Studying the lyrics of different types of songs

▶ Practicing the art of writing lyrics

. . . .

Think back to the first song you can remember hearing as a child. What part of that song really made a connection in the developing synapses of your brain? It could have been the beat, the sounds, or the singsong melody. But most likely, these parts wouldn't have had much impact on you if they hadn't been attached to words that somehow stuck with you. The words you noticed were probably very simple at first, perhaps a part of a game ("ring-around-the-rosie") and so on. As you grew up, you started gravitating toward songs that seemed to reflect the experiences of your expanding awareness. If you could turn to your friend and say, "Hey, that's me they're talking about," or "I've been wanting to say that myself," or "That's exactly what I'm going through, right now" — chances are you'd buy that song and play it till you wore it out. As a songwriter, it's the connection you make with a song's lyric, and how closely you can relate to the feelings of your audience that puts you in touch with them. Starting with what matters to you most is a very good place to start.

In this chapter, we look at the various ways that you as a songwriter can make an impact through lyrics. We break it down and discuss the various forms in which your ideas can be expressed, explaining the different devices the pros use to add impact and professionalism to their songs. Chapter 6 dives into creating your own lyrics.

Looking at Lyric Types

Webster's defines a *lyric* as "the words of a song, as distinguished from the music." Well, that's fairly cut and dried. But when the word is defined as an adjective, things get interesting: "songlike; specifically, designating poetry or a poem expressing the poet's personal emotion or sentiment. . . ." Now we're talkin'! You can think of lyrics as thoughts with rhythm and rhyme — and on rare occasions you can even dispense with the rhyme.

A great lyric is an idea with wings. Take a look at the different forms a lyric can take and see where some of your favorite songs took root before taking flight:

- ✔ Concept-driven lyrics
- ✔ Story lyrics
- ✔ Love lyrics
- ✔ Current events and protest lyrics
- ✔ Novelty and humorous lyrics
- ✔ Parody lyrics
- ✔ Inspirational and spiritual lyrics

When I sit down to write a song with someone, before even writing one note, I ask that person what's on his mind, what really matters to him right now. The ensuing conversation can often be a stepping-off point for a song that actually has substance, because it's important to that person.

Now, in the following sections of this chapter, we describe each type of lyric in detail and give you some song examples.

If you want to study the lyrics to the songs we dive into and are looking for the words to those songs, we suggest you purchase the lyrics or buy the CD. You can also find lyrics on the Internet — although you'll have to pay a fee; most songs are available at www.songfile.com. We also recommend you check out the articles (related to copyright issues and websites sharing lyrics and MP3s) posted by the Harry Fox Agency, Inc. at www.harryfox.com.

Concept-driven lyrics

Behind most great songs is a great idea or concept. A concept is a lyrical blueprint for the song (and its authors) to follow. A strong concept can increase your chances for a great song.

Write down the concept of the song in prose (the un-poetry) when you start the song, and refer back to it frequently to make sure your lyric stays on course. The concept is also referred to as a songs' premise — basically a one or two sentence sum-up of what the song is about. If you can't distill your idea into one or two sentences, perhaps your idea is too complex for one song, or you lack a clear idea of what you want to say.

In many of my songwriting sessions, I look back at the initial concept of my song and realize it has somehow morphed into something else. I then have to decide just which song I want to write! I may have two songs in one, and that's never a good thing. The focus of your song must be clear, or you run the risk of confusing the listener.

Don't let the word *concept* intimidate you. A concept can be extremely simple — in fact, most successful songs have very simple ideas that drive them. In the following, we take a look at a few popular songs that are concept-driven.

"Missing You"

This '80s classic written by Charles Sanford, Mark Leonard, and John Waite (former lead singer for The Babys and Bad English) was a top-ten hit and has been covered numerous times by other artists (most significantly by former Ikette, Tina Turner, in her soul-drenched version) largely on the strength of its telegraphic guitar figure and the underlying irony of its concept.

This song's concept revolves around the tortured hero who throughout the verses professes the many ways that life is no longer the same now that the love of his life is gone. He's in a quandary as to why she left and it sounds as though he's ready to stick his head in the oven when he's saved by the chorus.

The dichotomy between what he's saying in the verses (his gut-wrenching feelings) and the chorus (where he puts on a front for the world) is the unique concept for this song. No matter what his friends say, what he says, and how it may appear, he's not missing her at all.

It's often the contrasts in life that have the most impact — the difference between what our lips are saying and what our heart is feeling (for a good example give a listen to "Tears of a Clown" written by Henry Cosby, Stevie Wonder, and Smokey Robinson), or the way you feel about her as opposed to how she feels about you.

"Good Vibrations"

This collaboration between songwriters Brian Wilson and Mike Love of the Beach Boys is a good example of a great concept that got better and more commercial (in other words, more people could relate to it — so it sold zillions) through the process of collaboration. Brian was initially intrigued by the notion of vibrations in the universe (both good and bad) that dogs and humans pick up on.

His initial lyric didn't contain any reference to relationships and there was no romantic back story. Mike Love heard and loved the song, but felt that an element was missing. He felt that by adding "that boy/girl thing" they could expand their market and still stay true to the original concept of cosmic vibrations coursing through the universe. "I'm picking up good vibrations, she's giving me excitations" became the catch phrase for the Baby Boom generation with the song's brilliant juxtaposition of heaven and earth.

When you find a lyrical concept that intrigues you, see how you can make it as easy to relate to as possible. If the listener can see himself or his situation in your song, you may have put something into words that he could never quite express on his own.

"Superman (It's Not Easy)"

Of all the songs with this title (and there have been many), Five For Fighting's ode to everything he isn't, is perhaps the most touching (written by John Ondrasik).

The concept of the frailty of man and his search for identity is universal and one of the most soul-baring, gut-wrenching examples in recent memory, culminating in the poignant statement at the chorus's end, "It's not easy to be me." Much of the song's lyrical power lies in the contrast between Superman and mortal man — in admitting the differences, he's elevated to super-hero status.

Lyrics that tell a story

Songs that tell a story are as old as time itself. Even in days of old, songwriters realized that songs were a good way to put a relatively plain story into an attractive package and make everyone want to listen. Today, great storytellers often write in the style of country, but there are no restrictions on the genres that the story song can cross.

"Stan"

This modern-day fable of fan worship taken to the extreme, written by Eminem, Paul Herman, and Dido, sung by white rapper Eminem, is an example of how a musical style can update a sturdy lyrical form like the story song. This song is presented as a series of letters from a loyal fan of the rapper expressing his mounting frustration at Eminem's lack of response to his letters. His letters get more and more manic until he commits suicide while driving his car with his pregnant girlfriend tied up in the trunk.

When our star finally gets around to answering this fan's letters, it's too late — he realizes that the suicidal fan he just read about in the paper was in fact Stan, the author of the letters. Eminem's words, even without the music, have a chilling power. The chorus refrain, sung by English singer-songwriter Dido (or Elton John as performed at the 2001 Grammy Awards telecast) is really the only melody in an otherwise spoken presentation.

"The Chain of Love"

Now, take a good look at the lyrics to this story song (written by Rory Lee and Jonnie Barnett; sung by Clay Walker). It has a heartwarming touch and will remind you that what goes around — comes around!

"The Chain of Love" written by Rory Lee and Jonnie Barnett

Verse 1

He was driving home one evening
In his beat up Pontiac
When an old lady flagged him down
Her Mercedes had a flat
He could see that she was frightened
Standing out there in the snow
'Till he said I'm here to help you ma'am
By the way my name is Joe

Verse 2

She said I'm from St. Louis
And I'm only passing through
I must have seen a hundred cars go by
This is awful nice of you
When he changed the tire
And closed her trunk
And was about to drive away
She said how much do I owe you
Here's what he had to say

Chorus

You don't owe me a thing, I've been there too
Someone once helped me out
Just the way I'm helping you
If you really want to pay me back
Here's what you do
Don't let the chain of love end with you

Verse 3

Well a few miles down the road
The lady saw a small cafe
She went in to grab a bite to eat
And then be on her way
But she couldn't help but notice
How the waitress smiled so sweet
And how she must've been eight months along
And dead on her feet

Verse 4

And though she didn't know her story
And she probably never will
When the waitress went to get her change
From a hundred dollar bill
The lady slipped right out the door
And on a napkin left a note
There were tears in the waitress's eyes
When she read what she wrote

Chorus

You don't owe me a thing
I've been there too
Someone once helped me out
Just the way I'm helping you
If you really want to pay me back
Here's what you do
Don't let the chain of love end with you

Verse 5

That night when she got home from work
The waitress climbed into bed
She was thinkin' about the money
And what the lady's note had said
As her husband lay there sleeping
She whispered soft and low
Everything's gonna be alright, I love you, Joe

Love lyrics

Love is one of those dishes that can be served up a thousand different ways and still be a lyrical feast. Like Bubba's shrimp list in the movie *Forrest Gump*, if you made a list of all the song titles that use the *L* word, it would reach from "here to New Orleans."

The love song can range from celebratory to suicidal and all points in between and still be considered a love song. Because love is the driving force behind much of human activity, writers never seem to run out of inspiration. In fact, every generation seems to recycle some of the same emotions, situations, and predicaments that love seems to breed, each time around, totally unaware that it was said before by other generations. Look up the lyrics for some (or all) of the songs in Table 5-1 for examples.

Table 5-1	Categories of Love Songs	
Story love songs	*Songwriter(s)*	*Singers/Performers*
"Give My Love to Rose"	Johnny Cash	Johnny Cash
"Me and Bobby McGee"	Kris Kristofferson	Janis Joplin
Situation love songs	*Songwriter(s)*	*Singers/Performers*
"Always Something There to Remind Me"	Hal David, Burt Bacharach	Dionne Warwick
"Sunshine of Your Love"	Eric Clapton, Jack Bruce, Peter Brown	Cream
Concept-driven love songs	*Songwriter(s)*	*Singers/Performers*
"Love Is a Wonderful Thing"	Michael Bolton, Andrew Goldmark	Michael Bolton
"All You Need Is Love"	John Lennon, Paul McCartney	The Beatles
Protest love songs	*Songwriter(s)*	*Singers/Performers*
"Love Stinks"	Peter Wolf, Seth Justman	The J. Geils Band
"Love Hurts"	Roy Orbison	Nazareth
Novelty love songs	*Songwriter(s)*	*Singers/Performers*
"Love Potion #9"	Doc Pomus, Mort Schuman	The Searchers
"Love in an Elevator"	Steven Tyler, Joe Perry	Aerosmith
Silly love songs	*Songwriter(s)*	*Singers/Performers*
"Silly Love Songs"	Paul and Linda McCartney	Paul McCartney
"Oops I Did It Again"	Martin Sandberg, Rami Yacoub	Britney Spears
Parody love songs	*Songwriter(s)*	*Parody lyrics and vocal by*
"Stop Draggin' My Car Around"	Tom Petty, Mike Campbell	Weird Al Yankovic
"My Bologna"	Berton Averre, Douglas Fieger	Weird Al Yankovic
Inspirational or spiritual love songs	*Songwriter(s)*	*Singers/Performers*
"With Arms Wide Open"	Scott Stapp, Mark Tremonti	Creed
"My Sweet Lord"	George Harrison	George Harrison

In the following sections, we look at the variety of ways the subject of love can be treated.

"Love the One You're With"

This 1971 concept-driven love song (written and sung by Stephen Stills) spoke to the summer-of-love generation with its breezy notion, "If you can't be with the one you love, love the one you're with." Well all right then!

When writing a love song, try to find a fresh angle from which to approach this subject. Look at some of your favorite love songs and notice the ways in which the writers have set their song apart from the thousands of others.

I, like so many other writers, would be lost for words if not for the subject of love. (Desire is another staple in the writer's pantry.) The challenge, of course, is finding fresh ways to serve it up. When in doubt, follow your heart. If the sentiment rings true, you may have the start of a great song.

"This 1 Promise You"

This super-smash by 'N Sync (written by Richard Marx), has to be the fron-trunner for the "wedding song" of this generation, giving "The Wedding Song" (written by Paul Stookey; performed by Peter, Paul and Mary) and "The Search Is Over" (written by Jim Peterik and Frankie Sullivan; performed by Survivor) a run for their money. Take a look at the words of this inspirational love song.

> **"This I Promise You" written by Richard Marx**
>
> **Verse 1**
> When the visions around you bring tears to your eyes
> And all that surrounds you
> Are secrets and lies
> I'll be your strength
> I'll give you hope
> Keeping your faith when it's gone
> The one you should call was standing here all along
>
> **Verse 2**
> I've loved you forever
> In lifetimes before
> And I promise you
> Never will you hurt anymore
> I give you my word
> I give you my heart
> This is a battle we've won
> And with this vow
> Forever has now begun

Chorus
And I will take you in my arms
And hold you right where you belong
'Til the day my life is through
This I promise you, this I promise you

Bridge
Over and over I fall when I hear you call
Without you in my life baby,
I just wouldn't be living at all

(instrumental solo)

Chorus
And I will take you in my arms
And hold you right where you belong
'Til the day my life is through
This I promise you, this I promise you

Coda
Just close your eyes each loving day
And know this feeling won't go away
Every word I say is true
This I promise you
Every word I say is true
This I promise you, oh I promise you

Notice how the writer expands the scope of his love to cover "lifetimes before." That's a nice touch. Also see how the lyric starts with timeless concepts like "strength, hope, faith" and then gets intimate and physical at the chorus, "And I will take you in my arms and hold you right where you belong." The hook, "this I promise you," is saved for the end of the chorus. If your girlfriend's not melting by now, perhaps she's not the girl for you!

"Ghost Story"

This story song from Sting's 1999 release *Brand New Day* takes the love song into fresh new territory. This song (written and sung by Sting), which examines a complex relationship, has the singer looking back at his denial of love throughout the years. The audience is never quite sure who Sting is addressing — perhaps his father or a former lover. What we do know is that his "indifference was my invention," and through it all, "I must have loved you."

When you look up the lyrics notice that as the story unfolds, many devices (see Chapter 6 for more on devices) are used: personification ("his icy sinews" referring to winter), metaphor ("the moon's a fingernail"), anaphora (the repetition of phrases like "the same," "I did not," and "you were"), the use of only perfect rhyme, (suffer/tougher, stars/scars, measure/treasure), and others, such as the absence of a title as a hook and an innovative form. But, like with most great songs, the devices all become invisible as the listener becomes intrigued with where the lyrics of this unique love song are headed.

There are so many different ways to treat the subject of love. When I heard Sting crooning the hook "I must have loved you," I said to myself, "Leave it to Sting to find a unique way to use a song as a form of self-therapy." By getting the chance to peek inside his diary — his emotional journal — the listener becomes an insider, and that's a role that makes a fan for life.

Lyrics that draw on current events and social protest

What better way to make a statement than through a song. People are much more inclined to listen if an idea is attached to a catchy melody and a good beat — and as a songwriter, it's a great way to get things off your chest, raise awareness, and possibly even make a difference in the world. Certain artists have become well known for their ability to encapsulate world events into musical form and often sum up the feelings of the people. Take a look at a few examples of songs that use current events or social protests as their reason for being.

"Ohio"

Neil Young's powerful response to the four students killed by National Guardsmen at an antiwar demonstration at Kent State University on May 18, 1970, became the protest song of choice for an America that was sick and tired of its troops dying in the Vietnam War. "Tin soldiers and Nixon's coming, we're finally on our own, this summer I hear the drumming, four dead in Ohio." The photos in the newspapers told the story of the horrific event and this rock anthem became the soundtrack. ("Ohio" was written and sung by Neil Young.)

"Cop Killer"

This rap tune is the one that for several years caused all records to carry rating stickers (labels that indicate that certain language contained could be considered offensive and unsuitable for minors). The record was also banned by stores like K-Mart and Wal-Mart and incited many racial confrontations all over America. This song proved once again, the power a song can have — whether it's used as a positive tool or a negative one. ("Cop Killer" was written by Ernest Cunnigan and Tracy Marrow, sung by Body Count.)

"Blowin' in the Wind"

This hit song, sung by folk icons, Peter, Paul, and Mary and written by one of America's finest musical journalists, Bob Dylan, is perhaps, along with singer/songwriter Pete Seeger's "Where Have All the Flowers Gone," the prototype of the modern protest song. Covering war ("how many times must the cannonballs fly before they're forever banned"), freedom, and the environment, the lyric poses questions that Dylan begs us to answer. The song was soulfully covered by Stevie Wonder in 1966, thereby bringing the message to a whole new audience.

Novelty and humorous lyrics

One concept that is sometimes forgotten by "serious" songwriters is the element of humor in a song. A thread of wit running through an otherwise serious lyric can add a much-needed lift to a song. Bob Dylan is especially good at injecting humor into his songs — "the pump don't work 'cause the vandals took the handle" from "Subterranean Homesick Blues" is a good example.

Some songs, however, center most of their appeal on the novelty value of their concept. These "gimmick" songs have been around in various reincarnations since day one. They are often based on some current fad or craze, so their shelf life can be affected by the longevity of the craze they document. They are often based on current expressions or popular catch phrases. Some of these songs can actually outlive the phenomenon they describe. In the following sections, we take a look at a few examples of novelty songs that may or may not stand the test of time.

"The Thong Song"

This new-millennium smash by young urban artist Sisqo (written by Mark Andrews, Desmond Child, Marquis Collins, Tim Kelley, Joseph Longo, Bob Robinson, and Robert Rosa) shines a light on the current undergarment-of-choice of the club-hopping, hip-hop woman-on-the go: the thong. Girls in the audience of Sisqo's shows have been known to toss these articles on stage during his performances, causing the Lycra police to do double duty. His follow-up to "The Thong Song" did not rely on a gimmick for its hook, perhaps in his desire to be taken more seriously and not be typecast as the "underwear guy." He also left out this song in some of his shows to the bewilderment of many of his fans. Oh well, as they say, "The Thong Remains the Same." (We just couldn't resist!)

"Surfin' USA"

Brian Wilson of The Beach Boys certainly had his finger on the pulse of the youth of America when he wrote this song. He put the whole carefree West Coast feeling into songs like "Surfin' USA," "409" (his tribute to a hot Chevy with a 409-cubic-inch engine), and "Surfer Girl." (When you can combine a hot trend with a hot date, you got it made!) Based on "Sweet Little Sixteen" by Chuck Berry, "Surfin' USA" proves that you don't have to actually experience what you write about in a song to capture authenticity. (Brian didn't surf!) An audience can sit back or hit the dance floor and live vicariously though the soft-focus lens of a song. Songs based on fads and crazes have been known to "surf" the generations and have enjoyed popularity long after the fads that have inspired them have come and gone.

The gimmick or novelty song is another form to experiment with as a songwriter. The popularity and the longevity of the subject matter, however, will affect the popularity and longevity of the song itself.

Being a huge fan of the comedian Mel Brooks and his masterwork (along with Carl Reiner), "The Two Thousand Year Old Man," I was inspired to write a series of songs based on this famous, largely ad-libbed stand-up routine. The song is sung from his own perspective as he doles out hilarious health tips and wisdom from his alleged 2,000 years on Earth. The main hook of the song is, "Eat a nectarine every day." Although the song has never been commercially released, I got an enormous charge out of writing it (and playing it at parties), and I wait for the day when I get to play it for "The Man" himself. Until then, "You've been a great civilization!"

Parody lyrics

A parody lyric is a (hopefully) comical reinterpretation of someone else's more serious lyric. Some parody songs have gone on to be hugely popular, a few even rivaling the popularity of the original. Many times a parody artist takes a popular song and writes a lyric that is often topical and sometimes even in direct contrast to the original. If you look at the world in a humorous light and tend to see the comic or ironic possibilities in every situation, writing song parodies may be right up your drainpipe. Right now we'll take a look at a couple artists who've made a career out of spoofing popular songs.

"Weird Al" Yankovic

First breaking into Billboard's top 40 in 1984 with a parody of Michael Jackson's mega-smash, "Beat It" written by Michael Jackson (which he rechristened, "Eat It," complete with a hilarious accompanying video in which he plays a guy with a serious food addiction), Weird Al has carved a wide niche for himself with his clever and well-crafted take-offs. Through the years, he has lampooned some of the greatest songs in rock 'n' roll. In his hands, Tommy James' classic, "I Think We're Alone Now" (written by Ritchie Cordell and redone by Tiffany in 1987), becomes an ode to the emerging technology of "cloning" — "I think I'm a clone now, where every chromosome is a hand-me-down." Other popular parodies of his include "Lasagna" (a parody of "La Bamba," written and sung by Richie Valens), "Addicted to Spuds" (a send-up of "Addicted to Love" written and sung by Robert Palmer), "Like a Surgeon" (based on Madonna's hit, "Like a Virgin," written by Thomas Kelly and William Steinberg), and "The Rye or the Kaiser" (a parody of Survivor's "Eye of the Tiger," where presumably Rocky Balboa gets fat and weak and a delicatessen owner offering his customers roast beef "on the rye or the Kaiser"). Al just loves to take the grand statement of certain songs and cut them hilariously down to size.

When Frankie Sullivan (co-writer of "Eye of the Tiger") and I were approached by our label and publisher to grant permission to a new artist named "Weird Al" Yankovic to release a parody of our then current hit, "Eye of the Tiger," I must admit, I had my doubts. Two factors ultimately changed my mind: the excellence and wit of the comic concept, and the fact that the "The Gloved One," Michael Jackson, had just given Al permission for parodies on a couple of his songs. That gave instant legitimacy in my mind to the notion of poking fun at our big, motivational song.

Cletus T. Judd

Some would call Cletus T. Judd the undisputed king of the country music parody song. His send-ups (another term for parodies) of country hits include his hilarious parody of Deana Carter's hit, "Did I Shave My Legs For This?" (written by Deana Carter and Rhonda Hart) entitled, "Did I Shave My Back For This?" "If Shania Were Mine" (spoofing Shania Twain's hit, "Any Man Of Mine," written by Mutt Lange and Shania Twain), "Cletus Went Down to Florida" (taking off from "The Devil Went Down to Georgia," written and by performed by The Charlie Daniels Band), and of course, "Third Rock from Her Thumb" his parody of Joe Diffie's hit, "Third Rock from the Sun" (written by John Greenebaum, Tony Martin, and Sterling Whipple) boasting the lyric, "Nothing else shines like a zirconium, don't tell her what it's worth, third rock from her thumb."

Often times parody lyrics can serve a noble purpose by lightening up (and even shedding light upon) a troubling subject. In the wake of the tragedies in America on September 11, 2001, came many parodies designed to defuse the events, one of which was an Internet-driven parody of Harry Belafonte's "Banana Boat Song." A sample lyric from that song was: "Hey, Mr. Taliban, hand over bin Laden, daylight come and we drop de bomb." It may be difficult to laugh at this but almost impossible to ignore.

Inspirational lyrics

Lyrics of praise and worship, words of inspiration, and stanzas of belief have been the basis of many of the world's greatest and longest-lasting songs. A song is a powerful force that can change minds, shape nations, spearhead causes, and uplift the emotions. As a songwriter, it's a perfectly acceptable goal to make the listener want to wiggle ("Bootylicious" written by Beyonce Knowles, Rob Fusari, and Stevie Nicks; performed by Destiny's Child), giggle (see "Parody lyrics" featuring Weird Al), or jiggle, ". . . Baby One More Time" (written by Martin Sandberg; sung by Britney Spears). When a writer can inspire, however, he's helping to change the world. As songwriters, we have the unique opportunity to get our message across to potentially millions of people. Here are a few noteworthy examples in this wonderfully crowded category.

"Change the World"

This mid-'90s hit for singer Eric Clapton (written by Gordon Kennedy, Wayne Kirkpatrick, and Tommy Sims) centered on the ways we all can make a difference in this vast universe. It's a great example of how an old concept can be given a new lease on life through a fresh musical approach. The arrangement of this song is a unique combination of country-blues and soul.

"My Sweet Lord"

George Harrison was considered the Beatle "on a quest," and this song that he wrote is a wonderful documentation of his journey. As he explored religions of all peoples, he came to the conclusion that they all had one thing in common: a belief in something greater than us all. This song reflects his wide-eyed allegiance to his "Sweet Lord" and sweeps us away with producer Phil Spector's lush bed of 12-string and slide guitars.

In the 70s, George Harrison was involved in a lawsuit over "My Sweet Lord" when the publisher of the '60s hit "He's So Fine" sued him for copyright infringement claiming significant similarities between the two songs. In the end, George admitted that he had perhaps unconsciously incorporated a portion of the old song by The Chiffons into his song. When you're writing a song, be as sure as you can be that it's not too reminiscent of something that already exists. When in doubt, play it for your friends (and your publisher) to see if they experience a strong sense of déjà vu and feel as though they've heard it some place before.

"With Arms Wide Open"

This 1999 hit by Creed (written by Scott Stapp and Mark Tremonti) taps into one man's boundless joy over learning that he is soon to become a father. We can feel his awe and uncertainty in the journey that lies ahead for him and the woman he loves. He's ready and eager to be the child's tour guide on this planet, but wants to inspire his offspring to be even more embracing of life and its spiritual riches than he is himself, and to "greet the world with arms wide open."

Practice Makes Perfect

We've given you examples of the different lyrical types of songs in this chapter. As you develop phrases that work together with your general concept, see what lyrical type your phrases are fitting into, and then drive your message on home with the rest of the song. Take a look at what form your song is taking. Being aware of this form helps you keep consistency throughout your song. If you're telling a story, then tell the story. If your lyrics are situation-driven, don't lose sight of the situation that inspired the song in the first place.

Chapter 6

Creating Lyrics

· ·

In This Chapter

▶ Taking ideas from concept to completion

▶ Considering all aspects of the lyric

▶ Bringing in the element of music to your song

▶ Sorting out the use of poetic techniques

▶ Allowing yourself the freedom of flight

· ·

*L*yrics can make or break a great melody. But coming up with lyrics is often easier said than done. In this chapter, we fill you in on some tried-and-true techniques used by the pros when they're setting out to write lyrics. We also take you step by step and show you how to fit your lyrics into the common formats of songs.

Creating a Lyric

You've just bought yourself a brand-new laptop (the kind that burns CDs and DVDs). You've purchased a silver pen with your initials on it. You've rented a villa in the Caribbean. You also have a cassette recorder by your side, set on pause, to capture the cosmic overlap of words and music. The scene is basically set for a *Behind the Music* episode on VH1.

You're ready to write a great lyric. But where do you start? Start at the heart. Find the subjects that matter to you right now. Find the melodies that resonate in your soul. In this section, we show you some of the ways the pros get started on their journey to writing a great lyric. Take a look at using one of these suggestions as a starting point:

✔ A title from most any source that suggests a concept

✔ An idea or concept that suggests a title

✔ An experience you've had

✔ A cause you believe in deeply

- ✔ A storyline you've imagined or lived
- ✔ A catchy phrase
- ✔ A melody that suggests a lyric

Starting with a title

When you feel you have an intriguing title, the next step is to examine the possibilities of those words. Find unique ways to look at common words (or common ways to look at unique words!). Following is a list of some famous song titles. As a quick exercise, pretend you're seeing the title for the first time. Now imagine the storyline that the title may imply to you, as if you just stumbled across it in your own notebook. How would the concept of your song differ and how would it be similar to the hit. How would you put your own life experience into the lyric? (See Chapter 5 on how to search for lyrics on the Internet.)

- ✔ **"Heart of the Matter"** (written by Don Henley, Mike Campbell, and JD Souther; sung by Don Henley)
- ✔ **"Heartbreak Hotel"** (written by Mae Axton, Elvis Presley, and Tommy Durden; sung by Elvis Presley)
- ✔ **"Ain't No Mountain High Enough"** (written by Nickolas Ashford and Valarie Simpson; sung by Diana Ross and The Supremes)
- ✔ **"Night Moves"** (written and sung by Bob Seger)

Oftentimes, I use a good title as a stepping-off point for a lyric and song. At its best, a title can literally sum up what you're going to say in the song itself. I'm constantly jotting down potential titles from the words people say, things I see in newspapers or magazines, and phrases that seem to come to me out of thin air. "The Search Is Over," "Vehicle," "High on You," "Hold on Loosely" . . . in fact, most of the hits I've written or co-written have started life as ink stains between the lines of a spiral notebook, as a title I jotted down or one that someone suggested to me.

Example step #1: Developing a title idea

There are many ways to achieve a goal, and although in this example we're suggesting one particular method of writing lyrics from scratch, we encourage you to find a style you're comfortable with and one that works best for you.

If you start with only the title in mind, you'll want to develop that title into an idea. If you're not sure what the song is going to be about, then sit down and create a list of different ideas that could be expanded and covered by your title. Just for an example, we'll say you had a dream last night and the title "Deep in the Heart of the Night" jumped right out and you're convinced that this title was sent to you from the ethers to use in your next song. Your mission now, should you accept it, is to go about discovering just what the song will be about in relation to your title.

As you think about your title, "Deep in the Heart of the Night," make a list of all the things that you can imagine happening deep in the night. Your list may look something like this:

- ✔ Falling in love deep in the heart of the night
- ✔ Fantasizing that you're falling in love deep in the heart of the night
- ✔ Looking back at falling in love deep in the heart of the night
- ✔ Thoughts and feelings that only come to you deep in the heart of the night
- ✔ Waking up from a dream deep in the heart of the night
- ✔ Getting a phone call deep in the heart of the night
- ✔ Driving your car or truck deep in the heart of the night

After thinking over the ideas that you came up with, you decide to use "Driving your car or truck deep in the heart of the night." Maybe this is because you just bought some new wheels, or you're craving an escape to somewhere — anywhere. It's most likely that what you choose from your list will be one with which you feel the strongest connection. That affinity for your subject will become the fuel for your brain that will help you maintain your creative flow.

A title doesn't have to be clever or even unique to be effective. Sometimes a generic title can be infused with new life by using a different camera angle or shedding a new light on an old subject. Notice how one of the most common titles of all time, "I Love You," is presented in a fresh light in the context of the song performed by Martina McBride (written by Tammy Hyler, Adrienne Follese, and Keith Follese) of the same name. By using edgy, similar sounding words to set up the title hook like, "electrically," "kinetically," "erratically," "fanatically," "magically" the songwriters are adding contrast to the simple closing line of the chorus, "sure as the sky is blue, I love you."

Finding a place for the title within the song

After you hit on a good title, experiment by placing it in different spots within your tune to see where it works the best. Many successful songs place the title in one of the song's power spots to help hook the listener. Take a look at the following examples in Table 6-1.

Table 6-1	Power Spots for Titles	
At the end of each verse	*Songwriter(s)*	*Singer/Performer*
"Bridge Over Troubled Waters"	Paul Simon	Simon & Garfunkel
"Blue Eyes Crying in the Rain"	Fred Rose	Willie Nelson
"The Times They Are A-Changin'"	Bob Dylan	Bob Dylan
At the beginning of the chorus	*Songwriter(s)*	*Singer/Performer*
"Oops, I Did It Again"	Max Martin, Rami Yacoub	Britney Spears
"Baby, I Love Your Way"	Peter Frampton	Peter Frampton
"If It Makes You Happy"	Sheryl Crow, Jeff Trott	Sheryl Crow
At the end of the chorus	*Songwriter(s)*	*Singer/Performer*
"Where Have All the Cowboys Gone?"	Paula Cole	Paula Cole
"Wind Beneath My Wings"	Larry Henley, Jeff Silbar	Bette Midler
"One Sweet Day"	Walter Afanasieff, Mariah Carey, Boyz II Men	Mariah Carey and Boyz II Men
In both the first and last lines of the chorus	*Songwriter(s)*	*Singer/Performer*
"On the Road Again"	Willie Nelson	Willie Nelson
"Breathe"	Holly Lamar, Stephanie Bentley	Faith Hill
"I Can Love You Like That"	Jennifer Kimball, Steve Diamond, Maribeth Derry	John Michael Montgomery

In the first line of each verse	Songwriter(s)	Singer/Performer
"Just One of Those Things"	Cole Porter	Cole Porter
"Raindrops Keep Falling On My Head"	Burt Bacharach, Hal David	B.J. Thomas
"Over the Rainbow"	Harold Arlen, E.Y. Harburg	Judy Garland
In the last line of each verse	**Songwriter(s)**	**Singer/Performer**
"As Time Goes By"	Herman Hepfeld	Jimmy Durante
"He Ain't Heavy, He's My Brother"	Bob Russell, Robert Scott	The Hollies
"My Way"	Paul Anka, Claude Francois, Jacques Revaud, Gilles Thibaut	Frank Sinatra

So where should you put your song title? In as many places as you can without going overboard. Some songs take the concept of the title as a hook to the extreme and really hammer it home in this way. In the song "Let It Be" (written by John Lennon and Paul McCartney; performed by The Beatles), the title appears 42 times!

Don't force a title into numerous places within your song because you feel you have to — unless it really makes sense to do so. A good title has a way of sticking in your head even if it's only used a few times.

Much of the process of lyric writing is experimentation and trial and error. Many writers prefer to start a song with a co-writer and finish it up separately (often getting back together one more time to compare notes and finalize the song). Like viewing a painting, it's good to take a step back in order to see the whole picture clearly. There's no need to force a lyric. You'll find that if you just give it a little time (but not too much), the lyric will naturally come. It's great to come back after a break and get each other's fresh point of view.

Starting with an idea or concept

Whenever the process of songwriting seems to become more of a craft and less of an art — more of a puzzle and less of a passion — it's good to throw the tricks away (at least temporarily) and go back to theme and concept. Some of the greatest lyrics are remembered more for their idea or story rather than for their clever rhyme schemes, hooks, twists on title, plays on words, or expanded clichés. A theme that matters to you can draw out some amazing emotions in, and often as, a sidelight. As a bonus, it helps you to come up with some incredible titles, rhymes, and hooks.

Harnessing a concept

Just as I have reams of pages of hooks, phrases, and titles, I have nearly as many pages of potential concepts for songs. Many times in a co-writing session with another person (or co-writing with myself on an old idea), the idea of the song actually suggests the title of the song, the tone of the lyric (angry, sad, happy, nostalgic, and so forth), and an appropriate musical hook. In a songwriting world often driven by title and hook, it's refreshing to go back to concept and work the rest from there. Some writers say they write great songs when they're in the depths of depression, but it sure doesn't work for me. Even a great idea holds little appeal for me when I'm in the dumps. However, when I finally pull out of the trenches, I draw from the experience of having been there. You can learn to create from your sorrow, but for most songwriters, only *after* they've experienced it. Similarly, some writers insist on getting high before attempting to write a song. All I can say is that from what I've learned through the years it's extremely easy to be fooled into thinking you have a brilliant idea or song only to say, "What was I thinking?" once you get sober.

Example step #2: Expanding the concept

Once you have a concept — what the song is going to be about — you'll want to elaborate on that concept, and develop it into a story. Let your imagination run free. Going back to our fictitious example of "Deep in the Heart of the Night," try to picture yourself being deep in the night, and take note of all the emotions you might be feeling in the seat of your vehicle as you drive the night away. Make note of all that your imagination dictates to you — the stars, the clouds, the terrain, the glow of your dashboard dials. These are the images that will illuminate your lyric.

For "Deep in the Heart of the Night," you may decide that the song is going to be about driving to Tulsa late at night. Perhaps you chose Tulsa because you liked the way the word sounded. Maybe it was the wide-open plains of Oklahoma that held the attraction for you. Perhaps there is someone waiting for you in Tulsa. Maybe Tulsa somehow represents a fresh start for your life. Or it could be that Tulsa is just a random point on the map, and you're thinking "anywhere's better than where I am right now." When you're expanding on the idea of driving deep in the heart of the night to Tulsa, ask yourself questions such as the following:

- ✔ What is the motivation for driving?

- ✔ Why is the destination Tulsa, Oklahoma?

- ✔ Am I writing from the personal perspective or am I telling a story about someone else or from another person's point of view?

> ✔ Am I writing about the trip in the present tense, looking back at a past trip, or dreaming of one in the future?
>
> ✔ What is going through my mind as I'm driving?
>
> ✔ What emotions am I feeling as I drive along?
>
> ✔ Who or what is waiting for me when I finally reach my destination?

Asking these questions and making these decisions will influence the tone your lyric will take — angry, tender, joyous, full of longing, full of remorse, and so forth. These decisions will also influence the style of language you use from formal to hip- slang.

There are plenty of things to think about when developing your concept. When writing a screenplay for a movie, one of the tips in training is to decide how the story will end up before you even begin. And so it goes with developing the story for your song — think your concept through to the end of that drive to Tulsa — deep in the heart of the night.

Telling a story

Much like starting with a concept, putting a story into lyrical form has been the basis for many memorable songs. Story songs (see Chapter 5 for a definition of story songs) can be very involving for the listener because, for one reason, the listener is waiting to the end to hear the story's outcome. The effectiveness of songs as divergent as "Stan" (written by Eminem, Paul Herman, and Dido; sung by Eminem), which is the story of an obsessed fan of the artist himself, and "24 Hours To Tulsa" (written by Burt Bacharach and Hal David; sung by Gene Pitney), which is the tale of a man who was unfaithful to his wife just 24 hours before he was to come home to her, depends on how interested the audience is in the story the songs are telling. In the case of these two smashes the answer is clear.

Find a story that interests you from current events, a fictional account, or a history book. Now try to put the story into verse form using your own style.

Using a melody that suggests a lyric

Sometimes as a songwriter you get very lucky and hear a melody in your head. Other times, you're noodling around on your keyboard, guitar, mandolin, or trombone and stumble on a series of notes that sound good together. Then there are times when you're even more blessed and your vocal chords produce some primitive utterances that actually resemble words. In this way, a melody can literally inspire a lyric — as opposed to the other way around.

On occasion, when one of my co-writers or I hit upon an interesting melody, I'll sing it out with what I call *creative gibberish* — in other words, nonsense syllables that sound remarkably like words. (Another widely accepted term for such gibberish is "vocable.") I once sang a new but unfinished song for a friend with nothing but gibberish for words. Afterward, he told me it was one of my best lyrics. When I told him it was nothing but nonsense, he still insisted it was one of my most meaningful lyrics! The amazing part is that often, when you listen to tapes of these artificial lyrics, you hear sounds that you can actually develop into real words. When you become adept at the art of gibberish, it can be a tool to your lyric writing. When you're unencumbered by the English language (or whatever tongue you speak), you are freer to concentrate on the naturalness of the sound and the rhythm of the words without being hung up on their meaning.

When starting a song, try to put yourself in the most receptive mood possible. Many a song never got past the first verse because the writer was convinced it wasn't any good. Try to be as patient and caring with yourself as you would be to a friend in whom you're trying to bring out the best.

Finding the Format for Your Lyrics

Different sections of a song serve different purposes. Sometimes it takes a great deal of experimentation to find the best format for your song (see Chapter 3 for more on song forms). In the following sections, we cover ways that you can use lyrics to help differentiate the sections, as well as the lyrical techniques you can use to build and shape your song.

Jim Morrison of The Doors used to love to write poetry. He would sit in with a young local band that he liked and recite his poetry during their sets. He loved to use the rhythm of the music to move his words. (By the way, this band later changed its name to Kansas and went on to have a multi-platinum career of its own).

Verse lyrics

Songwriters generally use the verse to set up the idea or premise of the song. The *verse lyric* conveys the meat of the meaning of the song. First it draws the listener in with a catchy opening statement or question, and then sets up the song's premise or idea as it leads to the chorus. Each subsequent verse will add new information to the story — often looking at the premise from a different perspective. One popular technique is to start with a general or non-specific idea in the first verse and get more situation-specific in subsequent verses as the song develops. You may also want to set up your scene geographically ("In the town where I was born . . .") as to where the action takes place, or set the time perspective as to when the situation occurs ("Many, many years from now . . ."). The verses serve to set up the chorus of the song. In story songs, the verses are all-important, drawing the listener in as the tale unfolds. Tell it as simply and interestingly as you can, embellishing it with poetic devices such as rhyme, word rhythm, alliteration, imagery, personification, simile, metaphor, assonance, and anaphora (a-NA-phor-a). (Refer to "Using Poetic Devices in Lyrics" later in this chapter for more information.) You might also draw the listener in by posing a question in verse one, making him an interactive member of the song — "Is there anybody going to listen to my story?" which is the first line of "Girl," or as in "Roll up, roll up for the mystery tour" from "Magical Mystery Tour" (both of these songs were written by John Lennon and Paul McCartney; and performed by The Beatles).

Example step #3: Developing the verse lyric

On the fictitious song we are collaborating on, "Deep in the Heart of the Night," we've chosen one of most common forms in popular songwriting, the ABCABCD form that translates to verse, pre-chorus, chorus, verse, pre-chorus, chorus, bridge (for other options of song forms you can refer to Chapter 3). *Note:* We can always change it later as the song develops.

Now that we've decided on the basic concept or premise for the song, it's time to start brainstorming some verse lyrics. Since this is a chapter about words, we'll start with the lyrics, as opposed to the melody or chords (not that a melody or chord progression can't pop into your head as you're working on the lyrics). We'll suggest the opening two lines and you can take it from there. These lines can of course be substituted for others as you develop the song but it'll at least give you someplace to start:

- ✔ "Do you wonder why I'm sittin' here behind this wheel?"
- ✔ "Nowhere' circled on the map, 300 horses at my heel?"

These lines can serve as the set up to a hundred different scenarios to expand upon. Whatever concept you've chosen to illuminate the title "Deep in the Heart of the Night," make sure every line sticks to that concept and moves the action of the plot along. Try to use some descriptive words and intriguing visual images if possible (maybe "moonlight" in Line 3?). You may only want to work on the first verse for now and wait to write your second verse until after you've written your chorus (often the chorus will suggest where to take the second verse). You can also decide at that point if you need a third verse or a bridge.

Letting the verse express the concept

The opening line of your song is all-important. Try and capture the listeners' imagination and curiosity as to where your song is heading.

By looking at John Lennon and Paul McCartney's song "Eleanor Rigby" we see an excellent example of verse progression. The song consists of three verses and a chorus and uses the verse-chorus form. The concept of the song (loneliness and the basic futility of life) is shown through the interwoven lives of an elderly spinster named Eleanor Rigby and the town preacher, Father McKenzie.

The concept unfolds over the course of three verses. The first verse presents Eleanor Rigby picking up the rice at the church after a wedding. We immediately get a feel for the careful, prayerful type of person she is. In the second verse we're introduced to the pathetic Father McKenzie, who writes the "words to a sermon that no one will hear" and clandestinely darns his socks late at night as if it were somehow a sin. These two lonely people are joined in the final verse when Eleanor Rigby dies ("nobody came" to her funeral) and Father McKenzie buries her "Wiping the dirt from his hands as he watched from the grave." The good father accomplishes nothing in his life ("no one was saved"). The writers did a great job in telling a sad story and developing two memorable characters in a few short minutes of the song.

The verse is really where you first set up your concept and then expand upon it as the verses progress.

After you have your first and second verse written, try flipping them around. It's amazing how often the second verse sounds better as a first verse and vice versa.

Pre-chorus lyrics

If you feel your song needs a pre-chorus (see Chapter 3 for more details on pre-chorus), make sure it's doing its job lyrically. A pre-chorus can give the song some fresh chords to differentiate the verse and chorus. Lyrically, the pre-chorus (or *B section* or *channel*) is a place to further set up the action in the chorus. If the verse is very specific — mentioning names, dates and locations — you may want to make your channel more conceptual for contrast as you set up the hook. If your verse is general in nature (talking about love as a concept as opposed to jumping in bed with someone), your pre-chorus can get down to specifics before hitting the chorus.

Example step #4: Developing the pre-chorus lyric

In our fictitious song "Deep in the Heart of the Night," we have our title, have considered many concepts and chosen one, picked a potential song form, and started a verse. Since the form we've chosen includes a pre-chorus, it's now time to look at that element of our song. The specifics of where you've taken the verse will influence where you go on the pre-chorus. If your verse talks in very specific terms about the trip you are taking (the lyric, "Tulsa circled on the map," indicates a certain goal), then perhaps your pre-chorus (also known as a channel) could be very conceptual (perhaps something about your innermost thoughts as you are driving). Another pre-chorus approach might be if your verse is in the present tense, your pre-chorus could shift to a retrospective outlook, thinking about the events that led up to your decision to drive. For instance:

- ✔ "Wish that I could change your mind"
- ✔ "And claim the love we left behind"

This two-line channel could be expanded to four if you have more to say, but generally 4 measure pre-choruses are an appropriate length (refer to Chapter 8 for an explanation of measures). A good example of the two-line, 4-bar pre-chorus would be "You're trying hard not to show it (baby), but baby, baby you know it" ("You've Lost That Lovin' Feeling" written by Barry Mann, Phil Spector, and Cynthia Weil; performed by the Righteous Brothers).

Putting the pre-chorus to work

It's often the lyrical contrast between sections that keeps a song moving. Feel free to change your perspective from general to specific and past to present in a given tune. It's also okay to change the location of the action — and move the listener around from place to place.

Sometimes I'll be laboring for hours on a second pre-chorus or bridge, and when I'm done I realize that it just doesn't flow with the rest of the song. Be sure to keep referring back to your lyrical premise. Don't be afraid to go back to the top and read the lyric again and again to make sure all your lyrics belong in the same song.

Chorus lyrics

The chorus lyric is really the money lyric (the one that people remember first and motivates them to buy the record that makes the songwriter money!). When you've done a great job in your verse (and pre-chorus, if necessary), you want to sum it all up as simply and infectiously as possible in the chorus. This is generally where the hook of the title is placed. The chorus is sometimes just one or two words chanted over and over as in "Mony, Mony" (written Tommy James, Bo Gentry, Ritchie Cordell, and Bobby Bloom; sung by Tommy James), or can really expand and crystallize all that was said in the verse as in "Because You Loved Me" (written by Diane Warren; sung by Celine Dion). Whether the listener is hit over the head with the lyrics of the chorus or seduced by it, it must be something they want to hear again (and hopefully, again and again).

There is no law that says a chorus has to be exactly the same each time it comes around. Sometimes when writing a chorus, you have a few variations that are hard to choose between. If you can't decide on the one best option (at the risk of confounding a sing-a-long), use them all in unfolding choruses. Just make sure the title doesn't change too radically.

Example step #5: Developing the chorus lyric

In our future hit, "Deep in the Heart of the Night," our next step is to work on the all-important chorus of the song. We should consider keeping the chorus extremely simple, emphasizing the (quite lengthy) title, "Deep in the Heart of the Night." This is the area of the song where we emphasize the premise of the song in its most basic terms. Depending on the concept you've chosen, the chorus could be as simple as, "Deep in the heart of the night, I see you, deep in the heart of the night, I touch you." This section needs to be the part that people are compelled to sing along with.

Having the chorus make your point

Very often, the chorus is the first thing to be written because it can spring right out of the title and lyrically sum up the point of the whole song.

If you want to write a memorable song, one that people will fall in love with and sing forever — write a great chorus. The chorus presents the main point of the song, while the verses describe the details. This principle can be seen in many verse-chorus songs such as:

- "Goodbye Yellow Brick Road" (written by Elton John and Bernie Taupin; sung by Elton John)
- "Amazed" (written by Marv Green, Chris Lindsey, and Aimee Mayo; performed by Lonestar)
- "I Do (Cherish you)" (written by Dan Hill and Keith Stegall; sung by Mark Wills)
- "Circle Of Life" (written by Elton John and Tim Rice; sung by Elton John)
- "The Wind Beneath My Wings" (written by Larry Henley and Jeff Silbar; sung by Bette Midler)
- "Un-break My Heart" (written by Diane Warren; sung by Toni Braxton)
- "All You Need Is Love" (written by John Lennon and Paul McCartney; performed by The Beatles).

The chorus can be similar in tone to the verses, blending in with them, or it can become a surprise or a climax, such as we find in "The Night They Drove Old Dixie Down" (written by Robbie Robertson; performed by The Band).

Bridge lyrics

The bridge of your song can be an important element for a variety of reasons. It can serve to sum up in broad terms, the main idea of the song. It can expand upon or amplify the lyric's main theme, or it can simply be a respite or oasis from the intensity of the rest of your song. At the bridge of "What a Girl Wants" sung by Christina Aguilera, the song shifts feel from its intense groove, to a light, syncopated rhythm that adds contrast. It is the singer's chance to give her loved one, her heartfelt thanks for being there for her. The bridge is also your chance to reflect at what you've already said in the song and say it a bit differently (for example, "Don't let her slip away, sentimental fool, don't let your heart get in the way," as done on "Hold on Loosely" [written by Don Barnes, Jeff Carlisi and Jim Peterik]).

In my opinion, The Beatles wrote the book on great bridges. Often, John and Paul would supply each other with bridges for their songs (they called it the middle eight, referring to the standard length of a typical bridge — eight musical measures long). The lyrical shift from one writer to the other was usually enough to make the bridge a welcome section of the song, both musically and lyrically. John added the "life is very short" bridge to the otherwise optimistic tone of their song "We Can Work It Out," and in doing so added a much-appreciated contrast.

Example step #6: Developing the bridge lyric

In our imaginary song "Deep in the Heart of the Night," it's time to *build a bridge* to the end of our song. Having nailed down the concept in the verses, taken it to some contrasting ground in the pre-chorus, laid out the title boldly in the chorus, now it's time to change things up and shift the mood a bit. We need to give the ear something fresh to ponder and the emotions some new land to wander. If our verses and choruses are filled with a lot of words and fast syllables, it might be time to relax the pace of the words to supply contrast. If the verses and choruses unfold at a leisurely pace, it may be time to step up the frequency of the words. From a "meaning" point of view, it's time to perhaps reflect on the scenario that's been painted in the verse, pre-chorus, and chorus. You may also want to look ahead to what may be waiting down the road "Deep in the heart of the night," before heading into the third verse or the final chorus.

One of the best ways to learn about bridges, what they are and what they do, is to study them in a variety of different popular songs

Using a short form bridge in your song

If you have inserted your bridge in its most common location — after the second chorus, the listener has already had to process a heck of a lot of information. Many current pop songs are using extremely short (often two or three lines) to change the pace without extending the song too dramatically. Many writers are taking a cue from the "bridge masters," John Lennon and Paul McCartney from songs such as their "I'll Be Back" — "I love you so, I'm the one who wants you, yeah, I'm the one who wants you, oh, oh, oh, oh." Writers like Richie McDonald, Gary Baker, and Frank Meyers, who wrote the goose bump rendering 2001 release "I'm Already There" for Lonestar, make use of a simple, but triumphant, two-line bridge to sum up the message of the song: that even when the father and child are a thousand miles apart, the father is with him every minute and every mile in a thousand different ways. Similarly, the bridge in "This I Promise You" (written by Richard Marx; performed by 'N Sync) is short and sweet, adding a little new information, some fresh chord changes (starting on the 2 minor), and revealing that, "Over and over I fall, when I hear you call, without you in my life baby, it just wouldn't be living at all." And onward to the out chorus!

Moving Beyond Format to Sound

Building your lyrics around established song forms is a vital aspect of lyric writing. But making the words sound attractive and professional within that form, is an art in and of itself. In this section, we give you some concrete tips for making sure your lyrics have the right sound for the song.

Paying attention to the rhythm of the words

Whatever section of your song you're writing, you need to consider not only the meaning of your words but their rhythm as well. This often-overlooked element of the mechanics of lyric writing is the secret weapon of many successful songwriters. Often, the beat of the words is accelerated in a certain section of a song to add excitement. (Check out the chorus of the smash hit "Bye, Bye, Bye" written by Andreas Carlsson, Kristian Lundin, and Jacob Schulze; performed by 'N Sync.) Other times, just a few words are stretched over vast expanses of measures for a romantic or passionate effect of "You Are So Beautiful" (written by Bruce Fisher and Billy Preston; sung by Joe Cocker) and "Without You" (written by Peter Evans and Tom Ham; sung by Harry Nilsson).

The rhythm of the words in a song can be as important as the rhyme scheme and the meaning. This is a large part of the feel and appeal of rap music. The late, great Steve Goodman has an excellent song, titled "Banana Republics" (written by Steve Goodman, Steve Burgh, and Jim Rothermel) about the joys of "words you can dance to and a melody that rhymes." The original opening line for my song "Vehicle" (a number-one hit for my band The Ides Of March back in 1970) was "I got a set of wheels, pretty baby, won't you hop inside my car." It wasn't until I changed it to "I'm the friendly stranger in the black sedan, won't you hop inside my car" (a line inspired by one of those well- intentioned but corny government-issued anti-drug pamphlets) that the tune really started to move. Not only was the new version a much more visual line, but it also had a rhythm all its own that cut across the backbeat and the choppy rhythm guitar figure. I had no idea what was so special about that line at the time — so much of what we do when we're just starting off is purely instinctual. It took me years to know what I was doing right on the songs that became hits. I realized much later that the first line of "Vehicle," when spoken is similar to the rap rhythms that came into vogue some years later.

Even if you're not a great singer, try to sing the song you're in the process of writing to see whether the words flow rhythmically. Certain lyrics read well but sing lousy. If your tongue trips over a word or phrase time after time, you may want to consider modifying that portion. Is there too much room for certain words, and not enough for others? Is there enough contrast between sections in the rhythm of the words? Reading a lyric over is a good first step, but road-testing it with a singer can really reveal a lyric's true strengths and weaknesses.

Paying attention to the sounds of words within a lyric

Another often-overlooked element of lyric writing is the actual *sound* of the words themselves. Certain words and phrases roll off the tongue, and others just don't. The most popular songs are ones that people love to sing. If the words sound odd and awkward, it doesn't matter how deep the meaning of your lyric is, the message won't be delivered effectively. Sometimes a great writer will throw in an unusual word or an unconventional pronunciation as a special effect — listen how Elton John delivers the word *discarded* in his power ballad, "Don't Let the Sun Go Down on Me" (co-written with Bernie Taupin).

Example step #7: Making the words sound right

In our fictitious song, "Deep in the Heart of the Night," we have our title and have expanded on our concept, chosen our song form, and developed our verse, pre-chorus, chorus, and bridge lyric. Now it's time to make sure your words *sound* right. Notice that, going back to our starter opening lines, "Do you wonder why I'm sittin' here behind this wheel, 'Nowhere' circled on the map, 300 horses at my heel," we have already made some poetic and sound choices that make them sound professional. Notice the repeated "w" sound in the words "wonder" and "why" (this is alliteration, which is explained later in this chapter), the exact rhyme of the words "wheel" and "heel," and the rhythm of the syllables as they roll along (much like the rhythm of the wheels of the car).

Making the words flow

As you develop your lyric, try to include lyrical and poetic devices like these (and the many others we explore in this chapter) into your lyric. As these lyrics start finding a melody, be sure to try out your lyrics to see how comfortable they feel being sung.

One way to help ensure that the sound of your words will be an asset to your song is to write as you would talk. If a lyric is conversational and informal, it's more likely to be easy to sing and sound natural.

"Baby" is a word you'll find a lot in songs, yet few people still use it in conversation. Some popular writers would sooner die than use this word. Yet, others have made a career out of using the word "baby."

Noticing a lyric's point of view

Another important element of a lyric is the point of view from which the lyric is sung. Hit songs have been written from every perspective imaginable. "A Day in the Life of a Tree" (written by Brian Wilson and John Rieley; performed by The Beach Boys) is sung from the point of view of an endangered species of tree. In "I Am the Walrus" (written by John Lennon and Paul McCartney; performed by The Beatles), John Lennon takes on different personas as the song develops.

First person

The first person perspective is perhaps the most popular of all the forms. This is where the story is told from the singer's point of view — it's also the most personal of all the points of view. Take a look at this list of songs that illustrate the first person point of view:

- ✔ **"Every Little Kiss"** (written and sung by Bruce Hornsby)

- ✔ **"I'm Real"** (written by Martin Denny, Leshaun Lewis, Jennifer Lopez, Troy Oliver, and Cory Rooney; sung by Jennifer Lopez)

- ✔ **"Superman (It's Not Easy)"** (written by John Ondrasik; performed by Five For Fighting)

The first person approach to a lyric is many writers' favorite point of view. Maybe that's because so many of us use songwriting as a way of expressing what's in our hearts — getting things off our chests. The singer/songwriter era in the '70s spawned many songs from this perspective when the buying audience seemed fascinated by the innermost feelings of the introspective artists of that time — such as Dan Hill, Cat Stevens, and Jim Croce.

Even if you write a lyric from a personal perspective, before you finalize it, try changing the perspective to third person (see the next section) to see how you like it. Changing the perspective can sometimes add needed depth to a lyric.

Third person

The third person point of view is a powerful vantage point because the songwriter becomes the reporter, if you will, of the events taking place in the song. He's the storyteller, and the whole world wants to hear his tale. Though not as personal as first person, third person is an extremely effective point of view because, as a semi-detached observer, the singer is able to express feelings, comment, praise, and criticize without having to take complete responsibility. In "Well Respected Man" (written by Ray Davies; performed by The Kinks), the singer documents the hypocrisy of England's class system — while staying out of the line of fire, because he's just reporting the issues. The Rolling Stones like to mix their first-person songs ("I Can't Get No Satisfaction" (written by Mick Jagger and Keith Richards), with third-person songs ("She bitches 'bout things that she's never seen, look at that Stupid Girl"). Songs like "Dirty Laundry" (written by Don Henley and Daniel Kortchmar; sung by Don Henley) draw their power from the writer's ability to satirize and criticize the world of sensationalized journalism from a vantage point just left of center stage.

Example step #8: Setting the point of view, tone, and perspective

In the fictitious song, "Deep in the Heart of the Night," it's time to make sure we keep our perspective in mind and consider issues such as point of view and the tone of the lyric. In our dummy lyric, so far we have the beginnings of a verse, "Do you wonder why I'm sitting here behind this wheel, 'Nowhere' circled on the map, 300 horses at my heel." This is a story being told from the first person point of view; in other words, the story is unfolding in the life of the person who is singing. The lines that follow this can either stay in that point of view or change to the third person point of view. We might want to shift to the feelings of the woman who perhaps broke his heart and made him take to the highway. In the pre-chorus, we switch to a looking-back perspective with "Wish that I could change your mind, and claim the love we left behind." In the chorus, we go back to the present tense, "Deep in the heart of the night, I see you, deep in the heart of the night, I touch you." Also, whether you use these lyrics or not, when you're practicing writing this song, make sure the overall tone of the lyric is consistent throughout. An overly hostile lyric, for instance would be at odds with the wistful tone that we've set up so far in this song.

Experimenting with point of view

Sometimes a lyricist can change the point of view within a single song. In "Hold on Loosely," the song I co-wrote with Don Barnes and Jeff Carlisi for 38 Special, the pre-chorus starts in first person — "my mind goes back to the girl I met long years ago who told me." But when it hits the chorus, "Hold on loosely, but don't let go," the message now comes from the woman's point of view. When the words hit, "who told me," it's now the advice of the woman we're hearing — even though the singer is delivering her message. Until I stumbled upon this technique, the chorus was sounding "preachy," as if the singer was expounding this piece of wisdom. In any "advice songs" or songs where you'd like to be a step away from the action, consider placing the words in someone else's mouth (or quoting the words as if from a billboard or a magazine).

Experiment with changing the point of view of your lyric after you feel you've completed it. "She Loves You" (written by John Lennon and Paul McCartney; performed by The Beatles) wouldn't have been nearly as involving lyrically if John and Paul had chosen to call it "I Love You." By making the point of view third person, you allow the listener to be an observer of the situation alongside the singer — and most everybody loves being an insider.

Getting some perspective

The perspective of a lyric refers to whom a song is directed and who will deliver it. It also refers to the song's timeframe. As a songwriter, you may have someone specific in mind to perform the song you're writing. As you're creating, you're putting yourself in the mindscape of that artist and, depending on whether your target is male or female, rough or gentle, political or apolitical, religious or agnostic, sarcastic or sincere, you are tailoring the perspective of the lyric to fit.

Find out all you can about an artist before you begin writing a song with him or her in mind. Try to write a lyric that stays within the boundaries of that artist's persona. Discover the marital status, hobbies, passions, and philosophical leanings of this person by reading interviews and listening to other songs he's written or chosen to perform.

When you're writing a lyric, also be aware of the time perspective or tense in which you're writing. The present tense is very prevalent in popular songs because it's here and now and immediate. There's no time like now to get an urgent message across (a good example is "I'm a Survivor" [written by Anthony Dent, Beyonce Knowles, and Mathew Knowles; performed by Destiny's Child]). The past tense in a lyric looks back on a time or situation. The reflective nature of past tense encourages songs about what could have been and what should have been, but it can also celebrate the good times of the past. Bob Seger is an artist who found a future in the past with powerful songs like "Night Moves," his bittersweet ode to coming of age in the heartland of America and "Against the Wind" (both written and sung by Bob Seger). Future tense is also popular in lyrics. People love to fantasize and futurize. "We'll Be Together" (written and sung by Sting) is a good example of future tense.

I sometimes like to combine past and present tenses in the same song. In "High on You," (written by Jim Peterik and Frankie Sullivan; performed by Survivor), We describe a scenario from the night before — "There you stood, that'll teach ya, to look so good and feel so right." In the pre-chorus, I move to the present tense — "Now I'm higher than a kite, I know I'm getting hooked on your love." The combination of tenses adds movement to the action of a song. You can even add what I call a *someday section* to bring the story into the future. Songs that come around full circle get me every time.

Tuning in to the lyric's tone and style

Many factors weigh into the overall tone of a song. Musical factors are perhaps the biggest influence on the mood of a song. The lyric, however, has to match whatever emotional tone the music sets (or vice versa). The images you choose for a sad, tragic, or moody song are going to be very different from the images you use for a joyful, giddy, or humorous one. Images of light and color seem to infuse positive songs, while images of darkness and shadow permeate the more negative songs. However it is sometimes appropriate to mix the hues of emotional color and create a new shade.

If you choose informal language in a particular song (complete with slang, intentionally bad grammar and colloquialisms), make sure you don't suddenly become a Rhodes scholar at the third verse and blow your cover! If your tone is formal and intelligent (listen to Don Henley's song "Heart of the Matter" written by Don Henley, Mike Campbell, and J.D. Souther; sung by Don Henley for a good example of this), try not to slip into a John Mellencamp kind of style, which is far more "down home" than "downtown."

Most of the songs I write tend to be on the positive side. I've always been more of a "half-full" guy than a "half-empty" guy, and my lyrics reflect that. Even when I write a sad song, there's usually a light at the end of the tunnel (and it's not the lights of an oncoming train!). You'll probably have more luck writing lyrics that reflect your personality rather than attempting to write "against type."

The musical marketplace you're targeting with a particular song does, to some extent, determine the style of your lyric. Certain words, expressions, and phrases are appropriate for a rock song, but they just won't work for a country song. Many lyrics are genre-specific. For instance, the country market by and large doesn't tolerate any word that resembles a swear word or a coarse or crude reference (better to change your *damn* to *dang* and your *lust* to *love*). There's no such ban, however, on words like this in modern hard rock (good examples are Limp Bizkit, Korn, and Slip Knot). Certain phrases in country, Christian, and easy listening are not going to sound appropriate against a balls-to-the-wall Aerosmith track or the latest by Linkin Park.

Using Poetic Devices in Lyrics

Many times people ask what the difference is between poetry and lyrics, and they often get one of a number of stock answers. People may tell you that poems are usually read and not heard, yet if that were always the case, we wouldn't have poetry readings. In reality, poetry is a kind of music on its own. If you look up the word *lyrics* in Webster's dictionary, you'll find that it means "words expressing a writer's strong and spontaneous feelings in a poem or a song." The truth is that the principle of poetry applies to lyrics as well.

Through the centuries, poems have been set to music by composers. Some poems can be set to music virtually unaltered, while others must be tailored to fit the form of the popular song. Factors such as song form, rhyme, rhythm, song length, and singability all come into play.

Some songwriters are as much poets as they are songwriters. When you read the lyrics of songwriters such as Leonard Cohen, Bob Dylan, Joni Mitchell, and Jewel, it's obvious that these lyrics have considerable power even without musical accompaniment. This is the hallmark of the poet who also happens to be a songwriter as well.

Bob Dylan changed his last name to Dylan as a tribute to the poet Dylan Thomas. (Bob Dylan's given name was Robert Zimmerman.)

There is much to be learned by the songwriter from the reading and analyzation of great poetry. We'll now take a closer look at some of the poetic devices that'll serve to enhance the sound of your lyric and song.

Using repetition

Repetition is an important component in both poetry and songwriting. A kind of poetic music can be created using the repetition of sounds. The repetition of words, phrases (such as a title), verses, and choruses can help get your point or your songs across to your listeners.

Applying word and phrase repetition

In our discussion of repetition, we'll start with the repetition of words and phrases, the most obvious example being the title.

Titles can be repeated frequently in a song. An example is "Hey Jude" (written by John Lennon and Paul McCartney; performed by The Beatles). The title in this song is repeated at the beginning of each verse and over and over again in the songs lengthy outro (outro is the opposite of intro). The repetition of the "na na na na" phrase in that same outro forms a hypnotic backdrop to the instrumental chaos that is mounting.

Certain words can be repeated for emphasis or to adapt to a melody. Sometimes this occurs in the title, as in "Say, Say, Say" (written and performed by Paul McCartney and Michael Jackson) and "Hi, Hi, Hi" (written and sung by Paul and Linda McCartney/Wings). Sometimes parts of a song are built using a single word (often its title) such as in the song "Hero" from the 2002 motion picture smash *Spider-Man* (written by Chad Kroeger; sung by Chad Kroeger of Nickelback and Josey Scott of Saliva).

Utilizing verse repetition

Repetition can also be used effectively with entire sections of a song. Verse repetition is fairly common. This usually occurs when the first verse is repeated at the end of the song. An example is "California Dreamin'" (written by John Phillips; performed by The Mamas and the Papas). Sometimes the songwriter does this because he just cannot come up with another verse. Other times it's because the verse is really worth repeating, or perhaps the songwriter wants to emphasize something that was said earlier in the song.

Utilizing chorus repetition

The verse-chorus form lends itself to chorus repetition just by its very nature. A strong chorus can benefit by multiple repetitions in the song, or by being repeated over and over at the end of the song.

Examining poetic devices

Using poetic devices in your lyrics is kind of like seasoning your food. The right spices in the perfect amounts can add flavor, excitement, and romance to a dish, but using too much can mask the flavor and make the food inedible.

Viewing different poetic devices

Look at some of the following spices that gourmet songwriters use to enhance their lyrics:

- **Rhyme:** A regular recurrence of corresponding sounds, especially at the end of lines. Rhyme is one of the most basic spices that can bring out the flavor in any dish (or song). (Rhyme is covered in Chapter 7.)

- **Alliteration:** The repetition of the same sound, usually of the *consonant* (everything except A, E, I, O, and U) at the beginning or within two or more words immediately succeeding each other. Titles like the following are all good examples of the use of alliteration in a song title:

  - **"Bewitched, Bothered, and Bewildered"** (written by Lorenz Hart and Richard Rodgers; sung by Frank Sinatra)

  - **"Silent Lucidity"** (written by Chris DeGarmo; performed by Queensryche)

- ● **"She Sells Sanctuary"** (written by Ian Astbury and Billy Duffy; performed by The Cult)

✔ **Imagery:** Those magic words and phrases in a lyric that impress images into your mind, the descriptive words that help drive home lasting impressions, mental pictures created with words. Who can ever forget the "tangerine trees" and "marshmallow skies" of "Strawberry Fields Forever" by John Lennon and Paul McCartney? Imagery is the indelible stamp of a truly great phrase. For a wonderful example of the use of imagery (and many other poetic devices such as simile — "like Sinatra in a younger day") call up the lyrics to "Life In A Northern Town" (written by Gilbert Gabriel, Nick Laird; performed by The Dream Academy).

✔ **Personification:** When a poet or lyricist refers to a thing, quality, or idea as if it were a person and ascribes human characteristics to inanimate objects. Good examples of this poetic device would be "They Call the Wind Mariah" (written by Alan Lerner and Frederick Loewe; sung by Sam Cooke) and the great line from "Mrs. Robinson" (written by Paul Simon; performed by Simon and Garfunkel), "Where have you gone Joe DiMaggio, *the nation turns it's lonely eyes to you.*" Nations don't really have eyes except in wonderfully creative songs like these.

✔ **Simile:** Comparing one thing to a dissimilar thing by the use of *like* or *as.* "Love Is Like an Itching in My Heart" (written by Brian Holland, Lamont Dozier, and Ed Holland; performed by the Supremes) is a good example, as is "Your Love Is Like Oxygen" (written by Andy Scott and Trevor Griffin; performed by Sweet) and "Like A Virgin" (written by Tom Kelly and Billy Steinberg; sung by Madonna).

✔ **Metaphor:** This is a figure of speech where one thing is compared to another thing, as if it were that other thing (without using *like* or *as*). A few examples are, "Love Is The Drug" (written by Bryan Ferry and Andy Mackay; performed by Roxy Music) or "I Am The Walrus" and "Happiness Is A Warm Gun" (written by Paul McCartney and John Lennon; performed by The Beatles).

✔ **Assonance:** A partial rhyme where the stressed vowel sounds are alike, but the consonant sounds are not alike, as in *late* and *make.* In the Simon and Garfunkel classic "America" (written by Paul Simon) the long o sound is used 3 times in the wonderfully descriptive line, "The moon rose over an open field."

I always go for a perfect rhyme when I can find one, but I'll never eliminate a great line simply because it doesn't rhyme exactly. Assonance in two words is a perfectly acceptable substitute for rhyme in most situations.

✔ **Consonance:** According to *Webster's,* "a pleasing combination of sounds simultaneously produced." This word covers a lot of ground in lyric writing and harkens back to what we said on the subject of words sounding good and flowing well together.

➤ **Anaphora:** A figure in rhetoric and lyrics in which the same word or words are repeated at the beginning of successive lines. You'll find many good examples of anaphora in "The One I Gave My Heart To" (written by Diane Warren; sung by Aaliyah), "I Got Rhythm" (written by George and Ira Gershwin; sung by sung by Ella Fitzgerald, Jimmy Dorsey, Judy Garland, Lena Horne, or Mel Torme) and "From a Distance" (written by Julie Gold; performed by Bette Midler).

Anaphora is a very common technique probably used more in songwriting than in poetry, yet it's not commonly discussed in songwriting books. While the word itself may be new and unusual, you'll begin to recognize anaphora in many songs when looking for it.

Example step #9: Using poetic devices

We're at the final fine-tuning of our lyric for "Deep in the Heart of the Night." It's time to make sure we use enough poetic devices to invigorate the imagination. Again put yourself into the driver's seat of that car and take inventory of every emotion you might be feeling. Look around and observe the landscape as it goes rushing past. Look up in the stars that light the plains and feel the pull of the moon on your heart. Now take these feelings and observations and see how you can apply the various poetic techniques to your lyric writing. It'll help to make your song linger in people's memories long after the sun has risen on Tulsa and our solitary driver has found some peace of mind.

Practice Makes Perfect

At this stage in the game, you've probably got the itch to get going with writing some great lyrics, so start now by writing down the theme or concept that's buzzing around in your head at this very moment. Go ahead and have some fun putting phrases together.

As a starting off point, you might want to take a stab at writing a lyric by going back to the song form you came up with from Chapter 3, as well as the hook you created in Chapter 4, and combine them with your lyric work in this chapter. Try not to get bogged down or frozen. Very often, songwriters are afraid of writing something that sounds pretty stupid, so they hold back from the freedom of just writing whatever comes to mind.

The more you free yourself to just let go with the words, the more of an opportunity you've provided yourself to lay down something that works great in your songs. Always remember that the more times you allow yourself to practice writing down phrases and thoughts that fit a burning concept inside of you, the more opportunities you give yourself to "hit the mark" and write some great lyrics.

Chapter 7

Using Rhymes in Your Songs

*W*elcome to the wonderful world of rhyming! Many writers consider this to be the fun part of the songwriting process, because the art of rhyming is similar to solving a brainteaser or putting together a jigsaw puzzle. But finding the right rhymes while capturing the essence of your lyric is anything but easy.

Nothing puts the final coat of shellac on a song better than a well-constructed rhyme scheme. The careful and often clever use of exact or similar sounding words is the spice behind the meaning of the words that helps market the emotions of a song. Without rhymes (unless purposely not used to create a specific unschooled effect), songs tend to sound unfinished and "amateur" in nature.

In this chapter, we look at the types of rhymes and the various rhyming patterns, called rhyme schemes, used in songwriting. Plus we fill you in on the techniques you can use to find and create rhymes for your own songs.

Identifying the Types of Rhymes

There are two kinds of rhymes — *perfect rhyme and imperfect rhyme:*

✔ **Perfect rhyme:** When the syllables of two or more words contain the same vowel and final consonant sounds but begin with different consonant sounds (such as boat and coat or bullet and pull it).

✔ **Imperfect rhyme:** Also called *near, slant* or *false rhyme*, imperfect rhyme is an approximation of rhyme. The two most common forms of imperfect rhyme are assonance, where two words share the same vowel sound (for example, *prove* and *sooth*, and *love* and *hug*) and consonance, where two or more words share the final consonant sound (as in *young* and *song*).

Perfect and imperfect rhymes fall into various categories:

✔ **Masculine rhyme:** A single-syllable rhyme that can either be one syllable words (like *love* and *shove*, or *tears* and *years*) or words that end in a stressed, rhymed syllable (such as *command* and *understand*).

✔ **Feminine rhyme:** A two-syllable rhyme where the first syllable is stressed (such as, *lovin'* and *oven*, or *carol* and *barrel*).

✔ **Triple rhyme:** When the last three syllables rhyme (as with *embraceable* and *irreplaceable*, or *unbelievable* and *inconceivable* -in rare instances writers have been known to use quadruple rhymes, but an example would be *too naïve to disbelieve you*).

✔ **Open rhyme:** When a rhyme ends in a soft consonant so that the sound can be held out at the end of a line (as in *say* and *play*, or *sky* and *fly*).

✔ **Stopped rhyme:** When a rhyme ends with a hard consonant (such as, *clock* and *sock*, or *got* and *diddley squat*).

✔ **Internal rhyme:** When any of the above types of rhymes occur *within* a line of lyric as opposed to at the end of the line (as in "she *told* me she had *sold* out long ago").

Before the onslaught of the 1960s, near rhyme was considered non-rhyme by the songwriting masters of Tin Pan Alley (the nickname given to the American sheet music industry that existed in the first half of the twentieth century when music publishers exposed their songwriter's songs through colorfully illustrated folios of music). Many of the rhymes in the old standards, the great songs up to the 1960s, were perfect rhymes.

Looking at Rhyming Patterns

Rhyme falls into two main patterns: external rhyme and internal rhyme. External rhyme, also known as end rhyme, comes at the *end* of the lines. Internal rhyme, sometimes referred to as inner rhyme, occurs *within* the lines of the songs.

Understanding external rhymes

External rhymes, or end rhymes, are the near or perfect rhymes that occur at the ends of the various lines of your lyric. These rhymes can occur according to a definite pattern and when they do, this is called a rhyme scheme, or rhyming pattern. Your song's rhyme scheme can take many different forms — these forms are indicated by using lowercase letters (to distinguish rhyming patterns from the types of form described in Chapter Three). The letters indicate which lines have matching end rhymes. In the following sections, we take a look at a few of the most popular forms.

The abab rhyming pattern

This very common rhyme pattern occurs when the words are rhymed at the ends of alternating lines. This is the scheme of the verses of "Heavy Metal," the movie-driven hit for Sammy Hagar, co-written with Jim Peterik:

Head bangers in *leather*	(a)
Sparks flying in the dead of the night	(b)
They all come *together*	(a)
When they shoot out the lights	(b)
Fifty thousand watts of *power*	(a)
And they're pushin' overload	(b)
The beast is ready to *devour*	(a)
All the metal it can hold	(b)

© 1981 WB Music Corp. (ASCAP), Easy Action Music (ASCAP), and The Nine Music (ASCAP). All Rights o/b/o Easy Action Music administered by WB Music Corp. All rights reserved. Used by permission. Warner Bros. Publications U.S. Inc., Miami, FL 33014

Each line leads perfectly to the next as a night at a heavy metal show is described. The rhymes — some perfect, some near — emphasizes the vibe of the action and adds impact to the images.

When we wrote the song "Heavy Metal," Sammy and I put ourselves into the moment of the concert and started to draw from our own experience of attending and performing big shows. The rhymes just kind of came naturally from the conversation we were having at the time. It's not like we said, "Let's construct an *abab* type of rhyming pattern." We just started with the lines "Head bangers in leather, sparks flying in the dead of the night," and those lines seemed to dictate where the rhymes went from there.

In "Superman (It's Not Easy)" by John Ondrasik of Five For Fighting, the *abab* rhyme scheme is used to equally good advantage on its verse:

... stand to *fly*	(a)
... that naïve	(b)
... out to *find*	(a)
... part of me	(b)

The *abab* pattern is one of the oldest in pop-lyric writing. No matter what's being said, what sentiments are being reflected, and what style of language is popular at that particular time, this form has resilience in every era. Check out this vintage gem from the pens of Jimmy Van Heusen and lyricist Sammy Cahn, written as the title song for *The Tender Trap,* a film starring Frank Sinatra:

Some starry *night*	(a)
When her kisses make you tingle	(b)
She'll hold you *tight*	(a)
And you'll hate yourself for being single	(b)

In "Vehicle" written by Jim Peterik for The Ides of March, the *abab* scheme is also used:

I'm the friendly stranger in the black *sedan*	(a)
Won't you hop inside my car	(b)
I got pictures, got candy, I'm a loveable *man*	(a)
And I can take you to the nearest star	(b)

What's fascinating to me about the rhyming process is that it can actually be a tool to finding your storyline. The word *sedan* in the first line dictated the short *an* sound for the third line. In searching for a line, I worked with the word *man* until I came up with an adjective that fit the character of this "character" in the song (me!). *Hell of a* wasn't right, neither was *wonderful,* but *loveable* somehow captured the innocent creepiness I was groping for. On the alternate lines, creating *Won't you hop inside my car* necessitated an *ar* sound rhyme. I soon thought of the word *star* and started to figure out how to use it. When I stumbled on *I'll take you to the nearest star,* I knew I had created one of the strongest images of the song. It's kind of like the tail wagging the dog in terms of the meaning coming to the surface after the rhyme is found, but the technique is legal in most states as far as I know! Think of rhymes as your friend for fleshing out your story — I'd be lost without them.

Check out other *abab* songs, if you want to learn by picking them apart. Here are a few to start with:

- ✔ "Love Is Here to Stay" by George and Ira Gershwin, over 100 different recordings sung by such artists as Tony Bennett, Frank Sinatra, and Kenny Rogers

- ✔ "Live to Tell It All" written and sung by Vince Gill and Sonya Isaacs (The entire song has an *abab* rhyming pattern using near rhyme.)

- ✔ "Girl" by John Lennon and Paul McCartney; performed by The Beatles

Two good tools of the trade for creating rhyme are a rhyming dictionary and a thesaurus. There are many different dictionaries to choose from, each a bit different from the other due to the outlook, experience, and slant of their author. Books like *The Songwriter's Rhyming Dictionary* by Sammy Cahn (New American Library) and *The New Comprehensive American Rhyming Dictionary* by Sue Young (Avon) are just two of the many fine books you can lean on when you're stuck for a rhyme or need some fresh ideas. A thesaurus is good to have around while working on rhymes because if a word is virtually non-rhymable, you may be able to find a word of similar meaning that's far more "rhyme friendly."

The aabb rhyming pattern

The sturdy *aabb* form is where the first and second line ends in similar sounding words and the third and forth lines end in a different set of rhymes. Take a look at how one of America's most descriptive songwriters, John Mellencamp, uses the *aabb* form in the verse of his 2001 release entitled "Peaceful World":

...world is a *wreck*	(a)
...being politically *correct*	(a)
...didn't at *first*	(b)
...made it worse and *worse*	(b)

Another song in the *aabb* pattern is "Night of the World Stage" by Jim Peterik's new ensemble group, World Stage. The second verse goes like this:

You're sittin' at the phone with your every day *frustrations*	(a)
I'll take you to the zone for mood *elevation*	(a)
There's a whole rhythm section bangin' in your *head*	(b)
Your heart could be my drummer, let's run it in the *red*	(b)

In the last line you have the added bonus of internal rhyme with the similarity of sounds of the words *drummer* and *run.*

For more examples of the *aabb* pattern, check out the songs in Table 7-1.

Table 7-1	Songs with *aabb* Rhyming Patterns	
Song Title	**Songwriter(s)**	**Singers/Performers**
"I Hope You Dance"	Mark D. Sanders, Tia Sellers	Leann Womack and the Sons of the Desert
"Can't Take My Eyes Off of You"	Bob Crewe, Bob Gaudio,	Frankie Valli and the Four Seasons
"If You Ever Have Forever in Mind"	Vince Gill, Troy Seals	Vince Gill
"Marrakesh Express"	Graham Nash	Crosby, Stills, and Nash
"Your Song"	Elton John, Bernie Taupin	Elton John
"All Along the Watchtower"	Bob Dylan	Jimi Hendrix
"Because You Loved Me"	Diane Warren	Celine Dion

Other forms

The *aaba* is a popular variation on *aabb* in which the last line of the *quatrain* (the fancy way of referring to four successive lines of lyric) rhymes with the first two lines instead of the third. Check out the verse in the Survivor song, "I Can't Hold Back" (written by Jim Peterik and Frankie Sullivan):

There's a story in my *eyes*	(a)
Turn the pages of *desire*	(a)
Now it's time to trade those dreams	(b)
For the rush of passion's *fire*	(a)

The third line adds just enough sound variation to keep the whole verse sounding fresh. You can see how monotonous it would get if the pattern was merely *aaaa* by inserting the fake line *Now it's time to trade those lies* in place of the third line. In the original the long *e* sound of *dreams* is a welcome relief from all the long *i* sounds.

Often times you can get away with a minimum of rhyming and still have your song sounding top notch. The lyric to the classic hit recorded by Elvis Presley, "Can't Help Falling in Love with You" (written Luigi Creatore, Hugo Peretti, and George Weiss) has an interesting back story. The song, originally titled "Can't Help Falling in Love With Him," was then tailored to fit Elvis when he showed interest in the song. If you read through the lyric, it's apparent that all the rhymes were crafted to fit the original title. It would have been an *abca* rhyming pattern. Instead, it turned out to be the more unusual *abcd* form (and we bet it never bothered you in the least!). If you look at these lyrics and read it the way it turned out, try substituting in your mind the word *him* for *you* each time it comes around to see the difference it made.

When I was working on the lyrics for "Eye of the Tiger" (co-written with Frankie Sullivan), more emphasis was put on telling Rocky's story than rhyming up a storm. The word *rival* was originally there as an exact rhyme to the original working title, "Survival." When the (extremely wise) decision was made to make the hook "Eye of the Tiger," the word *rival* came along for the ride and became an "approximate rhyme" for the word *tiger*. Even though it may have been more desirable to find an exact rhyme for either "rival" or "tiger," the emotion of the lyric was well worth the trade-off. It's fascinating to look at the rough drafts of famous lyrics to see their raw beginnings, before they were refined and merely scrawls on a notebook page. Figure 7-1 shows one of the rough drafts of "Eye of the Tiger" taken from Jim's work notebook.

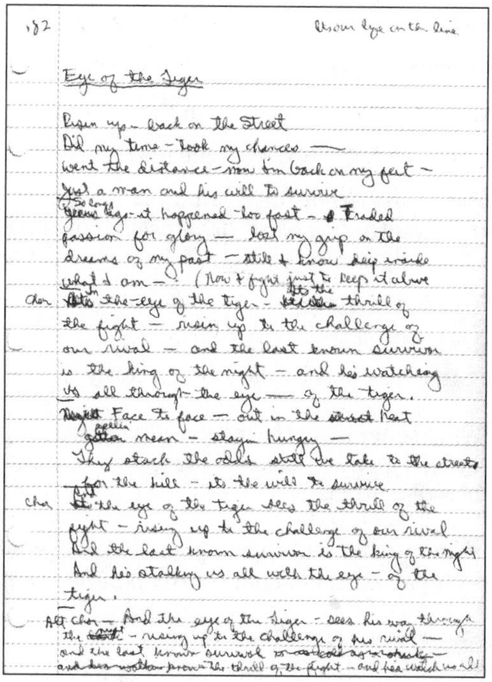

Figure 7-1: Lyric draft for "Eye of the Tiger."

Now look at an excerpt from the lyric of this ode to the human spirit to illustrate its lack of traditional rhyming techniques:

Rising up, back on the *street*	(a)
Did my time, took my chances	(b)
Went the distance, now I'm back on my *feet*	(a)
Just a man and his will to *survive*	(c)
So many times, it happens too *fast*	(d)
You trade your passion for glory	(e)
Don't lose your grip on the dreams of the *past*	(d)
You must fight just to keep them *alive*	(c)

Notice how the rhyme pattern actually spans two verses with the last line of each verse containing the rhyming word.

The chorus then shifts to the following pattern:

It's the eye of the tiger	(a)
It's the thrill of the *fight*	(b)
Rising up to the challenge of our *rival*	(c)
And the last known survivor stalks his prey in the night	(b)
And he's watching us all with the eye — of the *tiger*	(c)

© 1982 WB Music Corp., Easy Action Music, Holey Moley Music, and Rude Music. All Rights o/b/o Easy Action Music administered by WB Music Corp. All rights reserved. Used by permission. Warner Bros. Publications U.S. Inc., Miami, FL 33014

Sometimes you can fool the ear with an approximate rhyme. *Tiger* is such a strong word that it more than justifies the lack of exact rhyme.

Like many songs, the rhyme scheme on this one varies from section to section. This variance, in fact, further helps separate sections and makes them more distinct from one another.

As you can see, there are many different rhyme patterns used in popular songs. Here are some more patterns and some corresponding sample songs:

✔ *aaaa* **patterns** (where the first four lines rhyme):

• "Fortunate" written by Robert Kelly; performed by Maxwell

• "American Pie" written and sung by Don McLean

• "Every Breath You Take" written and sung by Sting

✔ *abcb* **patterns** (where the first and third lines don't rhyme with anything, and lines two and four do):

- "My Girl" written by Smokey Robinson and Ronald White; performed by the Temptations

- "Take Me Home, Country Roads" written by John Denver, Mary and William Danoff; performed by John Denver

- "God Must Have Spent a Little More Time on You" written by Carl Sturken and Evan Rogers; performed by 'N Sync (pop hit)/ Alabama (country hit)

- "How Can You Mend a Broken Heart?" written by Barry Gibb and Robin Gibb; performed by The Bee Gees

- "House of the Rising Sun" written by John Sterling and Eric Burdon; performed by the Animals

- "In My Life" written by John Lennon and Paul McCartney; and performed by The Beatles

The only real criteria for the validity of a rhyme pattern are not how many hits it's been used in, but how it sounds to the ear. Not coincidentally, most of the patterns used on the biggest hits happen to be the most pleasing to the ear.

Using internal rhyme

Rhyme isn't limited to the ends of lines. It can occur within a line or in the midst of two successive lines.

Internal rhyme is a common element in many of my favorite songs. Without knowing it, the audience is getting a nice portion of ear candy. It may not be nutritious, but it sure is tasty!

This line from the second verse of Survivor's "The Search Is Over" (written by Jim Peterik and Frank Sullivan) is a good example of internal rhyme used within a single line of lyric: "You followed me through changes and patiently you'd wait"/"Till I came *to* my senses *through* some miracle of fate."

Lyrical touches like this tend to be rather subliminal, but have the effect of making a song sound professional and "finished."

In the song "Long Day" by Matchbox Twenty (written by Rob Thomas), they use the technique of internal rhyme that occurs not only within a single line, but within successive lines. ". . . sitting by the overcoat"/". . . second *shelf, the note* she *wrote*"/". . . can't bring myself to throw away." The word *note* is an inner rhyme to the word *wrote* in the same line (which is an end rhyme to *overcoat* in the first line). *Shelf* is an internal rhyme to the word *myself* in the following line.

In John Mayer's song "No Such Thing" (co-written with Douglas Cook) he adds internal rhyme in the very first line of the song. ". . . she said to *me* condescending*ly*." He uses the technique again a few lines later ". . . the *dreams* of the prom *kings*."

Using Other Rhyming Techniques in Your Song

When writing a lyric, you can use various techniques to make your job a whole lot easier. Also note that it's not cheating to use inexact rhymes and play games like working backward from an end line and shifting pronunciations to make a rhyme work. Now look at a few of the methods that the pros use to complete a song.

Using perfect rhymes

It doesn't matter how the word is spelled as long as the sound of the word is the same. For example, *fight* and *ignite* are exact rhymes even though they're spelled differently (*night* and *ignite* are not rhymes because the two sounds are identical even though they are spelled differently). Conversely, *love* and *prove* are not perfect rhymes because, even though they are spelled the same (other than their opening sounds), they're not pronounced the same. Even the addition of an *s* at the end of a word technically prevents two words from being considered perfect rhymes. On the other hand *night* and *ignite* would not be considered rhymes because though the end of the word is identical, the preceding consonant needs to be different to be considered a rhyme.

Practically speaking, there is no compelling reason that I can see for insisting on perfect rhymes throughout an entire song. It's good work when you can get it, but don't sacrifice meaning and emotion for lack of a perfect rhyme.

Sometimes there are nuances between words that put their status as perfect rhymes in question. In the David Pomeranz and David Zippel hit "Born for You" (sung by Cathy Lee), they rhyme *stars* with *ours*. Though there's a slightly different vowel sound between the words, they sound virtually identical when sung.

Some writing teams of the past, like Richard Rodgers and Oscar Hammerstein II, always used exact rhymes in their lyric, otherwise they wouldn't write it. Look up the lyrics to "My Favorite Things" from *The Sound of Music* and check out the wonderful perfect rhyming schemes.

The argument for this perfection is the absolute neatness of all the phrases, kind of like the way the military demands its beds be made or the way the woman down the road keeps a perfect lawn. It sure looks nice, but you can decide for yourself if it's mandatory.

In Nashville, I wrote with a very successful songwriter who insisted on perfect rhymes. We wrote a few good songs, but I couldn't help feeling that some of the emotion was sacrificed on the altar of perfection. Sometimes the *perfect word* for a line does not happen to be a *perfect rhyme*.

Using near rhymes

Near rhymes are words that are close enough in sound to be similar, but not exactly the same. They are used extensively in all types of musical styles and seem to be getting more and more popular as rhymes are getting further and further apart. In "Take the Money and Run" (written and sung by Steve Miller), the line that you may remember most is his wonderful mangling of the English language when he rhymes *Texas* with *facts is*. This is a great example of the near rhyme taken to its extreme. More typically, rhymes will be closer as in the last verse of "Talent for Loving You" (written by Jim Peterik and John Greenebaum):

> And when the shadows fall *soft*
>
> And the lights are turned *off*
>
> And the moon beams are pourin' like *rain*
>
> Then you let your hair *down*
>
> And the night's only *sound*
>
> Is your voice whisperin' my *name*
>
> I could be the rock you lean on
>
> Or make the mountains *move*
>
> Cause I've got a talent
>
> I've got a talent for loving *you*

Also, notice that every rhyme is a near rhyme, but you probably would never have noticed had it not have been pointed out — that's the art of rhyming.

In "Can't Say It Loud Enough," Johnny Van Zant, Robert White Johnson, and I were stuck for a rhyme for the word *window*. Here's how we got around it:

> I see the eyes of a child barely five
>
> In a photo that sits by my *window*

I see the shadow of a man at my side

Feel his spirit each time the *wind blows*

Notice the inner rhyme of *eyes* and *five* in the first line.

"No matter how good a line or a thought is, if it doesn't please the ear in the context of the music, it's not gonna do what it's supposed to do, which is to make the listener enjoy the song. Poetry has to read well — lyrics have to sing well. Music is based in time and meter. A good lyric blends with melody, it doesn't fight it. It should be as ear-pleasing and interesting as possible. I use sound alike words as much as possible. Bouquet/day, problem/solve 'em, God/job; these were all in hit songs I've written. A good exercise is simply practicing rhyming words that don't easily rhyme; the ultimate being 'orange.' There is no perfect rhyme in the English language for 'orange' but there are plenty in songwriter-ese: i.e. 'storm,' 'born,' 'torn,' etc."

— John Greenebaum, noted Nashville songwriter —
co- writer of "Third Rock From The Sun" by
Joe Diffie and many more

Buy a rhyming dictionary and a thesaurus and spend ten minutes simply reading it every day. Even if you don't use these words when you write, the knowledge you gain will have a way of seeping in to your writing session.

Working backwards with rhyme

When working up a lyric you often have one key line, perhaps the first, to build up from. It would then be a good idea to create a *dummy lyric* for the next three or four lines (or however long your verse might be). As noted in Chapter 2, a dummy lyric is not intended to stay as a permanent fixture of the song, but exists mainly to block out the mechanics of the verse, marking parameters such as the amount of syllables per line and possible rhyme schemes.

I'm a big fan of the dummy lyric (I got it! How about a book called *Dummy Lyrics For Dummies*!). When I write with someone else, it's a great way to beat the writer's block that comes from thinking everything you write down has to be brilliant. I'll say, "Let's just come up with a dummy lyric for now to help us remember the melody." Almost invariably we'll then proceed to come up with at least one or two lines that are pretty darn cool in the climate of lowered expectations.

In creating your mock-up section (this technique works equally well for all sections of the song), you may hit upon a last line that is actually a keeper. Your next step may be to work back from that line to find appropriate rhymes for the rest of the verse.

"When I was writing the lyric to "Can't Say It Loud Enough" for The Van Zant album with Robert White Johnson and Jim Peterik, all we had was a great second line, 'My daddy said that the truth is the truth and there just ain't no space in between it.' We worked backward all day long to find the right line and the right rhyme for the first line. We finally came up with, 'Some people think that a lie ain't a lie if you find enough fools to believe it.' Working backward on a lyric, you can sometimes come up with some great stuff you never would've otherwise."

— Johnny Van Zant, lead singer of Lynyrd Skynyrd and member of Van Zant

Changing pronunciations to help rhyme

Sometimes, merely how a singer pronounces a word will dictate if a word will rhyme. *Thinking* is a perfect rhyme for *drinking*. If you're writing a country tune, however, you could easily rhyme *spankin'* with *drankin'* which is country past tense for *drinkin'*.

You can stretch the language only so far in search of a rhyme. When rhyming *pain* it would be out of fashion to pronounce *again,* so as to rhyme exactly.

Rhyming across verses

Take a look at this old standard, "In the Chapel in the Moonlight" (written and sung by Billy Hill), to see how the rhymes match up across the verses.

Verse 1

How I'd love to hear the organ
In the chapel in the moonlight
While we're strolling down the aisle
Where roses ent*wine*

Verse 2

How I'd love to hear you whisper
In the chapel in the moonlight
That the *lovelight* in your eyes
Forever will *shine*

Bridge

Till the roses turn to ashes
Till the organ turns to *rust*

If you never come, I'll still be there
Till the *moonlight* turns to *dust*

Verse 3

How I'd love to hear the choir
In the chapel in the moonlight
As they sing "Oh Promise Me"
Forever be *mine*

Words and music by Billy Hill © 1936 Shapiro, Bernstein & Co., Inc. New York Copyright Renewed/International Copyright Secured/All rights reserved/Used by permission

Notice the use of *lovelight* and *moonlight,* and the anaphora (the lyric technique where the same word or words are repeated at the beginning of succeeding verses or lines) used in this song: How I'd love to hear (1) organ, (2) whisper, (3) choir in the chapel in the moonlight. A picture is painted here: moonlight, the choir, the silence. Then the bridge provides the counterbalance: *rust* and *dust.* There is no rhyme scheme in the verses, the whole thing is tied together by the anaphora and the cross-verse end rhymes: entwine, shine, and mine. What a well-crafted gem this song is — no wonder it reached the Number 5 position and spent one third of the year on the charts in 1954.

To Rhyme or Not to Rhyme?

That is the question — you decide! Since the '60s, the use of rhyme in popular, rock, country, and R&B songs has changed greatly, with less and less of an emphasis on rhyme in many cases. Near rhyme such as assonance is used more as an embellishment nowadays — the same trend as poetry took at the beginning of the 20th century when free verse came alive.

Looking at songs with little rhyme

It's interesting to note that there's only one rhyme in the Paul Simon and Art Garfunkel-penned song "Bridge Over Troubled Water." Take a look at the following song, "Wild-Eyed Southern Boys" (written by Jim Peterik and performed by 38 Special) as another example of this — we've noted the few words that actually do rhyme:

Verse 1

It's a hot night at the juke joint
And the bands pumpin rhythm and *blues*
Gonna spill a little rock and roll blood tonight
Gonna make some front page *news*

Pre-chorus

And the ladies hate the violence
Still they never seem to look away
Cause they love those

Chorus

Wild-eyed southern boys
Wild-eyed boys
Wild-eyed southern boys

Verse 2

It's a southern point of honor
You got a get right in on the *act*
You can hear the outlaws holler
Fightin' for the lady in *black*

Pre-chorus

And she's just one in a million
But she's all I need tonight
Cause she loves those

Chorus

Wild-eyed southern boys

Wild-eyed boys
Wild-eyed southern boys

Check out some of these other hit songs that had very little rhyme schemes going on in the lyrics:

- ✔ "Let's Make Love" written by Chris Lindsey, Marv Green, Bill Luther, and Almec Mayo; sung by Faith Hill and Tim McGraw

- ✔ "Shape of My Heart" written by Max Martin, Rami Yacoub, and Lisa Miskovsky; performed by The Backstreet Boys

- ✔ "I'll Never Break Your Heart" written by Albert Manno and Ronnie Broomfield; performed by The Backstreet Boys

- ✔ "You Don't Have to Cry" written by Stephen Stills and Gold Hill; performed by Crosby, Stills, and Nash

Practice Makes Perfect

For this exercise, I'd like for you to look at the rhyme schemes of ten of your favorite songs by writing out the lyrics line by line and assigning a letter to every line. You'll start to see the various patterns of the rhyme schemes and the tricks writers use to make a lyric sound good while they're telling a story. Now go to a song you're writing and see how you might improve upon it by more exact rhymes, rhyming variations, inner rhyme, and dissimilar-sounding vowel sounds.

Next, choose one of your favorite songs and make a note of all the rhyming devices you find: external rhyme, internal rhyme (both within lines and between lines), perfect rhymes and imperfect rhymes, and the cases where a singer's pronunciation affects its R.Q. (rhyming quotient). Then take a look at your own finished or work in progress songs to see the workings of what you probably accomplished on pure instinct. Now figure out how the lyric could be made more "ear-pleasing" by the addition of some inner rhymes or some closer rhyming.

Part III
Creating the Music

In this part . . .

Although you probably don't analyze a song when you're on the dance floor or cruising in your car, the elements that create the music are what makes the song powerful and are important to understand when you're doing your own songwriting. In this part, we show you those musical elements that combust spontaneously to create magic. We take a look at how the synergy of rhythm, melody, and chords combine to help your song take flight.

Chapter 8

Using Rhythm in Songwriting

In This Chapter

▶ Understanding the dynamics of rhythm

▶ Creating a pulse for your music

▶ Getting into the beat

▶ Practicing connecting to the rhythm

● ●

*H*ave you ever noticed how, in certain songs, the words seem to dance across the music like they have "happy feet"? Have you ever started singing a song while walking down the street and found yourself picking up the pace as the song hits the chorus? It's practically a given that the biggest songs in pop history came right out of the box with a grabber word rhythm. Think of "Hot town, summer in the city, back of my neck gettin' dirty and gritty" ("Summer in the City" written by John Sebastian, Steve Boone, and Mark Sebastian; performed by The Lovin' Spoonful) or "Sir or Madame won't you read my book, it took me years to write, won't you take a look" ("Paperback Writer" written by John Lennon and Paul McCartney; performed by The Beatles).

In addition to the lyrical pulse, there is the musical rhythm of the song. In ancient times, messages were sent to distant villages using simple drum patterns to signal the news. Even today, to get the message of your song across, you need the persistent pulse of rhythm (drums, loops, and percussion effects) to communicate effectively. From the off-beat style of reggae music to the intricate rhythmic interplay of African, you can add flavor and interest to your song by interweaving divergent rhythm patterns (also known as *grooves*) into your song.

In this chapter, we'll look at how rhythm impacts your song — the rhythm of the words, the meter of the notes, and the underlying groove of the drums, by using some very basic examples from which you can expand upon as you write your song.

Looking at the Rhythm of Words

When you listen to someone talk, you'll notice a natural rise and fall in the voice as they express themselves in words. If not for this variety of speech, we'd all speak in monotone, and much of the nuance and expressiveness of language would be lost. The same is true in song. The *rhythm* of the words is the lilt or groove that the words possess even without the music. It's the beat you're left with if you were to substitute all your words for nonsense syllables like "ba ba, da da, do." The dynamics of a lyric can convey even more than the spoken word because lyrics have the added bonus of music underneath them to add even more interest. Such a deal!

Accented and unaccented syllables

When the voice rises in a phrase it's called an *accented* or *stressed* syllable. When the inflection of the voice lowers, it's called an *unaccented* or *unstressed* syllable. Take a look at some of the following lines of lyric and notice the natural rise and fall in the patterns of speech. The accented syllables are in capital letters.

> MAry HAD a LITTle LAMB

When you say that line, you can hear your voice rising on the accents (natural to the English language). The line has seven syllables and four accents.

To match this line *accentually* (counting the number of accents) and *syllabically* (counting the number of syllables), you'd create a second line following the same template:

> Its FLEECE was WHITE as SNOW

This famous example then goes on:

> And EVEryWHERE that MAry WENT
>
> The LAMB was SURE to GO

Just how Mary obtained the lamb and why the lamb in question was so eager to follow her has been the subject of heated debate throughout the years and frankly outside of our field of investigation.

Lines one and three now match each other and lines two and four match each other. You may have noticed, however, that line one has seven syllables, but there are eight syllables in line three. How do these lines match if they don't have the same number of syllables? They match because the first line is missing the first unaccented syllable, starting out with the accented MA syllable instead. Unaccented syllables at the beginning of lines can be dropped without affecting the meter of that line.

The pattern of a set of four lines with the four accents in the first and third lines and three accents in the third and fourth lines is called *common measure*. This particular pattern is often found in hymns. Now notice the common measure in the timeless hymn by John Newton, "Amazing Grace":

aMAzing GRACE, how SWEET the SOUND

That SAVED a WRETCH like ME

i ONCE was LOST, but NOW i'm FOUND

Was BLIND but NOW i SEE.

Now take a look at the cadence of the lyric of "Alcohol" (written by Stephen Page and Stephen Duffy; performed by Barenaked Ladies). Notice the stressed and unstressed syllables.

ALcoHOL, my PERmaNENT acCESsory

ALcoHOL, a PARty- TIME neCESsity

ALcoHOL, alTERnaTIVE to FEELing like yourSELF

o ALcoHOL, i STILL DRINK TO YOUR HEALTH

© 1998 WB Music Corp. and Treat Baker Music. All rights administered by WB Music Corp. All rights reserved. Used by permission. Warner Bros. Publications U.S. Inc., Miami, FL 33014

Notice how, even without the music, you start feeling a little tipsy due to the ups and downs of the accented and unaccented syllables.

Before you've written lyrics to your song, try mapping out the rhythm by creating a dummy lyric (see Chapter 2 for a detailed explanation) or blocking out the lines with nonsense syllables like "da dum, da dum, da dum" or "dum da dum dum, dum dum da dum dum," or whatever sounds good against the beat. For practice, find a lyric or poem by someone else and reduce it down to its "dum da dum" pattern to expose the rhythm's raw structure.

"When people think of rhythm in a pop song, they generally think of the beat — the dependable pulse you dance to. But that's only part of the story. Rhythm can also be used to make the melody more interesting or bring greater emphasis to aspects of the lyric. For instance, when in West Side Story, *Anita sings, 'I like to be in America . . .' the composer, Leonard Bernstein, uses rhythm to punch up and highlight the word 'A-me-ri-ca' from the rest of the thought. Looking at the subject of creative rhythm, we're really dealing with a combination of predictability and unpredictability and the artful mix of the two. I love a song that takes you for a predictable stroll down the street and all of a sudden takes a left turn — only to return to the familiar path again. Burt Bacharach, of course, is the master of this and, to me, this is why he and Bernstein are among the finest pop*

composers of our time. His use of rhythm is singularly unique. In "The moment I wake up, before I put on my make-up . . ." from "I Say a Little Prayer For You," he sets up Hal David's wonderful lyric with a predictable 4/4 pattern and on the words on my, he throws in a 2/4 bar! Completely unpredictable, but it works to excite because of Bacharach's setting the first lines up straight and returning back to 4/4 time. Essentially, rhythm not only makes a song groove, but at its creative best, can also make it an adventure."

—David Pomeranz, multi-platinum recording artist and writer of such hits as "Trying to Get the Feeling Again" and "It's in Every One of Us" (www.davidpomeranz.com)

Notice the rise and fall of speech patterns in the number one hit classic by Night Ranger, "Sister Christian," written by drummer/vocalist Kelly Keagy:

SISter CHRIStian, oh the TIME has COME

And you KNOW that you're the ONly ONE to SAY

oKAY.

WHERE you GOin' what you LOOKin' FOR

You KNOW those BOYS don't wanna PLAY NO MORE with YOU Its TRUE

"I must have performed "Sister Christian" thousands of times throughout my career, but it always feels like the first time for me. I enjoy singing it partly because it's written from personal experience and partly because of the conversational tone of the verses. The inflections of the words are just like talking to the audience."

—Kelly Keagy, founding member, drummer and vocalist of rock band, Night Ranger

Songs can also get their power from a succession of long, equally stressed words where every word carries an equal emphasis.

Many of the songs I write vary lyrical rhythm patterns from section to section. This is another way to create dynamics in a song. However, I like to try to keep corresponding sections as identical as possible in terms of the stressed and unstressed words and the length of syllables.

Syllable length

Another parameter that affects the rhythm of the words besides accented and unaccented syllables is the length of the syllables themselves. Short, fast words and syllables followed by long, slow words and syllables create interest by adding dynamics to a line and giving the ear some variation.

In the lines "We really NEED TO see this through" and "We never WANTED to be abused" from Blink 182's "Anthem Part II," we can see good examples of syllable length variations.

Notice the quick *pickup notes* (the unaccented notes that occur before beat one, the downbeat, of the musical bar — these terms will be explained later in this chapter) of "We really" contrasted with the long phrase "need to" (four beats to each word), then the mid-tempo "see this through" (one beat to each word). The next line follows the identical form with the quick "We'll never," the long "wanted," and the mid-tempo "be abused."

Looking at the classic Motown hit, "My Girl" (written by Smokey Robinson and Ronald White; performed by the Temptations), you can see the effective use of long and short syllables. When you know the devices of word meter, you suddenly start noticing elements that you previously took for granted.

> I've got SUNSHINE on a cloudy day
>
> When it's COLD OUTSIDE
>
> I'VE got the month of May
>
> **Pre-chorus**
>
> I GUESS YOU SAY
>
> WHAT can MAKE me FEEL this WAY
>
> MY Girl, talkin' 'bout MY GIRL
>
> *Words and music by William "Smokey" Robinson and Ronald White © 1964, 1972, 1973 (Renewed 1992, 2000, 2001), 1977 Jobete Music Co., Inc./ All rights controlled and administered by EMI April Music Inc./All rights reserved/International Copyright Secured/Used by Permission*

Notice how the word *sunshine* is stretched to match the vibrant feeling of the word. Also note how the pre-chorus section uses evenly stressed syllables (known as *spondaic rhythm*) to create a relaxed, peaceful feeling ("I guess you say"). When the song hits the hook, the rhythm of the words changes to the quick, punchy quarter notes of "My Girl" (and those wonderful background vocal echoes of "My Girl, My Girl") to drive the title home.

Looking at the Meter of Music

As important as the rhythm of the words is, it wouldn't mean much without the backdrop of the meter of the music. The meter of music is based on "beats" — the basic pulse of a piece of music. A beat is a recurring, regular pulse that defines the song's tempo (the speed at which the pulse is played). Beats are arranged into sections called *measures* or *bars* — with a particular number of beats in each bar.

The notes

Musical meter is written using a system of notes of different length values:

- **A whole note** has a length of 4 beats. It occupies a full bar in common time.

- **A half note** has a length of 2 beats. Only two of these can appear in a bar of common time.

- **A quarter note** has a length of 1 beat. Only four of these can appear in a bar of common time.

- **An eighth note** has a length of ½ beat. Only eight of these can appear in a bar of common time.

- **A sixteenth note** has a length of 1/4 beat. Only sixteen of these can appear in a bar of common time.

There are also dotted notes. When a dot is placed after a note, the value of that note is increased by fifty percent. A dotted half note therefore equals three beats instead of the two beats of a normal half note.

If no sound is to be made, then a *rest* is used instead of a note. Rests are the funny-looking symbols that we have shown in the figure. There is one that coincides with each of the notes (a whole rest, a half rest, a quarter rest, and so on). Also, rests can be dotted just like notes to increase their value by half. A rest in a piece of music simply indicates that no sound is made for the duration of the rest.

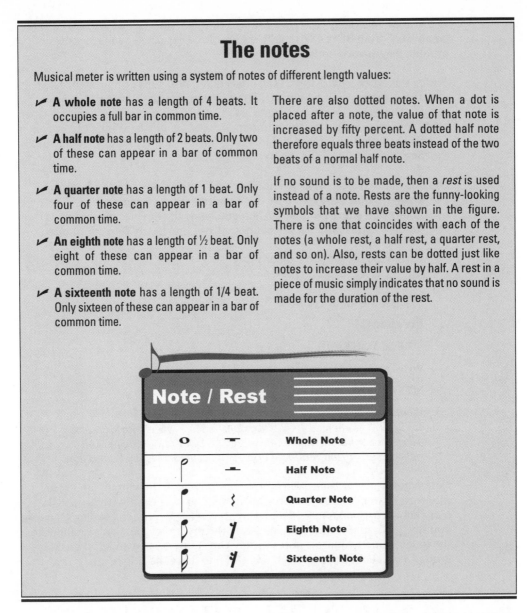

Note	Rest	
o	⊤	Whole Note
♩	—	Half Note
♩	ξ	Quarter Note
♪	𝄾	Eighth Note
♬	𝄿	Sixteenth Note

Even the silences between notes help create the pulse of what we hear. When combining music with words, rhythm is a vital unifying element. When creating melody and harmonies the force of rhythm helps shape what we come up with. Applying musical meter to lyrical rhythm is one of the most important facets of songwriting.

Placing beats in a bar

The pattern of four beats to a bar and eight bars in a section is the most commonly used of all beat structures. Four beats to a bar is called *common time* (or *4/4*). In these four-beat bars, the first and third beats are the strongest and usually receive an accented word from the lyrics (we call these *on beats*). The second and forth beats are weak, usually receiving an unaccented word (we refer to these as *off beats*). When a song is "in four" (or 4/4), it means there are four beats in each bar and each quarter note receives a beat. If a song is "in two" (also called *cut time* or *2/4*), there are two beats to a bar with a quarter note getting one beat. A song "in three" (also called *waltz tempo* or *3/4*) has three beats to each bar with a quarter note receiving the beat.

In each bar of music, you'll find notes of different value — a whole note in a bar of 4/4 will last for four beats (the whole bar), a half note for two beats (one half of a bar), and a quarter note for one beat (one quarter of a bar). A quarter note can be subdivided further into two eighth notes (the notes coming twice as fast as a quarter note), four sixteenth notes (twice as fast as an eighth note), and eight thirty-second notes (you guessed it — played twice as fast as sixteenth notes). It's this variation of note values that gives a melody its rhythmic movement.

JIM SAYS

Sometimes before I write a song, I'll pick a rhythm template to work off of. Perhaps I'm in a mellow mood and choose a waltz tempo — this is the signature of three-quarter time where there are three beats to every bar with the backbeat landing on the second beat — or a variation like in the song "Go Now" (written by Larry Banks and Milton Bennett; performed by The Moody Blues) where the backbeat is on the third beat. Or maybe I'll try noodling over a six/eight time signature where there are six beats to each bar with the backbeat landing on either the second or fourth beat — like on "Take It to the Limit" (written by Glenn Frey, Don Henley, and Randy Meisner; performed by The Eagles). Or, if I want to rock or write a big pop ballad, I'll usually stay "in four" (good old four beats to a bar with the backbeat falling on two) and simply play around with beats per minute (BPMs), which indicates the tempo at which you're playing (120 BPM is a popular tempo reflecting the average rate of the excited human heartbeat), and various rhythm patterns. By varying the emphasis within a 4/4 pattern you can change the feel from the "samba cool" of Burt Bacharach to the jungle overdrive of Bo Diddly and all points in between! In four, I also like experimenting with the "shuffle" feel pioneered by the early blues artists. A modern incarnation of this feel would be "Everybody Wants to Rule the World" (written and performed by Tears for Fears) and "Revolution" (written by John Lennon and Paul McCartney; performed by The Beatles). Sometimes the beat will give you just the needed direction for you to create a new song.

Applying notes to common time

Now we take a look at how notes and rests can be used to rhythmically notate music — with seven bars of common (4/4) time shown in Figure 8-1.

Figure 8-1:
This example shows how notes and rests can be used in 4/4 time.

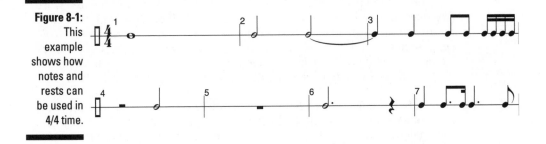

The example in Figure 8-1 starts out with the "time signature" of 4/4, meaning that there are 4 beats in each bar and a quarter note is equivalent to a beat. In the first bar of Figure 8-1, there is only one note: a whole note, which lasts four beats — the whole bar. In the second bar there are two half notes, each lasting two beats. But the second note has a *tie* to the first quarter note in bar three. When notes are tied together, that means that they have been joined to a single note: in this case, a note that lasts three beats.

In bar three, there are two quarter notes (the first tied to the half note in the bar before), followed by two eighth notes, those in turn followed by four sixteenth notes. The quarter notes each have a value of a beat, the eighth notes a half beat, and the four sixteenth notes occupy a full beat for themselves, the fourth beat of the measure.

In bar four, the first rest is presented, a half-note rest, and in bar five, a full-note rest, which makes the entire measure soundless. Bar six introduces the dotted note. Remember, a dot following a note increases its value by one half. In this case, the dotted half note equals three beats. It's followed by a quarter-note rest, which yields one beat of silence. The seventh bar shows how dots can be applied to quarter and eight notes, and *dots* all there is to it!

"In songs, there's a basic pattern that has been traditionally used in the accompaniment to help identify and reinforce the difference between the strong and the weak beats. The bass drum — also called the kick drum — plays on beats one and three, and the snare drum and high hat play on beats two and four. Rock popularized the heavy emphasis on beats two and four — the backbeats."

—Don Robertson, musician and composer

Putting Rhythm and Meter to Use in Your Songs

We've shown how lyrics have accents and syllables. Now take a look at how lyrics are applied to the meter of a song. For this we'll turn again to the familiar "Mary Had a Little Lamb" nursery rhyme, and adopt it to 3/4 time. (We could've chosen 4/4, or even 5/4 — 4/4 will work, but the 5/4 rhythm will feel awkward). Figure 8-2 shows how we set the lyrics to the rhythm.

"Mary Had a Little Lamb" has the honor of being the first words ever recorded on a phonograph! In 1877, Thomas Edison spoke these famous words into the first recording machine ever made in his laboratory in Menlo Park, New Jersey.

The observant reader will notice that the strong accents of the lyric (capitalized) have been placed on the strong (first) beat of each bar. Matching accents with strong beats, as we have pointed out, is what marries the meter of lyrics with the meter of music. It's the natural way that the two come together, although variations and exceptions will always be found — this is not a hard and fast rule, just a basic guideline.

Figure 8-2:
In this example of "Mary Had a Little Lamb," we apply the words to 3/4 time.

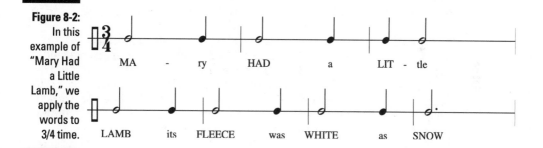

Now take a look at Figure 8-3 to see how one of the great songwriting/lyricist teams dealt with setting lyric to meter using the opening of "All the Things You Are" by Jerome Kern and Oscar Hammerstein II.

First of all, notice how all the strong syllables fall on strong beats (1 and 3). The opening words *you* and *are* are both strong and the songwriters wisely placed them both on the first beat of a bar (called the *downbeat*), giving them both a strong emphasis. *You*, the first word in the song, has a nice vowel sound (*ou*), therefore creating a nice effect when extended for a whole measure (which wouldn't of happened if the first word in the song was *zeke*).

Figure 8-3:
This is how
Kern and
Hammer-
stein
applied
lyrics to
meter at the
beginning
of the song
"All the
Things You
Are."

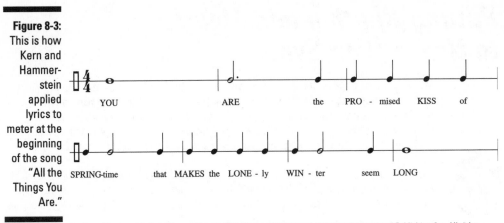

Songwriting with Syncopation

Syncopation is the shifting of a note from a strong beat to a weak beat. For some reason, the subject of syncopation is often overlooked in songwriting books, but it's important to understand when writing today's songs.

Syncopation entered the mainstream with swing music in the '30s. Arrangements were created where some of the notes of the song were shifted slightly to anticipate the *downbeat,* or to come just after it (listen to the string section hook in the song "1000 Miles," written and sung by Vanessa Carlton, to hear a current example of syncopation). We'll take a look at how this works using an excerpt from George and Ira Gershwin's "They Can't Take That Away From Me" with normal *straight* rhythm as shown in Figure 8-4.

Notice in Figure 8-4 that the word *hat* falls on the downbeat. If the Gershwin brothers had written it like this, with a strong syllable *hat* landing on the strong beat, it might have sounded too formal and a bit stiff for the song. In Figure 8-5, the phrase is actually written and sung, with the word *hat* antici-pating the downbeat by a half of a beat as it swings into the next measure.

Figure 8-4:
In this phrase from the song, "They Can't Take That Away From Me," you see that the accented word "hat" falls on the downbeat.

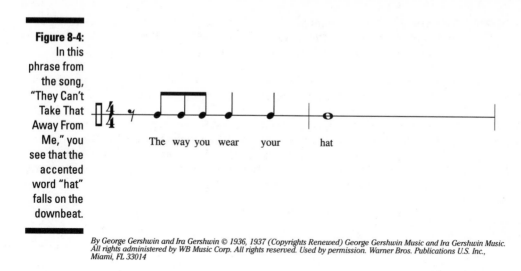

The way you wear your hat

Figure 8-5:
This is how the phrase from the song, "They Can't Take That Away From Me," shown in Figure 8-4 actually is sung, with a syncopated downbeat.

The way you wear your hat

The word *hat* now appears a half-beat in anticipation of the downbeat. This syncopation helps give the melody a swing feeling. In fact, it's this trick of syncopation that gave swing music its swing, and hence its name.

The next example shows how John Lennon and Paul McCartney similarly used syncopation in the song "I'll Be Back" (see Figure 8-6).

Syncopation is a standard feature in pop, R&B, jazz, country, and rock music and it's a major part of many songs not just as downbeat anticipation, but as a continual singing of words on the off-beat. Take a look at this excerpt from "Genie in a Bottle" written by Pamela Sheyne, David Frank, and Steve Kipner and sung by Christina Aguilera (see Figure 8-7).

Figure 8-6:
This is how John Lennon and Paul McCartney used syncopated downbeats in the song, "I'll Be Back."

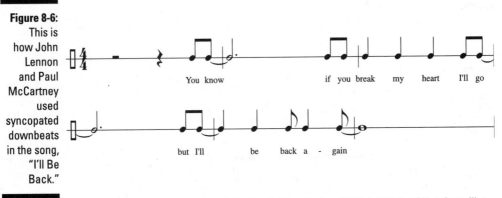

Words and music that work synergistically to create interesting rhythms is one of the hallmarks of a good song. Try syncopations in your lyrics so they cut across the beat as opposed to landing right on the beat. Consider if each word of the opening line from "Dance Hall Days" written by Jack Hues and performed by Wang Chung, "Take your baby by the hand," had landed squarely on the beat — sounds pretty boring, doesn't it?

Figure 8-7:
In this example of syncopation, from the song, "Genie in a Bottle," every beat is syncopated.

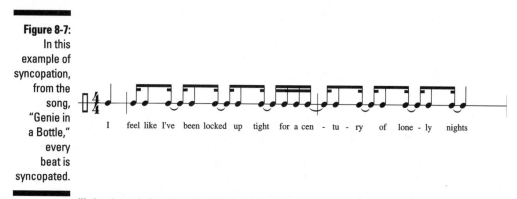

I feel like I've been locked up tight for a cen - tu - ry of lone - ly nights

Some genres, especially country and pop country, tend to insist on consistent word rhythm between corresponding sections of song from their writers. For instance, if a verse has a certain amount of syllables and accents per line, it should be exactly the same when the second verse comes around. Traditional Broadway songwriting is just as sticky about this rule as they are about exact rhymes. The theory is that this consistency makes a song more natural for the singer and easier to remember for the audience. This general rule isn't nearly as strictly enforced in other genres such as soul and rock. In fact, rap music thrives on the constant shifting in the accents of the syllables. Again, referring to the example of "My Girl" by The Temptations, the first line of the first verse — "I got sunshine on a cloudy day" — is replaced by a whole different word rhythm in line one of the second verse — "I got so much honey, the bees envy me" — even though the musical chords and rhythm remains identical. This technique provides fresh interest for the second verse — I can't even imagine it any other way!

Getting Your Groove On

Okay, we've discussed the rhythm of the words and the meter of the notes, now let's have some fun! The groove (the *feel* of the rhythm) that you choose as you write your song will not only inspire you to write a great one, but will influence the whole mood of the song and what marketplace it may best be suited to. The groove of the beat behind the song is what really markets the emotions within the words and music.

Often a producer or artist can reinvent a song merely by changing the arrangement's groove. For example, listen to how the group UB40 added their reggae feel (the backwards-sounding Jamaican rhythm that often puts the kick drum on the backbeat instead of the snare drum) to the Elvis Presley ballad "Can't Help Falling In Love With You" (written by Luigi Creatore, Hugo Peretti, and George David Weiss), or the way Joe Cocker and his arranger, Leon Russell, changed the 4/4 feel of The Beatles' "With A Little Help From My Friends" (written by John Lennon and Paul McCartney) to a gospel-influenced 6/8 feel.

As songwriters, we can draw inspiration from many of the great writers of today who are not afraid to experiment with grooves from different cultures. Artists like Sting, Peter Gabriel, Carlos Santana, and Paul Simon base much of their music around the reggae beats of Jamaica, the rhythms of Latin America, and African and Indian influences (featuring exotic, indigenous drums such as the djembe, doumbeck, and tabla) that combine to form what has come to be known as *world rhythm*. The inventive drum grooves that set the backdrop for groups and artists like Destiny's Child and Samantha Mumba and many others in the dance-pop genre are influenced by world rhythms. Many of these grooves are made interesting by taking a standard rock beat (4/4 time signature, bass drum on beats one and three, snare drum on two and four) and subdividing it with sixteenth notes (sixteen quick beats within the confines of one short measure.) For an example of this, listen to "He Loves You Not" (written by Steve Kipner, David Martin Frank, and Pamela Shayne; performed by Dream). This technique insures that the audience (and dance floor) will not lose interest even in a song with a slow *tempo* (the speed or beats per minute at which any groove is played).

Other grooves that a songwriter can work from or add to his song are shuffle, used in many blues songs (refer to "Pride and Joy," written by Stevie Ray Vaughan and Double Trouble; sung by Stevie Ray Vaughan) as well as pop songs like "Brand New Day" (written and sung by Sting), the 6/8 grooves such as in "Take It to The Limit" (written by Glen Frey, Don Henley, and Randy Meisner; performed by The Eagles), modified samba grooves contained in many songs by John Mayer plus "Fragile" (written and sung by Sting), and Cajun, New Orleans grooves (heavy on the eighth notes played on the hi hat cymbals) that can be heard on regional favorites like Buckwheat Zydeco and the more commercialized examples by the group, Little Feat. (Interestingly, Sting recast many of his reggae influenced early songs into the driving rock beat of his live album, *All This Time*.)

"To really get inspired by what rhythm and groove can add to your song, there's nothing like the "live music" experience. Performances by artists who are creative in their use of rhythm like Peter Gabriel or Santana never fail to give me fresh groove ideas. Certain theatrical productions spotlight the element of percussion. Shows like Blue Man Group and Stomp that feature intricate rhythms performed on unorthodox instruments like lengths of PVC plastic, hubcaps, garbage can lids, and brooms, demonstrate that rhythm transcends traditional instruments and cuts right to the soul."

— Ed Breckenfeld, session drummer and writer for *Modern Drummer Magazine*

Practice Makes Perfect

"Feel the rhythm. Feel the ride. Get on up. It's bobsled time." Do you remember this great chant from the popular movie about a Jamaican Olympic bobsled team entitled *Cool Runnings*? It's what the athletes chanted to get them into the rhythm and working together with the same beat.

It's amazing how rhythm is such a big part of our everyday lives. That's why it plays such a big role in the heartbeat of the song. How many times have you heard an athlete who's just accomplished major success say, "I just got in my rhythm," or how many times have you yourself said, "I'm really in a groove" when everything was going just right for you? When I played professional tennis, sometimes my heart would be racing seemingly out of control. To counteract this, between points I'd take a deep breath and create, in my mind, a slow steady beat that would keep me from rushing and losing my rhythm. Today, when I work with singers in the studio, I'll have them take a couple of passes at the song, then typically we'll have a talk and I'll ask them to take some deep breaths, relax and just feel the rhythm of the music. The more the singer gets connected with the rhythm, the greater the chance for pure magic to take place.

Now it's your turn as the songwriter to let yourself go, get into the groove, and let the rhythm in you come rising up to the surface. Lay down a basic beat on your cassette recorder using your "mouth percussion" (simply doing the beat with your lips, like "paa, pa pa paa, pa paa, pa pa" — mimicking the sounds of a drum kit). Now sing a dummy lyric over the beat letting it dictate the rhythm of the lyrics. When you come up with something compelling that inspires you to write more, go back to all those great phrases you've previously written down and cataloged. Pick an idea that fits the rhythm of the song, and start replacing those dummy lyrics with great ones that tell your story. Even though we might not have been able to shed any light as to why the little lamb followed Mary home, I hope the rhythm has gotten a hold of you.

Chapter 9

Making Use of Melody in Songwriting

*Y*ou've plunked down your hard-earned money to buy this book, and chances are you have some songs stirring in your soul already and a melody or two percolating in your brain. At this point, maybe you just want to know a little more about how to encourage and capture these "notes in conversation" and how to organize them into a song.

But what exactly is a melody? According to *Webster's,* a melody is "an agreeable succession of sounds, a sequence of single tones." (Fine, now if only you could look up "platinum smash hit" and get a definition for that, too!) Melodies are the ultimate "ear candy" of a song. It's the series of notes that transports the lyrics along, or in a musical piece without words, it's the "tune" that the main instrument plays. Where do melodies come from? Perhaps they are just out there, waiting to be harvested. Perhaps a melody comes "from nowhere" into your head. Perhaps you are the type to experiment on a musical instrument until a series of notes sounds good to you. Maybe writing various successions of notes on music (or staff) paper and playing them back is what works for you.

However you create a melody, the proof is in the beauty of the result. One of the measures of a great melody is its *hum-ability* (can the listener remember it after he hears it, and how long does it sticks with him?). Another is durability. Try to come up with melodies that wear well. The melodies that last, the ones people never tire of, are usually simple, but they have something unique about them that keep folks coming back for more.

Exploring the Basics of Melodies in Music

How do you create a great melody? Writers have been trying to pinpoint a way for years. Just what is the "Melody of Love" that you've heard so much about, and how do you write one of your own? The process is part technical and part inspirational. The following sections show just how important the melody is and how to come up with a melody of your own.

"Melody is the thread that ties a song together. If done poorly, every seam will be apparent and it will not hold together for long. When sewn together carefully, a song becomes a melodic whole with one section flowing seamlessly into the next."

— David Pomeranz writer of "Trying to Get the Feeling Again"
for Barry Manilow plus many others

When people ask me what my forte is in songwriting, I tell them I'm a melody man. Writing lyrics has been a craft I've worked hard on and have steadily improved at. The longer I live, the more stories I gather and the more grist I have for the lyric mill. Melodies just tend to enter my head from nowhere. However, the more you listen to and practice writing melodies, the luckier you get at spinning gold from thin air. Just as no one has to teach a bird to sing, it's much easier to write a melody than to tell someone how.

Knowing the power and emotion of a melody

If rhythm is the backbone of a song, chords the muscle, and lyrics the heart, then surely melody is the soul. Melody is the element that transcends all else and is remembered before the words are fully comprehended and long after they are forgotten.

When listening to, for instance, Christina Aguilera's Latin album, released in 2000 entitled *Mi Reflejo,* notice that she sings all her hits in Spanish. Whether you know that language or not, the power of the music comes through based on the rhythm, and most of all, the beauty of the melodies. You don't have to know what she's saying to feel the emotion.

Understanding the basics of a melody

Analyze the melody of one of your all-time favorite songs. Buy the sheet music, if it's available, and learn it on an instrument — a guitar or piano would be ideal, because you could then track both the melody and the way it works against the chords. Notice the intervals between notes, how many are jammed into one measure, the *range* of the notes (the distance from the highest note to the lowest), and the note's relationship to the chord (in the key of A, the note A is the root or dominant note of the chord). If the chord is changed to D, the same A note is now the fifth of the chord (five notes above the dominant) and therefore takes on a whole different mood. Notice also how the melody shifts between musical sections and how the minor or major mode of the melody is used to emphasize the mood of the song.

As a songwriter, your goal is to develop:

- ✔ **A keen sense of melody:** The more you listen to and analyze great songs, and the more you nurture your own melodic sense through constant experimentation, the sharper it will become.

- ✔ **A method for creating a melody:** Whatever works for you is the best way. It could be noodling around on an instrument until a melodic pattern emerges, meditating in a quiet place and letting the melodies find you, or creating beautiful melodies in the midst of total chaos. Discover what the wellspring of melodic ideas is for you and visit it often.

- ✔ **A way to collect and remember melodies:** Whether you record your melodies on a pocket recorder (if you forget your recorder one day, try the old trick of leaving the song idea on your home answering machine), or notate them in note or number form in a notebook or on staff paper, it is vital that you formulate a way to freeze in time your melodic tidbits.

- ✔ **An ability to incorporate melodies into a cohesive song:** The more you experiment and practice setting your melodies to music (finding just the right words that fit), the better songwriter you'll become. Don't be afraid to try a hundred different variations of your original chord pattern for your melody — you can always go back to your original if the others don't pan out. Try different lyrical approaches until the mood of the melody and lyric is a perfect match.

Just as with lyrics and chord patterns, the great songwriters have a unique melodic signature that signals who you're listening to before you even know for sure. The influence of melody masters such as Burt Bacharach, Paul McCartney, Elton John, Kenny Loggins, Todd Rundgren, Brian Wilson, and of course the classical geniuses like Mozart, Bach, and Chopin can be heard in many writers' melodies. Billy Joel seems to have taken melodic cues from Paul McCartney, whose melodies were influenced by the "rockin' fifties" and traditional Vaudeville and dance-hall classics. Whoever your influences might be, your goal is to assimilate them into a unique sound that is all your own.

Finding your melody

There's no right or wrong way of hitting upon a melody. Some people write their best melodies while working at something else — washing the car, shopping, driving, working in the yard, working out, hiking, or any pleasur-able or charitable pursuit. It seems that in casual, unguarded moments like these, the unconscious mind is free to do some creative play on the side. Often it's when you're not really trying to write a melody that your mind becomes a clear channel and starts picking up some strong signals. This is when you need to be ready with your cassette recorder (or staff paper if you know how to notate) to capture those often fleeting glimpses of inspiration.

"Sometimes cool melodies enter my head when I'm not really trying to write one It is often when I am doing something I enjoy, like driving — maybe that's because when we drive we have that wonderful feeling of being in control of our own destiny — eating, riding The Tube subway in London, exercising, or doing something nice for others. Certain seasons tend to bring out different melodies in me, different times of the day and different weather conditions. I also have my 'rainy day' melodies which are often bittersweet or reflective, and my sunny day melodies which are more expansive and optimistic."

—Kelly Keagy, writer of Night Ranger's smash "Sister Christian"

There are melodies all around — you just have to listen for them. Sometimes the vocal inflections of someone talking can suggest a melody. Other times, the sound of the ocean (remember "Sailing" written and sung by Christopher Cross) or the chaos of the city, can spark a mood that inspires a melody (listen to "Summer in the City," written by John Sebastian, Steve Boone, and Mark Sebastian; performed The Lovin' Spoonful). Other times, the simple sounds of nature can be the beginnings of a song.

The first time I wrote with Bill Chase — the virtuoso trumpet man whose cutting edge, high pitched wail helped define the sound of Woody Herman's Thundering Herd when he was a fledgling member — he told me an amusing story. One early Canadian morning while he was camping, he was awakened from his slumber by a particularly persistent bird chirping the same series of five notes over and over again. He shook himself out of a peaceful dream, grabbed some staff paper, dutifully notated the riff, and fell right back to sleep again. Of course, I loved the riff immediately once he played it for me — it became the signature horn riff and verse melody to "Run Back To Mama," perhaps the most requested song from Bill's Epic Records release, *Pure Music*. I wish I could say that we donated a portion of our songwriting royalties to the National Audubon Society, but let me take this opportunity, on our behalf, to thank that little bird and all of his fine feathered friends for inspiring our senses and routinely filling the skies with songs that brighten even an aver-age spring day.

Many writers have the most luck coming up with melodies as they're experi-menting at the piano or guitar, trying out the sound of different series of notes as chords are played. If you've come up with an intriguing chord pro-gression, record it on your boom box or handheld recorder (or get more sophisticated, if you like, recording the track digitally). Then play it back, experimenting with different melodies over the chords. Be sure to record the combination of music and melody on yet another recorder or on another track. After many repetitions you will inevitably land on one melody that seems to work the best (which is usually the one you keep going back to in the first place).

Lenny Kravitz presented Mick Jagger with a nearly complete track over which Mick added lyrics and melody to become the first single from his *Goddess in the Doorway* solo album entitled "God Gave Me Everything."

Many successful songwriters have learned the concepts of good melody writing from some of the courses taught at the various music colleges around the world — where classes are often conducted by masters at the craft. You can also enroll in other various songwriting workshops and seminars to learn the art of melody writing and melody appreciation.

I work differently with almost every different co-writer. Bill Syniar and Barbara Unger-Wertico — a Chicago-based writing team I often collaborate with — will present me a work track of chords and rhythm, complete with a proposed song structure and recorded very professionally to give me added inspiration. I then pop the CD or cassette in my car and, as I drive around doing my daily errands, I'll sing different melodies over the musical template they've given me. I'll have my cassette recorder running at all times on the passenger seat. We wrote "Under the Spell" for The Doobie Brothers in this fashion, as well as "Blinded by Emotion" and "You Still Shock Me" for the melodic rock band Mecca.

Giving goose bumps

There are many ways to gauge the impact your song is having on the world — how many pieces you are scanning per week at retail, how many requests you are receiving for co-writes and interviews, and how many local bands are doing your song at the club (and we won't even go into the burgeoning Karaoke scene). But to me the best indicator of the true soul-connection your song is having on other members of the human race is its ability to raise that involuntary response known as goose bumps. Almost always it seems to come at some point of the chorus when words and melody intersect like the confluence of rivers, and create that

moment of realization. Whether it has to do with galvanic skin response, heart rate, blood pressure, intervention from above, or simply too much caffeine, there are specific spots in certain songs that never fail to give me chicken skin. You can't write it into your song any more than you can tell the sun when to break through the clouds. It just happens when all conditions are right. As a songwriting "lifer," it's my highest honor to bring about this response in others. It means I have connected at a level deeper than words and higher than music. This intimacy between writer and listener is my greatest responsibility and most sacred privilege.

Making a Song More Memorable

Certain songwriters can make you feel a certain way, and the true masters always seem to have a very specific mood. Burt Bacharach can make you feel happy in a bittersweet way. Certain Paul Simon songs bring a sense of calm and introspection. Mick Jagger and Keith Richard are filled with the carefree recklessness of rock 'n' roll. What's especially intriguing is the intimacy the listener is experiencing with the artist by sharing the mood the artist was in when he or she wrote a particular song. Their brain chemistry at the time becomes your brain chemistry. The next time that you hear and really feel "Goodbye Yellow Brick Road," by Elton John and Bernie Taupin, you are, in effect, tuning into the masters as they were creating. In essence, you are becoming one with the composers — feeling and experiencing the distilled essence of what they might have been feeling at the time of creation. That's the power of what a song can do.

To get more specific on the art of writing a melody, we'll look at how melody can affect the mood or atmosphere of the song you're writing. We'll also give examples of how genre can determine the scope of your melody, and look at the different melodic requirements of the various sections of your song.

Finding a melody that fits the mood

Maybe you've been experimenting (creative noodling) for the last three hours at the piano and have come up with a sturdy set of chord changes that really sound cool. You've searched through your notebook and found a title or a lyric phrase that reflects the mood of the music. It's now time to experiment with melodies that best highlight the mood of the chord changes and the mood of the words:

- **Use a major key.** If the chord changes are based around a major key, and the title and concept is upbeat and optimistic, you'll probably find your-self gravitating toward an uplifting melody to complement your chordal and lyrical choices.

- **Use a minor key.** If your chord progression is in the minor mode, you'll probably choose a darker lyrical theme, and experiment with bluesier and more mournful melodies.

- **Make the melody complex.** If your music bed is extremely simple, you may have the luxury of making your melody more complex, using fast flurries of notes.

- **Make the melody simple.** If your music bed contains rapid and complex chord changes, it may dictate a more relaxed, simple, and sweeping melody to give it some needed contrast.

In certain situations, it's advisable to mate an optimistic set of chord changes with a dark and evocative melody that is technically at odds with the mood of the music. There are also many songs with a dark, minor key mood in the verse that benefit from the contrast of a shift to an optimistic, major key mood at the chorus.

In the song "Empty," which I co-wrote with artist Brian Anders, we set up a dark reflective mood in the verse as the singer describes his sense of alienation from self and those around him ("Now the fields are bare, I feel I'm breathing without air"). The key is minor and the melody is narrow and low in range. As soon as the song hits the chorus, it suddenly shifts into the major key (from D minor to D major), and the melody starts to soar. This move supports the lyrical shift from the singer's desolation in the verse to his search for truth in the chorus. As he reaches for answers, his voice reaches for higher and higher notes.

Figure 9-1 shows the song "Empty" notated musically and lyrically to illustrate how the words, chords, and melody work together to create the drama of the song.

Finding a melody to fit the genre

In the same way that every genre has certain lyrical tendencies and arrangement styles, so too, do they have different melodic leanings. Let's take a look at the melody trends prevalent in a few of the most popular genres.

Rock 'n' roll

Melodies sung over the simple blues-based chord changes of rock 'n' roll, are usually very simple and often *mono-tonal* (variations of only one or two notes). Charting the melodies of rock 'n' roll classics like "Johnny B. Goode" (written and sung by Chuck Berry) or a few of their latter-day offspring like "Travelin' Band" (written by John Fogerty, performed by Credence Clearwater Revival) or "Rock-and-Roll Never Forgets" (written and sung by Bob Seger), looks like a flat line of dots due to the linear, non-melodic nature of the vocal. Variation is achieved by vocal inflection (for example, when a vocalist changes his sound from smooth and calm to raspy and agitated) and chordal changes — the same note over a different chord gives the note a whole different mood and is often as effective a device as changing the note.

I'm a sucker for the big, soaring melody. Some of my favorite songs like "Waiting for a Girl Like You" by Foreigner (written by Mick Jones and Lou Gramm) have amazingly rangy melodies. This particular song achieves its range by changing keys upward from verse to pre-chorus and again to chorus. However, one of my biggest hits, "Vehicle," uses a narrow five-note range, similar to the early rock 'n' roll and blues songs, and achieves its impact through the changing chords (E flat minor to B flat minor) to give the melody its variety.

Figure 9-1:
The song
"Empty."

When you are writing a song, make sure it's singable. If it spans over two octaves, you are severely limiting the number of singers out there who can pull it off. Try singing it yourself to make sure it's in the realm of possibility. If the range is too wide, experiment with modifications of the melody.

Pop rock

Melodies in the rock genre range from the blues-based, two or three note wails (some call it screaming on key) by Robert Plant of Led Zeppelin ("Whole Lotta Love," written by Led Zeppelin, and "The Lemon Song," written by Led Zeppelin and Chester Burnett) to the octave leaps of Steve Perry, lead singer of melodic rock pioneers Journey ("Open Arms," written by Steve Perry and Jonathan Cain, and "Faithfully," written by Jonathan Cain). The newer pop bands and solo artists like Fastball ("The Way," written by Tony Scalzo), Guster ("Barrel of a Gun," written by Guster), and Barenaked Ladies ("Brian Wilson," written by Steven Page) take their melodic cues from The Beatles and The Beach Boys, who practically wrote the book on catchy melodies. For an example of a wide-ranging melody, listen to the jump of one octave when John Lennon sings "I Wanna Hold Your Hand," (written by John Lennon and Paul McCartney).

In every genre, you'll find a broad spectrum of melodic styles.

Urban and rap

To generalize, this genre is short on melody and long on attitude and vibe. The melodic nature of Rhythm and Blues (R&B) and soul with songs like the sweet "You Send Me" (written and sung by Sam Cooke, who, by the way, was a major melodic and stylistic influence on Steve Perry of Journey) and "Try a Little Tenderness" (written by James Campbell, Reginald Connelly, and Harry Woods; sung by the immortal Otis Redding) did not seem to make the transition to the gritty, urban streets because of the sophistication and craftsmanship of the song. Whether helping to set the style through choice or necessity, artists like Janet Jackson and Jennifer Lopez sing songs whose melodies toggle back and forth between essentially three or four notes. The songs gain their momentum through their insistent grooves and the vocal shadings and sexual nuances of the vocal delivery.

Obviously, rap being a spoken genre, any melody added occurs in brief interlude sections. When Will Smith reworked "Just the Two of Us," the great old Bill Withers tune, he created a rap for the verses and switched to the traditionally sung chorus. It was an extremely effective blend of old school and new.

I've endured recent criticism that the songs I've been writing for the urban marketplace have too many chord changes and are "too melodic" for the genre. When I listen to the radio, I can see what they mean. It's very attitude-based, where too much melody and too many chord changes can serve only to break the hypnotic groove of this type of music.

Finding the right melody for each section of the song

Take a look at how the element of melody can help you help your song be all it can be — section by section:

- ✔ **Finding the right melody for the verse:** The melody of this vital set-up section is crucial to the impact of the chorus, and whether your audience will continue to listen or press fast forward.

- ✔ **Finding the right melody for the pre-chorus:** The melody of this "gateway to the chorus" has to build from the verse, yet not eclipse what is soon to follow.

- ✔ **Finding the right melody for the chorus:** The mother lode of your song — the importance of the right melody in the chorus cannot be over emphasized.

- ✔ **Finding the right melody for the bridge:** As we cross the bridge, it's important to change up that melody.

It's not unusual for a writer to work on a song all day only to realize at midnight that the melody was written "on top of" another song (Nashville-speak for "you inadvertently ripped it off from another song, you hack!"). Instead of panicking or scrapping the song altogether, the next day, try modifying the melody to remove any similarities and make it your own. Sometimes if you keep a positive attitude, you can actually improve on what you had, and avoid a lawsuit at the same time.

The verse

The verse of a song is your chance to set up the premise, or idea, of the song. Because that is its primary mission, try to keep your verse simple melodically. With too many notes, or too varied and unusual a melody, you run the risk of overstepping the purpose of the verse and distract from the lyric. That's not to say it should be boring or bland — just not too wacky — letting the upcoming sections steal a little thunder from the verse, and giving your song a *build* (the continual rise of momentum which is the hallmark of many great songs). If you fire all the cannons melodically at once, you won't have any ammo left for the real battle — the chorus.

In Sheryl Crow's 1996 smash "If It Makes You Happy" (written by Sheryl Crow and Jeff Trott), it's difficult to identify the song until it hits the chorus. The catchy chorus is what you remember. The verse, however, is never a tune-out factor (when your hand involuntarily goes reaching to find another station); because even though it's short on melody, it's long on intriguing images ("scrape the mold off the bread and serve you French toast again"). The relatively tuneless verse also makes for a stunning contrast to the melodic feast of the chorus.

In the opening cut of Connecticut native John Mayer's major label debut, *Room for Squares* entitled "No Such Thing" (written by John Mayer and Doug Cook), he teaches a master's course in effective melodic build. The verse melody is sparse and conversational, pulling the listener in with the promise of the lyric, interesting intervals between notes, and nice spaces between phrases to give us time to process the previous phrase. The verse is followed by a nearly singsong pre-chorus, which cycles its five notes over shifting chords. When the chorus hits, the runaway melody mirrors the action on the set, "I wanna run through the halls of my high school, I wanna scream at the top of my lungs." When John sings "top of my lungs" he does so at the top of his lungs (and vocal range) for emphasis. All the wonders of the pre-chorus and chorus, however, would never have been revealed to his listeners if not properly set up by the verse.

"Even with my early attempts at songwriting, I always tried to keep it interesting and colorful. . . . I think because I began as a guitar player, my criteria for what was interesting was a bit more involved in what's happening on the guitar. I approached everything from the guitar neck up. . . . So I think by default, the music that I sang over was already a little more involved and interesting on its own."

—John Mayer, his major-label debut, *Room For Squares,* showcases his singer/songwriter talents as he takes an acoustic rock base and fuses it with jazz overtones; © Performing Songwriter, Issue #59

Think of the melody of the verse as the appetizer course — a bit of intrigue for the palette to get you in the mood for what is to follow. Too much, though, may spoil your appetite for the rest.

The pre-chorus

The purpose of the pre-chorus is to set up the chorus lyrically — with a little different approach than the verse, chordally — often injecting some fresh chords to come between a verse and chorus that happen to start on the same chord (if the verse and chorus both start on G major, try starting your pre-chorus on E minor or F major). The pre-chorus or channel (also known as the B section) melodically serves to further get everyone ready for the chorus. The melody of this section usually ascends higher in range (but not as high as the chorus) and changes up the rhythm of the words from the verse rhythm.

In Elton John's classic song from 1992, "The One," the pre-chorus sounds suspiciously like a chorus the first time you hear it ("In the instant that you love someone, in the second that the hammer hits"), as the suspended chords of the verse give way to pure majors and the melody starts to soar. It's only when the song hits the chorus ("And all I ever needed was the one"), that we realize Elton has upped the ante again with an even more majestic and compelling section.

A pre-chorus can be as good as you can make it, as long as you make sure that the chorus is even more memorable.

One of our producers (who also worked with Jefferson Starship, Led Zeppelin, The Who, and Bad Company) would always push Frankie Sullivan and I to write pre-choruses for the songs we were working on. He felt melodically it gave a song more build and created a further sense of anticipation for the chorus. In "High on You," we inserted a melodic pre-chorus in the relative key of E minor (the verse is in G) and elevated the melody ("Now I'm screaming in the night, I know I'm getting hooked on your love"). Each time this section comes around, it's like a mini-chorus due to the repeated words and the hookiness of its melody.

If a melody just isn't coming, don't "beat it into the ground." Leave it and come back to it after dinner, tomorrow, next week, or next year. If it's meant to get written, it'll happen at exactly the right time.

The chorus

If songwriting were an athletic event, the chorus would be the Olympics. It's every songwriter's chance to win the gold (pun intended). The chorus melody is generally what we go home singing after attending a concert, play, movie, club, or fest. It's the main course after you've been teased by the appetizer (verse), and eased by the salad (pre-chorus) — after the chorus are we then "pleased" by the bridge sorbet?

The chorus melody is generally the climax of the song, featuring the highest notes and often the widest intervals between notes. (Certain songs like Van Halen's "Love Walks In" actually take an opposite approach and come down dynamically at the chorus to add contrast.) Power ballads pride themselves on the big, melodically soaring chorus, such as:

- "All By Myself" (written and sung by Eric Carmen)
- "How Do I Live" (written by Diane Warren; sung by Trisha Yearwood as well as LeAnn Rimes)
- "Where Does My Heart Beat Now" (written by Robert Johnson and Taylor Rhodes; sung by Celine Dion)
- "Without You" (written by Peter Ham, Michael Gibbons, JC Molland, William Collins, and Tom Evans; sung by Harry Nilsson)

In "Day of Freedom" (written by Cindy Morgan, Brent Bourgeois, and Chris Eaton; sung by the young Christian artist, Rachael Lampa), the song features an Eastern-influenced melody in the verse (complete with sitar and tabla arrangement touches), a brief two-bar channel (pre-choruses need not be long to be effective), and then hits its sprawling chorus featuring long notes stretched over the 4 minor chord to the 5 seventh, and the words "We're all children of the faith, and though we walk in different ways, let's live our lives to celebrate the day of freedom." The power of the chorus comes from many factors: the deceleration of the velocity of the words (the verse is quite choppy and busy), the anthemic and universal nature of the lyric, and the melody, which sounds more unusual than it really is due to the unique chords underneath it. Try singing the same melody over the dominant chord of the key and see how common the melody now sounds.

When writing a chorus melody, make sure it's the high point of your song. If your pre-chorus or verse is more memorable than your chorus, keep working on it until it is the musical peak.

Certain songs use other melodic devices at the chorus to achieve impact. "One Week" (written by Ed Robertson; performed by the Barenaked Ladies) is a wonderfully twisted example of unorthodox song form. Basically the verse is a stream of non-sequiturs spouted by the temporarily deranged lead singer at the breakneck speed of a nervous auctioneer. When it hits the chorus, the beat relaxes to half time and the lyrics drape lazily over the melody. The chorus derives its power from repetition of its three-note melody, the slow down of the velocity of the words, and the staggering groove of the drums. If you read through the lyric of this song, and sing it to yourself, notice how the changing melodic patterns keep the song moving from section to section.

Here's one little-known trick of the trade that you can try: If you can't seem to find a chorus that is stronger musically than your verse (or channel) maybe it's strong enough to pull a flip-flop and make it your chorus. If that works, go back and rewrite the verse and pre-chorus to lead up properly to the new chorus.

In a song I co-wrote with Don Barnes and Don Chauncey of 38 Special entitled "Fade to Blue," we had this wonderfully melodic pre-chorus leading into this really lame chorus. Finally Danny Chauncey of the band suggested we just make that section the chorus and write another pre-chorus. I thought he was nuts until we tried it and the idea worked like a charm.

The bridge

Just what is the right melody for the bridge? Well, that would be dictated by the road leading up to that bridge. A bridge provides whatever is required to give the ear a change of pace. That change of pace could be rhythmic or chordal. In addition to these elements, the bridge can also change melodically. The bridge is your last chance to say anything lyrically, chordally, and melodically that has been left unsaid.

If you have nothing left to say in your song, you don't really need a bridge. It's one area of the song that's truly optional. When it works, it's something the listener waits for. When it doesn't, it's excess baggage that makes your song seem long and cumbersome.

Often an instrumental bridge is all your song needs. An *instrumental bridge* is where a solo instrument improvises or restates the melody. (The way the classical guitarist on Sting's "Fields of Gold" (written by Sting) interprets the musical theme.) Other times a simple extension of the chorus (listen to how the writers of Jo Dee Messina's hit "Burn" — written by Tina Arena, Stephen Werfel, and Pamela Reswick — use some chord substitutions to extend the chorus and create an effective bridge) is precisely what is needed.

When you finish your verse and chorus, try to see where the song could flow in terms of a bridge. Try a melody that's similar to the chorus, but try different chords underneath it. Or try changing keys and really reinvent the wheel. When you feel you have the bridge nailed, play the song in its entirety to see if it feels like it's needed.

Recently I had the pleasure of co-writing in Nashville with pop ace, David Pomeranz and gifted Nashville writer Tammy Hyler. We'd thought we had the music finished for the entire song that we were writing on that particular day, when David then came up with a wonderfully melodic and inventive bridge. Three hours and seven cups of coffee later, we still couldn't find the right lyric for that section. Finally, as we were just about to give up and admit defeat, I said, "Let's try it without the bridge." "Blasphemy!" everyone shouted, but when we played the song through, there was plenty of music without it — and more time to do some creative arranging on the last chorus.

Practice Makes Perfect

In sports, when a baseball player is on a roll and is hitting everything in sight, he'll often say that the ball looks as big as a watermelon and that it's coming towards him practically in slow motion. In contrast, when a player can't hit anything, you might hear a comment like, "Boy, that pitcher is really throwing BB's up there." Likewise, when a professional tennis player can do no wrong and is always in the right place at the right time, the ball actually feels so good making contact on the strings of the racquet that the player feels that she can hit it anywhere she wants. This is called being in the zone, and those who have experienced it know how incredible it feels. It's where all that preparation and hard work hits home effortlessly and you don't even have to think about all the little technique issues that you've worked so hard to develop over the year's — you basically "just do it."

Well, with most of my songwriting friends who've written hit songs, I hear similar comments about their sensational melodies that so captivate the masses — "It just comes out of nowhere," or "I was in such a groove, it just wrote itself." Know that for all the hard work you spend in creating songs, you're helping yourself to be prepared so that moments of "being in the zone" are allowed to take flight. An athlete can't ever know what it's like being in the zone unless he's practiced his craft over and over again, so he's prepared for those moments when preparation meets inspiration. The same goes for the songwriter — keep working at melodies that float in and out of your head. Maybe it's just a great start to a melody and you can't, at that moment, find the right direction for it. Write it down, or better yet, put it on tape so that the next time you're driving to the grocery store and you're least expecting it, the melody just takes flight in your mind. When you bring out the old notes or tapes, you can see how it's all connected and you're now in the groove to allow the song to soar to new heights.

Go ahead. Jot down or tape little melodies that are bouncing around in your head — no matter how small. Too many songwriters wait until it's more formed before they start writing down anything. Don't wait. The little notes you capture might just be the catalyst later on that helps you get into the zone.

I have a good friend (and very successful songwriter) who's really funny and outgoing, but seemingly out of nowhere he'll get a melody idea for a song. I always know when this happens, because all of a sudden he doesn't hear a word I'm saying and he seems to be way off in the distance. I know him well enough to realize that some magic melody idea just hit and he's repeating it over and over again in his mind until he can get to his tape machine before it's lost forever. Don't discard any thoughts or ideas because you think you'll be able to remember them later on — stop and write them down or run to the nearest tape machine before it's too late.

Chapter 10

Using Chords in Songwriting

Given the fact that you're reading this book, you may already have a basic grasp of chords on the instrument of your choice. You can use this knowledge of chords to play the songs you're in the process of writing for others. But, even if you're strictly a lyricist, you can use what you learn in this book to speak knowledgeably about chords with your co-writer. The more you understand the underlying chord structures of a song, the more appreciation you'll have for them when you hear a great song on the radio. The next step will be applying that knowledge and appreciation into your own song. Putting chords to work within the context of a song is what this chapter's all about.

If you have very limited know-how on an instrument, check out *Guitar For Dummies* by Mark Phillips and Jon Chappell, *Rock Guitar For Dummies* by Jon Chappell, or *Piano For Dummies* by Mark Phillips and Jon Chappell (all published by Hungry Minds, Inc.) for additional great tips and information.

Using Chords to Write Songs

Just like the concrete that forms the foundation of your house, think of chord structure as the foundation of your song. If the chord structure is solid, you can build a masterpiece on top of it; if it's weak, everything you lay on top of this foundation runs the risk of collapsing.

So what is a chord? A *chord* is a combination of three or more musical tones played simultaneously. Chords are constructed of different combinations of the half step intervals between the notes. You can locate these intervals by going to a piano and finding your way up and down the keyboard including the black keys. The specific intervals between the notes will determine the colors of the individual chord you use. The color of your song will depend upon the chordal intervals you choose. It's perhaps the most overlooked element of a song, because it does its job more or less invisibly. (When was the last time a friend came up to you and said, "Wait till you hear the chord progression on the new India.Arie release. It's awesome!") Nonetheless, great songs need great chords. They do their work " behind the notes," influencing a song's mood and where it'll turn melodically. A particular note or series of notes can sound entirely different depending on the chord it's played against.

When I'm listening to a new song on the radio, my ear usually focuses on the melody first and the lyrics second — the chord pattern is just the delivery medium. However, when a writer is daring enough to throw in an unexpected chord or two along the way, I take special notice and gauge whether it was a risk worth taking.

Believe it or not, your choices of chords can dramatically affect the commerciality of your song. Throwing in *odd intervals* (unexpected jumps between chords) can be too jarring for simple pop tunes, but it's practically required for grunge and alternative rock. *Diminished chords* (in which a musical interval is reduced by a half step are practically never used in country music, but they're almost a necessity in jazz-oriented songs. Knowing what genre your song fits into is a big part of choosing the right chords.

You can't copyright a chord progression (if you could, the estates of the pioneers of the 12-bar blues progression would be overflowing!). So unless you're particularly inventive with your chord progression, you're building melodies over ground laid by others. This is not to say you can't vary the changes and substitute chords to make them your own. Just don't be too surprised when someone else comes along with the same variation.

Getting started with chords

As a songwriter, even if your focus and strength lies primarily in lyrics, having a working knowledge of a chordal instrument like keyboard or guitar can help you find the proper chords for your song — or at least help you guide your co-writer. Learn some of your favorite songs on piano or guitar to see the chords sequences used and to notice the moods being set. Songwriters start as fans of different writers and songs, and then as they learn those progressions, they start to adapt and modify them to their own style.

"The first song I ever learned on the guitar when I was nine years old was the hit "Tom Dooley" by The Kingston Trio. With the sequence of just the two simple chords, A major to E major, suddenly I was making music — not to mention impressing my relatives and members of the opposite sex!"

—Don Barnes, 38 Special

The most basic and useful thing to learn when studying chords is that each key has seven different notes. From each one of these notes, you can build a chord — one through seven. When you hear someone refer to a "1, 4, 5 progression," he's talking about the one chord, the four chord (four notes up in the scale from the first), and the five chord (five notes up in the scale from the first).

Knowing your scales in every key will be an enormous help for you as a songwriter. In every key, you have three major chords, three minor chords, and one diminished chord. In a major key, a chord built off of the first note, the fourth note, and the fifth note will give you a major chord. This is the 1, 4, 5 progression of so many great rock 'n' roll and blues tunes. The chords built off of the second note, third note, and sixth note will give you a minor chord (a 2, 3, 6 progression). And the seventh note will give you a diminished chord. As long as you know what key you're in and what notes are in that key, you can begin to base your major and minor *triads* (three note chords starting with the *root* — or basic note — of the chord) off of each respective note. Technically, you can arrange them in any order (this is where personal taste and style comes in) and they'll all sound reasonably good together, because they contain notes from that key that you've chosen.

"When I'm writing a very simple pop-oriented tune, whether on guitar or piano, I definitely try to use the three major chords in a particular key — so if you're in the key of G, you'd have G, C, and E minor to give it a little color. G, E minor, C, and D are often called 'ice cream changes' because this chord pattern harkens back to the '50s and many of the doo-wop and rock 'n' roll songs heard in the old-fashioned ice cream parlors. This is kind of a cool way to start — just knowing the basics of which chords are major and which chords are minor in a major key."

—Mike Aquino, noted Chicago session guitarist

Blues and blues-rock chords

Blues and most forms of rock 'n' roll use a premise of a major key for the most part, using the 1 chord (the root), the 4 chord (the fourth), and the 5 chord (the fifth), which are the major chords. If you are in the key of A, you'd have an A major, a D major, and an E major. What blues and some rock do is to make each chord a *dominant* (the namesake of the key — if you are in the key of E, then E is the dominant — also referred to as the *root* or *tonic* of the chord) seventh chord. Your A will become an A seventh — an A major chord with a G natural on the top of it to give it that grindy or bluesy sound. To the D, you'll also add a dominant seventh of a C natural on top. The E will be an E major chord with a D natural on the top. When you're adding sevenths to your chords, you're actually going outside the notes contained in the major scale of that key and dipping into the notes of the minor key. It's that minor sound on top of that major chord progression that gives you the bluesy sound.

The minor blues progression is also a popular form from which to base your song. In the key of A, your one chord is now an A minor (lowering the second note of the triad from C sharp to C natural) with a G on top making it an A minor seventh chord. The D or four chord becomes a D minor chord with a C on top to make it a D minor seventh. Theoretically, your five chord — the E in the key of A — should also be a minor chord in a minor key, but often writers will make it a major or even a seventh to give it a more definite resolution back to the one chord. Songs like "Ball and Chain" (written by Willie Mae "Big Mama" Thornton; sung by Janis Joplin), feature the minor seventh on the five-chord turnaround and it sounds great.

Chord progressions don't have to be complex in order to be powerful. In fact, often a simple two-chord sequence can sometimes be the most powerful of all. Listen to the two minor chords (E minor to B minor) of "Fallin'" (written and sung by Alicia Keys) as a good example.

Pop-rock chords

Pop and rock chord progressions are all over the map in terms of style. The minor-key sound, however, may take the prize for being the most popular. The sound of songs like "Separate Ways" (written by Jonathan Cain and Steve Perry; performed by Journey) and "Eye of the Tiger" (written by Jim Peterik and Frankie Sullivan; performed by Survivor) are good examples of how the minor key mode can be used in the rock genre. In "Eye . . . ," you start with your C minor (the first degree of the scale) then move to G sharp major (the sixth degree of the scale), still keeping the C note in the bass. Then you move to A sharp major (the seventh degree of the scale), also with the C in the bass, and then back to home base, C minor. You can see that even though there are more major chords than minor, the verse still has a minor-key sound because of how that first chord sets the tone for the rest and how the common bass note C casts the minor mood on even the major chords.

Another popular progression in rock would be one to four, seven to three, and six to five. In the key of A minor, this would translate to A minor to D minor, then G major to C major, and finally F major to E major for your six to five change. Each of these chord pairs is all a fourth apart, just down one step from the previous pair.

Jazz chords

In jazz, instead of the 1, 4, 5 progression that you find so often in pop, rock and blues, you might use a repeating back and forth cycle of the 1, 6, 2, 5 chord progression. In the key of A major, this would be A major or A major seventh or sixth (adding the seventh or sixth note of the scale to the chord) to F sharp minor to B minor to E seventh.

In the swing era, to make this jazzy progression less "white bread," songwriters substituted an F sharp dominant seventh for the F sharp minor. Instead of B minor, they used a B dominant seventh and also kept the E as E seventh. In this cycle, there are always two notes in each chord that are a half step away from the next chord — known as *leading tones.* These leading tones help create smooth transitions from chord to chord. Tricks like these make things a little more interesting — adding color and opening up other notes from which to write your melody. Whenever you change a chord from minor to major temporarily, you're obscuring the actual key you are in.

Sometimes when I'm driving and am without a musical instrument in my hand (I'm still threatening to build a synthesizer into my dashboard), I hear a certain chord in my head, but I don't know its name. I'll actually sing the notes of the chord into my cassette machine, and when I get home pick the notes out on the piano.

Moving forward with chords

It's now time to get inspired by chords and to move forward. Get out your big acoustic guitar (the one with the low action and deep ringing tone), and sit in your favorite part of the house or under that tree in the backyard. Perhaps you'll want to plug in that electric guitar into an amplifier and even hook up one of those inspiring effects pedals like a *flanger* (units like the Electric Mistress flanger by Electro-Harmonics give your chords that shimmering 12-string effect you hear on Tom Petty and Rush records), so that each chord sounds profound. If you're writing hard rock, dial up some heavy distortion on an overdrive effects pedal (like a Ratt pedal by Pro-co). You could combine many effects into one by plugging into a Pod effects unit (made by Line 6 Electronics), which digitally models the sounds of classic effects pedals and devices, from vintage fuzz boxes, Leslie speaker effects (the rotating speaker sound that simulates the classic Hammond organ), phasers, wah-wahs, and other sound-warping mischief to get your juices flowing. Or sit behind your electronic keyboard and find an inspiring *patch* (one of those factory programmed settings that you fiddle around to find — as a last resort refer to the manual!). A good suggestion would be a piano setting combined with a touch of strings to give it a little cushion and grandeur.

Now play a nice big C major chord. Voice it fairly low on the keyboard or fret board so it sounds big and rich. Hold it for four beats. Now play a G major. Hold it for four beats. Play four beats on A minor, and then go with F for four beats. Sounds cool doesn't it? No charge! You just played a chord progression as good as the best. Now it's up to you to find some great toppings — melody, lyrics, and rhythm — and figure out where you want to go next in your chordal journey.

Play these chords over and over, experimenting with different tempos and different styles of chording from staccato (choppy and short) to legato (long and connected). Next try substituting a few of the chords for others to see if you like the sound of the progression even more. Perhaps it may spark a different melody. After the C major and the G major, try a B flat major instead of the A minor, and then to F major as before. Notice the edgier mood the chords now convey. Want edgier still? Follow the B flat major with an A flat major. Now, instead of changing your left hand with the chords (it had been changing with the dominant or root note of the chord) let that hand stay on the C root through all the chord changes (this technique will radically change the mood of the chords to a much darker perspective). Now go back to your original C, G, Am (abbreviation of A minor), F progression. What a difference! You can experiment endlessly with any number and sequence of chords till you come up with one that inspires you to find the perfect melody (or motivates you to call the perfect co-writer to help complete your vision).

The instrument you choose to write on and the sound you dial up can markedly affect not only your attention span of concentration on any given day but also the style of song you'll be inspired to write.

When coming up with a basic chord progression, not only try substituting one chord for another but experiment with different voicings of chords. For instance, a basic C major chord is the notes C, E and G. To give the chord a little more uplifting sound, make the lowest note of the chord the E and then add the G next and make C the top note of the chord. Also, a trick from the arranging style of Brian Wilson is to use a note other than the dominant. If you play a C major chord on the right hand, try playing an E on the left hand instead of a C. Notice how nicely that configuration slides into F major.

I love fooling around with substitute bass notes when I'm working on a progression. If a chord pattern is sounding a little commonplace, I'll search around with my left hand to see what color I can add to a chord. On "I Can't Hold Back," a song I co-wrote with Frankie Sullivan for Survivor, tension is added to the first chord of the chorus ("I can't hold back, I'm on the edge"), by putting the third of the chord on the bottom instead of the tonic (the chorus is in E major so the third of the chord would be three notes up — a G#). The last of three times the E major, A major, B major chord progression is repeated, the root of the chord is used for that extra solidity the last time around. This trick makes the chorus of this song much more unusual sounding. Go ahead and try this on the next song you're writing.

Now try a minor key progression. Start with an A minor chord, and stay there for two beats. Move to C major for two beats. Now to D major for two beats, then to F major for two. Sounds really cool and smoky doesn't it? Kind of like "House of the Rising Sun," written by Eric Burdon and John Sterling and made popular in the '60s by The Animals. Now try a few substitutions. Start with the A minor, then to the C major like before, then to F major to E seventh. Notice how the mood is retained, but you avoid the inevitable comments like "It sounds just like 'House of the Rising Sun.'" Now really shake things up and try A minor to D minor to G sharp seventh to G major. Wow! How cool is that? Just keep experimenting with different progressions and combinations until you have something you can't wait to come back to every day.

"Substitute chords are a staple in a songwriter's larder. For instance instead of using an A major chord, which contains the notes A, C sharp, and E, you can find another chord within that key or outside of that key that contains one or two of the same notes. If I want to stay in the key of A major and find a sub for the A major chord, I go to the sixth degree of the scale — F sharp — the notes in that chord are F sharp, A, and C sharp — which contains the A and the C sharp just like the A major chord. These substitute chords help add variety and create a different mood under exactly the same melody notes."

—Mike Aquino, Chicago session guitarist

A while back I learned a valuable lesson about substitution chords when listening to "Private Dancer," the hit for Tina Turner written by Mark Knopfler. At the end of the chorus under the lyric "and any old music will do," where it could've been totally predictable and gone to the one major of the key, it goes instead to the minor sixth. This technique is called a *deceptive cadence*, because you expect it to go home to the root but it goes to the relative minor. It creates an unsettling and unresolved mood that's in keeping with the bittersweet message of the lyric. Now, when I write, before I change a melody I experiment with the underlying chords to see if a simple substitution will add the needed interest.

Learn as many chords as you can on the instrument of your choice. If you're a guitarist, you can't do better than the old Mel Bay chord book: *Rhythm Guitar Chord System* (published by Mel Bay Publications, Inc.). Also, you might want to check out the Web site: www.melbay.com for more information. Countless rock, pop, and jazz guitarists have cited this book as their primary source of self-learning. Basically, if a chords not in this book, you've probably just invented it. The more chords you have in your arsenal, the more options you give yourself.

Many writers will find interesting ways of linking chords together by keeping certain notes within the chords the same whether they are at the bottom of the chord or the top of the chord — keeping the main note of the key common to at least two or three of the chords. This technique has the effect of holding things together. The chords are moving in a certain direction, but there's an element behind the chords that says, "We are all united."

 A course or two on music theory is a good idea for the aspiring songwriter. You'll come away with a better idea of why things work and don't work in chord sequences.

Choosing Your Style of Chordal Instruments

The type of instrument you choose as you write your song may influence the direction your song will take. Conversely, if you are attempting to write a song in a particular style, the appropriate instrument will help inspire the results you need. Take a look at the following sections for various chordal instruments and their stylistic strong suits.

Picking at the guitar

Depending on the type of guitar, this instrument can run the gamut of musical styles. For folk, country, light rock, and certain types of pop, a good acoustic guitar (also called a folk guitar) might be your first choice. With its airy, transparent sound, it's a beautiful texture to use to experiment with the chords needed in those genres of music.

When you want to write hard rock, (and all its different styles like alternative, punk, grunge, melodic and so on), choose an electric guitar run through an amplifier that's overdriven to various degrees. To make sure you don't lose your lease, amp manufacturers have come up with a master volume control, which allows you to dial in all the distortion your heart desires even at low volumes. You can write hard rock on an acoustic guitar, but it takes a lot of imagination to hear it differently. Also an acoustic guitar lacks the sustain of a distorted electric that helps extend the chords and create the signature riffs of this genre.

For Latin songs, a nylon stringed guitar (also called a classical or flamenco) may be your ticket to inspiration.

Using a capo on the neck of your guitar can be a useful technique while writing a song. A *capo* is a device that you clamp onto the neck of your guitar to change the key you are playing in without changing the way you form a chord. (For example, if you place the capo on the third fret of the guitar and play an E major, the chord will now become a G major without changing your fingering.) By wrapping a capo around the neck of your guitar at various fret positions, you can vary the key signature you're working in without changing the voicing of the chord. This is great when trying out various keys for a singer, but it also inspires different emotions from a songwriter since the chords take on a very different perspective and color when moved up and down the scale.

I'll use the capo device (good ones are available at any music store for about $15) especially when I'm writing country and folk. I'll place it generally on the third or fourth fret. I love the chimney, almost mandolin, texture it adds to the chording — it makes the song sound fresh. When I'm writing rock, especially alternative, I enjoy tuning the whole guitar a whole step down to give the instrument a grungy sound. I also enjoy tuning the low E down to D — this is the sound of the guitars on Aerosmith's "Draw the Line" (written by Steven Tyler and Joe Perry). Also, I recommend buying one of the several books on alternate tunings. Whether they are the tunings of Joni Mitchell on acoustic guitar or the tunings of Keith Richards of The Rolling Stones on electric and acoustic guitar, these alternates to the standard E, A, D, G, B, A tuning can elicit totally unique chord progressions and accompanying melodies. The group Creed bases their chordal sound on the D, A, D, A, D, D tuning, giving the chords an ominous power and droning quality.

Pecking at the keyboard

The keyboard (any instrument based on the piano) is one of the most versatile and widely used chordal instruments for the songwriter. For everything from power ballads to old-fashioned rock 'n' roll (Jerry Lee Lewis was perhaps the king of the rock 'n' roll piano), the acoustic piano would be the weapon of choice. Nowadays, we have electronic pianos that rival the sound of a real acoustic piano at a fraction of the size and cost. The majesty and honesty of a good piano (or sampled grand — the name that refers to the electronic variety) is second to none. For extra inspiration, you can purchase a keyboard such as the Yamaha S80 that not only contains a reasonably good grand piano patch, but also includes terrific electric piano — the sound of the Wurlitzer immortalized in "These Eyes" (written by Randy Bachman and Burton Cummings; performed by The Guess Who) or the Fender Rhodes piano featured in "You Are the Sunshine of My Life" (written and sung by Stevie Wonder). In addition, you'll find synthesized brass patches — useful when writing '80s style rock — listen to "Heat of the Moment" (written by

John Wetton and Geoff Downes; performed by Asia for reference), woodwinds, and a vast collection of strange and wacky synthesizer and bass sounds. R&B, gospel, jazz, new age, urban, and dance pop are all primarily the divinity of the keyboard. Because urban music is so simple chordally (generally one or two chords throughout the entire song) the texture of the keyboard sound becomes especially vital in setting the mood and creating variation throughout the song.

As fun as it is to experiment with chords on a keyboard or guitar, it's also interesting to call up a bass patch on the keyboard (perhaps synth bass or electric bass) or plug in an electric bass guitar and work with the simple dominant notes of each chord. It gives your imagination plenty of room to wander when not encumbered by a lot of chords.

Although you can write any genre on practically any chordal instrument (death metal on mandolin and acid rock on banjo being possibly the only exceptions) certain instruments seem to have a connection to certain genres. The more you experiment with different instruments, the more you'll find your true direction as a songwriter.

Practice Makes Perfect

Now that you've found some amazing chords and great ways of joining them in progression from reading this chapter, go back to some of those great melodies you came up with in Chapter 9, and experiment with laying down different chord patterns beneath it. Who knows? Maybe you'll create a chord pattern that takes the song to new heights, thereby letting you complete the melody that just keeps standing still — when in fact it's time for it to sway to the music.

Chord theories and progressions are certainly the more technical side of songwriting — and if it flows easily for you, great! But, if not, don't get discouraged. Keep practicing and experimenting, and allow yourself the freedom to create and to also make mistakes. Review the material presented here (over and over if necessary) until you get comfortable with the nuts and bolts of chords. Then get in the groove and let your creative juices go to see what magic can happen.

Regardless of all of this, when it comes right down to it, you'll need to rely heavily on your gut instincts and inner intuitions to find just the right chords.

Part IV
Writing Songs in Different Styles

The 5th Wave   By Rich Tennant

@RICHTENNANT

"Denise is a natural at helping me with the lyrics. She's been finishing my sentences for over 20 years anyway."

In this part . . .

Where does your taste in music lie? Are you heavy metal, easy listening, or one of the hundreds of shades in between? It's easy to argue that a great song is a great song; still, every song seems to live and breathe best in a particular style, or *genre*. In this part, we look at many of the different directions your song can take and study the devices that are the signatures of the various musical styles. We also give you directions for how to write and submit your songs for television, movies, and theater.

Chapter 11

From Country to Rock and Everything in Between: The Genres

As a songwriter, you're presented with a broad menu of styles or genres from which to choose. Many songwriters settle on two or three musical directions that they want to specialize in — usually mirroring their personal taste in music and drawing from their background and influences. Some songwriters can write outside their field of expertise and stretch themselves — often with the help of a collaborator versed in that genre. Other times, a writer's song that's intended for one marketplace can find a home outside its original genre by a clever recasting of the arrangement.

In this chapter, we look at the genres of popular music, and see how you can vary your style — both in writing style and arrangement. We explain how to tailor your lyrics, melodies, and chord progressions to fit each genre.

The various musical genres we take a look at, include the following:

- ✔ **Singer/songwriter:** When you write strictly for yourself, the rulebook goes out the window.

- ✔ **Rock 'n' roll:** This broad spectrum of styles ranging from hard to soft, with all stops in between, has been around since the mid-1950s, and there are some unique ways to create it.

- ✔ **Pop:** Ranging from Johnny Mathis to Billy Joel to Christina Aguilera, this genre is perhaps the most widely known and accepted.

- ✔ **Country:** Spanning from traditional to "new country," this genre continues to be a major goal for the serious songwriter.

- ✔ **R&B, urban, hip-hop, and rap:** This ever-developing segment of the music charts started life in the 1940s and hasn't stopped to catch its breath.

- ✔ **Gospel and Christian:** Defined today mainly by its lyrical content and subject matter, this genre now encompasses practically all of the musical styles.

- ✔ **Blues and folk:** The granddaddy of several other styles, the imprint of blues, both lyrically and musically, is undeniable.

Creating Your Own Style: Singer/Songwriter

Singer/songwriter is considered a genre of its own because it defines itself by often breaking traditional songwriting rules and depends on the unique vision of the artist. Success in this category depends on how well the artist's vision relates to public taste and whether the audience cares enough about the artist as a person to listen to what he has to say. The singer/songwriter genre tends to be very personal and sometimes confessional. It's a form that isn't so much learned, as it's lived.

A lyric that was once deep and thought-provoking might be considered whiney or self-indulgent, depending on how "in vogue" the singer/songwriter genre is in any given year.

If you're a performing songwriter, your goal should be to create a unique voice and persona through your songs. Although issues like good song form, effective use of poetic devices, and solid musical hooks and ideas are a given, the overriding objective is to separate yourself from everyone else and isolate whatever it is about you that makes you unique. It may be a point of view, a complete diversity of musical styles, or the unique way you look at life.

Whatever it is, you define this genre — not the other way around.

The list of singer/songwriters goes on and on, who invented for themselves a style all their own. To name a few are James Taylor, Joni Mitchell, Bruce Springsteen, Kenny Loggins, Paul Simon, Cat Stevens, and Melissa Etheridge. One characteristic that's shared by all these artists is this: There's no mistake about who you're listening to as soon as you hear them.

Back in 1984 when I was on the road with Survivor, we were staying in Beverly Hills when I wandered into the hotel bar to have a drink. As I drank a cold one, I noticed the young girl performing at the piano. As I started to focus on what she was playing and the words she was singing, I soon realized this was not your typical lounge singer recycling standards and top 40 hits. She was singing future classics. I went over and sat at the piano bar (one of those pianos with seats positioned all around it where the piano itself becomes your table), and I sat mesmerized by the stories of her life. When she finally took a break, I introduced myself to the young Tori Amos. Her sense of unshakeable confidence and knowing who she is totally bowled me over. Without any false modesty or boastfulness, she just *knew* that she would make it and that she had everything it takes to make it in this business.

If your primary ambition as a songwriter is to perform your own songs, study the lyrics of the artists listed above (along with any of your own favorites) to compare your vision, then ask yourself:

✔ Just who am I, and how can I best put my personal vision into a song?

✔ How do I reach deeper inside than ever to strip mine my soul?

✔ How can I develop a style of songwriting, arranging, and singing that, when it comes on the radio (or is heard from the lobby of the theater), will immediately be recognizable as mine?

The singer/songwriting category is one where being unique is not an option — it's a necessity.

Playing It Cool: Rock 'n' roll

Rock music was born in the mid-1950s from its ancestors: rhythm and blues. As a songwriter, this is one genre that can satisfy many cravings. The genre of good old rock music is the foundation of many sub-genres.

If this is your style of interest, take a look at the following subcategories of rock, and see where you might fit on the continuum, and how you can tailor your own writing to correspond.

As Chapter 4 mentions, the musical riff (often played on guitar) is a component in the rock genre. As a songwriter, if you're a bit weak musically, try to find a guitarist who can create an original signature sound for you in the same way that the Edge does for U2, Keith Richard does for The Rolling Stones, Eddie Van Halen does for Van Halen, Jimmy Page did for Led Zeppelin, or Slash did for Guns 'N Roses.

Old-fashioned rock 'n' roll

This genre that started in the wild mid-'50s when people were looking for the perfect escape with acts like Bill Haley and the Comets ("Shake, Rattle, and Roll"), Chuck Berry ("Johnny B. Goode"), and Buddy Holly ("Peggy Sue").

Today, this genre finds expression in a variety of acts such as George Thorogood and The Destroyers, Brian Setzer, Black Crowes, and Bob Seger. Opportunities for the songwriter are a bit limited in this genre (because it's full of bands and artists who usually write their own songs), but if you love it, then write it and pray that a new band is forming (or form one yourself!) and is ready to kick butt with some good old-fashioned rock 'n' roll!

Songs in the old-fashioned rock 'n' roll genre generally base their chord progression on the basic blues progressions ("Hound Dog" and "Johnny B. Goode" both use the 1, 4, 1, 5 progression — or E, A, E, B, E progression) and they just bump up the tempo. Messages are pretty straightforward, although Chuck Berry notably stretched its boundaries with the pretty darn literate lyrics (considered rock 'n' roll poetry) of "Sweet Little Sixteen."

Adult Contemporary

The Carpenters of the 1970s, with songs like "We've Only Just Begun" (written by songsmith Paul Williams originally as a jingle for a savings and loan company), Neil Diamond, Barry Manilow, and the music of Bread helped define the genre known as *adult contemporary*. This style, sometimes referred to as *soft rock*, takes its adjectives from being easy on the ears and not particularly controversial — either lyrically or musically — and that's not a musical slight. Sometimes the lighter side of rock is exactly what you need to help unwind and sooth your jangled soul. It's a genre short on story songs and long on first person observations on the trials of life and love. Today it has found expression in such adult contemporary and hot adult contemporary (the more modern, hipper, and slightly edgier version of the adult contemporary genre) acts like the following:

- **Five For Fighting:** Actually the creation of one man, John Ondrasek (the name was derived from the five-minute penalty for fighting in a hockey game), this music with its textures of acoustic 12-string guitar, upright bass, viola, B3 organ, and other pleasing sounds that certain unusual or unexpected instruments make goes easy on the ears and tough on the soul.

- ✔ **Lifehouse:** Originally a "praise and worship" group at their church, this group relies on gruff, raspy vocals to offset its "soft core" instrumentation — and the guitars, even when distorted, are smooth and pleasant sounding. The drums are never overbearing.

- ✔ **Train:** Although often a hard-rocking unit, Train's most popular songs, "Meet Virginia" and its Grammy-winning 2002 smash "Drops of Jupiter" are really hot adult contemporary due to their emphasis on acoustic guitar, piano, and real strings — they've crossed over into the mainstream from the alternative charts.

In terms of arranging, guitars are fairly polite (as opposed to the raunchy distortion of other rock genres, such as hard rock and heavy metal). Keyboards and strings are a staple, and vocals are on the smooth side. Drums are not bombastic, and they are used mainly to keep the groove as opposed to creating sonic effects.

The genre known as adult contemporary is as much a function of treatment as it is of substance. Recently, the soft rock Monkees hit "I'm a Believer" from the '60s (written by the soft rock king himself, Neil Diamond), was given a raunchy reworking by pop-rock czars, Smashmouth. Catapulted back onto the airwaves by its inclusion in the animated motion picture, *Shrek,* it proves not only the staying power of a great song, but how it can be "painted to suit" the modern palette of tastes.

When producing a demo of your latest song, you may want to try multiple versions. If your song started its life as a soft rocker, try a radical treatment putting it fiercely into the hard rock or alternative category. Likewise, if you started out hard, you can tone it down to a softer version.

Hard rock

As you turn up the decibels and distortion, mic up the drums from a distance (to capture the raw room ambiance), and focus your lyrics on more extreme, explicit, angry, and controversial topics, a genre comes into the focus known as *hard rock.* If your songwriting is verging into the hard rock side of music, it's time to look at the menu of choices to see just how loud, extreme, and radical you want to go. This genre includes many subgenres such as:

- ✔ **Heavy metal:** For example, Megadeth, Metallica, Static X, Stereomud, and Ozzy Osbourne. This subgenre is defined by overdriven and distorted electric guitars generally playing a minor-key, and an often classically inspired riff underneath manic, shouted vocals.

- ✔ **Speed metal:** For example, Dash Riprock, Slayer, and perhaps "the fastest guitar alive" Sweden's Yngwie Malmsteen (pronounced Ing-vay). This is where heavy metal is played as fast as humanly possible, and then sped up from there.

  The Swedish sensation, Yngwie Malmsteen, used to play for Stormer and then Keel — he's had and still has an amazing solo career and sells tons of CDs worldwide. *The Guinness Book of World Records* checked this guy out for his speed — that's how fast he was at his peak.

- ✔ **Alternative rock:** For example, Nirvana, Soundgarden, Mudhoney, Pearl Jam, Nine Inch Nails, REM, Stone Temple Pilots, and Smashing Pumpkins. Sometimes referred to by the media as *Grunge* (referring both to the grungy distortion present in the guitars and to the often negative themes of songs), this genre has been around for over 15 years and shows no signs of losing steam.

- ✔ **Punk rock:** For example, The Clash, X, Sex Pistols, Black Flag, Fear, The Ramones, and Green Day. This subgenre is all about alienation from society, and music with all its rough edges left in. Punk songs usually contain anywhere from 1 to 3 chords and are arranged in a stripped down fashion. Tempos tend to be exceptionally fast. Vocals are generally sung at the edge of hoarseness.

- ✔ **Progressive rock:** For example, King Crimson, early Genesis, Hawkwind, Rick Wakeman, Rush, Pink Floyd, plus Emerson, Lake, and Palmer (ELP). This is music with a grand vision, musically, lyrically, and visually. This genre incorporates expansive musical arrangements, sometimes written for full symphony orchestras, into what are essentially rock melodies. Progressive rock draws themes from classical sources both literary and musical. The style has actually experienced a bit of a rebirth in the early years of the new millennium, with many of the signature songs by progressive rock acts being sampled and scratched into new music by groups in the electronic sub-genre of rock.

- ✔ **Psychedelic/acid rock:** For example, Jefferson Airplane (and their splinter group, Hot Tuna), Love, The Grateful Dead, The Doors, Cream, and Traffic. This genre of music is influenced by, or reflects, the use of mind-altering psychedelic drugs (like LSD — also known as acid), typified by extended, free-form musical jams, and often cosmic, deep, or conscious-expanding lyrics. Though this form saw its heydays in the late '60s and early '70s, it's spirit is still alive in newer groups like Phish (and it's lead singer Trey Anastasio's solo work).

- ✔ **Modern rock:** For example, System of a Down, Staind, Nickelback, Puddle of Mudd, or Linkin Park. This category is a modern blend of decades and genres combining the slick production values (big guitars) and song craft (big choruses) of the '80s, with the attitude and anger of the new millennium. Modern rock also samples from other genres such as rap, metal, and hip-hop.

✔ **Hard rock:** For example Led Zeppelin, AC/DC, Bad Company, Aerosmith, Joan Jett, and Deep Purple. The bands themselves generate many of the songs written in the hard rock genre. Because hard rock is such a live performance–oriented genre, it's difficult to write it in the confines of a writer's cubicle at a publisher's office. It's also not a form that encourages the *outside song* (the song written by someone outside the band and pitched by that writer or his publisher). Songs are often fallen upon in open-ended jam sessions, where the musicians turn up the volume and interact musically until they fall into some sort of set pattern over which song structure and lyrics are eventually fitted.

When I was a member of Survivor, we would usually jam at *sound checks* (when a band checks its equipment, house amplification, stage monitors, and lighting, usually a few hours before a performance). I'd always have my cassette player rolling (some bands record every sound check through the mixing console) to catch any brilliance that might just happen to be flowing through the band that particular day.

If you're a songwriter with aspirations to write in the rock genre, put together a kind of songwriter's jam band, not necessarily to become a recording act (hey, you never know — crazier things have happened!), but to write songs in the rock genre for other artists.

Checking into the Limelight: Pop

Pop, or popular, music sometimes overlaps with rock (light rock songs and harder-edged pop), but it's also a style all to itself, and includes the subgenre of dance pop.

Usually what separates the rock from the pop is a sense of imminent danger that rock possesses and pop lacks. Rock songs walk terrain that pop songs often fear to tread (or choose not to). On the other hand, you'll probably not choose "Pit of Zombies" by Cannibal Corpse as your wedding song. Take a look at two of the most vital modern day subgenres of pop.

Contemporary pop

Evolving from the form called traditional pop (Barbra Steisand, Julio Iglesias, Neil Diamond, Barry Manilow), this genre, has been the songwriters' gold mine for a number of years. Usually represented by artists strong in the visual and performing arts (and not necessarily strong in the songwriting craft), it's an industry constantly searching for great songs to extend the careers of its stars. Artists such Mariah Carey, Celine Dion, Whitney Houston, Enrique Iglesias, and Marc Anthony have supplied the voices and talents to inspire (and feed) hundreds of songwriters.

Memorable melodies and catchy hooks are highly prized in this category, and ageless themes such as love, regret, faith, dedication, and family are the norm. Instrumentation can be innovative, but never harsh, and is subservient to the voice of the singer and the message he or she is putting across.

When writing a contemporary pop song, it's important to keep your lyrical themes fairly broad and universal if you want to be considered by the widest number of artists. If you're writing with a particular artist in mind, put yourself in his or her shoes, and see if you can picture your words and melodies emanating from that artist.

Dance pop

Songs for this category are based around the almighty groove. If a song just happens to possess a memorable melody, relatable concept, and interesting chord progression, all the better — but getting an entire dance floor pulsating to the diva gyrating on the stage is much more to the point. Madonna is the *grande dame* of this genre with the likes of Britney Spears, Christina Aguilera, Mandy Moore, Jessica Simpson, Jennifer Lopez, and Pink now grabbing the torch.

Keep your lyrics very simple in this genre and also positive and young. Reflect on experiences appropriate and relatable to your target audience — males and females in the 10–25-year-old categories. A lot of the depth and complexity you put into your pop and soul songs may get lost on the dance floor in this genre.

Lyrically, this genre tends to be on the risqué and suggestive side, but it's never explicit or filled with foul language — call it X-rated innocence, if you will. The female singers love to seduce you, and then tell you that they're "not that kind of girl." The boys, for all their strutting and posturing, would like nothing more than to "promise forever" to the girl of their dreams.

This genre uses big hooky power ballads, mid-tempo grabbers, and up-tempo dance vehicles such as the following:

- ✔ **"All Or Nothing At All":** Romantic power ballad by O-Town (written by Wayne Hector and Steve Mac)

- ✔ **"I Want It That Way":** Thoughtful mid-tempo by 'N Sync (written by Andreas Carlsson and Martin Sandberg)

- ✔ **"The Call":** Up-tempo hoofer by The Backstreet Boys (written by Martin Sandberg and Rami Yacoub)

Dance pop and boy/girl band is one genre often controlled song-wise by the producer himself. It's difficult (though not impossible) to have an outside song considered by one of these acts because their producer (who is usually a songwriter as well) will come into the project with songs in hand. He's also there to collaborate with the band when needed. I always feel, however, that a great song and tenacity will pay off. Just ask Richard Marx, who had one of the biggest hits of his career when 'N Sync recorded his song "This I Promise You."

As a songwriter, your demo for the dance-pop field will be especially important in getting your song cut. Slicker is better, and the more like the finished product it can sound, the better your chances are. This is truly a genre where sound is as important as content. Use a good programmer to do the drum track for you. Treat him well; he's worth his weight in gold records (you might even consider making him a part of your songwriting team in exchange for his services). There are many rhythmic devices that he'll know that'll keep your song cooking along even if it's a mid-tempo tune or ballad. Those inner rhythms will fool the ear (and the feet!) into thinking it's a much faster tempo.

I didn't quite get this whole dance-pop phenomenon until I took my nine-year-old son to see the, at that time, up-and-coming 'N Sync open the show for urban diva Janet Jackson. They took the stage in space suits and soon stripped down to their multi-colored, chick-magnet uniforms. The screams were high pitched and deafening (as opposed to the more muted din for Janet which seemed to be voiced about an octave lower because of the slightly older demographic of her segment of the audience). Each member had a distinctive persona and their own legions of fans. The songs, which seemed a bit clichéd and overly simplistic on the radio, took on a whole new power live when combined with the razor-sharp choreography and million-watt sound system. I gained a whole new respect for this genre.

Don't skimp on hiring the right singer for your song. This is one genre where the A&R representative (A&R stands for artist and repertoire — the person responsible for not only finding talent but also finding songs for the acts he brings in) will cut no slack for a "charming" rendition by a non-singer/songwriter. Bite the bullet, and spend the extra $200 on a great session singer and to increase your odds of landing a giant cover of your song. A great singer will most assuredly elevate your song.

"I just arrange my Boy Band songs when I demo them as if I was doing a record for an '80s rock band. Many of the songs in this category like 'Shape of a Heart' by The Backstreet Boys are like Journey, sideways. I then take it and add current sounds, effects, and rhythm patterns to make sure it keeps up with what is currently on the radio. A great song is a great song — it's mainly the arrangement that changes from genre to genre."

—Kurt Howell, Nashville writer/producer and member of Southern Pacific

Singing It Plain and Simple: Country

This broad and popular genre prides itself in being the heartbeat of the working class. Its common messages and plain language ("Write it like you talk it" is a popular saying among country songwriters) have been the benchmark of a form that started in the rural south and spread like a wildfire to all points North, East, and West. Nashville, Tennessee, has been this genre's launching pad since the '30s and is now Music City to practically all types of music. We'll break this category down into its two primary types:

- **Traditional country,** which includes hillbilly, country and western, and blue grass music
- **Pop country,** also known as *new country* is where pop rock arranging meets the more traditional style of country

If you live and breathe traditional country and it feels as comfortable as a broken-in pair of cowboy boots, then by all means, follow that old dusty road, no matter where you hail from. But if you don't really feel natural or are just trying to "cash in," you'd better know that no one can spot a wooden nickel quicker than country folk.

Traditional country

If you want to write country songs, it's good to know your roots — the flowers of today come from seeds of yesterday. The following segments will fill you in on the parts (or seeds) that can help you create your country song. Find some of the songs by the people or groups we mention and pick them apart to see what made them so successful.

Traditional country's appeal lies in its simplicity. It can be clever and intelligent, but it never aims over the head of the common man — nor does it talk down to him.

Traditional country music originally came from the Appalachian Mountains where people sang and played fiddles (violins), guitars, autoharps, and banjos. During the '60s, Johnny Cash became a superstar followed by Willie Nelson, and George Jones is considered to be one of the greatest, if not the greatest, traditional country singer around. One of the most popular traditional country artists today is singer/songwriter Alan Jackson. In 2002, he won three Academy of Country Music awards including: Top Male Vocalist of the year, and his song "Where Were You (When the World Stopped Turning)" won Song of the Year and Single of the Year.

There are two types of traditional country:

- **Country and western:** *Western* music came about when country musicians, many from Oklahoma and Texas, started using western themes (cowboys, life on the range, horses and cattle, and of course, the girl that waits back home) in their music and began wearing colorful western clothes. The biggest stars were Gene Autry and Roy Rogers. Country music grew dramatically in the '40s. In order to market both country and western music in the same genre, the record industry came up with the name "country and western" to include both genres.

- **Bluegrass:** This type of music is acoustic (meaning they use no electronically amplified instruments). Typical instruments used are the upright bass fiddle, acoustic guitar, *Dobro* (the metal-bodied guitar-like instrument usually played with a metal or glass slide), banjo, fiddle (violin), and mandolin (the small-bodied instrument comprised of four pairs of strings). With a continued up-shift in popularity of bluegrass music, you may want to consider songwriting in that genre. In order to become successful, it's necessary to immerse yourself in the music, especially in its roots. There are fine anthology CD sets available for Bill Monroe and the Stanley Brothers and that's a good place to start. Then familiarize yourself with current artists, especially Allison Krauss who finds herself regularly on the country charts, Ricky Skaggs, ex-Stanley brother Ralph Stanley, and the "new grass" sensation Nickel Creek — three talented songwriters/performers from California.

The bluegrass soundtrack for the movie *O Brother, Where Art Thou* won the Best Album of the Year Grammy award in 2002, to the shock, surprise, and delight of many in the industry.

Pop country or new country

Pop country is a wayward cousin of country who came to visit for the weekend and somehow became a permanent member of the household. In doing so, some of the rough edges of country were knocked off and substituted with some of the slick chord changes and production values of pop and rock.

Pop country is quite a different genre than traditional country. In traditional country, the songs were simple, using three-chords, and dealt with real-world issues. Pop country songs, on the other hand, are often simple pop songs with a country feel and usually use more chords than the typical three-chord traditional song (like using the 2, 6 and 3 chords more frequently and even other more tantalizing chords such as the diminished, half-diminished, and sustained forth chords). The hit song "Amazed" (written by Marv Green, Chris Lindsey, and Aimee Mayo; performed by Lonestar) that crossed over into the pop charts actually uses three separate keys: one for the verses, one for the pre-chorus, and another for the chorus.

The fact is that there is little difference in the structure of many pop country ballads and those sung by "boy-band" groups such as the Backstreet Boys and 'N Sync. The song "I Can Love You Like That" (written by Steve Diamond, Maribeth Derry, and Jennifer Kimball) and "I Swear" (written by Gary Baker and Frank Myers) were both number one country hits for John Michael Montgomery as well as hits on the Top-40 when they were sung by the group All-4-One. The song "(God Must Have Spent) A Little More Time on You" (written by Carl Sturken and Evan Rogers) was recorded not only by 'N Sync (reaching number eight on the pop charts), but by the country group Alabama (featuring 'N Sync), which hit the country charts as well.

When you're writing for the new country marketplace, remember that songs with a negative theme will have trouble finding a home. Also blatant "lost my baby and I'm gonna drown my sorrows in Jack Daniels" weepers go in and out of style — refer to today's music charts for reference.

Coming to Nashville for the first time to collaborate back in 1996 was kind of scary. Nobody seemed to care about my rock-and-roll resume. I was asked by one prominent publisher if I really thought I could write country. I answered honestly that I wasn't sure, but I told him I could write a good, simple song from the heart and that's really what country is all about anyway. Well, I guess I passed his pop quiz because he hooked me up with one of his top country writers who I continue to write with to this day — Mr. John ("Third Rock from the Sun") Greenebaum.

Arrangement-wise, many stylistic elements have been added in country's quest to cross over to the general populace. In the mix, there are now rock electric guitars (more distorted and hotter in the blend) and nontraditional elements like strings (Chet Atkins turned the country world on its head when he started adding string sections to county songs in the '50s), synthesizers, and even drum loops like the ones found on urban tracks. You can even hear the gimmick of mis-using the pitch correcting devices to create the robotic vocal effect heard on Cher's hit, "Believe" (written by P. Barry, M. Gray, B. Higgins, S. McLennan, T. Powell, and S. Torch). Certain elements from traditional country are often added to put in the "down home" elements listeners are accustomed to hearing, such as fiddle and *pedal steel* (that's the unit that sits on four legs in front of the player and is picked with finger picks, chorded with a steel bar, and pitch-shifted by manipulating levers with your knees — it supplies the "crying guitar" sound you hear on many country songs). Also incorporated are the banjo, *dobro* (the steel bellied guitars you see on the cover of the *Brothers in Arms* album by those English hillbillies, Dire Straits) and harmonica.

Sometimes a song can straddle more than a single genre by changing the arrangements, instrumentation, and vocal style. Producers can sometimes change a song from pop to new country with the addition of certain key Nashville instruments like pedal steel and fiddle. "I Swear" (written by Gary Baker and Frank Myers) was not only an R&B hit for All-4-One but a country hit for John Michael Montgomery as well.

Getting Your Groove On: R&B, Urban, Hip-Hop, and Rap

All these genres are united by one word: *soul*. This is music that touches the heart at the gut level, reaches inside of you, and twists. This music seems to touch on something through shared expression and oppression that brings its emotions explosively to the surface.

Rhythm and blues — R&B

This genre, derived from work songs and field chants, became commercialized in the '50s by artists such as Jackie Wilson, Ray Charles, and Solomon Burke. They paved the way for rhythm and blues artists of the '60s like Stevie Wonder, The Four Tops, Martha and the Vandellas, Smokey Robinson and the Miracles, and The Temptations. These acts, in turn, passed the baton to Usher, Boyz II Men, and R. Kelly in the present day. R&B is generally heavy on the back beat (the second and fourth beat of the musical measure). The vocalists of R&B songs often approach a melody in an interpretive or soulful manner, often straying from the written melody. Check out Stevie Wonder's soulful reworking of "For Once in My Life" (originally written by Ronald Miller and Orlando Murden), the standard made popular by Tony Bennett and written by Ronald Miller and Orlando Murden, and the R&B remake of the Gershwin brother's classic (co-written by DuBose Heyward) "Summertime" written by Billy Stewart. With these two songs you can clearly see the line where pop stops and R&B begins.

Urban

This seems to be the genre that everyone in dance pop is currently gravitating to. It reflects the sound of the city: the fads, lingo, styles, habits, priorities, and sensibilities of the young, hip, and tuned-in generation. Destiny's Child, Ja Rule, Michael Jackson, Pink, Janet Jackson, Mary J. Blige, Jennifer Lopez, and Ginuwine typify the direction many of the dance-pop acts like Christina Aguilera, Britney Spears, Backstreet Boys, and 'N Sync are moving towards in their music. They're looking for that sound and image that will give them street credibility with their hipper-by-the-day audience.

A hallmark of this style is an extremely simple chord structure, (often just one or two chords) with a simple, often 2- or 3-note melody that varies a bit from section to section for delineation. The grooves themselves are actually quite basic as well (light years from the complex counter-rhythms of dance pop and Latin). The kick drum (bass drum) samples used in the rhythm beds are big and bassy — think of the low-end sound that threatens to shake your muffler loose when that certain car pulls up next to you at the stoplight.

Lyrical themes in urban music are all over the map but are united by the casual slang lingo of the urban streets and a defiance that almost always burns through ("What Have You Done For Me Lately," written by Jimmy Jam and Terry Lewis; performed by Janet Jackson).

If you aspire to write for the urban market, get to know the genre. Hang out at the clubs. Listen to the right stations and keep your ear to the street in terms of what is being said and how it's being expressed. This genre is all about street credibility and if your song lacks it, it will never get cut.

Never assume you are writing urban just because you have developed a good groove for your song. Urban is all about attitude and if it ain't got that then maybe you should just give it up!

Hip-Hop and rap

In the beginning, rap was associated with break-dancing — amazing dance movements achieved by only the limber and soul-filled rhythm enthusiasts. The word *rap* originated from a '60s slang word for conversation, like "my wife was on the phone rapping all day with her friends." The music consists of chanted, often improvised, street poetry — complemented by samples of well-known recordings, usually from the disco, funk, or rock genres.

In the late '70s, *hip-hop* was born from rap — a genre that tears down recognizable sounds and songs, and rebuilds them as entirely new, unpredictable songs. While rap is mostly spoken word, hip-hop is mostly sung lyrics. Rap is more aggressively rhythmic, while hip-hop is based more on sensuous, hypnotic grooves. Though the beats of hip-hop and rap might sound the same to an untrained ear, there are a number of different levels to add rhythmic contrast to even the simplest song. Rap originally started with DJs playing drum loops and *scratching* (the rhythmic sound of the phonograph needle going against the groove) the records while rapping to rhythms. As the form evolved, the techniques used by rappers became quite varied in style — some were more extreme and complex using instruments such as hard-rock guitars, while others smoothed out the rough edges and emphasized the lyrics.

In the OutKast debut release, 1994's *Southernplayalisticadillacmusik*, ushered in a new period of hip-hop — southern style. 2000's *Stankonia* received universal acclaim and garnered the duo a handful of *Grammy* nominations. With a tip of their hat to the funk of Parliament and Funkadelic, OutKast's thought-provoking lyrics, clever phrasings, and incredible fashion statements have vaulted them to the forefront of the hip-hop scene.

Rap music has been criticized as a boastful promotion of violence and negative attitudes towards women, while others admire it as an imaginative manipulation of cultural idioms and credit many rappers with a heightened social and political awareness. Hip-hop currently features as many women as men (take a good listen to Lil Kim, Missy Elliot, and Queen Latifah) and appeals to a broad range of ages, races, and social strata.

If rap is your calling, take a look at the lyrics and listen to the current songs that are hitting the charts. See if you can identify just what separates the rap styles of some of the most popular ones like Snoop Dogg, Eminem, Outkast, Busta Rhymes, Ludacris, Method Man, and Ice T.

When writing in other genres such as rock, R&B, and dance pop, get creative and start experimenting with injecting rap sections and hip-hop rhythms into your arrangements. Listen to how Shaggy blends traditional smooth soul and reggae ("I Wasn't Me" written by Shaun Pizzonia, Orville Burrell, and Brian Thompson) with rap, and how Kid Rock mixes rap with rock 'n' roll ("Bawitdaba" written by Kid Rock, Matthew Shafer, Sylvia Robinson, David Parker, and Jason Krause).

Going to a Higher Level: Christian

The Christian genre, like all the others, is based on authenticity. Just as a true country aficionado can spot an insincere attempt at down-home songwriting and the hip urban crowd can see a poser from down the block, writing in the Christian field requires true commitment and belief in Jesus Christ.

There's a well-documented story circulating about the rock artist who released a Christian-slanted song to Christian radio. When the programmers went to his Web site, as directed, they found foul language and un-Christian attitudes. That was all that was needed to put the kibosh on his Christian crossover ambitions.

This rapidly expanding genre covers practically all styles of music from soft rock to heavy metal. Groups like Creed (who for the last four years have been one of America's top selling acts in *any* category and actually won a Grammy in a non-Christian category), Jars of Clay, Lifehouse, and P.O.D. are part of the newest movement in Christian where a spiritual message has entered the mainstream and is being programmed by not exclusively Christian radio as well as Christian-only stations. (The group Stryper paved the way for metal music in the Christian genre and Amy Grant was the first Christian act to make a major impact on the general pop charts.) Joining the more traditional Christian acts like Steven Curtis Chapman, Michael W. Smith, and Bill and Gloria Gaither on the contemporary Christian charts, this new breed of artist is helping to spread "the Word" to a broad marketplace.

It's not always necessary to use the words *Jesus* or *Christ* in every song in order for it to be Christian. The message and spirit of your song is the most important element.

A trend towards more "positivity" is being seen today on the radio. Contrasting the doom and gloom of the grunge era, a new message of hope is taking shape from Christian groups like P.O.D. and Audio Adreneline. Other acts, such as Lifehouse and Creed (though not marketed as Christian), are spreading good values and positive, life-affirming messages — the audience is often getting "the word" in between the lines.

If you're a singer/songwriter breaking in to the Christian world from rock, there may be some resistance and skepticism about letting you in. Just as the country world is hesitant to let "just anyone" be a part of country, the Christian market wants a high degree of proof that the artist is truly committed and walks the path of the Lord.

Getting Spiritual: Gospel

Today's contemporary gospel music combines jazz, R&B, and hip-hop with words of praise and worship. Some of today's top gospel singers are Yolanda Adams, Mary Mary, CeCe and Bebe Winans, Trin-I-Tee 5:7, Hezekiah Walker, and Kirk Franklin.

Like most other genres, the borders of gospel music have been blurring in the last few years to embrace more nontraditional musical styles. For every Shirley Caesar (more traditional), there is a Yolanda Adams (hip-hop gospel). Acts like Donnie McClurkin and Mary Mary are holding the gospel torch high while blazing new trails.

Stylistically, southern gospel has remained truer to its roots than any other genre of music excepting bluegrass. A tradition of family groups continues today with such groups as the McKameys and the Singing Cookes (both of which are Appalachian Mountain-style groups), and The Crabb Family, The Sons Family, and the Bowman Family. Such groups as the Isaacs Family and Jeff and Sheri Easter represent the Bluegrass Gospel tradition.

Music (the lyrics and the melodies) in all of the genres has a profound effect upon our emotions. Many people believe that listening to songs about Jesus Christ is healthy for the spirit, and oftentimes, certain Christian and gospel songs, especially performed live in church or concert, can take people into a state beyond description — where the audience shouts with joy, feeling goose bumps all over while tears roll down their faces. Take a look at the lyrics of the following song, and imagine being in a crowd of people filled with the spirit:

"From the Depths of My Heart" written by Ben and Sonya Isaacs

It hasn't been a bed of roses since I've started on my way

And Lord you know I'm not complaining

There's just something I should say

For I've reached desperation and I've stumbled since my start

I've grown weary through the years, now I'm crying bitter tears

From the depths of my heart.

Chorus

From the depths of my heart, Lord, I'm calling out to you

For I need you here to lead me, I've done all that I can do

Lord I'm trying to do my part to see that others make it through

And though I know I don't deserve you

Still I'm trying hard to serve you from the depths of my heart.

It's not a prayer just from the lips, it goes much deeper that words

It's not a worthless expression, I just need to be heard

For Lord, I need to reach your throne, I know exactly what I'll do

I'll just fall down on my knees, I know you will hear the pleas

From the depths of my heart

Words and music by Ben and Sonya Isaacs © Isaacs Family Publishing (BMI)

If you're interested in writing for this genre, there's an excellent resource called the "Singing News" magazine that can point you in the right direction. The monthly magazine features tour schedules of (and articles about) all the major artists. You can find them at www.singingnews.com.

Songwriting for the Soul: Blues and Folk

Blues and folk music are considered by some to be the original soul music, because it exists to document the trials and heartbreak of the human condition. This was music created not for commercial gain. The music was created by people who needed to tell their story and vent their souls through simple and heartfelt songs.

Blues pioneers like Robert Johnson, Blind Lemon Jefferson, and Memphis Minnie inspired Howlin' Wolf, Muddy Waters, Big Mama Thornton (who wrote and performed the original version of the Presley smash, "Hound Dog"), and

T-Bone Walker, who lit the path for later blues greats like B.B. (blues boy) King, Buddy Guy, Albert King, Freddie King, Etta James, and Elmore James. They, in turn, inspired a new generation of blues journeymen starting with Eric Clapton, Bonnie Raitt, Stevie Ray Vaughan, Robert Cray, and extending to current blues upstarts like Jonny Lang, Anthony Gomes, Shannon Curfman, and Kenny Wayne Sheppard.

For the ultimate guide to the blues, check out *Blues For Dummies* (published by Hungry Minds, Inc.). You'll love Cub Koda and Lonnie Brook's insight and humor.

As a songwriter, there are always plenty of blues and folk artists looking for good, simple, and honest material. Blues is one genre where it's okay to bitch and moan. But as you listen to the great blues songs, you realize that it can also be very vibrant and uplifting. For every song about a lost love, you'll find one about a found love. Often it's the juxtaposition of the jumping blues shuffle beat that energizes an otherwise mournful lyric.

Writing for the folk market is mainly a matter of colorfully documenting events and telling a good story, as done by Folk pioneers of America like Huddie Ledbetter (known as Leadbelly), Woody Guthrie, and Pete Seeger. Remember to keep the chord changes simple and the language fairly plain.

Every genre has specific ways of expression. In the blues and folk categories, avoid flowery and overly poetic phrases. Speak to the heart of the matter and tell the story clearly and honestly. Listen to the early albums of Robert Cray for a textbook example of how to weave a great story around an immediately recognizable hook ("Smoking Gun," written by Robert Cray, Richard Cousins, and Bruce Bromberg) in the context of a blues song.

Practice Makes Perfect

For the fun of it, experiment around and try your hand at several different styles of music, following the guidelines set up in this chapter. Remember though what you're most passionate about and focus on what genre you're most comfortable with — as this is most likely where your best material will be created. In the case with sports, there are not many athletes that can compete at a very high level in more than one sport. The same goes for songwriting — very few songwriters can write hit songs in all genres. Do what you can to find your passion and direction, and let that be your ticket to the level of gold and platinum.

Chapter 12

Writing for Stage, Screen, and Television

- -

In This Chapter

▶ Writing songs for motion pictures and television

▶ Coming up with jingles for commercials

▶ Creating songs for the theater

▶ Practicing the art of mixing music with visuals

- -

*W*hen a songwriter dreams, sometimes his flight of fantasy takes him to a gilded Broadway theater where his songs are being performed by the cast and orchestra of a long-running, live stage production. In his dream's next feature, he sneaks into the Cineplex for the 8:00 showing of the blockbuster movie where his music is underscoring the action, and his song is featured as the "end title." Just before he awakens, he hears another of his songs being used as the theme music for the hard-hitting drama just picked up by one of the networks for its fourth consecutive season. Then just after the credits roll and the morning sun is peeking through his curtain, he hears yet another of his compositions, which has just been chosen as the slogan and rally cry of a new multi-million dollar ad campaign. Ultimately, he wakes up — but the vision stays with him all that day and possibly a lifetime.

If you're anything like other songwriters, you've probably had some segment of this dream either in your slumbering or waking state. Dreaming is a big part of what songwriting is all about, and there's no question that writing for the stage, screen, and television is worthy dream fodder. Writing for these arenas can be inspiring and lucrative, as well as frustrating and asset depleting — depending on your luck, connections, perseverance, and talent. And yet, if any portion of this dream comes true, you'll leave a giant footprint on the road to success in the world of songwriting.

In this chapter, we show you some of the road signs, detours, entry ramps, curves, straightaways, and deceptive bends down the vast turnpike of stage, screen, and television — and we let you know how it relates to your songwriting.

Songwriting for Film

Whether it's creating the score for a motion picture or writing songs for specific scenes or areas in a film, this remains an incredible goal for every serious songwriter. The list of songs written for and inspired by motion pictures is long. Table 12-1 shows you just a few of the songs on that list.

Table 12-1	Songs Featured in Movies		
Song	**Movie**	**Songwriter(s)**	**Singer/Performer**
"A Whole New World"	Aladdin	Alan Menken, Tim Rice	Peabo Bryson, Regina Belle
"There You'll Be"	Pearl Harbor	Diane Warren	Faith Hill
"I Don't Wanna Miss a Thing"	Armageddon	Diane Warren	Aerosmith
"Can You Feel the Love Tonight"	The Lion King	Tim Rice, Elton John	Elton John
"Power of Love"	Back to the Future	John Colla, Hugh Cregg, Christopher Hayes	Huey Lewis and the News
"Eye of the Tiger"	Rocky III	Jim Peterik, Frankie Sullivan	Survivor
"Stayin' Alive"	Saturday Night Fever	The Bee Gees	The Bee Gees
"The Sound of Music"	The Sound of Music	Richard Rodgers, Oscar Hammerstein II	Julie Andrews
"Everybody's Talkin'"	Midnight Cowboy	John Barry	Harry Nilsson

The various categories of music in movies are:

✔ **Main title:** This is the song that opens the movie and is often heard throughout the picture in various styles and treatments. This song is vital because it pretty much sets the emotional tone for the entire movie.

✔ **Songs for specific scenes:** These are the songs that are in the background, setting the mood for a specific location in the movie — sometimes the lyric can echo the action on the screen. The song can be featured prominently with a minimum of dialogue (love scenes come to mind), or the song can be barely audible, coming out of some cheap transistor radio on the beach. A recent trend has been to stick songs by hot groups into a scene, randomly and barely audible, basically so that they can be featured in the movie's lucrative soundtrack.

✔ **End title:** This is the song that closes the movie and is another key position because it creates the impression that the movie leaves you with (and hopefully is the song that you'll be singing all the way home, like it or not). Generally speaking, the music supervisor likes to find a big artist for this "money" song.

✔ **Scoring music:** This is the music, usually instrumental in nature that runs through the entire film. It exists to create moods behind the action that emphasize what we are supposed to be feeling at the time. Great orchestrators are worth their weight in gold to a filmmaker because their work can actually make or break a film.

Understanding the role of the music supervisor

The *music supervisor* or *supe* is the right-hand man of the director and the producer of a film when it comes to finding the right music to go with the action on the screen. Music supervision is a relatively new position in film making (it came into its own in the early '80s), alleviating much of the chaos and last-minute scrambling for music that used to take place in this business. The supe is the person who must understand the script backward and forward, the motivation of all the characters, the mood that must be set overall and in each scene, and, not least importantly, the budget available to work with.

He usually has a great deal of financial incentive to get the job done right. His per-picture fee can run as high as a quarter of a million bucks and he often receives a substantial royalty on the soundtrack he puts together. That might more than make up for the nightmares of trying to make all the significant entities — film company, director, producer, songwriters, artists, actors, record companies, and music publishers — play nice together!

Although the budget for a major motion picture is in the $30 to 50 million dollar range, the budget for the music might be a mere $1 or 2 million. It's often the last thing considered by directors, who are far more concerned with the actors, editing, and storyline than they are with the underscoring or specific songs. It's only in recent times that music has become much more than just an afterthought.

Once the music supe meets with the director and producer to determine the film's needs, he then marks out the positions in the movie for specific songs (spots like main title, various key scenes, and the all-important end title as the credits roll). He'll also start making lists of artists and music producers to fill these slots, and contact songwriters, artists, managers, and publishers, while combing the record charts to find hot artists to include (especially if there's going to be a soundtrack album). He'll also contact some of his favorite scoring composers to write music that enhances the underlying mood of each scene and start sending copies of the script (often rough drafts) to the artists, songwriters, and composers he is considering.

Never say no to a music supervisor's suggestion. Instead say, "I'll try it." You may be surprised just how well the idea works — and you might also keep your job that way too!

Don't be too surprised if the song you labored over is practically lost in the context of the movie. Just like the ubiquitous *product placement* in films (that's when, say Hostess pays a film company megabucks for the heroine to munch their Twinkies after she and the hunky male lead make love), often songs are placed inconspicuously beneath dialogue, just so the film company can put the song on the soundtrack album. If you have enough clout, and/or a great attorney, try to get the usage of your song specified in your agreement.

The supervisor must also choose the perfect person to *score* the movie. Scoring is the job of creating music that plays behind the action of a film. Sometimes it calls attention to itself, like the dramatic scores of Hans Zimmer in *Terminator, The Prince of Egypt, Pearl Harbor,* and many more, and John Williams in the *Star Wars* trilogy, *E.T., Harry Potter and The Sorcerer's Stone, Jurassic Park,* and others. Other times, the background music is more subliminal, subtly emphasizing moods ranging from joyous to creepy. Try to think of the movie *Jaws* without hearing the ominous foreboding of sawing strings in the background as the shark is about to feast on human flesh.

Scoring is a different art than songwriting, although the two are related. Both crafts have to do with creating moods, but scoring does its job generally without words by laying textures of sound (from celestial to abrasive) on the musical palette with both subtle daubs and bold strokes. The score to a movie is often overlooked, but boy, would you ever miss it if it were gone.

Getting to the music supervisors

If you're getting the impression that music supervisors pretty much control the music to be considered in a film and that it might be important for you as a songwriter to establish good relations with them — you'd be right! But building a rapport with them, even if you are an established writer, is not always easy.

If you're signed with a major publisher, they'll undoubtedly have a wing of their staff that caters to the film industry. Many publishers will, in fact, put out monthly pitch sheets that list and describe films in the works that are in need of songs and even list the music supervisor in charge.

I used to be signed with a publishing giant who would routinely send out sheets to their writing staff listing movies that were looking for songs. Much of the time, it was on an *all-skate basis,* where you and a bunch of their writers would write a song on spec (in other words, you get no fees unless your song is chosen — I've learned another meaning for this abbreviation — "Don't spec to get paid!"). Many times I would bust my hump to get a song written and demoed only to hear the roaring silence as I waited for some response. I was never quite sure if the song got to the designated music supe, much less given a fair chance to be "tried to scene" in the actual film — when your song is actually put against the action to see how it works. If you get this far, consider yourself on the home stretch. I finally realized that I had to make personal acquaintances with the music supervisors themselves. When I did this, things started to pop. After one of the great "Music & Tennis Festivals" held in the '80s and early '90s (the brainchild of one of the authors of this book, "Coach" Dave Austin, along with his good buddy Phil Ehart, drummer for Kansas), I ran into noted music supervisor Budd Carr. He told me about a new John Candy movie he was advising called *Delirious,* and I ended up co-writing the end title, "Beyond Our Wildest Dreams" (beating out "Unforgettable" by Irving Gordon, if you can believe that!). No matter how good your publisher is, there's no substitute for personal contact.

"The best way to get music to me is 'proximity' at the right time. I was recently on a panel hosted by the Recording Academy and a songwriter asked 'How does one get songs to you?' I then asked if he had a demo CD with him — the answer was no, and I simply said, 'Missed opportunity.' Be ready for those special moments when opportunity meets preparation."

—Budd Carr, Music Supervisor for *Terminator, JFK, Wall Street,* and *Platoon*

There are specific magazines such as *Variety* and *The Hollywood Reporter* with Web sites that cater to the film industry and movie aficionados. Often they'll report on movies in the planning stage and films that are in progress. They'll usually list the film company, director, producer, and sometimes even the music supervisor. Start making inquiries and requests with your own professionally worded letter, or one from your music attorney, reflecting your interest in submitting songs for the project. If you have a publisher, have them make calls to music supervisors on your behalf or obtain lists from them of the ones that you can approach yourself.

Understanding the creative side of songwriting for films

Writing for film can be a wonderful, though sometimes frustrating, experience. At its best, it gives a songwriter a wonderful storyline, already created, to expand upon. When you get good at it, you can read a script and songs will seem to leap off the pages of certain scenes. Capturing the essence of a scene without being too obvious is an art in and of itself. If you are a composer scoring a movie (as opposed to writing specific songs for certain scenes), most film companies will send you *rushes,* or film footage, of the *dailies* (the scene shot that day) from which to score. There is usually a very short turnaround time in which to complete deadlines.

Personally, I love a song that spotlights, fairly literally, the action on the screen. "Let's Hear It for the Boy" (written by Dean Pitchford and Thomas Snow, sung by Denise Williams) from the '80s smash feature *Footloose* is a great example of a song illuminating the storyline. But many directors (and thus many music supervisors) are squeamish about songs being too literal to the scene. It strikes them as corny or *operatic* (where the songs virtually *are* the storyline). I learned that the hard way with "Long Road Home," which I was commissioned to write for *Backdraft.* In the end, it was disqualified for the line, "still we're keeping alive the flame" — flames being too literal to the fires that appeared in practically every scene.

"I look for music that makes the action in the scene comfortable or effective. When you are out to dinner at a romantic restaurant on a first date, Nine Inch Nails music is probably not as appropriate as a jazz piano — although at times in order to heighten tension or amplify action, music can play against the grain of a scene. When looking for a song, sometimes the movie needs a big name or a familiar song for the scene to help the movie — so I'm not looking particularly for the best song for the scene; I'm looking for a combination of the best song for the scene from the right artist. At other times, it is purely the song that works best for the scene regardless if the song is from an unknown or known artist."

—Budd Carr

Songwriting for Television

Billions of viewers can't be wrong! And as long as there's TV, there's got to be music to go along with both its brilliance and inanity. The synergy between songs and television and the exposure you can receive for one of your songs being on a program is staggering. Many songs have languished on shelves until some visionary director discovers it while station surfing in his Porsche and decides to feature it the next episode of his series.

Sometimes all it takes for a great song to be recognized is one person in a position of power to hear it at just the right time. When Michael J. Fox's first show, *Family Ties,* featured an obscure song by Billy (Vera) and The Beaters, "At This Moment" (written by Bill McCord), the phones at the radio stations lit up with requests for a song that had been ignored for six years! Television can be one of the most powerful stimulants to record success.

Knowing the kinds of songs used for television

Producers of television shows are constantly calling publishers to license preexisting songs for use in their episodes. But in addition to this, they also commission new songs, *incidental music* (the music that plays under specific scenes), and theme music to flesh out this season's "big push" series. Even though the budgets are slimmer for TV shows and time limits are tighter, they're still a worthy goal for the songwriter, due to the exposure received and the monies generated by repeated performances of the same show. Can you imagine being the composer of the *I Love Lucy, Dick Van Dyke Show,* or *NYPD Blue*'s themes? You could literally retire on those royalties!

The fees generated for writing the background music for a half-hour sitcom or drama might be around $10,000 (and you pick up the recording tab!). But for theme music, get ready to receive from $10,000 up to $100,000 for writing the main song for a "major push" series (and get the wheel barrel ready to collect the performance dollars that ASCAP, BMI, or SESAC will be sending to your door!). See Chapter 18 for more details on performance dollars.

When a song of yours is being licensed for a particular scene in a television show, your fee will be substantially lower than you might expect — usually between $1,000 and $10,000 — but don't forget the added bonus of performance fees generated by its use.

Recognizing the exposure value of television

Many songwriters and artists have been boosted to fame from exposure on television. Singer Vonda Sheppard found the public ear though her appearances on *Ally McBeal* (making major bucks for the songwriters featured in her inspired re-interpretations of soul and rock classics). In addition to Vonda-type stories, many songs have found an audience by being exposed on the small screen. You may find opportunities for title songs like "I'll Be There for You" (written by D. Crane, M. Kaufman, M. Skloff, P. Solem, D. Wilde, and A. Willis), the theme for the smash series *Friends* by pop-rock group The Rembrandts. Not only do they get their moniker on the *crawl* (the tiny and rapidly moving credits that roll as the theme music fades), but they get the added promotion of the weekly exposure on a network smash. This song was catapulted to number one because of its extreme catchiness and the mass acceptance of this show. The Rembrandts just happened to capture the essence and demographic of this inventive ensemble comedy.

Especially if you are a singer/songwriter, you can expand your chances of success by sending your songs to television production houses and *clearance services* (the agencies that specialize in licensing preexisting compositions for use in television shows). The song "Superman (It's Not Easy)" (written by John Ondrasik; performed by Five for Fighting) was brought to the public's attention by its inclusion in the WB channel's series, *Smallville* — the hook line, "It's not easy to be me," fit like a glove into the premise of Superman living among mortals in the small town of Smallville, U.S.A.

I received a request recently from *The Man Show* of Comedy Central fame, to license my song "Vehicle." The contract had provisions for its use for one year and an increased fee if the producers decided to pick it up for a number of additional years. It was a no-lose situation for me because it put a few dollars in my pocket, increased the exposure of one of my primary cash cows, and did nothing to disqualify it from consideration by any of the big commercial corporations that might consider my song for use. Even though the money wasn't huge, I happily agreed to its use. Judging from the response I received from the press and the returns I saw from ASCAP, I'm glad I did.

As a budding songwriter, make a list of songs you think would be appropriate for some of your favorite shows, or better still, target certain shows to write for. Even if they don't hit their intended goal, they may serve as songs you can use or pitch for other applications.

"I get asked all the time how a composer/songwriter gets their music into the right hands to be considered for television. My reply is simply: persistence in following your dreams. Keep your vision in front of you."

—John D'Andrea, MusicWorks, arranger and producer

Pre-fab groups like the Monkees and The Partridge Family (and okay, also The Brady Bunch) actually paved the way for songwriters for hire to submit songs to be considered by major sitcoms. As manufactured and artificial as these groups were, they inspired many catchy songs by the likes of songwriting teams like Carole King and Gerry Goffin, Neil Diamond, and John Stewart to do some of their best writing. Apparently TV is one of those media types that strike a responsive chord in people, whether you are merely watching or participating in its creation.

The hit show *CSI* uses The Who's classic, "Who Are You" to open every show. Aimee Mann's "That's Just What You Are" was regularly featured on *Melrose Place* and appears on the soundtrack for the show. It really doesn't matter the vintage or style of a particular song. In television, all that's in contention is the impact it has in context of the scene.

Getting to television music supervisors

Television, just like with movies, uses music supervisors and this is your first choice in submitting songs to get yours placed on a show. In fact, because music budgets in television are almost always smaller than movies, a new songwriter usually has a better chance of getting their song on a TV show than in a movie. The music supervisor for television usually doesn't have the budget for an established or current hit, so when a great song comes across their desk that fits what they need, it's a win-win situation — they can usually get the song under contract within their budget and the songwriter/artist gets valuable exposure, not to mention a great credit and a reasonable amount of money to add into their bank account.

Many times *The Hollywood Reporter* or *Variety Magazine* will list production schedules and the music supervisors signed on. An annual publication called the *Music Supervisor Directory* lists over 600 music supervisors complete with their contact information. If you're really adventurous, you can also explore who the picture editor is for a show (the person who takes the film dailies and pieces them together into a rough cut for the producer/director to review the work in progress) and send that person your song as well. The picture editor usually likes to create their rough cuts to music for added impact, mood, and ambiance. When a producer/director is reviewing the rough cuts, they might just like the song so much they'll ask the music supervisor to include that song in the final cut.

Songwriting for Commercials

Okay, so you didn't become a songwriter to sell beer and tires, but neither did a great many famous songwriters of our time, who created a win-win for themselves by helping to sell products without selling their souls. The *jingle,* as it has been called inexplicably for the last three decades, is a source of inspiration and income for songwriters and composers that could well be considered manna from Heaven. Many composers and songwriters make a very good living writing specific songs for specific products. Some of these songs have actually crossed over to the hit parade. Songs like "No Matter What Shape (You're Stomach's In)" written by Stormie and Michael Omartian, performed by The T-Bones (from an antacid commercial); "I'd Like to Teach the World to Sing (In Perfect Harmony)" written by William Backer, Roger Cook, Roquel Davis, and Roger Greenway, performed by the Hilltop Singers and The New Seekers (which started life as a Coke jingle); and "Percolator Twist" written by Lou Bideu and Ernest Freeman, performed by Billy Joe and the Checkmates (the Maxwell House coffee song) have all percolated into top 40 hits. Other songwriters have made millions by licensing their old hits to huge conglomerates for elephant bucks. Still others have actually found that leasing their latest release to a product line is a great alternative means to promote their record, especially when traditional airplay on radio can be so hard to come by.

Take a look now at the basic ways you can harness your songwriting talents to enter the world of commercials — and make big loot to boot!

Writing jingles from scratch

Writing a jingle from scratch requires the expertise of the songwriter to spotlight the product, service, or company in the desired light. Whatever the image of that company or product is — it's the goal of the jingle writer to cement that into the hearts and minds of the listening and viewing audience. Catchy melodies, rhythms, and catch phrases are the stock in trade of a good jingle. An effective jingle is like a hit song on speed — you only have 30 to 60 seconds (or less) to make your impression, get your message across, and set up the product you are helping to sell. Jingles are usually very simple, repetitive, and full of the kind of sound effects that catch the ear. To write a good jingle, it's important to get as much input from the client (the actual people writing the checks to the ad agency) as possible, and to get a clear-cut picture of the entire campaign they are planning. Oftentimes, a jingle house will do several treatments of the same slogan or catchphrase in an attempt to please the consensus at the company level. Many of the same principles we examine for writing a full-length song can be applied to writing a jingle. Rhyme, rhythm, and melody all come heavily into play. But remember, due to the time constraints of the average commercial, when it comes to the element of song structure, the jingle is often limited to chorus only.

Fees for coming up with a new jingle for a product can range as high as $50,000 and may include renewal fees for every period the lease is extended. In addition, the jingle writer will usually play on his own song, reaping heaps of additional income for radio, network, and cable television airplay from the musicians union. If he sings on the spot as well, he'll also receive payment from the Screen Actors Guild (SAG) and the American Federation of Television and Radio Artists (AFTRA). Now how does all that grab you?

Visiting a music house

Often an ad agency will come up with a concept for a product that they've been hired to represent. They'll then contact a *music house* (a company whose job it is to create and record commercials) for them to turn the concept into the sound of music — and money. On staff at the music house are various musicians who specialize in providing the ad agency and ultimately the product honchos with what they need to sell their product. Sometimes they'll be asked merely to do a *treatment* (basically a different arrangement) of a preexisting jingle. Other times they'll be asked to do a *sound alike* of a famous hit that they'd like to use. Other times they'll request a commercial (or spot, in the jingle jargon) based on the original recording of a hit. But what really defines a great music house is its writer's ability to create new jingles *from scratch*.

For many years, my voice was heard in the context of commercials. I had what the jingle houses referred to as a *beer and tires voice* — kind of gruff and macho. I came to really respect the songwriters behind the jingles I sang. Can you remember, "Look out for The Bull, look out for the Schlitz Malt Liquor bull" or "The friendly skies of your land, United Airlines?" These were a couple of the memorable songs I got to sing. I also sang a treatment of "Good Vibrations" for Sunkist Orange Soda — the new hook was "I'm drinkin' up orange vibrations, Sunkist Orange Soda taste sensation." Finally when my own hits started coming and I hit the road, I pretty much had to give up the jingle scene. But I'll never forget those jingle producers telling me to "put more smile in it!" the time I had to sing "like a rice crispy," or the cat food commercial where my one enthusiastic line was, "The meat/fish group!"

"Writing jingles from scratch makes up perhaps 50 percent of the work we do. The other 50 percent is adapting songs for new campaigns. Of the original songs I come up with, about 70 percent are instrumental tracks and 30 percent are sung. Fees vary greatly depending on the client's budget and the music house's reputation for success. Typical creative fees for a spot run anywhere from $5,000 to $50,000 (for a big campaign with a corporate behemoth like McDonald's.) The jingle writer can also look forward to performance money when the jingle is played, since both BMI and ASCAP monitor airplay activity on your commercial (but don't expect publishing income since it's pro-forma that the ad agency retains the publishing on songs it commissions). In addition, if you play and sing on your own spot, you'll be printin' money!"

—Matt Thornton, creative director of Track Attack music house

If you're eager to break into the world of jingle writing, put together a reel of some of your best material. You may even want to "mock up" some jingles for products that may or may not exist to give examples of the kind of work you are capable of. Go around to the ad agencies in town and introduce yourself and your work. Another way to go would be to take your demo reel to existing music houses to try to get hired there. Sometimes learning the ropes and making contacts at an established company is the best primer for moving on later to your own company.

Getting your songs in commercials

If you have a song or a number of preexisting songs that you think would be ideal for the commercial market, contact the various ad agencies and request permission to submit those songs to their musical supervisor. Whether you're an established songwriter or a beginner, this process is much the same. There are many well-known songwriters who compile samplers of all their hits to remind the various advertising agencies of their songs. All it takes is one "ear" at the agency to hear a song and say, "Hey, that would be perfect for our client's product!" Even as an unproven songwriter, if you put together a professional looking and sounding CD sampler of your songs (complete with lyric sheets and all contact information; see Chapter 17) one of them just might catch the imagination of an ad executive. Some of the big agencies you'd want to get your material to are Leo Burnett and ddb in Chicago, BBDO and Lintass in New York, and McCann Erickson in Troy, Michigan.

Songwriting for Musicals

The excitement and lure of the Broadway stage has inspired writers to come up with some of the greatest songs of all time. Before there were motion pictures there was the theater. Live dramatic presentations were the way playwrights and composers brought their stories to life. It remains, to this day, a vibrant messenger of emotion, song, and story. The excitement surrounding a top-notch musical can be electric. Songwriting teams like Rodgers and Hart and songwriters like the Gershwin brothers made their considerable fortunes from the songs they wrote for Broadway musicals.

Many songwriters I know draw a great deal of inspiration from the Broadway stage. To imagine your song being performed by a major star in the context of a powerful story is pretty good motivation to come up with a great one. After my wife and I saw *Cats*, I had all the ammunition I needed to finish a song I was working on at the time, "Man Against the World." That song may never make it to the stage, but as writers we can often draw from its power to bring a song to fruition.

Submitting your songs for musicals

If you're a songwriter eager to break into theater, it may be best to start at the local level in community theater. You'll start to get a grasp of the breakdown of responsibilities of the various people who comprise a theater company and get to try out your music in front of a sympathetic audience. Try to make acquaintances with local directors and discuss their musical needs. Attend as many theater workshops and round tables as possible (for a comprehensive guide to U.S. theater companies and workshops, be sure to check out the book *Songwriter's Market*). And above all, attend as many top-notch musicals as you can afford to see where the bar has to be set to make it all the way to Broadway! Make contact with the musical director if you can — she'll be the one making decisions on what songwriters will be involved in a plays production. Your demos can be sent in care of that person to the musical's main production headquarters.

Understanding the creative side of songwriting for musicals

All the business stuff won't mean too much if you don't have some great songs to go along with the excitement and drama onstage. This is your chance as a songwriter to get large, wear your emotions on your sleeve and your heart in your throat. The scale of most productions is big enough to accept songs that are sweeping in their panorama of feeling.

"I have learned to paint with broad strokes in the songs I write for the stage. I try to keep lyrics simple and not too busy because in an ambient theater, words are easily lost. All the great words in the world won't mean a thing if intelligibility suffers. Also, it is important to use musical devices that assure heightened drama — like key modulations at choruses and sometimes a second modulation upward at the final chorus. Extreme dynamics from loud to soft is another way to wake up your audience. Many of these writing cues were created for Broadway for specific dramatic effect. When I write rock 'n' roll, I have to hold myself back a bit from it from becoming too Broadway."

—Jimmy Nichols, musician and composer

Writing songs for musicals is much like writing songs for other purposes. Big titles and memorable melodic hooks become even more important in the theater. It's the goal of every songwriter who writes for musicals to send the people away singing the featured songs. Generally, the lyrics of these songs mirror the action and emotion of a particular scene. Keep in mind that the plot of a musical can be a constantly changing thing. With those changes, the songwriter has to be open to adapting his songs to the ever-changing shape and landscape of the play.

"In writing music for musicals, flexibility is the key. Unlike writing a popular song, where the composer is in total control of the musical and lyrical content, in musical theater, oftentimes the composer must be cognizant of the ever-changing facets of the book. In Broadway terms, the book means the script of the stage play. If the director cuts a scene or wants quicker character development, the book is always changing, therefore a song that was appropriate at one point of the play's development may no longer fit the new scene. Even when the play finally opens, there is inevitably fine-tuning of songs and scenes. Showboat was written 75 years ago and they're still fooling around with the book!"

—Dennis DeYoung, noted composer of the musical adaptation of The Hunchback Of Notre Dame and founding member of platinum rock band Styx.

Practice Makes Perfect

Throughout this book, we talk about preparation meeting opportunity. If you are serious about your songwriting, you can't do enough to prepare yourself for moments of opportunities. In this practice, I'd like you to pick three of your favorite shows. Record an episode of each on tape. Turn off the volume and begin imagining what music you'd put under the scenes, then also try your hand at writing a song that fits a particular scene — since these are your favorites, you'll probably know most of the lines anyway, so turning off the sound shouldn't hinder you much. As you do this, you may discover that you have a real knack and love for doing this kind of writing, so put your best work on a demo CD and get your networking shoes on. Who knows when you'll be at the right place at the right time, and when the opportunity to get your CD to the "right people" will arise?

Part V
Getting Down to Business

The 5th Wave   By Rich Tennant

Harriet Attempts to Promote Her First Song

Tasty Treat Ice Cream

"Okay, one more time past the music publishers house, and then I resume the route, and you're back to 'Pop Goes the Weasel.'"

In this part . . .

Just so all your best songwriting efforts don't languish on the shelf collecting dust instead of royalties, in this part, we get into the business side of music and songwriting. We tell you about the business team you can assemble to make sure your songs get to the right homes and are protected and collected on properly. You see how the right collaborator can help you complete your musical vision and the way you can make goals and deadlines work to your advantage. We look at the various ways your little ditty can make some serious dough. And we examine the networking possibilities that can increase your creative and business powers exponentially.

Chapter 13

Introducing the Business Players

- -

In This Chapter

▶ Assembling an effective business team

▶ Choosing and using a music attorney

▶ Navigating the roles of a publisher

▶ Considering the use of a song plugger

▶ Looking at the roles of managers and agents

▶ Managing your money and business affairs

- -

*W*hether you've just finished your very first song or you already have a CD full of completed gems ready to go, your next step is choosing the right people to help your "children" find a good home. Your success will depend not only on the quality of your song, but also on the specialized team that you assemble to market it. Your rock just won't roll unless your business team is rock-solid and your common goals are unified.

In this chapter, we look at the job descriptions of the various business players and give you some criteria for judging them. We discuss methods of locating the right people and suggest a few questions you can ask to improve your chances of making all the right moves.

Putting Together Your Business Team

A major step toward achieving success is choosing the right team to work together in getting exposure for your songs and you as a songwriter. Some writers thrive on the business side of the music industry, but more typically, writers prefer spending their time creating new songs — not filling out forms, reading contracts, and making follow-up phone calls to record companies and managers. If you're a songwriter in this latter category, you'll want to find people to help you so you can spend your time doing what you do best. You'll need one or more of the following experts on your side:

✔ **Music attorney:** The expert in all the legal questions that you'll encounter, especially as you get further and further along in the field of songwriting.

✔ **Song publisher:** The company — large or small, major or independent — responsible for one or more of a variety of duties on your behalf, including soliciting or shopping your song or songs to artists, record companies, producers, and artist managers; teaming you up with other writers and artists who write; and handling administrative duties, namely, filing copyright forms, and filing notices with agencies to collect your mechanical royalties (see Chapter 18 for more on mechanical royalties) or collecting the money themselves.

✔ **Song plugger:** The person who will, for a monthly retainer or a percentage of the publishing rights upon his getting an artist to record your song, shop your song around to the music world.

✔ **Manager:** The person who has the ability to put you together with music attorneys, song publishers, and song pluggers. A highly qualified manager can oversee your songwriting career in its entirety and help you to make the best-informed decisions.

✔ **Agent:** The person, who will, if you are a performing songwriter, secure live engagements for you to give your songs and you as an artist the much-needed exposure.

✔ **Accountant:** The person who keeps track of your songwriting income and the expenses you incur in getting your songwriting career off the ground. An accountant will also help you in your financial planning and tax accounting.

When you're just starting out, you may have to function as a kind of one-man band until you can afford the luxury of hiring the services of others. You'll have to be very hands-on when it comes down to cutting demos, copyrighting, shopping (the process of soliciting your song to artists and artists' representatives), and registering your songs. If you can't afford to hire representatives in each category, review the job descriptions and see what duties you can undertake yourself. We help direct you as to which jobs can be done on your own.

Music Business Registry, Music Business Attorney, Legal and Business Affairs Registry, Film and Television Music Guide (all published by Ritch Esra, The Music Business Registry, *The Musician's Atlas* (published by the Music Resource Group), *Billboard Musician's Guide to Touring and Promotion, Music Row,* and *Mix Masters Directory* are useful publications to get your hands on. Each of these directories are at least updated at least annually and give you information and contact resources for music attorneys, song pluggers, and publishers, as well as record companies, producers, and engineers. (For information and Web site addresses for these publications, turn to Appendix B.)

First Things First: Getting an Attorney on Your Side

A music attorney should be one of the first business associates you add to your team. This person can be your best friend and ally, so hiring your attorney in the beginning will start your team off with the right offense and defense. Good attorneys don't come cheap, but a good one is worth his weight in gold because he can help you avoid the pitfalls so many of us fall into and guide you into fair contracts with reputable people. Because of the importance of this person's role, some say, if you choose to handle your own legal representation, you may end up with a fool for a client.

Discovering what a good music attorney can do for you

A good music attorney will have contacts with artists' managers, publishers, song pluggers, record company artist and repertoire (A&R) people, and the artists themselves. With a good attorney, you don't have to worry about not having 35 years experience in the business. A desirable music attorney does all the following:

- Makes sure that every piece of paper that you are asked to sign is fully negotiated in your best interest and makes sure that you fully understand what you are signing.

- Puts you in touch with other potential team players such as publishers, managers, agents, accountants, and other songwriters.

- Promotes you among her friends and associates and raises your visibility in the music world.

- Adds credibility and prestige to you as a songwriter — if she happens to garner the respect of her peers in the business.

- Gets A&R people, record labels, publishers, and artists to listen to your work.

- Analyzes contracts previously signed for ways to permit her to renegotiate, expand upon, or even invalidate an unfair contract.

- Upholds and defends your legal rights in the case of a dispute and deals with any "breaches of contract" (when someone fails to live up to their part of the bargain).

If you start your team off with an attorney, the rest of the players will appreciate it. Many industry professionals prefer not to hear from you directly — they'd rather talk with an experienced music attorney.

Hiring a music attorney

For starters, make a list of potential candidate's referrals you receive through other musicians. You can also call one of the performance rights organizations such as ASCAP or BMI, as they can be helpful making a recommendation on a music attorney to handle your needs. There are also listings of music attorneys in publications such as the ones listed under "Putting Together Your Business Team" tip earlier in this chapter. By the way, an attorney need not be in your home town to be effective. Although face-to-face contact is always preferred, with phones, fax, and e-mail, long distance communication has never been easier. Write letters of introduction to those on your list and follow up with a friendly phone call. If they fail to call you back after a few tries, either they're too busy for you anyway, or they lack in the courtesy you're looking for. Keep searching and soon you'll be sure to find the one with the expertise you need who also happens to match your personal wavelength.

Although there are many top-flight, caring attorneys who reach out to bands, artists, and songwriters they've seen perform at various showcases to offer a helping hand (sometimes for free), they'll always ask the person if he already has legal representation. Beware of the ones that try to persuade you away from your current attorney.

After you make a solid connection with an attorney by phone, the next step, if at all possible, is to set up an interview at the attorney's offices. You need to be in harmony with the person who's going to help you make tons of money with your music, so be armed with specific questions when you have your interview. Let the attorney's answers to each of the following questions help you decide whether or not you want this person on your business team:

- ✔ **Is your practice limited to music?** A jack-of-all trade's attorney may not be the master of any. (Your dad's real estate attorney who "plays a little banjo," ain't gonna cut it.) Look for an attorney who specializes in music law. Next, find out what his specialty is within that broad category. For instance, if his forte is negotiating recording and publishing deals, make sure he also feels comfortable handling copyright issues and royalty questions, or has others on his staff that he can pass the baton to when the need arises.

- ✔ **Whom do you represent?** See if, on his list of clients, you recognize the names of any big success stories that have inspired you. Also, check for any conflicts of interest. For instance, does he represent any publishing companies that may want to sign you to a future deal? That's something you may want to avoid.

✔ **How much experience do you have?** This might tell you how much time he's going to have to spend with you. Find the one attorney who has enough experience in business to make you feel confidant in his services, but also whose workload won't make you feel like you're at the bottom of his totem pole.

✔ **How much will your services cost?** You can expect a variety of options, and there are pros and cons for any of the following fee arrangements:

- **Retainer:** Simply put, this is when you pay your attorney a fixed advance, usually monthly, from which his fees and expenses are deducted.

- **Hourly rate:** The attorney keeps track of the time spent on your behalf, and you're billed on a monthly basis. You can expect the hourly rate to be $100 to $500 per hour, billed in 15-minute increments. In addition to the billed time, all expenses for phone, postage, photocopies, and so on will be added to the bill.

- **Fixed flat fee:** Usually, this is a fixed amount that's proposed by the attorney when a deal is being negotiated for your project — like when you're offered a huge amount of money and you don't know how much of your attorney's time you'll need, and you want to call him at all hours of the night! The fee could be $5,000 or even $100,000 depending on the deal.

- **Reasonable fee:** This arrangement is similar to the fixed flat fee; however the amount is not arrived at until after the deal is completed — which could be sticky and lead to unpleasant surprises. If you're ever offered a reasonable-fee deal, be very cautious!

- **Percentage:** Now we're talking popular! Here's an arrangement most people would enjoy having. Typically, 5 to 10 percent goes to the attorney who negotiates the deal. This is based on whatever you receive, whether it's from an advance payment or from royalties down the road. With this type of arrangement, you get all the professional advice you need when you need it, and if there's no deal, there's no pay except for expenses — it's kind of like profit sharing with this type of arrangement. The attorney will be highly motivated to keep working with you when he sees big bucks added to his bank account.

The important thing is to establish a fee arrangement that you feel comfortable with *before* any work begins. Think about it — surprises are much more fun at birthday parties!

✔ **How strong are your contacts?** Let's face it. Networking and access are important aspects to consider as far as what this team player can offer you. An attorney's clients, contacts, and relationships are important aspects to consider in making your choice.

After completing your interviews, asking your questions, and checking up on references, it's time to decide. Look at your notes and organize them into a pros-and-cons list for each attorney. Why would this attorney be good for you? What are his strengths and weaknesses? Take a look at your lists and see which attorney best fits your needs. Perhaps it may be wise at this point to whittle down your choices to just two or three attorneys, and then take some time to digest each of their answers and reflect on their personalities and contacts before making a final decision. With all of this in mind, go ahead and try to make a choice.

Looking at Your Publishing Options

After finding the right music attorney, the single most important issue to consider is publishing. A publisher is the person or group of people who are responsible for managing the career of your songs. A good publisher, by being at the heart of the action of the music business, will be aware of all the opportunities available for your song. Check out this list of the functions a music publisher may provide:

- ✔ Soliciting your songs to artists, artist managers, agents, producers, A&R representatives at record labels, and to anyone else who has a connection to an artist looking for material.

- ✔ Finding opportunities for you and your songs in film, television, and theater.

- ✔ Putting you together with other songwriters in their publishing stable and even those outside of the company.

- ✔ Putting you together with the artists themselves to write songs.

- ✔ Providing you with inside information as to which artists are looking for material so that you may set your writing sites on those goals and scan your back catalogue of songs for appropriate *pitches* (a pitch, in publisher's lingo, is the act of putting the right song into the right hands).

- ✔ Critiquing your work and guiding the creative aspects of your growth as a songwriter.

- ✔ Helping to negotiate contracts on your behalf with other writers, foreign publishers, sheet music publishers, film companies, and so forth.

- ✔ Granting licenses to those who would like to use your song.

- ✔ Handling administrative duties such as copyrighting your songs, filing notices with performance organizations (ASCAP, BMI, and SESAC) for songs that receive airplay, registering your song with the various agencies like Harry Fox that collect your mechanical royalties, (the monies a writer and publisher receive on every record sold), collecting your mechanical royalties themselves, doing general accounting, and of course paying you your writers royalties (generally on a quarterly basis).

✔ Providing upfront money to a writer in the form of advances either in a lump sum, annually, monthly, or a weekly salary.

✔ Footing the demo bills on songs they've approved, and on occasion, even making the demos themselves. (Demos are the demonstration recordings of your song — see Chapter 17 for more details.)

✔ Advising you on all aspects of your songwriting career and finding every opportunity possible for your song (everything from television commercials to uses by choirs and marching bands!).

JIM SAYS

If a publishing company likes your work enough to sign you as a writer, they may also be nice enough to give you some money, so you can actually stay afloat while indulging in your passion of songwriting. This money will come in the form of advances upon your future royalties (did you think you wouldn't have to pay it back?), and it's doled out in either weekly or monthly portions, or it's given in one or two chunks during the year. Your music attorney may also specify in your contract with the publisher that the publisher will spring for your song demos, for lyric translations into other languages, and for the production of sheet music. If you happen to be an aspiring performer as well as a songwriter, they might even assist you in securing a record deal. The publisher will also administer your song — which means they'll take care of all the paperwork and registrations for your song, as well as collect all your royalties and disburse them to you, usually quarterly, along with a detailed accounting.

If it sounds to you like a music publisher plays a vital role in the future of your song and songwriting career, you guessed right. However, finding the publisher to fit your specific goals is not always easy. You need to find a publisher that is not only passionate about your songs, but has the connections to find placement for those songs. The right publisher will know your songs almost as well as you do in order to make well-informed pitches. Also, you must be sure to get adequate attention from the publishing staff. Take a look at the types of publishing companies from which you have to choose (for lists of companies in each category, refer to the publications listed earlier in this chapter or consult The Songwriters Guild of America):

✔ **Major publishing companies:** There are a few behemoths out there that are certainly worth your consideration. When a large company is running on all cylinders, it's hard to beat. Many of them have the staff and track record to go the distance with your song. They have developed clout in the industry through the big name writers and artists they are associated with. The major publisher will also have the cash flow to offer you an advance and be generous in demo budgets. Companies like Warner/Chappell, BMG, Zomba, Sony, Almo/Irving, EMI, and Famous all have great reputations for servicing their writers' needs. The fact that some of these publishers are affiliated with record companies seems only to be an advantage.

✔ **Mid-sized publishing companies:** These companies still have the advantage of an adequate staff to handle your many songwriting needs — though the companies themselves are not as large. Often their stable of writers will be smaller, and they may have offices in one or two cities as opposed to worldwide. If you want the advantages of a major, but are afraid you'll get lost in the shuffle, a mid-sized company may be right for you.

✔ **Independent publishing companies:** If you're not looking for big cash advances and want "a few good men (and women)" representing your songs, an independent publisher may fit your needs. These small independent companies will often make deals on a per-song basis — whereby you make a deal for one song at a time, usually with a two-year reversion clause, which means if they fail to place your song within that period, the publishing rights will go back to you. (The larger major companies will also make deals on a per-song basis, but focus more on acquiring song catalogues and signing songwriters as entities, as opposed to individual songs.)

No matter which publishing option you choose be sure to have the advice of a qualified music attorney on your side. Make sure every contract is fully negotiated on your behalf and that you understand what you are signing.

Whether you sign with a major, mid-sized, or small independent company, the range of compensation for representing your songs is the same. To understand better how a publisher is paid, think of a song you write as 100 percent. (If you wrote less than 100 percent of the song — for instance 50 percent, base your calculations on that figure being 100 percent of your share.) Of your 100 percent, 50 percent is the "writer's share" and 50 percent is the "publisher's share." Generally, when a publisher makes a deal with a new writer, unless that writer has a very powerful attorney or is an artist/writer about to break on his own, the publishing company will demand 100 percent of the publisher's share (in other words 50 percent of the income on the entire song). The length of your agreement is an important negotiation point, and whether you get the full rights to your songs back at the end of the agreement depends on you and your attorney's or manager's leverage in the business.

As a songwriter just starting out, you may have a better chance landing a deal on a per-song basis with a smaller publishing company because they'll incur considerably less financial risk on your behalf for this type of deal. You might also consider making an agreement with an independent song plugger — because although they are investing their precious time on your behalf, and because they're not advancing you money — their investment in you is fairly modest.

Co-publishing deals

Depending on your status as a songwriter and the power of your attorney, you can often enter into a co-publishing venture with an established publishing company whereby you get to split the publishing 50/50. Generally, the established company will want to retain administration rights, which will keep them in the driver's seat when it comes to many future decisions. (For instance, you as a co-publisher will not be allowed to sell your share of the publishing without the main publisher's consent.) Co-publishing deals are common for self-contained bands and artists with a built-in following that makes a publisher's job a lot easier. Co-publishing deals are also common for writer/producers with a built-in means for getting songs placed and songwriters with many contacts with artists and their representatives and record labels.

When my managers made my first publishing deal for me with a major (previously they handled my publishing themselves), I already had enough hits under my belt to warrant a co-publishing agreement — whereby I got to retain 50 percent ownership of the publishing. I didn't, however, have enough clout for my songs to revert back to me at the end of the contract's term. Therefore all my early songs published by Warner/Chappell will receive 50 percent of the publishing income for the "life of copyright" or 70 years longer than I live. In later deals, my attorney was able to negotiate the reversion of publishing back to me at the end of the contract's term.

Being your own publisher

Sometimes a writer will decide to be his own team player and handle the publishing duties himself. Here are some of the plusses of retaining your own publishing:

- You get to keep all of the income your song ultimately generates, the writer's share and the publisher's share.

- You have the freedom of making deals on a per-song basis with various independent publishers.

- You steer clear of the inter-company politics that have been known to exist within a company where one writer will receive advantage over another due to track record or personal alliances with members of the staff.

And, here are some of the minuses of being your own publisher:

- You have to do much of the business duties and paperwork and you have considerably less time to do what you do best — write songs.

> ✔ You may lack the contacts to fully exploit your songs.
>
> ✔ You lose the advantage of working with other writer's on a publisher's roster.

If you have contacts of your own in the music business, have a flair for salesmanship, or you're an artist recording your own songs and therefore do not require song pitching, self-publishing may be an option for you. Here's a list of the steps to take when forming your own publishing company.

1. **Become a member:** Set up your company with one of the performing rights organizations — ASCAP, BMI, or SESAC. Generally they'll require that a recording of one or more of your songs is about to be released for sale, heard in a movie or on a television program, or has been broadcast on the radio.

2. **Choose your name:** Come up with three choices of names for your company in order of preference. The performing rights organization will then do a computer search for names already taken and advise you accordingly. Unless your given name is extremely common, it's a good idea to name your company after yourself. Using your own name is another way of getting your name out in front of people. The other option is finding a highly creative name for your company that in all likelihood has not been used. Be prepared for a modest application fee and annual fee in order to belong to one of these agencies.

3. **File your name:** Once you've locked in your name, go to your local county clerk's office and fill out the necessary forms to set up a DBA (doing business as) with the same name as your publishing company. (If your name is the name of the publisher, you can skip this step.) You should then open a separate business banking account under that name You must also give notice through a local publication that gives the required notice that you are doing business under that name. (The county clerk's office can direct you in these matters.)

4. **File your copyrights:** Register the songs in your new company with the U.S. Copyright Office (Library of Congress). If they are already copyrighted, you'll want to register them again as published works.

5. **Register for royalties:** Be sure to notify your performing and mechanical rights organizations of all songs that'll be hitting the airwaves either on radio, television, or motion pictures (or sold to the public), so they can pay you and your company the performance royalties. (For an explanation of royalties refer to Chapter 18.)

Although it's relatively simple and cost effective to set up your own publishing company, the proof is in the pudding. If you can handle all the detail work necessary to be effective, and have the willingness to hit the phones to make contacts and follow up — more power to you. Your own publishing could be an enjoyable and profitable venture. If not, you're better off to enlist the help of an already established company.

Working with administration deals

A good half-way point between signing away your publishing to a publishing company and doing the publishing yourself, is entering into an administration deal. In this arrangement, a writer would have his own publishing company, but would sign a deal with a publishing administrator to handle all the paperwork involved in running his company. For a commission of between 5 and 15 percent of the publishing royalties for the contracted period (typically 1 to 3 years), the administrator's job is to register copyrights, fill out ASCAP, BMI, or SESAC forms, grant licenses to those who wish to record your song, and negotiate synchronization fees for those wishing to use your song in films or commercials. (A synch fee is paid to the writer for the right to "synchronize" his music with the action on film.) In addition, the administrator will collect your royalties and pay them out to you on a quarterly basis. Some administrators will use the services of an outside collection agency such as The Harry Fox Agency to do the royalty collection — others do it themselves.

Here are some plusses in making an administration deal:

- ✔ The administrator takes a massive burden off the songwriter who runs his own publishing company, freeing him up for the creative side, including writing and *song casting* (getting the right song to the right artist).

- ✔ You can retain your publishing rights since the administrator generally doesn't have ownership of the song, but instead is paid a percentage of the song's earnings for the contracted period.

- ✔ You can harness the administration skill of a large experienced publisher without signing over the publishing rights.

- ✔ If you are a self-contained singer/songwriter or have a deal with an independent song plugger (see following section on independent song pluggers), you may not require your songs to be shopped to other artists, and may only need someone to do your paperwork and disburse your money. So, why give up a major portion of your publishing share to a publisher.

And, here are some minuses of administration deals:

- ✔ No monetary advances in the form of weekly salaries or yearly guarantees are made in administration deals. You must be solvent financially to handle all of the expenses incurred by you, the publisher.

- ✔ Since generally speaking administrators do not do song solicitation, the burden falls on you to hawk your songs and get them into the right hands.

- ✔ There is generally no one at the administration level that gets involved in the creative nurturing and "songwriter's matchmaking" that many songwriters need to get their songs to the next level of excellence.

Dealing with foreign sub-publishing

Whether you decide to sign with a publishing company or act as your own publisher, collecting moneys from foreign countries will be a factor when you start having worldwide success. The local publisher in the various foreign countries is called a sub-publisher. The huge publishing conglomerates have branches in practically all territories which is certainly one of the advantages of going with a major. For the smaller companies and the songwriter with his own publishing, deals must be made on a territory to territory basis. A qualified music attorney can set up deals for you with the various sub-publishers worldwide. Generally a sub-publisher will collect all revenue on behalf of the main publisher on a given song and keep 15 to 25 percent for himself. If the sub-publisher actually gets someone to record another version of your song, he'll then retain 40 to 50 percent of the songs publishing revenue. Even though the world of foreign sub-publishing is a bit of an inexact science, it behooves the songwriter to make sure that his interests are being looked after worldwide — after all, it's estimated that between 55 and 65 percent of the international music market is actually outside the United States.

Using an Independent Song Plugger

A song plugger is someone who actually solicits your songs to artists and their representatives on your behalf. Every publishing company employs a song plugger who listens to their writers' songs, decide who might be an effective pitch, and proceed in getting your material to that person. A song pluggers' main talents would include a great phone personality, as many personal contacts as possible, and the ability to hear a song and be able to not only assess its quality, but determine which artists might be a match for those songs.

Sometimes a person with these talents will work on his or her own — independent of a publishing company. Here's an inside peek at the various aspects of an independent song plugger.

Putting a song plugger to work

Generally an independent song plugger will work on a retainer basis (the big ones in Nashville command anywhere from $500 to $1,500 dollars per month to pitch your songs). The reputable ones will only take you on if they feel you have material they can "get cut" (Nashville lingo for getting someone to record your song).

In addition to a monthly retainer, some successful song pluggers ask for and receive a bonus for getting a song recorded on an album, a further bonus if the song is released as a single (the cut that is pushed to radio), and additional bonus if the song reaches the top 30, top 20, and top 10 of the music charts.

Other independent song pluggers will make an agreement with a writer that he will receive anywhere from 10 to 50 percent of your publishing, if he gets you a cut. Generally the song plugger will retain this share of your publishing for *life of copyright* (life of copyright on songs written after 1978 is the life of the last living author of a song plus 70 years).

Agreements with song pluggers are generally one year in length so that at the year's end everyone can assess the success of the relationship. Some pluggers actually operate on a month-by-month basis, giving a writer the option of terminating his services at any time.

Deciding on using a song plugger

There are pros and cons to the various roads you can take as a songwriter. If you go with a song plugger, you can quite possibly retain ownership of your song and you can receive the extra degree of attention afforded by a song pluggers' generally smaller roster of songwriters and songs to pitch. However, a publishing company can offer you advance money, pitch your songs, and administer your catalogue all in one fell swoop — but this service may be at the expense of giving up a significant portion of your songwriting income and freedom to do whatever you please with your songs. There is no right or wrong way — it all comes down to weighing the needs of your own personal situation.

To decide if a publisher or a song plugger best fits your needs, there are certain questions you'll want answers to regarding their services.

- ✔ Are they specialized in the type of songs you are writing? Just like with publishers, some song pluggers' contacts run more toward one style and market of music than another. On the other hand, most publishing companies have individuals who specialize in all the various genres.

- ✔ Does the company have a true passion for you and the songs you are writing? Do they see the bigger picture of your career as a whole or will they take any opportunity on your behalf just to make a quick buck?

- ✔ Are you comfortable with their style of doing business? Do they get back to you on the phone and treat you with the respect you deserve? If not, they may not be getting back to potential producers or artists either.

- ✔ Can you negotiate a performance type agreement where you give up no portion of your publishing unless the song plugger gets your song cut? If so, and he fails to find a home for your song, at the end of your agreement you're free to offer the song to another plugger or publisher.

I have been with just about every size and shape of publishing company from the behemoths (Warner Brothers and EMI) to tiny companies owned by well-meaning managers. Currently, I have my own publishing company, employing a song plugger and administrator to help carry out the functions required. I can tell you one thing: It's all about the people working on your behalf and their belief in you. It doesn't matter how big and impressive their roster is if you end up getting lost in the shuffle.

Using a Manager or an Agent

As mentioned in the beginning of this chapter, a big step toward achieving success in the business of songwriting is choosing the right team to work together in getting exposure for your songs and for you as a songwriter. Managers and agents can play a big role in this mission, and here is a look at each of these roles.

Do I need a manager?

A *manager* does what his name says: He manages your business career. Choosing someone to guide you is a very personal decision and comes down to chemistry as much as it does ability, experience, and contacts. As a songwriter, a manager is not a necessity since your publisher is really the "manager" of your song catalogue and your music attorney can handle many of your business affairs. A manager comes more into play if you are a performing songwriter. It's then all the more important to add this point person to your team.

Here's what a good manager can do for you:

- ✔ Helps you decide who the players will be on your business team.
- ✔ Assists you in getting signed with a publishing company.
- ✔ Assists you in securing a recording contract as an artist.
- ✔ Advises you on all aspects of your songwriting and performing career.
- ✔ Makes sure that all your other players are working for you to their full capacity — applying pressure if necessary.
- ✔ Networks and makes contacts on your behalf.
- ✔ Makes sure you get every dollar you have coming your way.
- ✔ Inspires you to do your very best work.

Managers consult with you on every aspect of your musical career. They help you decide whether you should have a song plugger or a publisher, and then hook you up with one. Managers can also be a help in getting you connected with the right music attorney and accountant if you don't already have one.

A manager is the one who can do all these things for you, so if you're not really into the business side of songwriting, and you would just like to work on the creative side of things, hire a manager to be out there fighting for you on a daily basis. Your manger can be the one to assemble your entire team.

Some singer/songwriters like to be hands on and become their own manager. Why would you want to do this? Because no one cares more about you than you do. You can have a manager out there working for you, but if he already has four or five other clients that are earning him a decent living, he may tend to point all his energy in that direction. A manager really has to believe in you to give you the time you deserve. List the pros and cons of using a manager to see if having one meets your needs and circumstances.

Steer clear of a manager who asks for a fee upfront against future commissions. This could be a red flag that he's either in dire financial straights, or that he doesn't really believe in you and is hedging his bets. Reputable managers don't charge for their services upfront. They make their money when you do, by taking a percentage. It's a good arrangement because the better you do, the better they do! That's pretty good motivation to try to make you a household name in the songwriting world.

Shop around. Be aware that there are different levels of managers, from the heavyweight who handles the superstars, to the well-respected middleweight, to the friend-who-loves-your-music featherweight who would fight for you to the finish. Compile a list of referrals from musician friends and look in Appendix B for sources for names and phone numbers of managers. You may want to look for a manager in your geographical region — there is nothing like close proximity for good communication. However, if your manager is located in a music hub like Los Angeles, Nashville, or New York, he may do more good for you there. (Especially if you live way out in the boondocks!) Then set up interviews and prepare your list of questions, which may include the following:

- ✔ **Whom do you represent?** Listen for any names you recognize and take note of any powerhouses.

- ✔ **How much experience do you have?** You need to find a manager with far more experience than you have yourself. You don't need to be spending your time educating them — it should be the other way around!

- ✔ **What genre of artist do you specialize in?** Look to see if this manager falls into your genres of choice.

- ✔ **What is the cost for your services?** You can expect to hear a range of between 15 to 20 percent of your gross income. If a manager is really good, he'll more than make up for the money you're paying him.

✔ **How many artists do you manage?** If his roster is large, does he have enough staff to cover all the detail work? Make sure you meet his entire team, from the front desk receptionist to any partners he may have. Make sure you're not relegated to one of his assistants without your full approval.

✔ **How strong are your contacts?** Don't be afraid to ask just who his friends are in the music business. His reputation and connections directly impact how effective he'll be on your behalf.

Do I need an agent?

In addition to a manager, a good agent may help you to reach your committed goals. If you're a performing songwriter you'll need the right agent to find you steady work to promote your career whether you're at the club, county fair, or arena level. As a songwriter, there are specialized agents that handle television, advertising, and film score placement for your songs. There are agents that find opportunities for writers in the video and interactive game market as well. Just as with managers, music attorneys, song pluggers, and publishers, reputation and connections are everything! Ask them where their strengths lie as an agent and make sure that coincides with your career goals. Whether they earn their 10 to 15 percent commission will depend on the quality of the shows they schedule for you, and how well they can interface with the other members of your team. When there's good synergy between your manager and your agent, you have a better chance of succeeding in this very competitive business. Listings of booking agents can be found by searching Web sites mentioned in Appendix B, and you might also get referrals from your music attorney and your various musician acquaintances.

You're in the Money: Hiring an Accountant or a Business Manager

Accountants are people who are skilled and trained in accounting — they are the numbers crunchers. Their role is to give advice and/or handle financial accounts, and depending on your particular circumstances, an accountant can be hired to do as little as your annual tax returns or a great deal more. If you just need one to do your taxes, then you can probably get by without one who specializes in the music industry. But if you feel more comfortable with a music expert, then get an accountant who really knows the ins and outs of the music industry. The financial accounting business is complex when dealing with royalties and musical rights — very different kinds of animals that an everyday accountant might not fully understand. Taking this one step further, if you have your accountant handle your entire financial situation, what they have basically become is your *business manager* — one who handles all of your business affairs. However, please note that due to ever-changing rules and availability of Schedule C deductions, that even for start-up songwriters it's absolutely important for anyone in the entertainment industry to obtain advice from a licensed tax practitioner, enrolled agent, or CPA with experience in entertainment industry reporting. These specialists usually don't cost any more than a regular tax professional but, depending upon where you live, it may be more difficult to find one.

The accountant is usually the last person to join the team because he can't play until there is money in the bank. Actually, he doesn't *want* to play until you have money to work with! For a fee, he can receive and deposit all your royalty checks, pay your bills, do your income tax, help you invest your money — and help you spend it, too!

Knowing what a good music accountant or business manager can do for you

You may want to hire an accountant who specializes in sources of revenue that apply specifically to a songwriter. You need to basically go through the same process you did when hiring your music attorney. Although you can consider an accountant who is a little more of a jack-of-all-trades, he still must have some understanding and experience in music accounting.

A desirable music accountant or business manager provides all the following services:

- ✔ Helps you set aside (hopefully) large chunks of money to pay your taxes, which he'll calculate and submit on time?

- ✔ Helps you understand such things as tax deductions and will get you saving all those little receipts for expenses that are business related.

- ✔ Handles your money (makes deposits into and balances your bank accounts — pays the bills that you've had forwarded to his offices).

- ✔ Provides you with a monthly financial statement of what your incoming and outgoing finances are, known to him as *accounts receivable* and *accounts payable.*

- ✔ Gives you advice on investments, or refers you to professionals who can better advise you on what to do with your money.

- ✔ Reviews your royalty statements and makes sure you're being paid accurately and on time.

Employing a music accountant or business manager

Because the music accountant or business manager is probably the last person to add to your business team, you have plenty of time to find just the right one — unless, of course, you make it big overnight, in which case you'll have to put it into overdrive and find someone you can really trust right away.

Considering that by now you have an attorney and maybe a publisher, your search for referrals just got easier. Many times these music professionals work together, or at least have some experience or knowledge about others in the industry. In any case, round up a list of people to interview and book some appointments.

Every person on your business team is important, and the accountant or business manager is the one who handles what everyone seems to care about most — your money! You really need to feel good about this person, so be prepared with crystal-clear questions when you arrive for your interview. Let the answers to each of the following questions lend a hand in your decision to sign on your music accountant or business manager and to complete your team of players.

- ✔ **Whom do you represent?** Take note of any recognizable names. (Although this in of itself does not guarantee your money is safe, as many "big names" have been known to get ripped off!)

- ✔ **How much experience do you have?** He can have all the big-dollar clients in the world, but the music business is a unique animal. Listen to what knowledge he has about royalties, performance, and mechanical rights. Get a feel for his music knowledge and expertise.

- ✔ **How much will your services cost?** Accountants are similar to attorneys in this regard. Most of them charge by the hour, with a monthly retainer or percentage payment made upfront.

When choosing an accountant or business manager, be absolutely sure that he has the background and experience to do what it is that you're asking him to do (handle your professional career and earnings!). Make sure that he has some music-industry knowledge and know-how before signing him on. Then just keep those hit songs coming, so he can become a long-term team player!

Chapter 14

Looking at the Legal End: Dealing with Paper Work

In This Chapter

▶ Understanding contracts

▶ Registering copyrights

▶ Organizing all the paper trails

*B*eing creative, working with melodies and lyrics, and producing songs can be very time-consuming. And on top of all this, having to deal with paperwork issues can be boring, overwhelming, and cumbersome — especially for artistic people. Nonetheless, this part of the songwriting process can make a big difference in improving your chances for ultimate success.

Creative and linear thinking rarely go hand in hand, and most people tend to be stronger in one way of thinking than they are in the other. But in order to really be in control of your creative output, the more you understand about the business side, the more successful you'll be at meeting your goals. Even if you put together a business team to help you with the inevitable paperwork of songwriting (those versed in publishing, legal, administration, and accounting), it's still your name that's scrawled on the bottom of the paper, so you can't completely sit back and "watch the wheels go round and round." Taking the approach of, "Hey, I'm an artist; I don't need to know that stuff!" just ain't gonna cut it. Even with the best possible players, your basic understanding of the business is vital in helping your team function at 100 percent.

In this chapter, we discuss signing contracts, filling out forms, and keeping track of all the paperwork that's involved in songwriting.

Legal Deals: Creating Win-Win Contracts

"The best for all concerned" is certainly what you strive for when you're coming up with a contract. Although the music industry is full of stories about people getting taken to the cleaners, when structured right, it is possible for everyone to come out on top.

Getting things clear upfront, before you begin any business adventure, is always best. That way, you eliminate (or at least reduce) confusion about who gets what and how the credits and money are handled. In other words, get rid of any disagreements before signing any agreements.

My least favorite part of the music business is the "business of music." I'd rather spend all my time creating and performing songs. Unfortunately, without the business side of things, many of my songs would remain unheard or the income they generate will not be looked after properly. Over the years, I've come to value the various paperwork issues involved in my chosen field, whether it's protecting my song with a copyright, registering it with a performing rights group, signing with a publisher, or filling out administration forms. The business side of songwriting isn't all as weird and mysterious as it first appears, and the better you understand what you're signing, the better you and your songs will be taken care of in the long run.

Understanding different kinds of contracts

Contrary to popular belief, contracts *can* be made simple. Some deals are sealed with only a handshake (however, this is not a recommended practice!), and others can be as simple as a one-page agreement between you and a co-writer or musical-team player, outlining who gets what, when, and how. As your songs become hits, the contracts will definitely get longer and more complex — and your attorney will undoubtedly make sure that every *i* is dotted and every *t* crossed. See Appendix A for descriptions of the various contracts you may encounter.

Never let an unscrupulous publisher, manager, artist, or anyone else pressure you into signing a deal without fully understanding and agreeing to its terms. A popular ploy is to get you to sign on Sunday when lawyers' offices are closed. Another is to say that if you don't sign "right now," you'll blow the entire deal. You're better off letting the whole deal fall apart than having to live with an unfair contract. Beware of anyone who says they represent you *and* the other party in a contract. It's a common practice for the representative of one party (publisher, producer, co-writer, and so on) to approach a featherweight songwriter saying, "Hey, we have to do this deal NOW because. . . ." "Since I'm already working for [so and so] why don't I just go over the paperwork with you now, so we can get this show on the road?" Stay away from this type of situation at all costs. Songwriters need their own independent representation.

The day will undoubtedly come when you, as a songwriter, will have to sign on the dotted line to consummate a deal. In fact, you'll probably encounter several different kinds of contracts, and it is wise for you to be familiar with each of them ahead of time. In the following sections, we guide you through what to expect before you sign your name.

Publishing and co-publishing agreements

When a songwriter finishes the music, lyric, and/or music-with-lyric of a song, the songwriter is automatically the publisher of that song unless they've assigned their publishing rights to another company. (There is specific paper-work to setting up your own publishing company as discussed in Chapter 13.) However, since most songwriters lack the clout or industry connections to act as their own publisher and get their songs into circulation, it's usually necessary for songwriters to assign all or part of their publishing interest in their own songs to a third party. This third party can be a publishing company, record company, or manager acting as a publisher, song plugger, or song administrator.

A publishing or co-publishing agreement is the often-complex contract you're asked to sign when making a deal with a publisher (see Chapter 13 for more about what a publisher does). Whether the company you're considering is large or small, be sure to read and understand *every* word of the contract. If you're entrusting your precious songs and pledging half of the income (or a quarter of your earnings in a co-pub deal) from these songs, you'll want to:

✔ Make sure that the publishing company is treating you fairly regarding issues such as advances, demo costs, length of term, and *reversion of copyright* (if you don't get the rights to your song back at the end of your deal, they should treat you especially well financially speaking).

✔ Make sure that your *submission quota* (the number of tunes you must create and turn into your publisher within a period of time) is reasonable. Often an unscrupulous publisher will specify an unrealistic number of songs to be completed each quarter, just so they can put you in breach of contract and stop paying you advances.

✔ Make sure that the publishing company doesn't make you, the writer, responsible for obtaining a set number of *cuts* (the industry term for getting an artist to record and release one of your songs) — getting cuts is the publisher's job! Unless you are a really hot producer with a built-in avenue for your songs or a signed singer/songwriter — watch out for this one.

Only so much can be spelled out for you in a contract. How hard the company will work on your behalf, and how many of your songs they'll find homes for, are factors you have to gauge by the company's track record, their reputation, and your own gut feeling about the people you'll be dealing with. That piece of paper is all you have to hold them to their promises, so make sure you understand it and that it's as comprehensive as possible.

Performing rights agreements

A performing rights agreement is the contract you'll sign with ASCAP, BMI, or SESAC — the agencies that monitor the airplay on your song and collect money on your behalf. The contracts are fairly simple and nonnegotiable. Your main concern should be that you understand the length of the agreement and how you can terminate the agreement if you're unsatisfied with their performance for any reason. More important than the actual contract is your understanding of how your performances are being calculated. (See Chapter 18 for more details regarding your songwriting income.)

It used to be that one of the determining factors for songwriters when they were choosing a performing rights organization was which one offered the largest advance of dollars against future royalties. Much too many songwriters' chagrin, both BMI and ASCAP stopped that practice back in the late '70s.

Performing rights forms

Performance royalties are the monies songwriters and publishers receive when your song is played (or in old terminology, performed) on the radio, network and local television, commercials, juke boxes, Muzak (the smooth versions you generally hear at the supermarket or mall), or in live performances, stores, night clubs, by marching bands, sung by choirs, at work-out clubs, for film, and anywhere else your song is helping to enhance people's mood and elevate the day. Performance royalties are paid by one of the performance rights groups such as ASCAP, BMI, and SESAC. Once you have joined one of these groups, in order to get paid, you'll need to fill out certain forms they supply (by mail or online — the latter being the obvious choice when wishing to contact one of the foreign performing rights agencies) when your song is about to be released. The forms require you to supply accurate information regarding: your name and publishing company, any co-writers and their publishing affiliates, address and the Social Security numbers of all parties, all contact information, date of release of the product containing your song, and the writer's splits (the percent of each song that each writer has a share in). Take extra care in making sure all entries are correct, since this is the only record they have to ensure you'll be paid correctly.

Mechanical rights agreement

Mechanical royalties are the monies that the songwriter and publisher receive from the sale of compact discs, tapes, videotapes, and DVDs. (The term *mechanical* stems from the old days and referred to devices "serving to mechanically reproduce sound.") There are certain forms that you or your publisher need to fill out for your songs that get recorded, in order to assure you get paid on the units sold (if someone else wants to record one of your songs, they must also contact your designated mechanical rights agency). Whether you sign up with the Harry Fox Agency (many of the larger publishers actually hire Harry Fox to perform mechanical rights collection) or one of the smaller companies that specialize in royalty collection, you'll still get paid according to the statutory rate, set by Copyright Royalty Tribunal, of 8 cents per unit sold. (If you wrote 50 percent of the song, cut that figure in half.) If you are signed to a publisher, that company will handle this paperwork on your behalf. If you handle your own publishing you'll want to team up with an administration agency to take care of your mechanical royalty collection and the issuing of song licenses. Record companies must account to them as to the sales of the units containing your song so you can be paid properly. The Harry Fox Agency is the largest administrator of songs (in fact, many publishers use Harry Fox themselves to do their administering as well), but there are other smaller administrators who do an excellent job too. Most of these royalty collection services command anywhere from 5 to 10 percent for their services, Again, be sure to understand the scope of the agreement, the percentages withheld, and the term of the contract.

If you chose a giant mechanical collection agency like the Harry Fox Agency, try to make a few personal acquaintances at the company so that you're more than an account number. There also needs to be one or two specific people you can count on to answer your questions as they arise. No matter how big the company is that you are dealing with, remember, it's ultimately *you* who are keeping *them* in business, so don't be afraid of asking questions and requesting explanations of their business practices.

Mechanical license payment rates are standardized, with all songwriters being paid equally according to a formula that changes occasionally over time. You can contact the Musician's Union or Harry Fox to give you the current rates.

Copyright forms

Copyright forms are important documents for you as a songwriter. Before you send your song out to the immediate world, you want to protect it from theft through copyright. Fill out these forms carefully and accurately. (You can find more information on copyrights later in this chapter.)

Synch rights agreements

Whenever someone wants to use your song in a movie, video, commercial, or any use where a song is synched up with the action on the screen, the company will issue you or your publisher a synch rights license for you to sign. The figures involved vary widely and are dependant on the popularity of your tune and how badly someone wants it. Thoroughly read the agreement and pay attention to the terms and the specific ways your song will be used.

Commercial music agreement

When a commercial manufacturer wants to use one of your songs to hawk his wares, he'll contact you or your publisher and offer you a contract to cover the song's use. These are actually quite simple and specify the following:

- ✔ The product being advertised
- ✔ The geographic area that the commercial will cover (anywhere from Southern Idaho, for example, to the entire world)
- ✔ The media concentration (radio, TV, Internet, or all of the above)
- ✔ The amount of the song being used
- ✔ How long they want to use the song (if asked for an option of more time, make sure you or your negotiator up the ante for the next time around!)

Having your song used in a commercial can be a great opportunity for you and your song. But after a song is used for a specific product, it may be eliminated from future use with other products — so make sure the deal you make is lucrative enough to make it worth your while.

Co-writer agreement

Whether it's scribbled on a napkin or specially worded by a high-priced attorney — this is the agreement between the songwriters as to how the songwriting credits will be divvied up. Standard forms can be obtained from the Songwriter's Guild or supplied by any good entertainment attorney.

Contracts are only as good as the parties involved and trust is still the number-one factor when signing a deal. When in doubt, rely on your gut and a reputable music attorney.

As soon as I've completed a song with a co-writer, I find that it's best to decide right then and there what the writing splits are going to be — when everyone can still remember the degree to which they've contributed. I've made the mistake in the past of waiting too long, only to have some confusion and fuzzy memories just before the song was about to be released.

Knowing when to put the pen to the paper

When you are making a deal with someone regarding your career, property rights, potential earnings of your song, or whatever, get it in writing! If you think that you've found the right person with the right connections — whether it's an attorney, a publisher, or a song plugger — make sure that you spell out your mutual goals and set time limits to reach them. In other words, create a contract. It can be simple or complex, but the main thing is that you convert your mutual goals into a written level of understanding between those who'll be representing your songs, style, and ethics. Take a look at Figure 14-1 for a checklist of what a contract between a songwriter and a publisher should contain.

There's often a lot of hype prior to actually signing a deal. Try to use your instincts to know when it's the appropriate time to consummate an agreement. Again, here's where having an attorney on your team will help you decide when the time is to sign on the dotted line.

Songwriter/Publisher Contract Checklist

☐ **Date of Agreement:** The birthday of your agreement.

☐ **By and Between:** Your name and the publisher's name.

☐ **The Composition:** List and define (title, words, and music) the song or songs that you assign and/or transfer to your publisher.

☐ **Time of Agreement:** Beginning on the date that you sign the contract for the length of time that you agree to work together (generally the time varies anywhere from 3 to 25 years) and also include some provisions to extend or terminate the contract.

☐ **Existing Agreements:** The contract should be subject to any existing agreements that either party is already affiliated (such as performing rights organizations).

☐ **Exclusive and Original Work:** Identify that you have the right to make the agreement for your composition(s) as exclusive and original work and that no other claim to the composition(s) has been made.

☐ **Rights and Responsibilities:** Clearly define who has the right to do what, and what each party is responsible for. Make sure you get credit where credit is due.

☐ **Publisher Agrees to Pay Writer:** An advance on royalties; upfront costs to produce a demo(s); percents of the: wholesale price, all net sums for foreign countries, piano copies, orchestrations, band arrangements, song books, licenses to reprint lyrics in books and magazines, and so on; fees for synchronization with sound motion pictures; and any other source not now known which may come after signing the agreement.

☐ **Method of Payment:** Include the when and how you will be paid by the publisher for each portion of the income. It should also be spelled out how the publisher will compute and credit your account, and your right to inspect the bookkeeping process.

☐ **Recording the Composition:** Set a date for the publisher to release a commercial recording of the composition and create a clause to terminate the agreement if they do not.

☐ **Defining the Writer:** If you are a co-writer and share the royalties, you need to clarify who the other writers are and how you divide up the writers' portions.

☐ **Time to Comply:** Define what and when items in the agreement should happen and identify all the "if this" or "if that" happens. Here's where you'll really need an attorney!

☐ **Termination:** If and when you or your publisher terminate the agreement, you need to include all the reasons and methods to do so. Also make sure that all of the compositions that you have assigned to the publisher are transferred back to you.

☐ **Arbitration:** In the case of an argument, you need to define just how you will settle the differences of opinion.

☐ **Cost for Legal Action:** Define who pays for what in the case of a legal battle.

☐ **State of Law:** The agreement will abide by the laws of (choose a state) for settling any legal action.

☐ **Signatures:** You, a witness, and the publisher all sign on the dotted lines: including names, addresses, and dates.

Figure 14-1:
A checklist for a songwriter/ publisher contract.

Before you sign your name to any kind of contract, have a trusted music attorney look it over to make sure that it's both fair and properly written. In addition, ask yourself the following questions to see if you're ready to sign:

✔ Do you understand everything you're agreeing to?

✔ Do you trust the people you're signing the deal with?

✔ Are you satisfied that you're getting the best deal possible?

✔ Can you live with the term length of the contract and its possible restrictions?

✔ Do you feel the agreement will help promote your career?

✔ Will this contract motivate you to do your best work?

Also, it's a good idea to watch out for any red flags in each agreement that you're asked to sign. Here is a list of ten of the most common offenders:

✔ **Publishing agreements that ask a writer to pay a fee to publish the song.** Reputable publishers take their agreed-upon percentage from the back end of monies earned. (In fact, publishers who take upfront fees to publish your tunes are generally not allowed to belong to the various performance rights groups!)

✔ **Publishing contracts that take a cut of your writer's royalties (as opposed to a piece of the publisher's share).** This practice is acceptable only in certain cases — be sure to consult your attorney before agreeing to this.

✔ **Publishing deals that make the writer responsible for getting a specific number of songs cut by artists.** This is the publishers' job — if you can help in the process, all the better, but the total responsibility shouldn't be on the shoulders of the songwriter.

✔ **Agreements between other individual songwriters that limit your percentage of the song to a set amount — no matter what portion of the song you've actually written.**

✔ **Publishing contracts that specify an unrealistic quota of songs that must be submitted in order to avoid suspension.**

✔ **Publishing contracts that don't count a song against your *submission requirement* (the amount of songs you agree to turn in quarterly) unless you are at least a 50 percent writer of that song.**

✔ **Contracts that have an unrealistically long term (usually anything over three years) and put all the reasons for termination on the publisher's side of the court.**

✔ **Publishing contracts that restrict you to writing only with other songwriters signed with that same publishing company.**

✔ **Publishing contracts that take 100 percent of your publishing without offering some kind of upfront or weekly monetary advance.**

Because of the slightly depressed condition of the retail record business, many record companies, when signing an artist or a band, will demand their publishing rights as another way to recoup on their investment. If you're an artist about to sign a record deal, have your attorney do his best at retaining at least half of your publishing.

✔ **Any contract that you are pressured to sign without the advice and counsel of a good attorney.**

Breaking a contract can be costly — so understanding exactly what you are agreeing to is vitally important. After all the explanations from your professional guides, discussions with friends and family, even hashing it out with the guy next door, go on your gut feelings and the information that you've gathered. More often than not, you'll know when and what to sign.

When you have questions about the meaning of some wording or language in a contract, it's worth the money to have it looked over, explained, and perhaps modified by an attorney.

Protecting Your Songs with Copyrights

Before you solicit your song, protect yourself with a copyright. Your publisher or attorney can handle the filing of your copyrights, or you can do it yourself — just make sure that the job ultimately gets done.

A *copyright* is basically a form of protection that is provided by the laws of the United States to the authors of "original works of authorship," which includes you, the songwriter. The small print and details may look a bit overwhelming at first, but in this section we make it simple for you.

The moment you've committed your song to tape, it's in what is known as *tangible form* and it's technically protected by copyright laws. However, if your copyright is ever challenged, you'll have a hard time proving the exact date of your song's creation if you don't actually file a copyright registration. This is why registering your song with the federal government is always a good idea — you'll be better protected in the event of a copyright infringement suit. You'll also be listed at the Library of Congress in Washington, D.C., if someone wants to look up the songs you've written.

Although no longer considered a legal substitute, a *poor man's copyright* is the old technique of recording your song on a cassette (or CD) and sending it to yourself. If you don't open the envelope after you receive it back, the postmark will serve as a record of the date you originally created it. This method should only be done *in conjunction* with a government copyright, for additional proof as to the date of a song's creation.

Copyright forms are available on-line — it's easy to fill out (these are not difficult to decipher since their revision in the early '90s), the filing fee is relatively inexpensive (currently $30) and the copyright lasts for the lifetime of the composer (or the lifetime of the last surviving co-writer) plus 70 years. (That's the new law for all songs written after 1978.)

Rounding up the right forms

The Copyright Office of the Library of Congress has all the forms you'll ever need for filing your copyright. They can provide you with the necessary paper work and instructions for registering copyrights, changing your mailing address, changing the name of your song, updating a lyric, and myriad other options. You can either call them to request the forms, or you can download them online (using the PDF format). The Library Of Congress's Web site is the best place to find all the most up-to-the-minute info regarding copyrights. They even include links to some related sites such as performing rights societies (ASCAP, BMI, and SESAC) and to the Harry Fox Agency. The folks at the copyright bureau are usually quite willing to walk you through any questions you may have regarding forms or procedure.

Here's how to contact the Copyright Office:

> Register of Copyrights
> Library of Congress
> Copyright Office
> 101 Independence Avenue, S.E.
> Washington, D.C. 20559-6000
> Phone: (24 hour hotline) - (202) 707-9100
> Web site: www.loc.gov/copyright

As a songwriter, you'll want Form PA. This form is used for published or unpublished works of the performing arts including:

- Musical works, including any accompanying words
- Dramatic works, including any accompanying music
- Pantomimes and choreographic works
- Motion pictures and other audiovisual works

When you mail off your package to the Copyright Office, you'll need to enclose the following materials:

✔ Application Form PA

✔ Deposit material: Two copies of your recorded song

✔ A nonrefundable filing fee in check or money order payable to the Register of Copyrights (As of the time of this book's publication, the filling fee is $30, but it's always good to check with the Copyright Office first in case they've changed it.)

Copyright protection by law is legally granted you as soon as your song is in fixed form. (That means recorded on any recording medium.) However, for additional protection we would always recommend filing an official Library of Congress Copyright to back up your claims. When you solicit your songs, always affix the copyright symbol (©) and/or the written word "copyright," followed by the year of the song's creation and your name, to the CDs, tapes, sheet music, and lyric sheets you send out.

Filling out Application Form PA

Each songwriter's situation is a little different, so read the instructions before filling out your form. If you have a publisher or an administrator, they'll handle the filling of this form on your behalf. Figure 14-2 is an example of Form PA filled out for a songwriter who has completed a demo and is ready to send it off to artists, record labels, or other music-industry people. We've named our fictitious up and comer, Jennifer Songsmith.

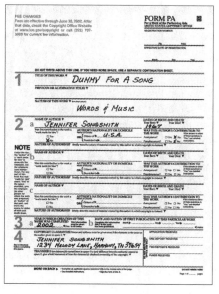
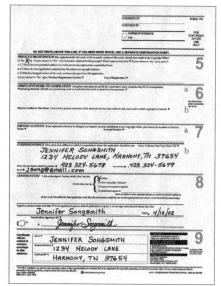

Figure 14-2: A completed sample Form PA.

The Copyright Office can take several months, sometimes longer, to return your form with it's official number — so don't panic (The office routinely gets 8,000 pieces of mail every day!) After you've mailed your application in, you can breathe a lot easier knowing that the song you worked so hard on has an extra degree of protection.

Using the copyright notice

For published works, the law provides that a copyright notice (©) must be placed on all publicly distributed copies. Doing so is your responsibility! Here are the three things that, together, make up a copyright notice:

✔ The symbol (©)

✔ The year of creation

✔ The name of the owner of the copyright

Here's an example of how the copyright notice will look:
© 2002 Jennifer Songsmith.

Filling in the Blanks and Being Organized

As a songwriter you have to be as good at the *organizational* elements of the business as you are at the *creative* aspects in order to give your songs the best chance for success. The bottom line is that you need to get organized.

Records are everything. When I send out a particular song, I keep a record of when and to whom it was sent. When I make follow-up calls on the song, I log the listener's responses. When I file my copyrights, I keep a duplicate for my records (which I destroy when the finals come back from Washington). When I write with someone new, I take down all their personal info — their name, address, phone number, date of birth, publishing company, and social security number. (These facts really come in handy when I'm filling out forms or supplying information to my administrator regarding the song we wrote.) It doesn't really matter if your method is high tech (sophisticated computer software that offers various organizational templates), or primitive (written down in a spiral notebook); the important thing is to have a system and to stick to it.

Endless organization methods are out there — you just need to find the one that works best for you. One method is to create a standard form with blank lines to fill in while you're on the phone or when you send out packages. Just make blank copies or print them right from your computer as needed. In the following sections, we provide a few sample forms that you can use to give you an idea. Naturally, you can come up with your own system by customizing the fields of information to include on the various forms (or tracking sheets) that you design.

If you're a computer whiz, you may want to you use a database such as Microsoft Access for keeping track of your information.

Using a prospects-and-contacts form

Figure 14-3 is an example of a form you can use to keep track of whom you know and who you want to know — your contacts and prospects. This is your personal note-taking organization. Getting referrals from friends and associates is an excellent way to get in the door (and on the phone with) music-industry people. There are numerous industry sourcebooks in which you can find all the big names with their phone numbers; however, unless you're very lucky, you'll most likely have worked your way to the top in order to actually get through and talk with the "bigwig" personally.

If you make contact with someone who says no to a specific request, you may have, ask her if she can refer you to someone else who may say yes. Also, ask if she has any other suggestions for you to help achieve your goal (of finding a record label, attorney, or artist to sing your song, and so on).

Creating a song-history tracking sheet

When you start sending your songs out, you'll want to keep track of who has a copy of your song, and how it's faring on a submissions rating scale (such as forget it, keep trying, possible interest, highly potential, and best of all, signed the deal on such-and-such date).

The importance of good organization

If you don't have a secretary (and even if you do), keep notes about what you've sent to whom, and when it was mailed. You're developing rapport with new contacts, so write down the names of everyone from the receptionist to the assistant of the person you sent your package to.

Organization can make a big difference. If the head of A&R of Polysutra Records gives you a call, you'll want to be quick about responding to exactly what he has in his hot little hands. If you've sent dozens of packages out and can't remember what you sent to whom, well, you won't appear very professional!

Songwriter Prospects & Contacts   (#) ≡

☐ Artist
☐ Manager
☐ Produce
☐ Publisher
☐ Record Company
☐ Song Plugger
☐ Other _____

Name

Title

Company

Address

City/State/Zip

Phone

Fax

E-Mail

Web Site

Referred By

Referred To

Notes

Follow-Up

Figure 14-3:
A prospects-
and-
contacts
form.

Figure 14-4, the song-history tracking sheet, is an example of the things to keep track of regarding your song.

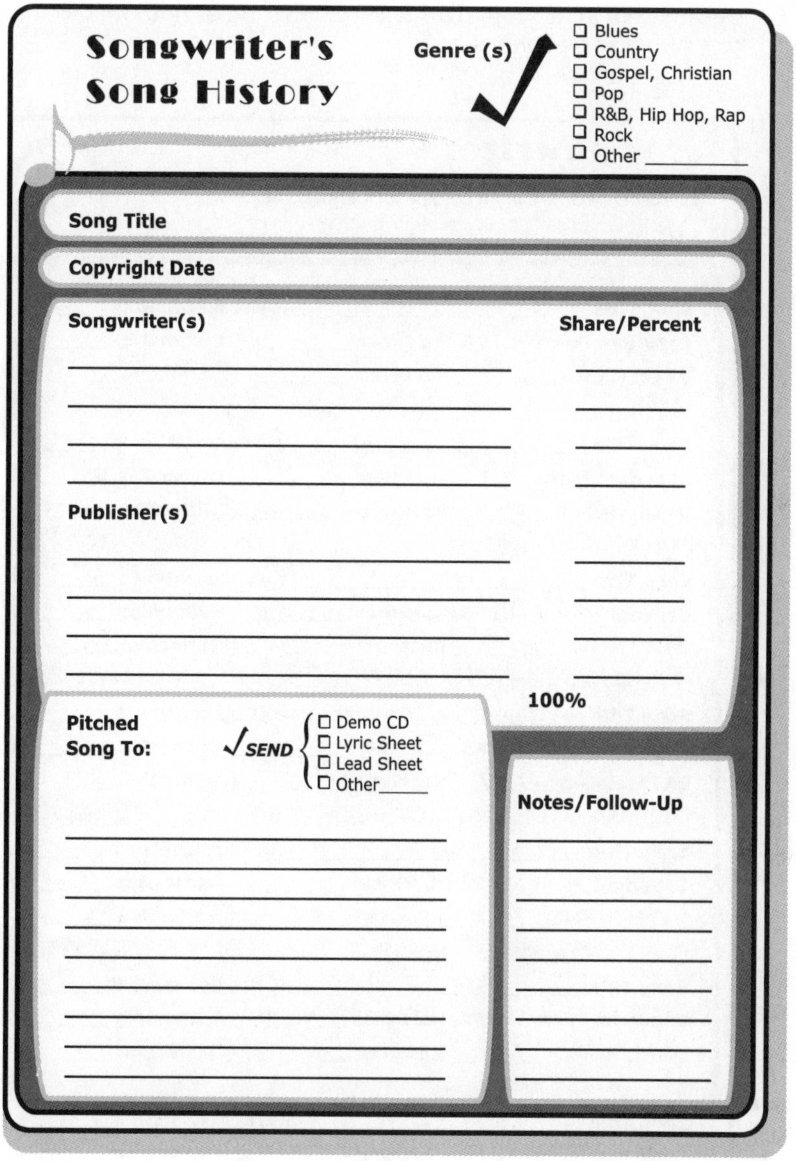

Songwriter's Song History

Genre (s) ✓
- ☐ Blues
- ☐ Country
- ☐ Gospel, Christian
- ☐ Pop
- ☐ R&B, Hip Hop, Rap
- ☐ Rock
- ☐ Other _____

Song Title

Copyright Date

Songwriter(s)   **Share/Percent**

Publisher(s)

100%

Pitched Song To: ✓ *SEND*
- ☐ Demo CD
- ☐ Lyric Sheet
- ☐ Lead Sheet
- ☐ Other_____

Notes/Follow-Up

Figure 14-4:
A song-history tracking sheet.

Keeping track of your copyright registrations

As you go along writing tons of songs, you'll see how time flies. So use the simple form shown in Figure 14-5 is used to help remember whether you've already sent in the copyright registration form or not. Organization has a nice way of replacing confusion.

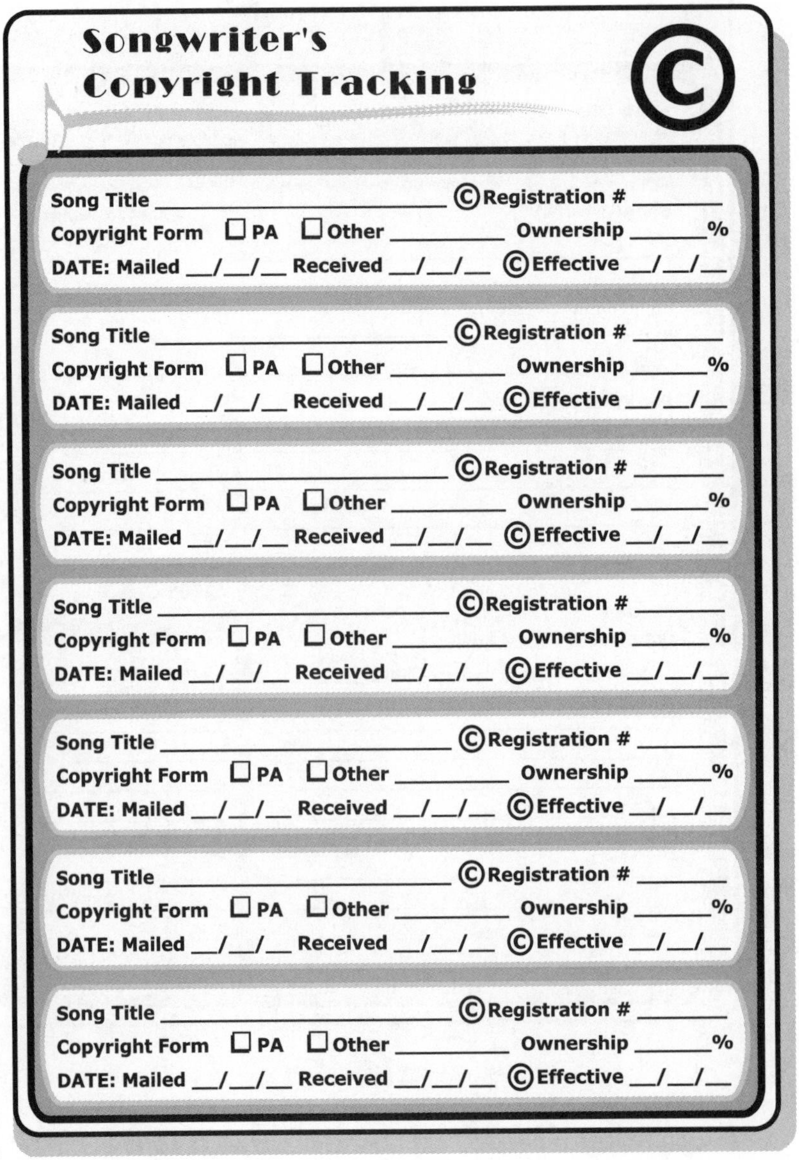

Figure 14-5:
A copyright tracking form.

Chapter 15

Bringing Talent Together: Songwriting Collaboration

*Y*ou may be one of those rare individuals who can literally do it all when it comes to the creation and presentation of your song. But more than likely, you're like most mortals who, in the process of bringing your songs to fruition, need to team up with other talented people. If so, you've come to the right place. This chapter is all about the fine art of collaboration — an all-important element of songwriting.

Finding Your Strengths and Weaknesses

Collaboration is a great way to write a killer song. When a team gets hot — look out! The sparks (and hits!) can really start to fly. But before you call your potential Paul McCartney on the phone, do a thorough self-inventory, asking yourself, "What is my strong suit?" Take a look at these specific areas of song-writing to help define your own role in the process:

✔ **Melody:** If you're the kind of person who goes about his business every day with a tune in his head, whether it's your own or another's, your talent may lie in the area of melody. A strong melody is an important element in practically every style of songwriting, so your talents will be well put to use as a member of a collaborative team.

- **Chord structure:** The chords are often called the *foundation* of a song. If chord progressions are your specialty, you'll be a useful and effective member of any songwriting partnership.

- **Lyrics:** If you're the kind of person who is very observant of life and loves jotting down ideas, philosophies, insights, and so on — even putting these inspirations in some kind of poetic form — your strength may lie in the field of lyric writing. In every collaboration, one or more partners must excel in this area.

- **Rhythm:** Maybe you're the kind of person who is constantly pounding out a beat on your desktop or steering wheel. Perhaps you love to spend hours on end programming exciting beats on your electronic rhythm box. Writing teams today can surely use this type of talent, because many current songs are actually built up from these rhythmic grooves.

- **Musical hooks and riffs:** An often-underrated element of a song is the repeating musical series of notes known as a *riff*. Everyone remembers the signature fuzz-tone guitar figure at the beginning of "Satisfaction" (written by Mick Jagger and Keith Richards, performed by The Rolling Stones), the guitar part at the top of "Day Tripper" (written by Paul McCartney and John Lennon; performed by The Beatles), or the intro horn riff of "Vehicle" (written by Jim Peterik; performed by The Ides of March). If riffs are your musical forte, you can undoubtedly be an asset to any writing session.

- **Editing and overview:** Knowing what's good and what isn't is a talent in itself. In many great songwriting teams, there is one great overview person who acts as a kind of sounding board for all ideas that are flying around the room. Not that he doesn't have creative ideas of his own, but his main strength is knowing what's hot and what's not. It's a good idea to have a person with this talent on your team.

- **Some combination of these talents:** You may be one of those unique and lucky people who have all the preceding talents (or some combination of them in varying degrees). All the better! However, try to be honest with yourself and spend time doing what you do best — knowing there are others available who can help round out the team.

A great writing team is one of balance, where one partner is especially strong in those areas in which the other one is weak (and vice versa). If your talents skew toward the music side, find a brilliant lyricist. Many poets are simply songwriters without a melody. If your passion runs to expressing your heart through words, but you only have a passing acquaintance with a musical instrument, track down that guy that you heard jamming down at the Guitar Center — the one who made everyone's jaw drop.

Maybe you hear rhythms in your head and you're dying to set them to music. Or maybe you're just one of those people who has that gift of knowing a great musical idea when you hear one, and you just need to be around the right inspiration to bring all the pieces together. Whatever your strengths and weaknesses, the right collaborator can be the missing piece in your songwriting puzzle.

I've had experiences where two excellent songwriters who attempt to write a song come up short because their strengths, shortcomings, and attitudes are too similar. They basically are two of the same and end up canceling each other out. Sometimes a skeptical way of looking at things can actually complement someone else's positive outlook. When Paul McCartney wrote the words, "It's getting better all the time," in the Beatles song of the same name, John Lennon chimed in, "Can't get no worse!" It was the bitter mixed with the sweet that made their collaborations so rich in texture.

Songwriting workshops are a great place to locate other songwriters to collaborate with. Refer to Appendix B for songwriting associations that can lead you to such workshops in your area.

Seeking the Chemistry of Collaborative Songwriting

Many times publishers will often put writers together in a sort of see-what-happens, blind-date sort of way. This process often seems very impersonal and cold, so it's a good idea before writing even one note, to go out for a cup of coffee to get to know each other a bit and find out a little about what makes the other person tick. In doing so, a better song may be the result.

Collaborative songwriting is as much about the chemistry between people as it is about individual talent. Take note of other factors that enter into a session and affect the vibe, such as the writing environment, the time of day, the weather conditions, and the mental and physical condition of the various partners. Although in the end, if a song is meant to be written, it'll happen — even under the worst possible conditions.

As a good collaborator, knowing when to step forward with an idea and when to "wait in the weeds" and let the talents of others shine through is important. Also, try to stay open about where the session goes, and don't be too strict in following the agenda that you may have planned out. Accommodating all the possibilities of the moment may yield a song that is totally beyond the boundaries you create on your own. Always expect the unexpected and allow for the possibility of pure musical magic.

The most important lesson I've learned through the years is to let go of pre-conceived notions. We can be so ingrained with being in control of our lives that we're afraid to let a writing situation run wild. I recently had the pleasure of writing with Henry Paul and Dave Robbins of the platinum country-rock act Blackhawk. I came armed with my usual sheaf of ideas earmarked for the band. But as the three of us sat behind our guitars and keyboards in the warm glow of the neon beer sign in Hank's studio, the brotherhood between us suddenly seemed a lot bigger than any idea I had intended on showing them. As we sat talking, just idly strumming our guitars, chords started lining up, words started flowing, cassettes started rolling, and the first of two songs started emerging — "Brothers of the Southland," a sincere ode to the brotherhood of southern rockers past and present. It was not a song we had planned to write, but it was the right song for that day. On the following day, guided by the same patient muse, we wrote "Spirit Dancer," a tribute to Van Stephenson, one of the founding members of Blackhawk, who recently succumbed to cancer at the age of 47. A brilliant songwriter himself — "Bluest Eyes In Texas" (co-writers: Van Stephenson, Dave Robbins, and Tim DuBois), "Every Once in a While" (co-writers: Van Stephenson, Henry Paul, and Dave Robbins), "Modern Day Delilah," (co-writers: Van Stephenson and Jan Buckingham) and many more. We used references from some of his best-loved songs and even used the Native American translation of "I love you, I miss you," which became a chant throughout the song. I have learned that letting go of what you think you know about songwriting is as important as knowing the craft itself.

Be honest with your co-writer. If she shows you an idea that you have absolutely no affinity for (or if you out and out think it stinks!), let her know diplomatically. You could say, "That's a great idea, but it's really not my style. Let's hear what else you have." Songwriters can exchange ideas all day long before they find one that strikes both of their fancies. Don't settle until you find that common ground. Find a writing partner who can challenge, inspire, push, and sometimes annoy you into being the best you can be.

Finding strength in numbers: How many geniuses does it take to write a hit?

There are no hard-and-fast rules as to the optimum number of collaborators. For The Beatles, the magic number was two; out of the many songs Lennon and McCartney wrote, only 27 of them were written together (even though they shared credit on their entire catalogue), but their undeniable chemistry seems to be present on all their tunes, even in each others absence. For the Brothers Gibb (better known as The Bee Gees), the writing was split three ways no matter how much each brother may or may not have contributed. In the following sections, we outline some popular writing configurations, along with their pluses and minuses.

The two-way split

The image of two songwriters in a dingy room with a broken-down upright piano somehow creating musical magic is one of the most enduring and inspiring images in movie memory. The fact is, however, this mythical image has plenty of basis in truth. Duos through the years like Rodgers and Hart, Bacharach and David, and Jagger and Richards have proven that, as in the words of Harry Nilsson, sometimes "One is the loneliest number you can ever do," and as Nick Ashford and Valerie Simpson crooned, "What two can easily do, is so hard to be done by one." It's hard to argue with the statistics — songwriting duos have had more success than any other combination — three can truly be a crowd especially if the chemistry is not right. Duos, in general, may be so successful simply because there aren't too many ideas being generated in the room and it's therefore easier to focus on the good ones. Too many opinions can lead to "a camel" — a horse designed by committee — and camels are just not as sleek and beautiful as a well-groomed steed.

The three-way split

There are times in songwriting when three is not a crowd however — in fact, it's the perfect number. If each person in a three-way split has a particular strength, it can become a triple threat. Also, if two of you are deadlocked on the validity of an idea, the third wheel can break the tie and act as a kind of arbiter over the proceedings.

When a three-way is bad, it's really bad, with three times the disagreements of doing it alone. If the third member of the team is a negative influence (perhaps he's a "my way or the highway" type or is not open to the other's ideas), he'll more than likely suffocate the creative process. In that case, three really is too many.

More than three

Sometimes when you're part of a band, or writing for a band, three, four, five, or even more people will be in a room attempting to write a song. Though this arrangement can sometimes work, getting a consensus in the room with everyone fighting for their own idea can be extremely difficult. And, from a business point of view, a collaboration like this splits up the publishing pie into sliver-like pieces and makes it difficult for anyone to make any real money (unless the song becomes a huge hit). On the other hand, you should never limit the size of a writing party merely to maximize each person's individual share. Just make sure that everyone is pulling his weight and that no one is just taking up space. Having coffee with everyone is nice, but it's not necessarily great in songwriting.

Take notes after each session as to who did what and whom you'd consider writing again with. If there were any bad working habits displayed, make note of those as well, before memories fade.

Collaborating with a band or an artist

Knowing how to write with a band or an artist is an art in itself. It means becoming like an extra member of the group or an extension of the artist you're working with. Every band or solo performer has a style of his own; the outside writer's challenge is to adapt his style to that of the artist. It's not that you can't bring your personality and vibe to the party, but you should never obscure or try to change what the artist is all about. Try as you might, most artists won't allow you to tamper too much with who they are. It's also impor-tant to be a statesman and discover the politics of each situation. Every band has a unique dynamic, and the more you can find out about who does what, the better. Also, if they're new to the outside-writer game, taking it slow and easy is best. Get to know each other personally and musically. Here are some tips on how to work with a band or artist:

- Listen to as much of a band or artist's recorded work as you can prior to your writing session to get familiar with their sound, direction, and flavor. It's also a good idea to see them perform live, to get a feel for their presentation and the kind of audience that they attract (this applies especially if you are writing with a new act that has limited recorded work).

- Learn as much about the artist or band members as you can so you feel as if you know something about them before you even meet (we're not talking about doing background checks — we're talking about reading their interviews and getting info off of their Web site).

- Arrange a meeting with the artist or band to scope out their dynamic, individual strengths as songwriters, and to determine their objectives for the project you're writing for. Discuss whether they would like to stay with their current sound or try to break some new ground.

- Find out what they hope to accomplish with their new project and what they're hoping you'll bring to the writing table.

- Ask to hear their ideas first, when you're at the writing session, before suggesting that they work on one of yours.

- If they're open to hearing your musical or lyrical ideas, have confidence in your presentation, but avoid being too pushy. If they reject an idea, try not to sit there and sulk for the rest of the session.

- Don't be afraid to offer constructive criticism regarding their songs. But be a good statesman and make sure you present it in a diplomatic way. For instance say, "It might be better if we came up with a memorable hook for this song," as opposed to, "Hey you morons, haven't you ever heard of a hook?"

✔ Don't belabor a song that you don't all have a mutual affinity with. It's okay to say, "This is a good idea but I might not be the guy to help you with this one." Make sure they know to be just as upfront with you.

Years ago, I had the opportunity to write with one of my favorite artists, Sammy Hagar, the "Red Rocker." He picked me up at the airport in San Francisco and whisked me off to his Mill Valley spread in his brand new Ferrari Daytona. After a few cups of high-octane coffee, we picked up our guitars and proceeded to stare awkwardly at each other for about an hour. He finally broke the silence and told me he'd never written with anyone face to face before and was afraid he'd say something dumb or play something that wasn't absolutely brilliant. He was used to messing up only in private! I eased his mind and told him that we were both bound to lay out some pretty embarrassing stuff — and I proceeded to prove my point. After that, things started to fly — and in two hours, we'd written and recorded a demo for what became the main title for the animated classic *Heavy Metal*. Sammy obviously got rid of his jitters permanently and went on to collaborate on countless hits as a member of the band Van Halen.

Collaborating with a script

Though not a true collaboration, many writers consider the script of a movie to be a silent member of the writing team. The songwriter often uses the storyline, characters, language, and style as an inspirational stepping-off point for the song.

Songwriter Frankie Sullivan and I were lucky enough to have the nearly finished *Rocky III* movie to watch as we wrote its theme, "Eye of the Tiger." Having those powerful visuals to inspire us and the motivational story to guide us, it's no wonder we came up with a lasting song. The movie footage was like a third person in the room. Similarly, when we wrote for *Rocky IV*, we worked from the finished script and were able to find key phrases in the dialogue to help us flesh out the lyric. The result was the song "Burning Heart."

You can try your hand at writing for film by picking a movie that you really like and can get into. If you don't already own it on video or DVD, rent it so you can see it over and over if necessary. Use the storyline or script as your writing partner, and let the feeling and emotion of the movie inspire a song or two within you. Use some of its dialogue as a starting point and go from there. If nothing of substance materializes, pick a different movie — one that may give you more to work with for practice.

Collaborating with yourself

Though not technically a songwriting team (unless you happen to have a split personality!), you can often make use of the popular writing technique known as *self-collaboration*. If you're having a case of writer's block in a given week (and it happens to the very best), it's a good idea to go through your stock-pile of notebooks and cassettes to find the gems that maybe you couldn't quite finish at the time. Often, so much time has elapsed that you can barely remember writing what you were working on back then, and it almost feels like you're collaborating with someone else — plus, you have the advantage of gaining perspective on an idea that you couldn't quite bring home the first time around.

Interestingly enough, with the passage of time, you can almost always tell why you were unable to finish a song in the first place. You're able to gain the per-spective a collaborator usually has on your own work. You can see the flaws, the missing pieces, the lack of focus, and poor organization that you couldn't see before, and you're now able to take steps to correct those problems.

Dividing Up the Credits

When a song is finally finished, it's a good idea to decide then and there how the songwriting credits will be divided. At the risk of blowing the mood, while everyone's memory is fresh, put down on paper who did what. If you want to make it more official, you may want to consider a songwriting con-tract between the collaborators that everyone signs to make the splits offi-cial. The Songwriters Guild of America can supply you with various standard forms to use. Some writers' use their ASCAP or BMI forms to make the writers' splits official.

In the absence of an agreement, any of the writers technically could claim an equal share of the song regardless of their contribution, so putting it all in writing is a really good idea.

There are many philosophies as to how the writing credits should be split up, but there is no standard method. In the following sections, we provide some guidelines as to the most common ways to cut up the pie.

The Nashville method

Nashville is to some the songwriting capitol of the world. It's the town where practically everyone you run into is there for one thing — to be where the action is in the field of songwriting. Whether they're waiting tables, playing at the local bar, or showcasing at The Bluebird Café (*the* happening showcase room for songwriters, often hosting roundtables where three or four of the world's most successful songwriters will take turns playing on each other's hits), they're all there for the same reason.

Nashville is also the mecca for collaboration. The way it usually works is that one of the many publishing companies will hear about a particular artist who is looking for material for their next release .The publisher rounds up her best writers and plays cupid, putting different writers together (usually two-way writes, but sometimes three). Sometimes a publisher will call another publisher if there is someone in that stable she feels could bring something unique to the party. The established writers in town are very familiar and comfortable with this kind of roulette, where they might write with three different groups of writers on any given day. It's not unusual for a writer to have completed five or six songs by the end of the week and have them demo-ed by Wednesday of the following week.

In the Nashville method, whoever is in the room actively writing a song gets an equal share of the writer's credit. This has been the etiquette in Nashville for many years, because its writers have learned that they would rather be writing the *next* song then arguing about who did what and for how much on the *last* one. If someone ends up getting equal credit when he didn't pull his weight, he just won't be asked back.

JIM SAYS

No matter how the seasoned pros do it in Nashville, it's better to write one great song than five mediocre ones. However, they're not all going to be gems no matter what you do. Sometimes you'll find one great song in ten you've written. I recently collaborated with a songwriter who was a huge success as a member of a super-popular '80s band. He seemed to be afraid that the songs we were writing together weren't going to live up to his old hits, and he had no idea if what we'd come up with was good enough. Try your best not to let past successes (or failures) affect your present situation. Keep a positive outlook and stop comparing everything you write to other successes and other songs. The art of letting your inspirations fly takes a fresh and open mind.

The honor system

The honor system is where, when a song is finished, the splits are discussed with all partners present. Besides the common 50/50 split, it isn't unusual for percentages to be divvied up 60/40 or 70/30 for a two-way collaboration. In a situation where one person wrote all the music and the other wrote all the lyrics, it's practically always a 50/50 split. For a three-way write, it's not unusual to see 50/25/25, 40/30/30, and other variations. Try to avoid goofy fractions that will make accounting a nightmare (and will mean next to nothing in the long run), and make sure the percentages don't add up to more than 100. (Don't laugh — it happens!)

He said, she said. . . .

Fortunately, songwriting is one of the few fields where gender discrimination just doesn't exist. Talent is talent, a great song is a great song, and that's all that matters to people. There have been some fabulously successful women in songwriting, like Diane Warren and Beyoncé Knowles of Destiny's Child, giving the men a serious run for their money. And there have also been many great husband-and-wife teams (Felice and Boudeleax Bryant, Carole King and Gerry Goffin, Barry Mann and Cynthia Weil, and Burt Bacharach and Carole Bayer Sager). It really comes down to the chemistry between people, not the issue of one's gender.

The Spinal Tap system

The Spinal Tap method is basically once the song is done, everyone has a few drinks and starts arguing about who did what. One guy might start counting the words he contributed and try to affix a percentage to every word. The other guy will claim 50 percent on the strength of the riff he created for the song — until the bass player reminds him that it was actually *his* lick from another song. At that point, the roadie comes in and reminds everyone that it was his girlfriend that inspired the song and that he should get a piece (of the song, that is!). He's cut short by his girlfriend, who just arrived and recognizes the belly ring described in the song as hers and demands payment for the procedure from future royalties. Scenes like these really do happen, which can take the fun out of songwriting and create bad feelings all the way around, not to mention driving up everyone's blood pressure!

If a song is successful, there'll be plenty of money to go around. If it's a stiff, then all the nitpicking you do won't matter anyway.

It's hard to make any generalizations on the differences between writing with men or women. You can't necessarily say that women are more sensitive writers than men or any other such stereotypical nonsense. I've written with guys with the heart of a poet and with some women who are as tough as nails — it really doesn't seem to matter if you're an X or you're an O.

Looking at Famous Collaborations

In the following sections, we take a look at few notable writing teams to see who does what and what makes their songs tick. (For a further in-depth study, take a look at Chapter 21.)

John Lennon and Paul McCartney

John Lennon and Paul McCartney were the main writing force behind The Beatles. John and Paul were both equally gifted in words and music. In the early days of The Beatles, they wrote in the same room (or van), each one bringing to the party the start of an idea for the other's input, until they had something good enough to show the rest of the boys. Oftentimes, the other one was there to add a bridge to an otherwise complete song. Later in The Beatles' career they would write more on their own, only showing each other their songs for comments after they were practically finished. By nature of their original songwriter's agreement, however, they always shared the copyrights 50/50, figuring (correctly) that their individual contributions would even out in the end.

What made their collaborations truly special were the different ways John and Paul looked at life. John's cynical nature made a good counterpoint to Paul's oftentimes Pollyanna optimism. When The Beatles broke up and they no longer wrote as a team, John's songs often seemed abrasive and a bit defensive — with some notable exceptions, like "Starting Over" and his master-work, "Imagine" — while Paul's sentimental streak dominated songs like "Silly Love Songs" and "My Love," which might have benefited from a dose of John's clarifying wit. In the end, they both continued to write great songs on their own, even without the contrast provided by each other's own unique worldview.

Burt Bacharach and Hal David

The hits of this gifted team just go on and on with "What the World Needs Now," "Alfie," "Do You Know the Way to San Jose," and "I Say a Little Prayer for You." Their songs have been recorded by countless artists and are constantly being redone and updated by contemporary artists.

In the case of Bacharach and David, their duties were well delineated: Burt supplied the music and Hal wrote the words. The integration of words and music would take place in any number of ways. In some instances, Burt would supply a portion of the music and Hal would write the words to that section with the two of them collaborating in the same room on the next part. Other times Hal would supply Burt with a lyric or a portion of a lyric and he would set it to music. Basically every means of combining music with words was used in creating the classic songs of Burt Bacharach and Hal David. Not that there weren't some successful misunderstandings in the process, like when Hal received a tape from Burt with the music that would become "Magic Moments," a big hit for Perry Como. Hal wrote the extremely busy lyric — the part about the hayride and the sleigh ride — over the section the Burt had intended to be the intro! The chorus was then written where the verse was supposed to go. A happy accident indeed, yielding a song perhaps more unique than Burt had originally imagined.

Bernie Taupin and Elton John

You'd be hard-pressed to find a more prolific and successful writing team in popular music than these two. Like Lennon and McCartney, who mainly wrote with The Beatles in mind, Bernie and Elton exist mainly to supply a steady stream of hits to one artist: Elton John. Answering Bernie's ad in the personal column of a London newspaper, Elton John (Reginald Dwight at the time) found his partner of destiny with one fortuitous phone call.

Bernie was a poet without a song, and Elton was a brilliant piano player and songwriter in search of words. Usually, Bernie would drop off a few sheets of lyrics and Elton would put them on his piano and go through them one by one until something struck his fancy. Often the song was completed in 45 minutes or less (to this day, if it takes Elton more than half an hour to finish a tune, he'll move on, often never to revisit it). Songs like "Your Song," "Goodbye Yellow Brick Road," and "The One" are all timeless testimony to the power of their collaborations. They both have written successfully with other partners (most notably the songs Elton has written with lyricist Tim Rice for *The Lion King, Aida,* and other works), but the songwriting team of Bernie and Elton will probably define each of them for years to come.

Chapter 16

Creating Goals and Meeting Deadlines

· ·

In This Chapter

▶ Setting goals for the featherweight, middleweight, and heavyweight songwriter

▶ Dealing with pressure and deadlines — head on

· ·

The business of songwriting is, like so many other businesses, a matter of being at the right place at the right time with the right song. Luck really means opportunity meeting preparation. This chapter is about making a habit of "getting lucky" by being prepared — creating goals for yourself, achieving goals set for you by others, and ultimately meeting deadlines.

Creating Goals

When players in various sports use the word *goal,* they're referring to their trajectory reaching its intended target. Their score depends upon an achievement toward a goal in which effort is directed. If you've not yet completed a song, but have that burning desire to be a songwriter, think ahead and dream up or imagine what you'd like to accomplish.

Getting set to write for the first time

Put together an *action plan* — some kind of goal-oriented schedule that you hold yourself to. Your individual action plan will depend on your personal goals, but the process is an important step in getting started as a songwriter. A beginner's action plan might look something like Figure 16-1.

Put a timeline on your imagination. Don't be discouraged if you don't meet every goal on time. A schedule like the one shown in Figure 16-1 is meant to be a creative tool, not a pressure cooker.

Jennifer Songsmith's Songwriting Goals
Featherweight Level

○ **Logging ideas:** I will gather up all the napkins, barf bags, grocery receipts, and other scraps of paper with scribbled notes of lyrical ideas, rhymes, and concepts, and organize them into one notebook. Or better yet, I will log them on my computer. I will log these ideas under specific headings like "Song Scraps," "Finished Verses," "Possible Titles," and "Song Concepts." And I will make sure to back them up regularly or keep them in a safe place.

○ **Preparing the place to write:** I will designate an area of my living space as a writing room (probably the spare bedroom that my brother has finally vacated). I will start to research the marketplace for simple and economical equipment to document musical ideas and to eventually demo my own songs. I will also look into the cheapest way of soundproofing the room.

○ **Getting myself ready to write:** I will bring my brother's old guitar over to Joey, the repair guy, to get it put into playable condition. I will then get my calluses back in shape by practicing along with every CD I own.

○ **Learning the craft:** I will look for various songwriters' workshops and seminars in town to learn more about the craft and business of songwriting and hopefully find a co-writer to allow for feedback and to help put my ideas into a more tangible form.

○ **Getting to know the masters:** I will enroll in a music appreciation class at the community college to get a better feel for the songs written by the masters in this field and buy at least one biography of a great songwriter or writing team.

○ **Completing a song:** By midyear, I will complete an entire song and perform it for my friends.

○ **Completing a demo:** By fall, I will complete a demo of my completed song.

○ **Mailing out a demo:** I will research the process of soliciting songs and compile a list of everyone I wish to send my song to. I will learn the guidelines, submission requirements, and etiquette, and I will mail out and follow up with everyone on my Prospects and Contacts list.

○ **Spending my royalties:** By this time next year, I will be in Cancun swimming with dolphins and spending my songwriting royalties.

Figure 16-1:
An action plan for the feather-weight songwriter.

JIM SAYS

Even as a beginning songwriter, I was very goal-driven. Although I hadn't yet learned the value of writing down goals in any kind of action plan, I'd always set my sights on a particular target. I told my seventh-grade class that I'd written a song before I had actually written it. Although I don't recommend this technique, it was perhaps my way of creating an unmovable goal for myself — if I didn't produce, I'd have been the laughingstock of Piper Elementary! Even though I didn't know the first thing about writing a song, I followed my instincts and used my rudimentary guitar skills to come up with "Hully Gully Bay" (sample lyric, "Where the sea is choppy and the shore is rocky and those hully gully sea gulls are wingin' our way"). The point is, I created a goal for myself and, through necessity, wrote a song.

Venturing out with your songs

If you're past the stage of figuring out the how-to's of songwriting, you've written or co-written several or more songs, and you'd like to get to the next step in your career, goals become even more important. Your action plan might look something like Figure 16-2.

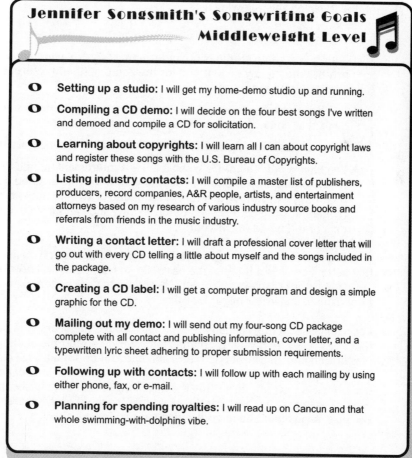

**Jennifer Songsmith's Songwriting Goals
Middleweight Level**

- **Setting up a studio:** I will get my home-demo studio up and running.

- **Compiling a CD demo:** I will decide on the four best songs I've written and demoed and compile a CD for solicitation.

- **Learning about copyrights:** I will learn all I can about copyright laws and register these songs with the U.S. Bureau of Copyrights.

- **Listing industry contacts:** I will compile a master list of publishers, producers, record companies, A&R people, artists, and entertainment attorneys based on my research of various industry source books and referrals from friends in the music industry.

- **Writing a contact letter:** I will draft a professional cover letter that will go out with every CD telling a little about myself and the songs included in the package.

- **Creating a CD label:** I will get a computer program and design a simple graphic for the CD.

- **Mailing out my demo:** I will send out my four-song CD package complete with all contact and publishing information, cover letter, and a typewritten lyric sheet adhering to proper submission requirements.

- **Following up with contacts:** I will follow up with each mailing by using either phone, fax, or e-mail.

- **Planning for spending royalties:** I will read up on Cancun and that whole swimming-with-dolphins vibe.

Figure 16-2: An action plan for the middle-weight songwriter.

It's not enough to merely write out an action plan. Try to read it over weekly to monitor your progress. Keep the plan in front of you at all times to remind you of goals achieved and yet unmet.

For me, goals were always a big motivational tool — they were not always that cosmic. My first goal was to be popular with the opposite sex (music has a way of transcending social standing and physical appearance). My further goal was to make enough money with my passion of songwriting to afford a brand new Datsun 240Z. Of course, trying to enhance the world through creating great music can be the ultimate goal of any songwriter, but never underestimate the power of material goals in tandem.

Setting goals as a pro

If your songwriting career is finally up and running, you can most likely check off the items on the following list:

- ✔ You've just signed a nice co-publishing deal.

- ✔ Your home demo studio is up and running (you've even paid back your brother the money he lent you for the equipment and returned his guitar after buying a better one).

- ✔ You have an entertainment attorney you are happy with to negotiate any deals that come along and answer your legal questions.

- ✔ You even have a song on the debut album of a brand-new artist.

- ✔ You have a *hold* (a hold is when a label is interested enough in your song to ask you to stop shopping your song until they've decided if they'll be recording it or not) with a time limit of one or two months imposed (sometimes the hold is even put in writing and can be from another label on a brand-new song of yours).

Because you're on your way to being a big-time songwriter, you may figure that setting goals is a thing of the past. Not so fast! Goals will now become more important than ever. Figure 16-3 shows what the action plan of an established songwriter might look like.

I have amassed a huge catalogue of songs through the years, and one goal that I've set before myself is creating a master computer file of all the songs I've written and all the vital info for each one. It'll be something I can refer to when I get a call from someone looking for a particular kind of song. My major goal is to continue writing the best songs I can, but my secondary goal is organizing my back catalogue so that it's more easily accessible — because songs don't do anyone any good sitting on a shelf!

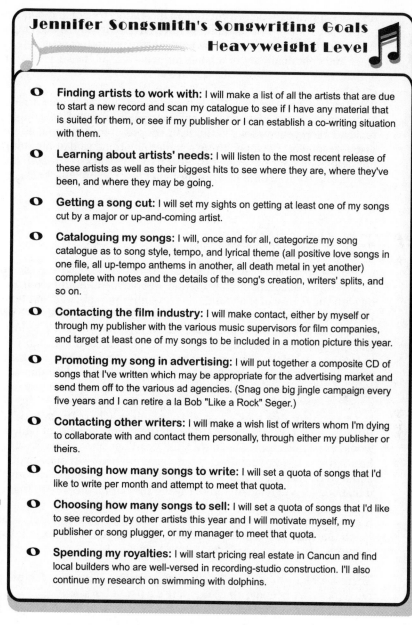

Jennifer Songsmith's Songwriting Goals Heavyweight Level

O **Finding artists to work with:** I will make a list of all the artists that are due to start a new record and scan my catalogue to see if I have any material that is suited for them, or see if my publisher or I can establish a co-writing situation with them.

O **Learning about artists' needs:** I will listen to the most recent release of these artists as well as their biggest hits to see where they are, where they've been, and where they may be going.

O **Getting a song cut:** I will set my sights on getting at least one of my songs cut by a major or up-and-coming artist.

O **Cataloguing my songs:** I will, once and for all, categorize my song catalogue as to song style, tempo, and lyrical theme (all positive love songs in one file, all up-tempo anthems in another, all death metal in yet another) complete with notes and the details of the song's creation, writers' splits, and so on.

O **Contacting the film industry:** I will make contact, either by myself or through my publisher with the various music supervisors for film companies, and target at least one of my songs to be included in a motion picture this year.

O **Promoting my song in advertising:** I will put together a composite CD of songs that I've written which may be appropriate for the advertising market and send them off to the various ad agencies. (Snag one big jingle campaign every five years and I can retire a la Bob "Like a Rock" Seger.)

O **Contacting other writers:** I will make a wish list of writers whom I'm dying to collaborate with and contact them personally, through either my publisher or theirs.

O **Choosing how many songs to write:** I will set a quota of songs that I'd like to write per month and attempt to meet that quota.

O **Choosing how many songs to sell:** I will set a quota of songs that I'd like to see recorded by other artists this year and I will motivate myself, my publisher or song plugger, or my manager to meet that quota.

O **Spending my royalties:** I will start pricing real estate in Cancun and find local builders who are well-versed in recording-studio construction. I'll also continue my research on swimming with dolphins.

Figure 16-3:
An action plan for the heavy-weight songwriter.

All the goals you set before yourself in the featherweight and middleweight phases of your songwriting journey have paved the way to even higher goals. Remind yourself every day of the reasons you got into songwriting in the first place and continually set new goals for achieving all the success you desire — and deserve.

If you're the sensitive type that's prone to getting easily discouraged or disappointed in yourself, try not to set your goals unrealistically high. Dream real and keep your visions in the realm of possibility to avoid unnecessary discouragement. However, there's something to be said about not putting limitations on your own success. Reach for the stars in strength if you so desire, and try to let the disappointments just roll off your back.

Meeting Deadlines

Deadlines are a necessary part of the business of songwriting, so you may as well try to make them your friends. People are conditioned from preschool on with the reality of time limits — remember pop quizzes and ten-minute essays? It's no wonder that people seem to thrive on this kind of pressure later in life. People often take as much time as they're given, but the passion and urgency can be lost if they take *too* much time. You probably won't have to think hard before memories of being under the gun and sweating deadlines start surfacing in your mind. Making these inevitable situations work enables you to have more fun with deadlines and be creative in the process.

I was a student that took a casual approach to school (usually doodling song ideas in notebook margins) until exam time came around, at which point I would cram like crazy. Give me a solid deadline, and my work will generally be sharper and more focused. If you have the reality of one of your songs about to be recorded, you're already imagining how embarrassing it would be if that song isn't great, so you're raising the bar all the way to that moment.

Having all the time in the world can be a song's undoing. When you have too much time and opportunity to change, second-guess, and solicit too many opinions you can ruin a perfectly good song.

There are many areas in the field of songwriting when time factors and deadlines may become an issue. Here's a list of but a few:

✔ **Publisher's deadlines:** Often your publishing contract will specify a set number of songs that you must deliver each contract year. If you fail to meet that quota deadline, they may fail to pay you your final advance payment for the year or forget to renew your contract entirely.

✔ **Movie deadlines:** If you're lucky enough to be commissioned to write a song for a motion picture, you may also be unlucky enough to develop an ulcer as you struggle against an unrealistic shooting schedule. Not only do you have to read the script, view the *rough cut* of the movie (that's the version that looks like it was edited by a machete), and write the song, but it generally has to be demo'd (and demo'd real well!) — all in about one week's time.

I'm certain that given enough time and opportunity I would have over-thought and ruined some of my best songs. When Sylvester Stallone con-tacted Frankie Sullivan and I to write the main title for his upcoming *Rocky III* movie, I enjoyed the pressure of the tight deadlines we were presented with. When you keep the finish line right in your sights, it tends to sharpen your focus. The question is frequently asked as to how long it took to write "Eye of the Tiger." The correct answer is about a week. Perhaps the more insightful answer is that the song had been silently taking shape for a lifetime, and finally in 1982, opportunity met preparation and a song was born.

✔ **Album deadlines:** When top-selling artists like Faith Hill are looking for songs for her new album, you can bet that every writer in Nashville is trying to come up with something fresh that will pique her, or her pro-ducer's, interest. However, good as that song may be, if Faith and her team have already chosen the songs for her next album, unless your song is the next "Breathe," you're a dime short and a day late for that one. In contrast, there's also such a thing as being "early on a project" — where it's so early in the song-searching process that your song may be forgotten by the time the songs are being selected for the record — so it's best not to be too early or too late. Usually your publisher or song plugger will have the most current info on who's looking and when the deadlines for submissions are. Also there are various "pitch sheets" that you can subscribe to (such as Row Fax in Nashville: www.Music Row. com) that give you a week-by-week snapshot of the artists currently look-ing for songs, specifying the kind of songs they need and if co-writes are being considered, and what their timetable is for sending tunes.

I had an extremely embarrassing brush with deadlines early in my song-writing career. I'd just been signed as a writer with Warner Brothers Publishing, and I was overly eager to impress. My mentor at the com-pany informed me that a prominent singer/guitarist was looking for material for his upcoming album. I had a song started called "San Pedro's Children" and was told that if I could finish it and demo it by the following week, I had a good shot of getting it cut. I finished it quickly, demo-ed it, and sent it in. Then I waited. The only thing that bothered me was that, because of the time constraints, I had to rely on my rudi-mentary grasp of the Spanish language (two years of study in high school) to create the section where the Mexican children could be heard singing God's praises just before the song hit the last chorus. On the demo, I started the section, "Viva Diablo con Noche. . . ." and so on. I figured who's gonna know anyway, and it sure sounded Spanish-y. Well the artist loved the tune. So much in fact that he was soon in the recording studio singing those words, "Viva Diablo. . . ." when one of the engineers of Mexican descent interrupted the session and asked John why he was singing, "The devil lives at night?" The singer then ripped my publisher limb-from-limb and he, in turn, tore into me. How does this story end? I took the time I should have taken earlier and got a proper Spanish interlude for my song with the help of the Spanish Council of Chicago. The song was completed the following week and the story had a happy - ending. But every time I see a photo of this artist, I picture him with the veins popping out of his forehead over the audacity of that new kid signed to Warner Brothers.

Pinpoint what stage of the game you most likely fall into — whether it's just getting started or as an established songwriter. Then get organized and set your goals for the next 12 months and commit to achieving them one by one. Songwriting is a creative process, but you still have to treat it as a business if you plan to make a decent living out of it. The more you structure your time, stay focused, and remain disciplined, the better your chances will be for success — and you'll tend to have other songwriters out there saying "man, you sure get lucky."

What to say when you miss a deadline

Rather than turn in poor work as a result of trying to meet a songwriting deadline (or is it rather a "dread" line?), look at this handy checklist of excuses the next time you are under the gun, and out of bullets:

✔ "The dog ate my song notebook" (the old standby).

✔ "I'd written the lyric on an airsickness bag on the flight to meet with you, but the person next to me needed the bag."

✔ "The demo was all finished when the Pro-Tool system went berserk and substituted my son's interactive Pokemon game. Do you have any kids?" (It's always wise to blame it on a computer glitch since many of us have

the uneasy feeling that computers are out to get us anyway).

✔ "The song would be finished except that I'm writing a new and better one right now, and giving you a piece of the publishing for your patience!"

Seriously, unless you are writing songs strictly for personal use, to play for friends and/or to creatively express yourself, you'll want to stay up with the flow of traffic on the music industry freeway, That means setting and meeting goals (at whatever level you are), meeting the deadlines you've set for yourself (or have been imposed upon by others) and finding ways to motivate yourself to do your finest work.

Chapter 17

Getting Your Songs Heard: Making the Demo

The day will come when you've finally finished your song and it's time to put your heart and money on the line and share your creation with the world. After all, your song won't do anyone any good sitting in your notebook! The first step in getting your song out there is to make a demonstration of the song — better known as a *demo*. A demo is a prototype or template from which the right industry people who are interested in your songs can elaborate. It's like a sketch from which a fully realized masterpiece can then be painted.

In this chapter, we give you the inside scoop on how to prepare and produce a demo of your song, and we let you know how to get it to the right people.

Paying Attention to Details

First and foremost, a demo should be an effective representation of your song. It can be simple or complex, depending on the song itself. The demo doesn't have to be totally polished. However, the more professional it sounds, the better the chance it has of being appreciated by the right people.

Picking your format

The compact disc (CD) is rapidly becoming the format of choice for demos. In the past, demos were always presented on cassette, but thankfully — because they sometimes run at wrong speeds, the quality is poor, occasional dropouts can be heard, and you can't just skip automatically to the song you want to hear — cassette tapes are soon to be a thing of the past. By using a CD, you can get away with having more songs on one demo presentation, simply because if the person you're sending it to doesn't like one song, he can quickly jump forward to the next one.

New technology has enabled the equipment that creates CDs from your master tracks to become more and more affordable. This equipment is often built right in to home computers and laptops. But don't donate your cassette deck to charity just yet — submission policies of some companies still specify cassettes, so always check before you send.

Choosing the number and length of songs

Ideally, your demo should contain no more than three or four songs total. The producer, artist, or A&R person probably cannot absorb much more than that at one time — and because he's leaving for Aruba on Saturday, his time is kind of tight anyway.

Making sure the songs on your demo aren't too long, or too short, is very important. However, don't compromise the song just for its length. Ultimately, the song dictates the length of the demo.

Ideally, a song that you're pitching should be under four minutes in length, but there are no hard and fast rules here. If the song is good at seven minutes, then let it be that long — just make sure you're not kidding yourself and that those seven minutes really work (please note that a seven-minute song is an extremely long one). Also, keep intro lengths down and get to the first verse as quickly as possible.

Play your song for friends' — this is a good road test. The bottom line is to see if you're holding their interest. Good friends will call a spade a spade and a clinker a clinker — and hopefully they'll still be your friends the next day! If they nod off while listening to your demo, consider editing the song (or finding some new friends!) — your song and demo should keep moving and building. Try to engage the listener's attention at all times.

Keeping it simple

Demos generally need to be very simple. Try to leave room for the potential singer to imagine what he can do to it to make it his own.

A good demo song is an effective representation of:

- ✔ The lyric
- ✔ The melody
- ✔ The chords
- ✔ The feel
- ✔ The direction or genre
- ✔ The heart and soul of the song

Overall, when creating your demo, always keep in mind that this is the way your song will be heard by the world. Make sure when all is said and done, whether the arrangement is simple or complex, or the production is rough or sophisticated, that it represents the song the way you think it should be heard. Take pride in the presentation at whatever level your budget dictates. If it gets across the essence of the song, it really doesn't matter how much money you spend on it, the song will shine through.

Picking the Players

After you've finished your song, unless you're a one-man-band, you'll need to create a team of musicians, programmers, and engineers to help see your vision through. (Refer to Chapter 15, for collaborating roles in greater depth.)

Deciding whether to use musicians or machines

Many times, nothing beats the sound and chemistry of real musicians playing together. But often, due to financial restrictions or lack of contacts, you may be wise to consider programming your demo on a computer. A programmer can sequence the sounds of drums, keyboards, and bass. However, you may want to add a real guitar player after all the other pieces are on, in order to humanize the sound of the track. (The guitar is one instrument computers have not yet mastered!) And of course, vocals are still — for the time being at least — the domain of actual human beings!

Often times, I have a programmer do practically everything on the song demo: the drums, percussion, bass, keyboards, brass, and strings — whatever is needed for that particular song. Then I bring in maybe one additional musician to humanize the track — perhaps a guitar player. Also, sometimes I replace the synth bass myself with real bass for that more organic sound and feel.

Using musicians

If you decide to go with real live musicians, instead of a computer, to create your demo, you'll quickly see that there are no shortcuts to finding the perfect team of musicians to work with — it's all trial and error, and finding the right combination can take years. You'll need musicians who are intuitive to what's in your head and are a supportive presence to your talents. Creating a demo is like putting a puzzle together — you can only see the whole picture when all the pieces are in place. Look for reliable people who you believe hear what you're hearing in your head and can expand on that vision.

Finding musicians

Finding musicians isn't as hard as you might think. Start by going to clubs where bands are playing. During a break, introduce yourself as a songwriter looking for musicians. Often times, they'll be eager to do studio work (especially if there's pay involved) because it's a welcome change of pace from their "live dates." You can also check in the back pages of your local music publication for musicians for hire (request a tape of their work before booking them), or place an ad yourself, seeking top-notch studio musicians. (Or check out one of the many networking Web sites listed in Appendix A.) In addition, by attending various writers' nights and showcases you'll inevitably find qualified people who are in attendance, or quite simply by "word of mouth." You can also find talent by keeping your ears open at your local guitar center, as musicians are trying out gear.

Working with musicians

In music, as in life, sometimes human interaction is the magic behind the music. Whether you're making a quickie demo or a big-budget master, the synergy created between musicians is often what brings a song to life.

Before I really had my music team together, I'd write a song, and sometimes by the time it was in demo form, it had morphed into an entirely different song — not the one I wanted to hear. Finding great players isn't enough. Try to use the people who don't feel they need to show off in order to earn their keep — find the ones that support the song and bring out the best in it and in you!

Using machines

It used to be that all instruments had to be played by actual human beings. But the advent of drum machines, samplers (a digital recorder that captures — or "samples" — any sound source for playback onto your track), MIDI (which stands for musical instrument digital interface whereby a musician can program his computer to communicate with a vast array of sound sources), and computers has changed everything. Much of the music you hear on the radio today is created and perfected on computers. As a songwriter, this can be good news. By learning the craft of programming, you can literally be a one-man or one-woman band — and courses are offered at recording institutes and community colleges that can educate you in this amazing and ever-changing technology.

As a songwriter making a demo, learning programming or finding a team player who's proficient at it is important — especially if you're pitching your song to any of the areas that rely on programming so heavily, such as urban, hip-hop, rap, and dance/pop.

Programming your demo can have these advantages in certain situations:

✔ Keeping your costs down by not having to hire as many musicians

✔ Making your demo have a more current sound in certain genres

✔ Adding flexibility to your demo by giving you the ability to build it up slowly and make modifications at the eleventh hour

Recently, I came across the original demo I had made for "Hold on Loosely," which I co-wrote with Don Barnes and Jeff Carlisi for 38 Special. I thought it was pretty hot when I did it using a drum machine and playing all the parts myself. I couldn't believe how stiff and mechanical it sounded when I heard it recently after being used to the finished hit version, which uses all the members of the band, giving it that human feel that only comes through human interaction. Whether it's the actual musicians playing together or the person who's programming the computer, it still comes down to the heart and soul of an actual human being.

Deciding who is going to sing

There are varying opinions and considerable debate on whether the songwriter should actually sing his own demo. On the one hand, the songwriter knows the song from the inside and whatever he lacks in vocal ability is made up for in soul and feeling. However, the industry is accustomed to hearing polished vocals — so it may be best to give up a little feeling for the range, vocal texture, and overall technique of a great singer. The best of both worlds, of course (unless the songwriter happens to be a great singer), is finding a singer who really gets into the song and sells it for you with professionalism *and* the correct mood or feeling.

Making an Arrangement

The term *arrangement* refers to the musical shape that your song will take. Years ago, the arranger was arguably more influential than the producer in determining how a song would end up sounding. When Frank Sinatra changed from arranger Nelson Riddle to other arrangers, his whole style changed. In those days, the arranger wrote out the parts that virtually every instrument would play and the dynamics (louds and softs, playing and laying out) with which they would be played. Even the rhythm and feel were notated on paper.

At the demo stage, the arrangement is important because it serves as a template of how you envision the final version. The type of arrangement that you create will depend on the type of song you've written. The arrangement of a song indicates what marketplace you'll be targeting and how effective your presentation will be. For example, ballads often can be presented in a simple piano and vocal version with minimal percussion, if any. This approach showcases the melody and lyrics, which are the most important elements of a ballad. On the other hand, up-tempo songs — whether they are rock, R&B, country, gospel, or whatever — rely as much on the rhythm as anything else. You'll want to add powerful drums, pounding bass, cutting guitar, brass, and whatever else you feel is necessary to give the listener the full impact.

In any case, allow the person who's listening to your demo *feel* the song, not just hear it. And, when creating the arrangement for your song demo, keep in mind that a strong musical hook is often as important as the song itself. It won't make a bad song great, but it sure can elevate an average song and make it a slam-dunk. Often, it's those little intro riffs and figures that stick in your head well after the song has faded.

Ask your band members or studio musicians to add their own creative touches to bring musical spice to your song.

A lot of times, the artist, manager, or producer who's listening to these songs has had it up to his ears with fancy demos. Don't give them anything not to like. Many hit songs were originally presented as a demo with only piano and voice. Some have been cut on the strength of one voice singing into an answering machine. But there are other examples where the excellence of the arrangement and performance actually sold the song — some writers create what sounds like finished products to showcase their song. Ultimately, you have to go with your gut instinct and do what's right for you and your song.

A good producer or publisher that you present a song to will see right through any gold paint and sparklers that you may have added to the demo thinking it would help compensate for what you feel your song may be lacking otherwise. If the song isn't solid at its core, you won't be able to disguise it with a fancy production. Let production be transparent, and let the song itself shine through. As they say in Nashville, you can't polish a cow chip!

Creating a chart

The songwriting team should come to a session with a *chart* of the song — a rough draft of the chord structure of the song. Chord charts can be presented in two different ways:

- ✔ **The note chart:** This is the traditional method, in which each chord is assigned a letter in accordance with its root or tonic note (the root or bottom note of a chord — if you played a C major chord — C, E and G, the C would be the root) — from A to G, in minor or major.

- ✔ **The number chart:** Also known as the Nashville system, this is a method in which each chord is indicated by its number and a plus or minus sign to indicate major or minor (see Chapter 10 for more information).

Notations should be made on the chord chart as to the sections of the song, clearly marking intros, verses, pre-choruses, choruses, bridges, repeats, instrumental sections, and whatever else. Often, musicians make their own notations on their chord charts to remind them of certain arrangement ideas.

Beyond that, it's up to the songwriter and his team of musicians to create a *head arrangement.* A head arrangement is where everyone makes mental notes (hence the word *head*) and suggests ideas as to style, feel, rhythm, genre, musical breaks, musical riffs, and hooks — all the nuances that take a basic chord chart and make it magic. Sometimes the spaces you leave in a song are as important as the notes you play. Arranging a song is all about the give and take between musicians — the sections of a song where one instrument will drop out, allowing another one to shine. These techniques will make your song demo more compelling to the listener.

If you come to your session without at least a chord chart, you'll waste precious studio time waiting for the musicians to write out their own charts as they listen to the song.

As the writer of the song, you'll probably have a pretty good idea of how you want your song to sound, but try to be open to the input of others you trust. Your arrangement choices will help to determine the following:

- ✔ The musical direction your song will take
- ✔ Which market is best suited to your song
- ✔ How effective your presentation will be
- ✔ What demographic target your song will find

Often there is a very fine line between the genres — and actually a lot of crossover among them. For instance, the borders are currently quite blurry between pop/rock and country. I sometimes change the instrumentation of a song slightly to tailor the same song to two different marketplaces. Often, the addition of a pedal steel or fiddle can tip a pop song into the country market. Conversely, the addition of a distorted power guitar can beef up a country pop song enough to be pitched to rock artists. Sometimes, the vocal style has to be altered accordingly, but the drums, bass, and keyboards can often stay the same. Similarly, a pop/rock song can change into a dance/pop song by altering the feel of the arrangement and usually by substituting programming for live musicians.

Using an arranger

Having a team player called an *arranger* — the person who puts all the musical pieces in the right place and adds sonic musical color where it's needed — is well substantiated but not always required. If you've assembled a good team, the musicians and the engineer can all become the arranger. The songwriter can also act as the arranger, but then the songwriter must put the arranger hat on and think like an arranger.

The days of hiring an arranger at the beginner's level are long gone. When you get your song cut and have a budget for, say, $10,000, then you can bring in an arranger and ask him, "Okay, here's the basic track, what do you hear?" He'll then say something like, "Oh wow, I hear an organ here, sleigh bells right there, and a 40-piece string section on the chorus."

As the songwriter, your arrangement of your song will set the tone for how you want the record companies, the artist, and the managers to perceive it. Start with a mission statement of the marketplace (or marketplaces) you think your song can fit and make decisions accordingly.

Recording the Demo

Whether you decide that you're going to be using real musicians, programmed instruments, or a combination of both, you must also decide on how and where your song will be recorded.

Deciding where to record

Generally, your finances dictate where you'll record your demo. If you can afford it, use a professional studio. They can offer you a trained staff, top-notch equipment, and great coffee so you can concentrate on what you do best: creating music. If money is tight, perhaps you know someone with a decent home studio who wouldn't mind helping you out (plus making a few bucks on the side). Maybe you could even barter your musical talents in some way against free studio time. The most cost-effective way, of course, is to do it yourself on modest equipment you've installed in your basement or spare bed-room. If you have a fairly high aptitude for the technical, this may be your first choice. Just be sure not to let the technical details totally bog you down.

Doing it yourself

These are great times to be living in if you're a songwriter on a shoestring budget. You can buy a relatively inexpensive but superb digital multitrack recorder such as the Zoom MRS-1044CD hard disc recorder (which for around $1,000 combines the capability of recording instruments on 100 virtual tracks, effects like reverb and equalization, and an onboard drum machine), a MIDI keyboard such as the Yamaha S80 (around $1,200) two Rode NT2 microphones (around $400 each) and for less than $3,000 total, create a recording studio in your spare bedroom. Becoming efficient at this will allow you to rival the pro-duction quality of what could only be done in the major studios just a short decade ago.

Of course, there are sonic differences between an inexpensive digital recorder and the professional setup at the downtown studio. But at the demo stage of a song, those differences won't determine whether your song will be well received or not. In fact, Alanis Morrisette's 13x platinum album *Jagged Little Pill* was recorded entirely on the Alesis ADAT system — a technology even at the time considered to be primarily a demo recording format. If the song is there and the soul is intact, that's all that really matters. Currently, there even exists a budget system called ProTools DIGI 0.1 — the disk-based digital recording system that is rapidly becoming the standard of the home and project studio industry. It can go head to head with the sound of the big ProTools system, although it's not nearly as flexible.

Lots of songwriters make their own demos and record all the instruments themselves — one overdub after another. They lay down the drum tracks or computer-based drum samples first, do a sequence, and then play all the instruments over that, adding vocals just before the mix-down phase.

To learn the technology of digital home recording you can often find classes offered by local colleges. Check with The Recording Academy (NARAS) to see if they have any recording workshops on the horizon or if they can point you to one. Look in the back pages of home recording magazines like *EQ* to find schools that specialize in the recording arts. Music stores often have company sponsored seminars on the recording gear they sell. Of course, as a last resort, you can always read the owner's manual and learn the old fashioned way — trial and error till you get it right!

A songwriter/producer I work with in Nashville does some of the best demos I've heard, and does it very economically. He plays almost every instrument himself, then calls in a really good singer to do the vocals and does the mix right there — all for a couple of hundred bucks to get a demo that would have cost $5,000 to do 20 years ago.

Using a professional studio

With the numerous improvements that have been made in home recording, many songwriters still choose to bite the bullet and spend bigger bucks in hiring professional recording studios. A commercial studio:

- ✓ Supplies top quality engineers and staff.

- ✓ Provides a musically conducive environment away from your everyday home or office atmosphere.

- ✓ Provides you with more equipment options at a level of higher sophistication on every aspect, from a wide assortment of microphones to sound processing like de-essing (getting rid of those spitty s's) and pitch correction.

- ✓ Provides a place where your musicians can meet and not invade your private space.

- ✓ Allows you to concentrate on patching up your song instead of running patch cables.

- ✓ Furnishes you with generally some of the strongest darn coffee north of Brazil!

Furthermore, professional studios make their reputation on service and reliability. If a machine goes down at home, the session is off until you can get it fixed. At a big studio, they'll generally have backups for just about every piece of gear — so the creativity and the momentum of your session rarely has to be broken up because of broken equipment.

If you aren't inherently a technical person, it may be wise to use a professional studio. Many songwriters get so bogged down watching meters, reading manuals, and troubleshooting problems that the music gets lost in the shuffle.

By any definition, I am not a technical person. I'm the guy whose VCR is always blinking "12:00." I rely on engineers and programmers to help me create my demos and final products. I would rather be writing another song than poring over another operations manual written in every language but my own. I envy those writers who can do it all — it's a great asset.

Currently, you can rent a good demo studio equipped with an engineer for about $35 to $60 an hour. Call around and find a good price, and avoid the expensive studios. Some studios specialize in cutting demos (as opposed to actual final album work). Studios like this make it easy by booking the room in three-hour session blocks, complete with recording engineer and often a selection of session musicians they'll supply for a package price. Studios like this (County Q in Nashville has made its reputation on this principal) pride themselves on total efficiency. If you come well prepared with songs and charts, you could cut as many as six or seven songs in a three hour session.

Finding demo services

In the back of many songwriting newsletters and music magazines, you can find listings of mail-order demo services. The deal is, you send them a rough tape of your song (or the sheet music) and for a set fee, they'll produce a finished demo for you. The quality of these services range from rip-off to wonderful, so be sure to request samples of their work before you hand over your precious song. And always copyright your song before sending it anywhere (refer to Chapter 14 for the example and details).

Paying for the demo

How much you're able to spend on your demo will be determined to some extent by who's footing the bill. If you're signed to a publisher, there may be provisions in your contract that specify the conditions of making demos and the maximum cost allowable per song. Usually the expense is paid upfront by the publishing company and recouped from royalties due to the songwriter (often a good attorney can negotiate for only 50 percent of that cost, to be paid back from your earnings). There may also be language in the contract that states that all demos must first be approved by the publisher — which means you'll have to do a great job of singing your song over the phone or do a decent boom box version for their approval. At any rate, it still behooves you to keep your cost down — you'll be paying it back someday!

Packaging the Demo

For a songwriter, the packaging that goes into selling your song doesn't need to be elaborate. In other words, your demo CD need not look like a CD in a record store with four-color printing or fancy artwork. The song — seldom the writer — is the star of the show. Few people really know what Diane Warren looks like, yet she is the writer behind scores of top ten hits. You'd walk right past Max Martin (who writes songs for the Backstreet Boys and others) and Mutt Lange (the writer behind hits for Shania Twain, The Corrs, Def Leppard, and Heart) without ever knowing it. Take note that it isn't necessary to have a photo of yourself on your demo package, unless you're presenting yourself as an artist as well.

When packaging your demo, it's not about you — it's about the song. Presentation is important with a song demo, but it doesn't have to be fancy or elaborate to get attention.

Including contact information

Information is everything when pitching your songs. Next to the music itself, it is the single most important element.

There have actually been cases where a song has been passed over by a producer who could not find a contact phone number on the label. Maybe the writer's information had been on the cover letter that accompanied the disc, but the letter had been tossed out. Producers get hundreds of songs a month — it doesn't take much to disqualify one for reasons like this.

The best and most economical way to package your song demo is to house your CD in one of those clear, slim-line jewel cases. Then put all the pertinent information on the sticky round label that gets affixed to the CD itself. That information would be:

- The titles of the songs on the disc and their running lengths
- The names of the songwriters
- The name of the songwriter(s)' publishing company (if any) and performing rights group (ASCAP, BMI, or SESAC)
- A contact phone number
- An e-mail address (if you have one)
- The copyright date (the date you recorded your demo)

Keep the information as simple as possible on the sticky label. For instance, if there is more than one writer, don't bother listing issues like who wrote the lyrics and who wrote the music. Similarly, there is no need to cram the label with every publishing company involved in a song. After your song is cut, there will be plenty of room on the final product to go into greater detail.

The audio CD is the best medium for presenting your song in terms of quality and convenience for the listener. CD labels, jewel cases, and front insert cards (which are optional — see Figure 17-1 for an example) can be purchased at your local office supply or computer supply store. You can buy blank CDs in bulk on spindles quite economically, and you can easily learn how to *burn* them (copy them) by using an inexpensive CD-ROM burner, a piece of equipment that connects to, or is included in, your computer.

Sometimes, putting a simple graphic behind the information on your CD sticky label can add a nice dimension to your presentation (check out the example in Figure 17-2). When I was sending various radio stations the demo version of the song I wrote with Johnny VanZant of Lynyrd Skynyrd, "The Day America Cried," my wife found a nice image of the Capitol building and an American flag. It made for a more compelling package.

There are many software programs on CD-ROM that you can load into your computer to add graphics to your demo presentation. CD Label Maker by Memorex is very popular. But if you don't have access to a computer or label maker, you can still type onto a sheet of sticky labels (available at your local office supplies outlet) all the pertinent details and label the CD yourself.

Always have your contact number in two places: on the CD *jacket,* which is the card tucked inside the case, and the sticky CD label.

Other elements to go out with your song package include:

- ✔ **A cover letter:** A typewritten letter from the songwriter or publisher introducing you, the songs, and the songs' intended target. This page should include all your contact details.

- ✔ **A lyric sheet:** A typewritten listing of all the songs included on the demo, along with their lyrics. This sheet, too, should include all your contact details in case the other sheet gets lost.

Requesting permission to send a demo

If you send a demo without it being requested or *solicited,* you run a high probability of having it returned unopened. The record industry seems to be particularly vulnerable to lawsuits, so whenever someone listens to a song they have received unsolicited in the mail, they're leaving themselves open to possible copyright infringement litigation. If you can't hire a music attorney to solicit your song, send a letter (like the one shown in Figure 17-3) to the record company, artist, and others requesting permission to send a song to them for a specific purpose.

Also, when you call, ask if the recipient uses or requires a code word or an identifying mark on the outside of an approved submission package.

As soon as you get an okay and you're ready to send your material, be sure to write on the envelope "REQUESTED MATERIAL," and any code or identifying mark if required. Make sure you have your name or company prominently displayed along with your return address on the package.

A little protocol can go a long way. As a songwriter, you need every advantage you can get.

Making a lyric sheet

Including a typewritten lyric sheet with the song you submit is a good idea. Some A&R people, producers, and others will ignore the lyric sheet and rely on their ears alone, while others will follow along as they listen. Some will read the lyrics only after the song has initially grabbed them — so your words need to be intelligible on your demo. The lyric sheet then becomes icing on the cake. Take a look at Figure 17-4 for an example of a lyric sheet.

Jennifer Songsmith

1234 Melody Lane
Harmony, Tennessee 37654
(423) 324.5678 - jsong@email.com

April 12, 2002

Mr. Sean Starmaker
A&R Department
Starmaker Music
4321 Chartmaker Terrace
Nashvegas, CA 95351

Dear Mr. Starmaker,

My name is Jennifer Songsmith. I am a 25-year-old songwriter from the tiny town of Harmony, Tennessee.

Although I do not yet have a hit to my credit, I have written over thirty copy-written songs and won my county's songwriting competition in 1998.

I would like your permission to send you a song for your artist Billy Bob Boyband. I feel I have one that would fit him to a tee. It is up-tempo pop with a bit of an alternative edge with what I feel is a very catchy chorus. Because I cannot yet afford to hire my own music attorney, I am asking your kind cooperation.

Looking forward to hearing from you by phone, fax, e-mail or mailing address.

Sincerely,

Jennifer Songsmith

Jennifer Songsmith

Figure 17-3:
Requesting permission to send a demo is a critical part of the submission process.

The words to a song are as important as the music. Make sure they stand out in the mix and that they are well enunciated!

Figure 17-4:
Include a lyric sheet in your demo package. Here's the song example Jim wrote with our fictitious Jennifer Songsmith — "Dummy For A Song."

If your demo presentation has a lot of unnecessary information, the listener will have a hard time finding the important stuff — like your phone number. Conversely, if a key element is left off the demo, it may end up in the circular file — otherwise know as the wastebasket.

Putting the Demo in the Mail

You've just written a song, finished the demo, and created a simple and attractive package for it. Now you'd like a certain artist to hear it — who is the best person to present your song to them? Try hitting as many people involved with your target artist as possible.

Getting your demo to the right people

It has been said that the definition of good luck is when opportunity meets preparation. Now that your song is prepared, you need to know the people who can give your song that special opportunity! They include the following:

- The A&R person at the record label
- The president or CEO of the label
- The artist's producer
- The artist's manager
- The artist's music attorney
- The artist
- The publisher

We cover each of these people in the following sections.

The A&R person

A&R is an abbreviation for Artists and Repertoire and indicates someone whose job it is to find talent and search out great songs for the record company's or publisher's artist roster. When you're a songwriter or an artist, this is a good person to get to know, because he usually sits at the right-hand side of the CEO (who is usually too busy wining and dining to actually sit down and screen songs). You can find record company A&R executives by checking out the reference guides (Web sites, magazines, and agencies) listed in Appendix B or on the Cheat Sheet in this book.

Sometimes the A&R person works hand in hand with a manager to get an artist together with a song. Survivor had one song left over after recording our first album. It was a song Frankie Sullivan and I had written called "Rockin' Into the Night," and our producer felt it didn't quite fit in with the rest of the album. Our A&R person gave the song to 38 Special's manager, who played it for the band, they loved it and the song became 38's first hit record.

The president or CEO of the label

In certain rare occasions, the head honcho at the label actually gets in the trenches and actively hunts for great songs for his artist. Sending two copies of your song to the label wouldn't be a bad idea — one to the A&R department and one to the president.

The artist's producer

Sending a song to an artist's producer really improves the odds of getting your song cut. The producer has a lot to say about what an artist will hear for a project, and if he has the confidence of the artist, he can influence what will and won't get recorded. Often, a producer will have a *listener* working for him — someone who screens for appropriate songs so the producer doesn't have to wade through thousands of songs himself.

Producers are usually looking for one particular type of song for a specific artist. Don't send a song to a producer unless you have one you think will fit. I once sent a producer friend of mine a song I knew deep down did not suit the artist. I mainly wanted to impress him with the song. Guess what? He wasn't impressed. If you go to the tool cabinet looking for a screwdriver, you may find a beautiful wrench but it won't do you much good. Don't wear out your credibility by sending inappropriate songs.

The artist's manager

The actual hands-on involvement of the artist's manager varies widely. Even if a manager doesn't listen personally to the songs submitted for his artist, he may pass them along to the producer or record company — especially if the songwriter has a proven track record.

A few years back I received a call from the manager of a major rock group, asking me if I had any songs for their upcoming album. With my usual zeal I told him I had tons of stuff that would be perfect for them. He replied that whenever a songwriter says that to him, he pictures a big dump truck pulling up at his office and unloading thousands of songs. He said, "Jim, all I really need is one great one." From that lesson forward, I learned that songs are evaluated one at a time — not weighed by the pound!

The artist's music attorney

Because of the trust built up between an artist and his attorney, this is a really good office to get your song to. It isn't as conventional as some other places, and therefore falls into the "Gee, isn't he clever and enterprising" category. The champion in this category is the young songwriter who has companies interested in her songs by recording pieces of her best ones on executives' answering machines in the wee morning hours. Although we cannot go on record as recommending this practice, we do admire her fearless ingenuity.

The artist

If you could pitch your song to only one person, the artist would be the number one choice. No matter how strongly those around the artist believe in a song, it is still the performer who has to connect with it. The artist must believe the song is right for him in terms of direction, emotion, message, and feel. Collaborating with the artist can be so effective precisely for this reason: A co-writer can really get into an artist's head to see what makes him tick.

The publisher

Getting a song to the artist's publishing company may seem contrary to logic, because they have their own songs to push. However, if they like your song enough, they just may pass it along to the artist or perhaps even suggest a collaboration between the two of you.

All of the above

Hitting as many bases as possible with a given artist is never a bad idea. If enough people in the artist's inner circle start talking about a song or a song-writer you can create quite a buzz — and generally, the more bases you can cover, the better your chances of having a home run and getting your song cut.

Producers get songs pitched to them all the time. It's important that the song you send them is in keeping with the style of the artist that producer is working with. Even if the song is great in and of itself, it won't be considered unless it's artist-specific. Focus on the artist you're trying to reach or you may not get a second chance.

Don't make apologies for the song or demo. A producer may lose interest in a song before he even hears it if all you can do is make excuses for the presentation. Don't send a song until you're confidant you've captured the essence of the song — then of course, no apologies are needed.

Following up

After you've sent your solicited song or songs to a producer, artist, A&R person, manager, and others, you need to follow up with a phone call or e-mail to confirm it was received. Once that's done, the next step is finding out whether it was listened to and how they liked it. You can do all of this with one phone call if you're lucky; but you may need to make several calls to get all the information you need. Persistence is a key element here, but you need to be sure not to come off as too much of a pest. Make sure your phone manners are pleasant and that you don't sound as desperate as you most likely are. Make sure you're not screaming at the kids, blasting the radio, or eating potato chips (bananas are okay) while you're talking to the head of A&R at Zomba Music! It's also a good idea to have a pen and paper ready — with a list of things you want to cover in the phone call. If you've tried and failed repeatedly to get a response on a song, it may be the interest is just not there!

Chapter 18

Pennies from Heaven: How Your Song Makes Money

- -

In This Chapter

▶ Predicting future funds

▶ Selecting your performance rights organization

▶ Making money from retail sales

▶ Allowing your song sell a product

▶ Using your songwriting talents for motion pictures

- -

*I*f you've written a song and someone wants to record it, you're now at the point in the songwriting process where you get paid for your hard work. In this chapter, we introduce you to some important organizations to know — the ones that handle the royalties. We also discuss how your song can find opportunities in commercials and movies.

Forecasting Financials

Most write songs because we love to. Songs help us to express some of our deepest feelings and allow us to share them with the world. It's nice to know, however, that there can be a pot of gold at the rainbow's end, that we're not only doing it for our mental health — we're earning a living at it!

Sources of income

The major sources of income for a songwriter are:

- ✔ **Performance royalties:** The performing rights organization that the songwriter and publisher is affiliated with (such as ASCAP, BMI, or SESAC, all covered later in this chapter) calculates this sum every time his songs are played — whether it is through radio, television, movie theaters, or anywhere else in public.

- ✔ **Mechanical royalties:** Songwriters and publishers get paid on every CD, cassette, video, DVD, or other product sold that contains their songs.

- ✔ **Commercial use:** Songwriters and their representatives negotiate fees to be paid when a company wants to use their song to sell a product.

- ✔ **Motion pictures:** Motion picture companies that wish to use one of your songs must first work out a deal with you and your publisher.

Splittin' up the pie

The amount of money you earn in the categories listed in the preceding section depends upon the following variables:

- ✔ **How well you and your business team function as a unit.** For example, you'll have trouble receiving your performance royalties if you or your administrator fails to register your song with one of the performing rights societies. Also, when a film company inquires about the use of one of your songs, an inexperienced publisher, music attorney, or administrator may quote a fee that's either too low (thus underselling you) or higher than the market will bear (thus blowing the whole deal).

- ✔ **How many people are sharing in the writer's credit.** Obviously, the more wedges cut, the narrower the slices will be.

- ✔ **How your publishing is split.** Some songwriters own their own publishing companies, and others have co-publishing deals. Writers who have signed away their publishing rights will make half as much money as those who own their own publishing companies. (See Chapter 13 for more on publishing companies.)

There's gold in them thar hills!

The number-one worldwide song of the year is likely to generate $1.6 million in revenue (for one year of sales and airplay). A single song could command $4,000 or more when used in a popular television show, and a standard popular song's lifetime earnings could total $11 million or more. In case you didn't know already, songwriting has the potential to generate a lot of revenue!

Joining a Performing Rights Organization

After you've recorded your music, it's important to join one of the performing rights organizations. The three major performing rights organizations — ASCAP, BMI, and SESAC — all are recognized by the United States Copyright Act of 1976. Their job is to monitor all music that is played in public and make sure that you get paid all royalties that you're due. Performing rights organizations collect license fees from the businesses that play music to the public, and then distribute them as royalties to the writers, composers, and publishers they represent. These three performing rights organizations collect over $1 billion a year.

If you act as your own publisher, the fee for joining a performing rights organization is different for each organization. These agencies bring in most of their money from the small percentage (around 4.5 percent) they take from money collected on your songs. If you are signed to a publishing company already, they'll usually take care of your performing rights paperwork (just requiring your signature) and pay the initiation fee for you.

There is always a debate among songwriters as to which performing rights group is the best. I once wrote a fair-sized hit with a writer who belonged to BMI. Because I was with ASCAP, we decided it would be interesting to see who made more money on the song per quarter, and determine once and for all which organization did a better job of collecting our royalties. The first quarter I won by a few thousand; the next quarter my co-writer won. By the end of the fourth quarter, the tally was just about equal. Even though the two societies have very different ways of calculating performance royalties, at the end of the day, they seem to do a comparable job.

Choosing a performing rights organization is an important decision, so be sure to find out as much as you can about these agencies and their collection methods before you make your final decision. But keep in mind that if the organization you join isn't working out for whatever reason, you can always change — you are not bound by a lengthy term.

ASCAP

The American Society of Composers, Authors, and Publishers (ASCAP) a nonprofit performing rights organization founded in 1914, has its headquarters in New York with offices in Atlanta, Los Angeles, Nashville, Chicago, Miami, London, and Puerto Rico.

In 2001, ASCAP distributed about $511 million dollars in royalties to the 130,000 composers, lyricists, and music publishers in all genres of music. Annual membership dues are currently $10 for songwriters and composers, and $50 for music publishers.

Performance money is primarily collected through a blanket license. After operating expenses are deducted, ASCAP sends the balance to its member writers and publishers and to affiliated international societies.

A *blanket license* is the annual fee paid by music users (radio, restaurants, television, and so on — see the long list later in this chapter). The music user pays each of the performing rights organizations this modest fee for the legal right to play all copyrighted music as much as they wish. In other words, one fee gets unlimited use for any music. The performing rights organizations require a quarterly report detailing what songs (and how often) the music user is playing to determine the fee that is charged.

Members who have belonged to ASCAP include such classic songwriters as Irving Berlin, Johnny Mercer, Richard Rodgers, Harold Arlen, and Jerome Kern, as well as current artists and songwriters such as Garth Brooks, Dr. Dre, Bruce Springsteen, Madonna, Stevie Wonder, James Horner, Joni Mitchell, Wynton Marsalis, Beck, Stephen Sondheim, Jose Feliciano, and many, many others. ASCAP also licenses tens of thousands of international music creators such as The Beatles, The Rolling Stones, Charles Aznavour, and Julio Iglesias.

ASCAP has a searchable database of performed works, along with writer, publisher, and recording artist information on the Internet at www.ascap.com/ace/ACE.html.

BMI

Broadcast Music, Inc. (BMI), a non-profit performing rights organization founded in 1940, has its headquarters in Nashville and offices in New York, Los Angeles, Atlanta, Miami, London, and Puerto Rico.

BMI distributes annually about $540 million dollars in royalties (less general and administrative expenses) to approximately 350,000 songwriters, composers, and music publishers in all genres of music. The current registration fee (for publishers only) is $150 for an individual and $250 for partnerships, corporations, and LLCs. There is no registration fee for songwriters.

As with ASCAP, BMI uses a blanket license to collect license fees. It then distributes the monies received to its writing and publishing members.

Where your songs may be played

By securing a license from these organizations, any song in the performing rights organization's repertory can be played legally. Without this license, music users are in danger of copyright infringement. The following list (not all-inclusive) gives you an idea of just how many places there are that might play or use your song and pay for that right. It's pretty awesome to think that your song could end up being played in so many different environments and that you would receive royalties from each:

- Airlines background/foreground music service
- Buses
- Campgrounds
- Carnivals and circuses
- Colleges and universities
- Concerts and recitals
- Conventions, expositions, industrial shows
- Meetings and trade shows
- Dance clubs and associations
- Dancing schools
- Drive-in theatres
- Family shows
- Festivals
- Funeral establishments
- Halls of fame, wax museums, and similar establishments
- Hotels and motels
- Ice-skating rinks
- Laser shows
- Motion picture theaters
- Museums
- Music-in-business
- Playgrounds
- Professional speakers
- Private clubs
- Radio stations
- Restaurants, taverns, nightclubs, and similar establishments
- Retail stores, shopping centers, and shopping malls
- Sporting events
- Symphony orchestras
- Telephone music services
- Television stations
- Theme and amusement parks
- Train cars
- Training and development sessions, educational or informational seminars
- Video services.

Members who have belonged to BMI include such classic artists as John Lennon, Chuck Berry, Dave Brubeck, Willie Nelson, Carlos Santana, Elton John, The Beach Boys, Aretha Franklin, The Who, and Leadbelly, as well as Janet Jackson, Michael Kamen, Faith Hill, Sting, Jennifer Lopez, Sheryl Crow, Jay-Z, 'N Sync, Britney Spears, Eminem, Mariah Carey, Kid Rock, Elvis Crespo, Oasis, Sarah McLachlan, Faith Evans, Snuffy Walden, Shakira, and Snoop Dogg.

SESAC

SESAC is a for-profit performing rights organization, with headquarters in Nashville and offices in New York, Los Angeles, and London.

SESAC was founded in 1930 as The Society of European Stage Authors and Composers. Since that time SESAC has significantly expanded the number of songwriters and publishers represented, and its repertory now includes all music genres. As a reflection of this change S.E.S.A.C. became SESAC, Inc.

SESAC's repertory, once limited to European and gospel music, has diversified to include today's most popular music. Members who belong to SESAC or have performed SESAC-affiliated songs include such artists as Garth Brooks, Jim Brickman, Eric Clapton, U2, Luciano Pavarotti, LeAnn Rimes, Mariah Carey, Alan Jackson, Cassandra Wilson, Jagged Edge, Jimi Hendrix, Ricky Martin, Christina Aguilera, and UB40.

SESAC is the smallest of the three U.S. performing rights organizations; however, they believe that their size is the largest advantage, because they're able to develop individual relationships with both songwriters and publishers.

SESAC has a selective policy of affiliation — they audition songwriters and publishers before they become a member, and once accepted, there is no fee to join.

Knowing What Happens When Your Songs Hit the Shelves

As a songwriter, not only do you make money every time your song is played on the radio, television, or in a variety of public places, you also get paid on the sales of every CD, cassette, video, or other product that contains one of your songs. The money from this source is called *mechanical royalties*.

The word *mechanical* appeared in the 1909 Copyright Law referring to payments for devices "serving to mechanically reproduce sound." It's been a very long time since those original mechanical devices were used to reproduce sound, but the name lives on, and all the money paid to copyright owners for the manufacturing and distribution of records are still today called mechanical royalties — the rights to reproduce songs in recordings are called mechanical rights.

If an artist and her record company wants to record and release one of your songs, or if a company of any kind would like to use your song for a variety of other purposes (the latest application is cellular phone companies who are licensing hit songs for users to download as their ring-tone), they must first obtain a mechanical license from you or your publisher. When a song is used on a CD, if it's the first time that song is being used, the artist or label must get the writer's written permission first.

If a song has already been recorded and released for commercial sale, according to copyright law, anyone is free to record that song as long as the songwriter and publisher are paid and accounted to in accordance with what's known as a *compulsory license.* (The artist or label will usually attempt to obtain a traditional song license from you initially. If you, as the songwriter, fail to cooperate, they will just issue you a compulsory one.)

If you are a songwriter who handles her own publishing, you can obtain samples of mechanical licenses from your music attorney, administrator, or organizations such as the Songwriter's Guild of America. Or contact the largest of all mechanical royalty collection and licensing companies, the Harry Fox Agency, for information as to how to employ their services.

Songwriters receive royalties from the first record sold and from the first time it's played on the radio or in public. On the other hand, artist's royalties are only paid out after the amount of money the record company has spent on production and promotion of the album has been recouped — and they're out of the red and into the black.

As of January 2002, the standard mechanical (also known as *statutory*) payment that the songwriter and publisher split is 8 cents per song. (That rate is reassessed every 2 years.) Doing the math, if you are the sole writer of a particular song, you will earn $80,000 on a million-unit seller. Often a record company will ask a writer for a reduced rate such as 75 percent of statutory rate. Your willingness to be marked down will depend on just how badly you want a particular artist to record your song.

Using Your Songs to Sell Products

One of the single most lucrative situations for you as a songwriter is when a product manufacturer decides that your song is to become the imagemaker for his company. It used to be that practically all songs used in commercials were created specifically for a product by ad agencies and *jingle houses* (companies that specialize in writing jingles for commercials).

But today, it seems that more and more major corporations are going with hit songs from the past and present, and they're creating their campaigns around these songs. "Revolution," performed by The Beatles (written by John Lennon and Paul McCartney), is now synonymous with the Nike brand. "Like a Rock," the platinum hit for Detroit's Bob Seger, will forevermore conjure up images of Chevy trucks climbing impossibly rugged terrain. The Ides Of March smash "Vehicle" (written by Jim Peterik) has become a rally cry for the entire G.M. line. Foreigner's smash "Double Vision" (written by Mick Jones and Lou Gramm) was certainly never originally intended to be the music behind Burger-King's Double Whopper, but who would have guessed? As a songwriter, you'll never be able to plan these magical pairings. However, when you're writing a new song, it *is* fun to fantasize! (Refer to Chapter 12 for more about jingles.)

At the time "Eye of the Tiger" was released, I never dreamed I'd see Joe Isuzu working out to that tune as part of a nationwide Isuzu ad campaign. All a songwriter can do is to try to write a great song with staying power, and someday the right product might just find *you!*

The money you can earn for the use of your song in a commercial depends on:

- ✔ The size of the product's advertising budget
- ✔ The popularity of the song
- ✔ How much of the song is actually used in the commercial
- ✔ The length of time that the song is contracted for
- ✔ The area of the country (or world) that the ad covers
- ✔ How good you or your publisher is at the art of negotiating
- ✔ How desperate the advertisers are to get the song
- ✔ If the song will be used for radio, television, the Internet or all three

A big hit song performed by a major artist for a major product can command upwards of $1 million for a year's usage. A more typical deal might bring $25,000 to $75,000 for an average-sized hit that's used in an ad campaign for a medium-sized company for a one-year period of time.

Even as an unproven songwriter, there may be opportunities for you to pitch your songs for commercial use. Contacting advertising agencies and jingle producers isn't as hard as you think. Use the same care with submitting material to them as you would with a record company or producer. And don't forget about local manufacturers, restaurants, dealers, and services that you could approach directly with your ideas for how your songs could be used to stimulate their business (and yours!). Check out Chapter 12 for more information on getting your songs into the right hands.

Making Money in the Movies

How many times have you walked away from the multiplex humming the title song of the movie you just saw? That's the power and synergy of combining the right song with the right scene. Motion pictures can be a great inspiration to a songwriter, as well as a tremendous source of income. Songs can be submitted to film companies, producers, and directors through your music attorney or your publisher — or you can do it yourself using the proper etiquette described in Chapter 12.

Due to my involvement in soundtracks in the '80s, I've had a fair amount of opportunities to try and repeat those successes. I've had some good experiences writing "Beyond Our Wildest Dreams" for *Delirious,* starring John Candy (co-written with Cliff Eidelman), and some disappointing ones as well. In 1990, I was commissioned to write the end title for the Robert DeNiro movie *Backdraft.* The movie supervisor sent me the script and a rough cut of the movie. I was blown away by the visual power of the film and the turbulent, yet loving, relationship between the two brothers in the film. I was also totally jazzed that the movie took place in my hometown of Chicago, and that my song would be playing underneath a majestic, smoke-tinged view of Chicago's skyline at dawn. I turned in what I thought was one of my best songs ever, entitled "Long Road Home." The music supervisor loved it, the stars loved it, but the director wasn't quite sure. The day before the film's deadline, he decided the lyric contained the word "fire" and was too literal to the story. He went with another song written and sung by Bruce Hornsby. I spent the next three days in my bathrobe! (By the way, that director was Ron Howard, and I haven't watched an episode of *Happy Days* since.)

Figuring out how much money to expect

Getting your song into a film, or writing one specifically for a movie, is definitely something to shoot for. It would not be unusual for a song that was used in the beginning or end-title slot of a major motion picture to command anywhere from $25,000 to $100,000. Songs that are used in lesser scenes might bring in anywhere from $10,000 to $20,000. A complete score by a well-known composer could bring in $100,000 or more.

Of course, if your song is included in a hit soundtrack album, and your performance and mechanical royalties start kicking in, then order that Hummer H2 you've been drooling over — compliments of those royalties!

Every time a movie is shown on television, the songwriter gets money from the performance society he belongs to in accordance with established rates. Unfortunately, the songwriter gets no royalties when the movie plays in a theatre, so try to negotiate a decent flat fee upfront to compensate for this.

There are many ways to turn your passion of songwriting into cash, but try to make sure money is not the main motivator. Let the cash be the fortunate result of your creative talent, hard work, and fair negotiations.

Chapter 19

Networking for Songwriters

· ·

· ·

*M*usical sparks can ignite when there's an open flow of ideas between like-minded individuals and a free exchange of information. These conditions have paved the way for various creative wellsprings that have emerged through the years such as the hit factory known as the Brill Building in New York City in the '50s and early '60s, which spawned such writers as Gerry Goffin and Carol King, Neil Sedaka, Neil Diamond, Barry Mann and Cynthia Weil, and more, plus Motown (Berry Gordy's creative Camelot in Detroit in the early 1960s that grew into a multimillion-dollar entertainment conglomerate that's still active four decades later). These were situations in which people weren't afraid to help one another, knowing full well that by combining creative juices they could achieve more than they could on their own.

In this chapter, we highlight places where you can reach out to song-writers and others in the music business — and make yourself available for others to reach out to you. We suggest that you check out these places to get a healthy exchange of ideas (plus e-mail addresses!) and see how great music can not only be created, but where it can find an audience as well. The main sources for networking (covered in more depth later in this chapter) include the following:

✔ **Writers' nights:** Intimate club-type gatherings where you can interact with songwriting associates, watch or perform new songs live, and make new friends.

✔ **Writers' organizations:** By researching the various organizations — big and small, international and local — you can find out which ones best suit your needs.

- ✔ **Writers' camps and cruises:** Getaway places in the woods (or out on the sea) for workshops that promise to be filled with inspiration and education for the aspiring songwriter along with instructional advice from songwriting pros.

- ✔ **Internet roulette:** A place to get the ball rolling (the mouse ball that is) by surfing the Net. There's more information on the Internet than you'll ever need — it's just a matter of finding it and having enough spare time to use it.

- ✔ **Seminars, workshops, conferences, and symposiums:** Educational and inspirational programs that offer opportunities to learn from and network with others. Plan to get on mailing lists that provide the calendar of dates for these places. Expand your abilities with these resources — some events are even free.

Hanging Out at Writers' Nights

The writers' night is a phenomenon that came into form and popularity in the "beatnik" coffee houses of the '50s (along with usually avant-garde poetry readings) and has been gaining steam and prestige with every passing decade. They're usually held at fairly intimate (that's code for "cramped and smoky") clubs and sponsored either by the visionary club owner or a nearby writer's association. They generally take one of two forms:

- ✔ Showcases where writers take the stage one at a time and perform a few of their songs (usually kept to around 20 minutes by a soundman with his eye on the clock).

- ✔ Showcases where a group of usually three or four songwriters perform together (often in a roundtable formation) and take turns accompanying and harmonizing (even trading verses) with each other on their songs.

Even as a member of the audience, you can get a lot out of these nights. You can observe the songs that are and are not working, and then try to gauge your own songs and performing readiness against what you've heard. Be sure to introduce yourself to as many people as you can (including the club owner, sound technician, industry representatives, and all the performing writers). See if you can convince the organization to include you the next time there's a similar writers' showcase.

The word of mouth you can receive within the songwriting industry is perhaps more important than the exposure you get from the audience in general. At events such as these, as much activity takes place off stage as it does on stage with phone numbers exchanged, co-writes planned, and ideas brainstormed.

I've attended and performed many writers' nights throughout the years. They're always fun and stimulating to my own creativity. I've also made contacts including A&R representatives (who come to have a drink and search for songs and new artists), writers willing to co-write, and even artists looking for new material. It's a great way to try out new songs and see which ones work — and which ones stimulate movement to the restrooms!

Make sure you follow up with the people you meet in these types of events. It's easy to make promises to call or get together in the glow of the night, after a few beers, but even more important is your following through.

If you can't find an existing writers' night or showcase in your area, why not organize your own? It's not hard to put a flyer up at the local music store or post it on your Web site. Just mention that you'll be hosting a writers' round-table at your home (or convince a club owner that it'd be good for building business on an off-night). A $5 entrance fee should more than cover the refreshments and overhead. Plus, a workshop of your own is a great way of making new acquaintances and contacts.

Joining Songwriting Organizations

Many organizations are designed to aid the songwriter in every stage of the game. Almost all major cities (and many smaller ones) have established songwriters' guilds and clubs to help develop and market your songs. Whether you live in Pittsburgh or Portland or any point in between, you'll find it relatively easy to locate those who share your same passion for songs. Here are a few organizations that can help your network talents in the songwriting field.

National Songwriters Association International

NSAI is a not-for-profit songwriters' organization based in Nashville (but it covers the U.S and a few foreign countries). Besides being an effective defender for the rights of the songwriter (fighting for royalty protection and so on), it's a terrific resource for the songwriter at any stage of his development in the craft and business of songwriting. In fact, there are four levels of membership:

- ✔ **Active:** For songwriters who have at least one song contractually assigned to a music publisher ($100 U.S. / $75 International).
- ✔ **Associate:** For songwriters who are unpublished or persons who wish to support songwriters ($100 U.S. / $75 International).

✔ **Student:** For full-time college students (12 or more hours) or students of an accredited senior high school ($80 U.S. / $75 International).

✔ **Professional Membership:** Pro membership is for songwriters whose primary source of income is derived from songwriting and/or who are generally recognized as professional songwriters by the professional songwriting community ($100 / 1-year membership).

When you become a member, you can take advantage of their song critiquing service (where pros evaluate your song for you — free of charge) and attend symposiums, song camps, cruises, and workshops. You'll also benefit from their quarterly newsletters, special events, and use of their office facilities when needed.

Authorized NSAI branch chapters and workshops are sprouting up all across the U.S., and you can find them by contacting the main NSAI headquarters at

NSAI
1701 West End Avenue, 3rd Floor
Nashville, TN 37203
Phone: (615) 256-3354 or (800) 321-6008 (toll-free within the U.S.)
Fax: (615) 256-0034
Web site: www.nashvillesongwriters.com

I had the pleasure of being asked to speak and perform at the NSAI symposium held in Nashville — and I've never had such a receptive audience in my life. You could literally feel the passion for a song in the air and certainly see it in the eyes of the 300 students and fans of the craft who attended. Afterwards, I got to meet many writers, young and old, with whom I shared some off-the-record tips, and I took home with me a few (very good) demo tapes. I was just one of many writer/speakers in an event that helps define the term *network*. Even after many years in the business, I learn a lot at the NSAI publishing seminars by listening to lectures and asking questions of the industry insiders enlisted by NSAI.

Songwriters Guild of America

The Songwriters Guild of America (SGA or simply the Guild) offers a wealth of information and services for its members, including sample songwriter's contracts, reviews of publishing contracts, and a copyright renewal service. SGA has offices in Los Angeles, Nashville, and New York, with their administrative headquarters located in New Jersey.

In 1931, three leading songwriters (Billy Rose, George M. Meyer, and Edgar Leslie) formed the Songwriters Protective Association (SPA), known today as The Songwriters Guild of America. They formed this organization after they had made numerous unsuccessful attempts to organize the contract arrangement between songwriters and publishers relating to the payment of royalties. Finally, the Guild was able to establish a standard and uniform contract. After 20 years of efforts, the Guild was successful in shaping the "author's bill" and educating Congress as to the needs of the songwriter. The result was the Copyright Act of 1976. The "author's bill" included legislation regarding the Term of Copyright and the Statutory Mechanical Rate.

The annual dues for members range from $70 to $400 depending on whether you are an Associate Member (unpublished), Regular Member (published), or Estate Member (an heir of a deceased songwriter), and depending on the amount of royalties collected by the Guild from your publishers during the prior year.

The songwriter's benefits and all the details regarding the Guild's services, history, sample contracts, and resources can be found on their Web site at www.songwriters.org. You can also contact the Guild at

Songwriters Guild of America
1500 Harbor Boulevard
Weehawken, NJ 07086
Phone: (201) 867-7603
Fax: (201) 867-7535
E-Mail: SGANewJersey@aol.com

For contact information for the New York, Nashville, or Los Angeles offices, visit the Web site.

Hello mudda, hello fadda. . . .

Since 1992, NSAI has been hosting song camps for aspiring songwriters to polish their skills with the guidance of professional songwriter mentors. Their curriculum has been described as a "transforming experience" for songwriters. They position you in a unique atmosphere combined with the finest faculty of professional songwriters anywhere, which translates into an experience beyond compare.

If you like retreats and honest feedback, sign up for one of their camps and have breakfast, lunch, and dinner where everyone is focused on songwriting for days on end. You'll be part of small-group sessions, personal song critiques with pros, and practice writing sessions. It'll cost some bucks and the groups are limited in attendance, so plan ahead. When you apply, they'll probably want you to send them two of your songs on tape or CD as well as other information.

You can find out the details by contacting their office at: Director of Camps/Cruises, NSAI, 1701 West End Avenue, 3rd Floor, Nashville, TN 37203; phone: (615) 373-7872; Web site: www.nashvillesongwriters.com.

I only wish I had known about organizations like the Songwriter's Guild of America years ago when I was starting out. Even now, they're a great source of knowledge when it comes to songwriting contracts, writer contacts, and performing (for a below-standard industry fee) many of the functions of a publishing administrator such as filling out and filing songwriting forms and other paperwork. Their song critiquing service and rewrite workshops could've really shaved a lot of time off my craft learning curve if I'd been smart enough to take advantage of organizations like these. (But as the saying goes, "it's never too late!")

Songwriters Guild Foundation

Based in Hollywood, the Songwriters Guild Foundation is the not-for-profit part of SGA. They offer a series of workshops with discount prices for SGA members and cover such topics as these:

- ✔ **Ask-A-Pro/Song Critique:** Present your song and receive feedback from pros. This is a great place to meet industry people, make contacts, and get answers to your questions.

- ✔ **Jack Segal's Songshop:** Spend nine weeks in a workshop that focuses on taking your song through to perfection — from the title and ideas to rewrites and pitching your song.

- ✔ **Building a Songwriting Career:** One-day workshops that help you discover how to establish a career in songwriting — featuring professional songwriters and music business executives in panel discussions about the trade — all free of charge.

- ✔ **Special Seminars and Workshops:** Check on the various dates and places held throughout the year — covering everything from lyrics to MIDI machines.

You can find out more information about current workshops by contacting them at

Songwriters Guild Foundation
6430 Sunset Boulevard, Suite 705
Hollywood, CA 90027
Phone: (323) 462-1108
Fax: (323) 462-5430
Web site: www.songwriters.org

Don't get discouraged by criticism, especially from the pros; consider it an opportunity to improve your songwriting. However, if you really believe in an idea, no one's opinion is more important than your own.

Getting help from the performing rights-organizations: ASCAP, BMI, and SESAC

In the beginning, the performing rights organizations were established to collect and distribute money to songwriters, composers, and publishers, but they've blossomed into providing resources as well. Whether you join ASCAP, BMI, or SESAC, you'll be amazed at the wealth of benefits as an information base and networking resource they provide to their members (and paying non-members).

Besides going to bat for songwriters' legal rights and new legislation to protect you, they'll provide you with tons of resources that'll help you succeed. And why not? The more you make, the more they make — it's a win-win situation. If you need medical and dental insurance, they've got it. If you need workshops and seminars, they're scheduled often and in a town near you covering subjects that are right up your alley. They also have contests, awards, parties, and networking opportunities for many genres.

You can find information about the performing rights organizations in Chapter 18 and contact numbers in Appendix B.

Playing Internet Roulette

The Internet is coming on strong as a primary method of soliciting your songs and networking with others. Because the Net covers the world, there are really no geographical boundaries and transmission is practically instantaneous. That's the up side.

The down side is that the Internet is really only the first step to true human interaction, which still requires actual contact between parties where a person's mannerisms, vibe, and voice can come through. Sometimes it is difficult to generate chemistry between people by merely sending e-mails and sound files back and forth. Sooner or later, after initial connections are made, it's important to get in the same room with the contacts you've made on-line. Whether it's co-writing a song, networking a business plan, or testing out a song, there's still no substitute for in-person interaction.

That being said and done, take a look at the ways you can harness the power of the Internet to find information and opportunity, gain exposure, and help network your talents with others.

Creating your own Web site

One of the best ways to get the word out on what you are up to as a song-writer is to create your own Web site. In this day and age, having a Web site is practically a necessity if you want to make the most of your career. Use your own name as your domain name, if you can (the domain name is the part between the *www* and the *.com*).

Many books are available that can fill you in on how to set up an effective Web site, including *Building a Web Site For Dummies* and *Creating Web Pages For Dummies,* both published by Hungry Minds, Inc. But if you'd rather not devote much of your time to it, you can always hire a pro to create a Web site for you.

The goal here is to create a kind of space-age press kit for yourself complete with photos, biography, accomplishments, goals and aspirations, strong suits. Let it be known what kind of people you're looking to connect with. In addition to this, include any songs that you feel best represent your work so that others can download and listen. Include all of your writer's affiliations, contact material, and anything else you want to share with the world.

Having the best site in the world will make no difference if no one knows about it. Be sure to get the word out any way you can that you have a Web site. Put your Web address on your business card and business stationery and post it on the myriad of musical sites and at local music stores. And whenever you send out an e-mail message, include an automatic signature at the bottom of the message, where you mention your Web site as well.

Your Web site can also be a useful forum for ideas. You can pose questions for others who visit your site to answer; you can solicit opinions on songs or lyrics you have posted (get ready for some very honest responses — it's easy to hide your true identity on the Internet so people tend to be more candid than they would be otherwise). You can also have other writer's stream music to you for opinions and collaborations.

Your Web site is only as good as how current you keep it. If visitors see no changes in the site after visiting a few times, they'll stop visiting altogether. If inquiries go unanswered, you will get an unfavorable reputation.

I was the original "who needs the Internet" guy until a fellow named Tom Soares created a Web site for me (`www.jimpeterik.com`) and my whole perception changed. Not only was it a great way for people to purchase my CDs, but it's also a way for them to get information on my past, present, and future. I get feedback from others on what I'm doing right and wrong from around the world. And I can post bits and pieces of new things I'm working on as they occur. After I got over "Web anxiety" and found a capable Webmaster, I found my Web site to be an indispensable component of my career.

Taking advantage of other people's sites

There are a growing number of music and songwriting sites that can be helpful to you in creating awareness for your talent and finding collaborators and contacts. You can set up an information page on www.MP3.com and also post your creation there for others to listen to and even download — just make sure you have filed the copyright papers for your songs before you share them with the world. You can also post your music and list your songs on a variety of sites such as:

✔ TAXI (www.taxi.com)

✔ TONOS (www.tonos.com)

✔ SongScope (www.songscope.com)

✔ SongCatalogue (www.SongCatalogue.com)

✔ Just Plain Folks (www.jpfolks.com)

Not only is the Internet a great way for others to hear your songs, it's also a good way for you to hear and evaluate the work of others.

Locating resource, advice, and information sites

Besides being a means to get your songs and information broadcast to potentially millions of people, the Internet can be the ultimate source for up-to-date information, contacts, and those looking for what you've got. For instance, to learn more about the craft of songwriting, check out www.jasonblume.com, where you will be transported into the classroom of one of the best songwriting authorities around, Jason Blume. Or you could go online with Muse's Muse (www.musesmuse.com), another great songwriter's resource site. A don't-miss site for all the tools, tips, and services you need to enhance your songwriting career is TONOS at www.tonos.com where networking is global. Because it was founded by Oscar/Grammy-winning professionals, you'll surely enjoy and benefit from everything the site offers. TAXI (www.taxi.com), of course, has been a fountain of accurate information and opportunities since its inception in 1992.

You can start your search for information and exposure at the more established sites and find links from there to many newer, smaller but often cutting-edge Web addresses.

I'd like to thank the Academy. . . .

Better known as The Recording Academy, NARAS (National Academy of Recording Arts and Sciences, Inc.) is most notably known for its annual telecast of the Grammy Awards. However, The Recording Academy is much more than just an annual awards show.

By becoming a member of The Recording Academy, you can get involved in the various music issues within your own community, and you can also network with other members who are making their living in the music industry. There are many local and regional programs and functions that you can become involved with through being a member of The Recording Academy and you can learn about these and see exactly what the advantages are of becoming a member just by logging on to their Web site at www.grammy.com.

There often are subscription fees that come along with these various music sites especially the ones that offer shopping services and song listings and provide weekly or monthly *tip sheets* (exclusive listings of artists and producers looking for songs, writers looking for collaborators, and so on). Make sure you understand the fee structure, and decide if it can be justified as far as how it benefits your career.

Attending Seminars, Workshops, Conferences, and Symposiums

Every writers' club, society, and organization puts together song workshops and seminars for the songwriting community. This is where you can get together with other songwriters and hear lectures by great writers and industry hot shots and participate in roundtable discussions on the craft with other songwriters at all stages of development. There may be a talk from a lyricist, a composer, a producer, an A&R rep, a commercial writer, a film scorer, and a publisher. These workshops are an indispensable tool to the serious songwriter.

There are virtually hundreds of these events around the world. Besides the most famous ones like the South By Southwest Music and Media Conference held each year in Austin, Texas, you can find many others on music sites on the Internet and in songwriters' resource books such as *Billboard Musician's Guide to Touring and Promotion,* published by Billboard Music Group, *The Musician's Atlas* published by Music Resource Group and *Songwriter's Market* published by Writer's Digest Books.

When you mingle with like minds, you're expanding your opportunities exponentially. You've probably heard the saying, "It's not what you know, it's who you know." Well, it's really both. It's just not enough to "have the gift," you've got to "work the gift." Workshop, seminars, writer's nights, and songwriting camps and cruises are your opportunity to combine forces with other "gifted" individuals, to make the best music of your life. Next time that up and coming songwriter is searching for the perfect collaborator for the movie writing assignment she just landed, she just might think of you!

Part VI
The Part of Tens

In this part . . .

In this part, we go out on a limb and show you some noteworthy (ouch!) songwriters, songwriting teams, and songs. Just so the limb doesn't break, instead of calling it "The Ten Best," we simply call it ". . . You Should Know." These shining examples of songwriters and their craft are sure to inspire budding songwriters. Over time, you'll surely create your own list of the songs and songwriters that really "float your boat," but this is as good of a place as any to start your voyage.

Chapter 20

Ten Songwriters You Should Know

The task of picking the definitive ten best songwriters of all time is extremely daunting considering the wealth of talent that has come and gone. Here are ten songwriters we have chosen because of their innate genius, dedication to the craft, and their contribution to the soundtracks of all of our lives.

Irving Berlin (1888–1989)

Proving his precocious hit writing abilities at age 23 with "Alexander's Ragtime Band," Irving Berlin would go on to become one of the most successful songwriters of the twentieth century. His ear for a great melody, his head for a hook, and his heart for a good earthy lyric has created such standards as "Blue Skies," "Let's Face The Music and Dance," "The Song is Ended," "Easter Parade," and "Always." Successful in both Hollywood and on Broadway, he scored 17 musicals and won the academy award for Song of the Year in 1942 for "White Christmas." His songs continue to be performed and reinterpreted by each passing generation.

Cole Porter (1891–1964)

To his emerging piano and violin skills, a six-year-old Cole Porter added his rhyming talents, and by age ten had written his first song. You don't have to have seen the plays that inspired songs such as "From This Moment On," "I Love Paris," "I've Got You Under My Skin," and "In the Still of the Night" to feel their lasting power. His sophisticated words and music gave popular singers of the '30s and '40s such as Billy Holiday ("Easy to Love") and Libby Holman ("Love For Sale") something to really sink their hearts into. He also supplied some of the best of that era's bands such as Tommy Dorsey and His Orchestra ("Night and Day") and Artie Shaw and His Orchestra ("Begin the Beguine") with some certified show-stoppers.

Bob Dylan (1941–)

Moving to New York City from his native Minnesota in 1960, Bob Dylan began trying out his observational songs at the folk music clubs of Greenwich Village. By the mid-'60s, he was impacting the world with songs filled with wit, wisdom, and social commentary. Many great songwriters through the years site Dylan as their primary influence and the reason they became songwriters themselves. Landmark songs like "Blowin' in the Wind," "Like a Rolling Stone," "Just Like A Woman," and "Mr. Tambourine Man" helped to define a generation. To this day, with his 1997 release of "Time Out of Mind" and his 2000 Academy Award for "Things Have Changed" (from the film *Wonderboys*), Bob Dylan proves the staying power of true genius.

Paul Simon (1941–)

"Somewhere in a burst of glory, sound becomes a song." This opening line from "That's Where I Belong" from Paul Simon's 2000 release *You're The One*, could very well describe the moment of inspiration that fuels his genius. As at teen growing up in Queens, New York, he teamed up with neighborhood friend, singer Art Garfunkel. They scored a minor hit as *Tom and Jerry* in 1957 with the Simon's, "Hey Schoolgirl." It wasn't until they evolved into Simon and Garfunkel, in the mid-'60's that Simon's songwriting gifts would become apparent with memorable songs such as "The Sound of Silence," "Homeward Bound," "Fakin' It," "America," "Mrs. Robinson," and perhaps the mother of all epic ballads, "Bridge Over Troubled Water." As a solo artist he continued his musical legacy with "Mother and Child Reunion," "Still Crazy After All These Years," and "American Tune." Never afraid to experiment with musical rhythms and influences from all over the globe, Simon took it all the way with his Grammy-winning album, *Graceland* in which he set his songs to the backdrop of the South African rhythms (recorded on site) of native musicians, and "Rhythm of the Saints" in which he worked with Brazilian instrumental textures and rhythms.

Brian Wilson (1942–)

As a typical American teenager growing up in middle class Hawthorne, California, Brian put together a band of brothers and cousins called The Beach Boys, which became a launching pad for his emerging talents as a songwriter. Starting with simple, fad-oriented tunes about hot rods and surfing ("409," "Surfin' Safari"), he soon expanded his song franchise into more weighty subjects like social acceptance ("I Get Around"), love ("Wouldn't It Be Nice"), and cosmic connections ("Good Vibrations"). Musically, his near-jazz chord progressions, brilliant use of modulation, and ear for melody

created a sound never before heard in pop music. His harmony arrangements, influenced by the intricate inversions of the jazz doo-wop group, The
Four Freshmen, are second to none. Wilson's triumph however came after he
stopped touring with The Beach Boys and in 1966, decided to create an album
that would transcend everything that he'd ever done. Teaming up with lyrist
Tony Asher, he created *Pet Sounds,* an album that would change rock 'n' roll
music and influence and inspire almost every major rock musician, including
such luminaries as Paul McCartney, Neil Young, Bob Dylan, Pete Townsend,
Stevie Wonder, and Elton John.

Joni Mitchell (1943–)

Joni Mitchell is perhaps the most influential female singer/songwriter of
our time. She started out as the ultimate coffeehouse folk singer in her native
Canada in the early '60s. But she soon relocated to the United States, where
she was discovered by (besides an adoring press and public) David Crosby
of The Byrds, who produced her self-titled concept album debut for Reprise
Records in 1967. A succession of highly acclaimed albums was to follow:
Clouds and *Ladies of the Canyon*.

Never one to stagnate musically, Mitchell started tinkering with her sound,
adding smoky blues elements to her *Blue* album and started easing into jazz
starting with *For the Roses* — featuring the hit, "Turn Me On (I'm A Radio),"
and the Tom Scott–influenced jazz of *Court and Spark* featuring "Raised On
Robbery" (actually an aberration, being more of a rock 'n' roll tune), "Help
Me" and "Free Man In Paris." With subsequent albums like *Hissing of Summer
Lawns* and *Don Juan's Reckless Daughter,* she continued her experimental
journey into practically all musical forms, even pushing the boundaries of
improvisational jazz. Her unerring melodic sense, obvious love for the word
play of the English language, and deep and often confessional lyrics make
her one of the great contemporary songwriters.

Jimmy Webb (1946–)

Jimmy Webb took his precocious songwriting, arranging, and producing
skills to Los Angeles in the late '60s and soon afterwards was at the right
hand of noted producer/engineer Bones Howe, lending his talents (keyboard
and songwriting) to *Up, Up and Away* the breakthrough album of The Fifth
Dimension. Continuing his Fifth Dimension roll with songs like "Carpet
Man" and "I Think I'll Learn How To Fly," he went on to write the brilliant
"By the Time I Get to Phoenix" and the haunting "Wichita Lineman" for
Glen Campbell, and wrote and produced the arranging tour de force of
"Macarthur's Park" for actor Richard Harris. The consummate song crafter,
he combines classical song etiquette (loving perfect rhymes and symmetrical
cadence) with soul and passion — a rare combination indeed.

Billy Joel (1949–)

Billy Joel started invisibly as a member of The Hassels, a psychedelic-era rock band. Who would have thought that he'd emerge from the other side of the tunnel as "The Piano Man" reinventing himself as the quintessential piano-picking singer/songwriter. With one of the most supple tenors in rock and one of the best piano techniques, his songs like "Just the Way You Are," "Uptown Girl" (written about his wife of that era, supermodel, Christie Brinkley), "Say Goodbye to Hollywood," "Honesty," "Only the Good Die Young," "New York State of Mind," and his emotional ode to the steel workers of "Allentown" have stood the test of time. Though we hear the influence of the songs and vocal styling of The Beatles, Joel has forged a sound that is uniquely his and a persona that is stubbornly American.

Sting (1951–)

As the bassist, lead singer, and lead songwriter behind the platinum success of the British trio The Police, Sting was on the leading edge of the new wave movement of the late '70s. Starting with his first solo album, *Dream Of The Blue Turtles*, which contained the hit singles "If You Love Somebody Set Them Free" and the majestic "Fortress Around Your Heart," and extending through his next five studio albums, Sting experimented with arranging his songs using some of the top jazz, world beat, and even classical musicians to flesh out his musical ambitions. Songs like "All This Time" from *The Soul Cages*, "If I Ever Lose My Faith In You," and "Fields of Gold" from *Ten Summoner's Tales* stand up to the best pop songs of all time.

Diane Warren (1956–)

In 1986, she penned "Rhythm of the Night" for DeBarge, which became a hit. Diane has since become the most prolific and successful songwriter of recent times with over 80 of her songs charting in the Top 10. Additionally, she has crossed the genre barriers. Her song "I Don't Want to Miss a Thing" sung by Aerosmith in the movie Armageddon received an Oscar nomination, while another version of the same song by Mark Chestnut hit number one on the country charts. She has even had songs at the top of the R&B, country, and pop charts all at the same time. Her hit song "How Do I Live" (a hit by both Trisha Yearwood and Le Ann Rimes) has gone on record as being the longest running song in the history of Billboard's Hot 100 chart. Other hits include "I Turn to You" (Christina Aguilera), "Music of My Heart" ('N Sync and Gloria Estefan), "Unbreak My Heart" (Toni Braxton), and "Because You Love Me" (Celine Dion).

Chapter 21

Ten Songwriting Teams You Should Know

In This Chapter

▶ Teaming up for success in songwriting

There are musically creative people who are masters at writing the lyrics and there are those who write great melodies. When you combine these two kinds of people, you get what's known as a songwriting team. Sometimes, individually, they can write both the words and the music, but when collaborating as a team, they're surely more than the sum of their parts. Some of the biggest hits are created in the crossfire of diverse personalities. The following songwriting teams are ten of the many we think you should know.

George and Ira Gershwin

In 1924, the brothers worked together to create the smash hit musical *Lady Be Good.* During the same year, George composed the immortal orchestral piece "Rhapsody in Blue." After the success of *Lady Be Good,* George worked most consistently with Ira — George writing the music, Ira, the words. Together, George and Ira created the music and songs for more than 20 musicals and films until George's untimely death in 1937. Together, the Gershwin brothers wrote some of the most memorable American standards that continue to live in both popular and jazz music today; such songs as: "Embraceable You," "Fascinating Rhythm," "A Foggy Day," "I Got Rhythm," "Love Walked In," "Someone to Watch Over Me," and "They Can't Take That Away from Me."

Richard Rodgers and Lorenz Hart, and Rodgers and Oscar Hammerstein II

Richard Rodgers wrote his first song when he was 14. Two years later he met Lorenz Hart and started a collaboration that would last for 25 years — Hart writing the words, Rodgers writing the music. By 1925, they'd gotten their songs into Broadway musicals; and *The Garrick Gaieties* was produced using their music. Rodgers and Hart premiered their debut complete show later that year with *Dearest Enemy*, as well as *The Girl Friend, Peggy-Ann,* and *A Connecticut Yankee.* Even though the musicals were moderate successes, several songs from these shows became hits ("Mountain Greenery," "Thou Swell," and "With a Song in My Heart"), and are still popular today. They wrote for Hollywood in the early 1930s, returning to Broadway in 1936. Their 1937 show *Babes In Arms* introduced the hit songs "My Funny Valentine" and "Lady Is a Tramp." During these years they wrote a number of musicals from which many standards emerged, including "There's a Small Hotel," "Spring Is Here," "Bewitched," "Falling in Love with Love," and "Where or When." After their breakup, Rodgers began writing with Oscar Hammerstein II. Rodgers' collaboration with Hammerstein II was a fruitful one as well and out of it came a revolution in the style of Broadway musicals and the most popular series of musicals ever produced: *Oklahoma!, State Fair, Carousel, South Pacific, The King and I,* and *The Sound of Music.* Collectively, the Rodgers and Hammerstein musicals earned 34 Tony Awards, 15 Academy Awards, 2 Pulitzer Prizes, 2 Grammy Awards, and 2 Emmy Awards.

Burt Bacharach and Hal David

The music of Burt Bacharach and the words of Hal David are surely one of the great musical synergies of our time — a songwriting team that also had the advantage of an "in-house" producer and arranger in Burt Bacharach. This team was able to find vocal interpreters commensurate with their brilliance in singers like Jerry Butler ("Make It Easy on Yourself"), Jackie DeShannon ("What the World Needs Now Is Love"), Gene Pitney ("Twenty-Four Hours from Tulsa" and "Only Love Can Break a Heart"), Bobby Vinton ("Blue on Blue") and of course, Dionne Warwick ("Don't Make Me Over," "Alfie," and "I Say a Little Prayer").

Bacharach and David made a fortune by never underestimating its audience's I.Q. or E.Q. (emotional quotient). Their songs are highly literate without being "high brow" and adventurous musically without sounding complicated. The heart and soul of the lyrics and the music are always on the same page, which is as much of a testament to Bacharach's inspiring musical beds as it is to David's grasp of every mood that is set. Through the years, and to this day, their songs are being re-interpreted by new artists of every generation. From the reverent readings of their "Windows of the World" (sung by Luther Vandross) to the irreverent version of "Little Red Book" performed by Love, somehow their songs remain deeply touching and uniquely theirs.

John Lennon and Paul McCartney

The power of a songwriting team cannot be better illustrated than by gazing at the collective works of Lennon and McCartney. Working closely together in the early days of The Beatles, they came up with such musical gems as "She Loves You" and "I Wanna Hold Your Hand," and ushered in a whole new era of music. Both influenced by the American sounds of The Everly Brothers and Chuck Berry, they echoed their mentors and upped the ante with a new British slant that somehow twisted the genre into a package that the world could not resist. The dichotomy of styles and personalities between the two is legendary: McCartney's do-good, people-pleasing optimism and work ethic, contrasted by Lennon's rebellious and often cynical posturing, made for the potent charge of the duo's output.

Even though they wrote more individually as the years went by, each man's mere presence in one another's other's lives profoundly influenced their solo writing. Each knew he'd be held responsible by the other for his output and so tailored their offerings to suit. Whether it was the majestic, timeless quality that gave the power to McCartney's "Hey Jude," or the thoughtful anarchy of that single's flip side of Lennon's "Revolution," the songs most assuredly couldn't have happened without each other's life force.

Elton John and Bernie Taupin

One of the most successful teams of any era in music, this duo has made its name writing songs specifically for one act, Elton John. Fortunately that franchise has been more than enough to sustain them through the years. The music and melodies of Elton John are among the most creative in the business. Taupin's lyrics are "outside" and quirky enough to counteract the more traditional nature of John's melodies and song structures to create interest in every track.

Waking the world up with "Your Song" in 1970, John literally designed a niche in music with his introspective and sensitive looks at life and love. His breakthrough self-titled album contained lushly arranged ballads (like "Your Song," mentioned earlier) as well as gospel-influenced rockers like "Take Me to the Pilot." Jumping between musical styles became his trademark, going from the serious portrait style of a man named "Levon" and the eerie mood of "Rocket Man" to the rambunctious high jinks of "Honky Cat" and "Crocodile Rock."

Taupin's fascination with all things American, especially the American West of the cowboy era, took form in the amazing song cycle of "Tumbleweed Connection," John's second album. Melodic feasts like "Goodbye Yellow Brick Road" also reflected the pair's love of the folklore and icons of Americana.

Jerry Leiber and Mike Stoller

It's hard to believe that two regular guys from Baltimore and Long Island, respectively, could turn the rhythm and blues and rock 'n' roll worlds on their ears in the mid-'50s with songs like one of Elvis's first mega hits, "Hound Dog" (originally recorded by Big Mama Thornton) and his movie classic, "Jailhouse Rock"; "Kansas City" by Wilbur Harris (and covered by a host of others, including The Beatles); "Stand By Me" by Ben E. King; "On Broadway" by the Drifters; and three major hits by The Coasters, "Yakety Yak," "Poison Ivy," and "Charlie Brown." Somehow this writing team captured the lexicon of American slang and wrote songs that were instantly relatable to the record-buying public. They helped to serve up the essence of rhythm and blues in an accessible and memorable form. They were pioneers in the uncharted territory of taming controversial raw rock and blues into pop music for the masses. For this, they have received a permanent place in popular music history.

Gerry Goffin and Carole King

If you look up the term *songsmith* in your Funk and Wagnall's, you just might find a picture of Gerry Goffin and Carole King. Writing some of the all-time classics of the '50s and '60s, this team's melodic sense and finger on the pulse of teenage taste kept them at the top of the charts for nearly a decade. They always had a gentle way with a song: The searching emotions of "Will You Love Me Tomorrow," the sweet sentiment of "Take Good Care of My Baby," the reflective mood set by "Up on the Roof," the goose bump relate-ability of "When My Little Girl Is Smiling," and Aretha Franklin's classic reading of their "(You Make Me Feel Like A) Natural Woman" are all examples of this duo in their prime. After all of King's solo success, where she handled both the music and the words, those old songs still sound as fresh as the day they were written. And that's the proof of a truly great song and songwriting team.

Eddie Holland, Lamont Dozier and Brian Holland

"Reach Out I'll Be There" performed by The Four Tops, "Heat Wave" performed by Martha and The Vandellas, "Where Did Our Love Go?" performed by The Supremes — three songs, three different groups, and one brilliant writing team: Eddie Holland, Lamont Dozier, and Brian Holland. This is another textbook example of the power of a team of songwriters. They were responsible for the lion's share of hits on Berry Gordy's Motown label between 1965 and 1968, making up for what they lacked in musical education (many of the Motown session players groused about their sketchy or non-existent musical charts at sessions) in sheer musical and emotional instinct.

In Levi Stubbs of The Four Tops, they found a powerful vocal instrument to broadcast their aching tributes to undying love like "Reach Out I'll Be There," "Bernadette," "Standing in the Shadows of Love," "It's the Same Old Song," and "I Can't Help Myself (Sugar Pie, Honey Bunch)." In Diana Ross, the ethereal lead singer of The Supremes, they found the perfect persona for songs like their first breakthrough hit, "Where Did Our Love Go," and others like "Baby Love," "Come See About Me," "In and Out of Love," "Stop! In The Name Of Love," "You Can't Hurry Love," and "I Hear A Symphony." In Martha Reeves of Martha and the Vandellas, they found a raw-voiced female messenger who could deliver urgent memos like "Heatwave," "Quicksand," "Nowhere to Run," and "Jimmy Mack." As writers and producers, Holland-Dozier-Holland stretched the boundaries of R&B into classical and electronic music. Their constant evolution charted the progress of the emerging rhythm and blues market of the mid-'50s and will stand the test of time.

Andrew Lloyd Webber and Tim Rice

The British team Andrew Lloyd Webber, born in 1948, and Tim Rice, born in 1944, are arguably the most successful team writing for musical theater in our time. They first teamed up in 1965 on the musical *The Likes of Us* (Webber the composer, Rice the lyricist), a musical that never reached the stage. Next they wrote the highly successful *Joseph and the Amazing Technicolor Dreamcoat*, which lead to the platinum selling cast recording in 1969. The two had dared infuse their work with elements of rock music, and for their next production they continued along the same lines, creating a full-blown rock musical called *Jesus Christ Superstar*. When the writers were at first unable to finance the production, the rock musical was released as a two-record set instead and went on to sell millions. Productions were soon mounted and the work became a huge success on Broadway and in London; a film followed in 1973. During that year, Webber and Rice went to work composing a musical based on the life of Eva Peron, the wife of Argentine president Juan Peron, called *Evita*. The album was released in 1976 and the song "Don't Cry for Me Argentina" hit the top of the charts in both Europe and the U.S.; the production, which opened in 1978, went on to win seven Tony Awards.

Rice and Webber severed their relationship after *Evita*. Webber went on to create a number of shows, including *Cats* and the *Phantom of the Opera*. Rice worked with other composers creating the musicals *Blondel* and *Chess*. In

1992, Rice worked on the Disney animated film *Aladdin* and the song from the film "A Whole New World," written with composer Alan Menken was a chart topper and won an Academy Award. Rice remained with Disney, teaming with Elton John in 1993 on the *Lion King*; "Can You Feel the Love Tonight" won an Academy Award for Best Original Song. Rice continued to work with Elton John on the 1998 musical *Aida* and the animated feature *The Road to El Dorado* released in 2000.

Mick Jagger and Keith Richards

As the lead singer and main guitarist of the legendary Rolling Stones, Mick and Keith have cast an equally giant shadow as perhaps one of the greatest pure rock 'n' roll songwriting teams of all time. Whereas Lennon and McCartney spread their songwriting talents in many directions, The Stones, with a few notable exceptions ("Lady Jane," "As Tears Go By," and "Wild Horses" come to mind), were all about raw, unabashedly sexual, and raucous rock 'n' roll. Not that there wasn't a strong thread of intelligence and humor running through their anthems — it's just that the audiences first instinct was to shake first and to think later.

Their most resilient songs like "Honky Tonk Woman," "(I Can't Get No) Satisfaction," "Jumpin' Jack Flash," "Tumbling Dice," "Paint It Black," and "Brown Sugar" are a combination of Keith "The Human Riff" Richards's knack for simple yet original guitar figures (often played in unorthodox tunings) and progressions, over Mick Jagger's insightfully clever and hooky lyrics and melodies. Not that there wasn't some healthy cross-pollinating between them, with Keith doing the lyrical and musical honors (like on "Wild Horses") or with Mick coming up with the odd guitar riff. Like with most great teams, the friction between them seems to create the spark of rubbing two stones together (pun definitely intended). From the moment their first producer, Andrew Oldham, allegedly shut them in a room and told them not to come out until they'd written a song (their first self-penned hit, "Tell Me"), they've kept on rolling. Although heavily influenced by rock 'n' role model Chuck Berry and blues greats like Muddy Waters (they got their name from Muddy's "Rollin' Stone"), they expanded on the form with innovative chord progressions, heart-wrenching lyrics, and a real reverence for good song craft. Their reverence for the hooky title and signature musical figure is second to none and will stand against the great, rock 'n' roll masters through the ages.

Chapter 22

Ten Songs You Should Know

There are endless lists of "Best Songs." Some lists are based on the opinions of the authors; some are gauged by chart positions and sales figures. Whichever way you tally it, the great songs of any generation are the ones that matter the most to people. Here's a list of some strong song contenders and some of the reasons why they've resonated throughout the years.

"Amazing Grace"

"Amazing Grace" is an old-fashioned hymn that is virtually timeless. Composed by John Newton in the mid-1700s as a testimony about his own life, it has been a mainstay ever since. When Judy Collins sang it a cappella on her album *Wildflowers* in 1970, it reached Number 15 on the pop charts. Many artists including Hank Williams and Elvis Presley have recorded it. The song was used in the Star Trek movie *Wrath of Khan* where it was played during the funeral of Mr. Spock. "Amazing Grace" may very well be the most easily recognizable hymn ever written. It's been recorded by popular singers, performed on TV, used in commercials, and it was even played in its entirety during the broadcast of the women's gymnastic competition of the 1996 Olympics. Countless people who've never set foot in a church can recite the first few lines and maybe even the whole first verse.

"Over the Rainbow"

Once in a while, a song comes along that's so great that it just never goes away. One such a song is "Over the Rainbow," composed by Harold Arlen in 1939 with words by E.Y. "Yip" Harburg — the pair who wrote the songs for the film *Wizard of Oz*. The melody suddenly came to Arlen while driving in his car He had a tremendous feeling about the value of the melody and took it to Harburg, but Harburg didn't like it. To settle the matter, they drove over to

Harburg's friend Ira Gershwin's house and asked him how he felt. Gershwin felt that Arlen had indeed come up with a great melody, and Harburg reluctantly wrote the words for "Over the Rainbow." Judy Garland sang the song in the movie, but the studio pulled it saying it didn't fit the plot, and that it was too slow. They only reluctantly put it back in the film after the associate producer, Arthur Fried forced them to do it. The rest is history. "Over the Rainbow" was voted by the National Endowment for the Arts (NEA) and the Recording Industry Association of America (RIAA) as the number one best song of the century, and it's been recorded by hundreds of artists ranging from Tori Amos to Zoot Sims.

"White Christmas"

One of Irving Berlin's most memorable songs, "White Christmas" has reached legendary status. Originally composed in 1942 for the film *Holiday Inn* (winning the Best Song Academy Award), it immediately caught on. Over 215 versions of the song have been released in all genres including pop, jazz, and R&B, by such artists as Louis Armstrong, the Beach Boys, Booker T, the MGs, Garth Brooks, Bing Crosby, Neil Diamond, Gloria Estefan, Vince Gill, Willie Nelson, New Kids on the Block, Elton John, Elvis, and many more. You've probably even sung this one a few times in your life! It's definitely an example of the staying power of a great holiday song.

"You've Lost That Loving Feeling"

This epic ballad of fading love was brought to "bigger than life" by the blue-eyed soul duo The Righteous Brothers, reaching the top of the charts at the tail end of 1964. This massive Phil Spector "wall of sound" production received its power from the soaring Barry Mann, Cynthia Weil, Phil Spector melody, their majestic chord changes, and the interplay between Bill Medley's huge baritone (many DJs thought they were cueing up the song at too slow a speed when they first received the record!), and Bobby Hatfield's choir boy tenor. Some-how it never seemed odd that this song was sung in duet form by two males because it never appeared like they were singing to each other. That is the genius of the song and its arrangement. And who could forget that memorable moment when it was featured in the '86 film *Top Gun*?

"Yesterday"

"Yesterday," written by John Lennon and Paul McCartney, has been played on American radio over 7 million times. No other song has been played more since it first hit the airways in the mid-'60s. It also holds the *Guinness Book of Records* title as the most "covered" song in history. The story is told that McCartney woke up one morning with this tune running through his head — the song just came to him without a flaw. The Beatles and their producer George Martin recorded "Yesterday" with just a string quartet, acoustic guitar, and Paul's vocal. This song is well served by the simplicity of its production. "Yesterday" ranks third place in BMI's Top 100 Songs of the Century. According to BMI's calculation, 7 million performances are the equivalent of approximately 350,000 broadcast hours, or more than 39.9 years of continuous airplay!

"God Only Knows"

With haunting vocals by the late Carl Wilson, "God Only Knows" is considered by many to be the ultimate Brian Wilson song. Ironically, shunned by certain radio stations for its use of the word "God," this song climbed to the outer reaches of the Top 40 in 1966. This ode to a love that can't quite be verbalized properly features some of the most sensitive chord progressions of Wilson's career. With lyrics by one of his most inspired lyricists, Tony Asher, this song, along with "Wouldn't It Be Nice," is one of the cornerstones of The Beach Boy's masterwork, *Pet Sounds*.

"Imagine"

"Imagine" was John Lennon's ultimate message to the world. John composed the song one morning on the white grand piano made famous in films and photos of him sitting at the keyboard. Lennon captured pretty much everything he believed in and stood for within this song — we are all one country, one world, one people, without boundaries or borders. "Imagine" is the most commercially successful of all Lennon's post-Beatles works. It peaked at #3 on its initial 1971 release, but ten years later was re-released and hit #1 — heralding the inner dynamics and longevity of the message.

"The Wind Beneath My Wings"

One of the most stunning moments of American television came when theatrical singer Bernadette Peters appeared on *The Johnny Carson Show* and sang a brand new song called "The Wind Beneath My Wings" — bringing the jaded *Tonight Show* audience to its knees. Written by former Newbeats lead singer, Larry Henley (remember his falsetto vocals on their 1964 hit "Bread and Butter") and Los Angeles–based songwriter, Jeff Silbar, it's one of those songs that pulls you in with every line until you're totally immersed. The title alone is one of the song's strongest assets and the concept of someone standing behind you in the wings, lifting you up is one that most everyone can relate to. Bette Midler brought this song to its ultimate chart position reaching number one in April of 1989 — this song's inclusion in the nostalgic motion picture *Beaches* gave it the connection needed to finally give this song its permanent place in the sun.

"This Is It"

This is one of those songs that continue to have a positive impact on our lives. Inventive musically and lyrically, it's main theme (inspired by the defeatist attitude of Kenny Loggin's father just before going in for major surgery), is that we all "have a choice in how it goes." We are not powerless observers of our life, that to some extent we direct its course and must "stand up and fight" for it. The triumphant suspended chords of the chorus emphasize the strength of the thesis — attitude has everything to do with survival and when looking for a miracle, look no further than your own life because — "This Is It!" Co-written with Michael McDonald, Kenny won the 1980 Best Male Pop Vocal Performance Grammy with this Top Ten song.

"Heart of the Matter"

There are certain lyrics that hold a potent emotional charge just reading them off the page. "Heart of the Matter" written by Mike Campbell, J.D. Souther, and Eagles member Don Henley is just one of those lyrics. As he describes his bittersweet regret over a former lover finally finding the illusive happiness he couldn't provide ("And the work I put between us, doesn't keep me warm") and the quest for forgiveness in himself, the brilliance of the melody, chord changes, unusual song structure (this is one song where the chorus is not signaled — it just kind of sneaks up on you), and the understated yet powerful vocal delivery are just icing on the cake. This is a song that gets better each time you listen to it. "Heart of the Matter" took its time reaching number 21 back in 1990 partly because of its steep learning curve (it's not exactly a sing-a-long karaoke delight), but its quiet pleasures and ring-true sentiments give this song legs to travel for many decades to come.

Part VII
Appendixes

The 5th Wave   By Rich Tennant

"Get me the ant spray, honey. My B-flat just became an F-sharp!"

In this part . . .

We thought it might be helpful to have all the little
details for contracts, resources, contacts, and definitions in one place. So, we've put together this collection
of appendixes to make life a little easier for you. Turn to
Appendix A for contract information, flip to Appendix B
for the lowdown on what information to get where, and
check out Appendix C for definitions of a whole bunch
of songwriting terms. Have fun!

Contracts: Where to Find Them and What to Look For

● ●

*W*hile the right side of your brain is engaged in the creative pursuit of writing a song, challenge the left side and make sure it understands your legal rights and responsibilities. This will assure that eventually the fruits of your labor will be served properly and you'll find some peace of mind.

In this appendix, we steer you toward resources and supply some short form definitions related to the business side of songwriting.

Online Resources

The Internet is a great place to start when you're in search of contract information. It also allows you to see some sample contracts, so you know what to expect. Here are two trustworthy sources of legal information geared specifically toward songwriters:

- ✔ **The Songwriters Guild of America** (www.songwriters.org): The Songwriters Guild of America is a great resource for all songwriters, regardless of how long you've been in the business. When you get to the Web site, click on Contracts, and you'll find numerous helpful resources to get you started.

- ✔ **Songwriters Directory** (www.songwritersdirectory.com): Songwriters Directory provides links to other sites that provide contract information. Click on Resources and then click on Legal Information to get where you want to go.

Books

In this section, we list books that can help you get business savvy. Visit a bookstore or library to narrow down your choices to the one or two books that meet your particular needs and situation. Even if you've already hired a lawyer, getting familiar with some of the points he'll be negotiating for you in your contracts isn't a bad idea.

- ✔ *All You Need To Know About The Music Business* by Donald S. Passman, published by Simon and Schuster
- ✔ *Contracts for Songwriters* by Vito Fera, published by Network Sound Productions, Inc. and SPIN
- ✔ *Legal Aspects Of The Music Industry: An Insiders View* by Richard Schulenberg, published by Watson-Guptill Publications
- ✔ *The Music Business: A Legal Perspective* by Peter Muller, published by Greenwood Publishing Group
- ✔ *Music Business & Entertainment Law Contracts for Indie Recording Artist, Labels, Songwriters, Composers, Producers, Managers and All Others in the Record Industry* by R. Williams, published by Platinum Millennium
- ✔ *Musicians Business and Legal Guide* by Mark E. Halloran, published by Prentice Hall
- ✔ *The Musician's Guide Through the Legal Jungle: Answers to Frequently Asked Questions About Music Law* by Joy R. Butler, published by Sashay Communications, LLC
- ✔ *101 Music Business Contracts* by R. Williams, published by Williams Publishing

Eleven Common Song-related Contracts

Think of contracts as your friends. They assure that you and your hard work will be duly rewarded, your song protected and that the proceeds end up at the correct address — yours!

- ✔ **Single Song Agreement**: This agreement is used by music publishers to acquire songs from a songwriter on a song-by-song basis. A copyright assignment of the songs from the songwriter to the music publisher is always attached to this agreement or is included in the verbiage of the actual agreement. Publishers often use this agreement in order to develop a relationship with a writer before offering an exclusive agreement to that writer.
- ✔ **Exclusive Songwriting Agreement (ESA):** This agreement is used by music publishers to acquire all songs written by a songwriter over a period of time (for example, for a period of three years or for a period

equal to the term of an exclusive artist agreement if the songwriter is also signed to an artist deal with a record label). Since you cannot assign an interest in property not yet created, a publisher will either issue individual assignments or songwriter agreements that parallel the terms of the ESA, once the songs are written and turned into the publisher. There may also be a "Schedule A" attached to the ESA whereby the publisher wants to acquire some or all of the songs of a songwriter that were written prior to the term of the ESA. Each of those songs would be listed on the Schedule A.

✓ **Copyright Assignment**: This document is usually a one- or two-page document that contains the formal wording for an assignment of copyright in a composition from the songwriter to the music publisher. Most publishers require that these assignments be notarized by a notary public in order to confirm that the person executing the assignment is actually the songwriter named on the document.

✓ **Co-publishing Agreement**: This agreement is similar to a Single Song Agreement (for an individual song) or an Exclusive Songwriting Agreement (for songs written over a period of time), except that the songwriter retains for itself a portion of the publisher's interest in the song (for example, 50 percent of the publisher's interest so that the songwriter retains 100 percent of the songwriter's portion of the songs and 50 percent of the music publisher's portion of the song).

✓ **Administration Agreement**: This document is an agreement for a third party to administer the rights to a certain number of songs in a given country or territory. This agreement is usually executed by the music publisher or by a songwriter that has formed his or her own publishing company and needs someone to issue licenses (mechanical, sync, print, etc.) on their behalf and to collect the income generated by those licenses. This agreement usually covers administration only and does not include the active pitching of songs. Many music publishers use The Harry Fox Agency for the administration of their catalogs in the United States.

✓ **Sub-Publishing Agreement**: This agreement is similar to an Administration Agreement except that this agreement is usually made between a publisher and another publisher outside of the United States (the "Sub-Publisher"). The Sub-Publisher is usually involved in the active pitching of the domestic publisher's songs and takes a greater share of the income from those songs if the Sub-Publisher secures a cover recording of that song in its home territory.

✓ **Performing Rights Society Affiliation Agreement**: Before a songwriter or music publisher can collect performance royalties for the performance of its songs (via airplay of the music by radio stations and performance of music in public venues), the songwriter and music publisher must execute an agreement with one of the performing rights societies (ASCAP,

BMI, or SESAC) for that organization to administer the "performance" right in those songs. Those societies issue licenses to all major radio stations and major clubs and venues, and collect substantial revenue from those licenses. The performing rights societies pay the songwriter and music publisher directly (usually on a 50/50 basis) for any performance income collected. This direct payment usually insures that a music publisher cannot collect the songwriter's share of performance income to recoup any outstanding advances paid to the songwriter by the music publisher.

✔ **Mechanical License**: This agreement is usually a short form document whereby a music publisher grants to a record label the right to record, manufacture, and distribute records embodying a specific song.

✔ **Print License**: This agreement is usually a short form document whereby a music publisher grants to a print music company (in the United States Warner Brothers, Mel Bay, and Hal Leonard are three of the major print music companies) the right to transcribe, manufacture and distribute print products (for instance, sheet music, personality folios, songbooks, etc.).

✔ **Synchronization License**: This agreement is usually a short form document whereby a music publisher grants to a movie or television producer the right to sync music to visual images and to either broadcast that video or manufacture and distribute the video in videocassette or DVD format. Most producers of video content will attempt to secure rights for both broadcast and home video; however, most music publishers will want to retain home video rights so that it may negotiate a better fee if the television show or movie is commercially successful. This license does not cover the use of the sound recording, as the producer of the video work must also negotiate and secure a license with the copyright holder of the master recording.

✔ **Digital Licenses**: Most licenses for content to be distributed via a digital medium (such as the Internet) are a combination of the mechanical, synchronization, and print licenses depending upon whether the material will be merely "broadcast" or whether a digital copy of the song will be actually delivered to an end user. This area of rights management is in its infancy and continues to develop as new means of digital distribution and expression are introduced to the marketplace.

Appendix B

Resources and Contacts

. . . .

As a songwriter starting out, you are bound to have more questions than answers about the craft and business of writing songs. Even as a seasoned pro, with policies and rules constantly changing, it's vital to know where to turn for the most up-to-date information. In this section we supply you with places to find the answers when there's a gap in your knowledge base.

Organizations

✔ **American Society of Composers, Authors, and Publishers (ASCAP):**
www.ascap.com

- **New York:** One Lincoln Plaza, New York, NY 10023;
  phone: (212) 621-6000; fax: (212) 724-9064

- **Los Angeles:** 7920 West Sunset Boulevard, Third Floor,
  Los Angeles, CA 90046; phone: (323) 883-1000; fax: (323) 883-1049

- **London:** 8 Cork Street, London W1X1PB England;
  phone: 011-44-207-439-0909; fax: 011-44-207-434-0073

- **Nashville:** Two Music Square West, Nashville, TN 37203;
  phone: (615) 742-5000; fax: (615) 742-5020

- **Miami:** 420 Lincoln Road, Suite 385, Miami Beach, FL 33139;
  phone: (305) 673-3446; fax: (305) 673-2446

- **Chicago:** 4042 North Pulaski, Chicago, IL 60641;
  phone: (773) 545-5744; fax: (773) 545-5792

- **Puerto Rico:** 510 Royal Bank Center, 255 Ponce de Léon Avenue,
  Hato Rey, Puerto Rico 00917; phone: (787) 281-0782;
  fax: (787) 767-2805

- **ASCAP Membership:** PMB 400, 541 Tenth Street NW, Atlanta, GA
  30318; phone: (404) 635-1758; fax: (404) 627-2404

- **ASCAP Licensing:** 2690 Cumberland Parkway, Suite 490, Atlanta, GA 30339; phone: (800)-505-4052; fax: (770) 805-3475

✔ **Broadcast Music, Inc. (BMI):** www.bmi.com

- **New York:** 320 West 57th Street, New York, NY 10019-3790; phone: (212) 586-2000; fax: (212) 245-8986

- **Nashville:** 10 Music Square East, Nashville, TN 37203-4399; phone: (615) 401-2000; fax: (615) 401-2707

- **Los Angeles:** 8730 Sunset Boulevard, Third Floor West, West Hollywood, CA 90069-2211; phone: (310) 659-9109; fax: (310) 657-6947

- **London:** 84 Harley House, Marylebone Road, London NW1 5HN, England; phone: phone: 011-44-171-486-2036; fax: 011-44-171-224-1046

- **Miami:** 5201 Blue Lagoon Drive, Suite 310, Miami, FL 33126; phone: (305) 266-3636; fax: (305) 266-2442

- **Atlanta:** P.O. Box 19199, Atlanta, GA 31126; phone: (404) 261-5151; fax: (404) 261-5152

- **Puerto Rico:** 255 Ponce de Leon, East Wing, Suite A-262, BankTrust Plaza, Hato Rey, Puerto Rico 00917; phone: (787) 754-6490; fax: (787) 753-6765

✔ **Recording Industry Association of America (RIAA):** www.riaa.org; 1330 Connecticut Avenue NW, Suite 300, Washington, D.C. 20036; phone: (202) 775-0101; fax: (202) 775-7253

✔ **The Society of European Stage Authors and Composers (SESAC):** www.sesac.com

- **Nashville (Headquarters):** 55 Music Square East, Nashville, TN 37203; phone: (615) 320-0055; fax: (615) 329-9627

- **New York:** 421 West 54th Street, New York, NY 10019; phone: (212) 586-3450; fax: (212) 489-5699

- **Los Angeles:** 501 Santa Monica Boulevard, Suite 450, Santa Monica, CA 90401-2430; phone: (310) 393-9671; fax: (310) 393-6497

- **International:** 6 Kenrick Place, London W1H3FF England; phone: 020-7486-9994; fax: 020-7486-9929

✔ **United States Copyright Office:** www.loc.gov/copyright; Library of Congress, 101 Independence Ave. S.E., Washington, D.C. 20559-6000; phone: (202) 707-3000; faxes are not accepted

Songwriting Resources and Internet Links

- ✔ **Association for Independent Music (AFIM):** An organization representing the Independent Music Industry, formerly known for 25 years as NAIRD; www.afim.org.

- ✔ **American Composers Forum:** An organization concerned with the entire spectrum of creation, presentation, and reception of songwriting, offering programs that focus on each of the links of this chain; www.composersforum.org.

- ✔ **American Federation of Musicians:** The association serving the world with over 250 Local Unions throughout the United States and Canada — the largest entertainment organization in the world; www.afm.org.

- ✔ **American Music Center (AMC):** The group that provides official information for new American music; www.amc.net.

- ✔ **American Songwriter Network (ASN):** An organization that provides leads for music industry professionals, especially good for songwriters and publishers who demo their own material; www.tiac.net/users/asn/index.htm.

- ✔ **The Century Music Group:** An organization that helps the development of singers, songwriters, and groups in all genres of music. Located on Music Row in Nashville, Tennessee; www.centurymusicgroup.com.

- ✔ **ASCAP Nashville — Murphy's Laws of Songwriting:** Ralph Murphy (instructor for NSAI's Song Camps, and Assistant V. P. for ASCAP Nashville) provides numerous tips (laws) for songwriters; http://www.ascap.com/nashville/murphy.html

- ✔ **It's Only Words**: A group that promotes the opportunity for writers to easily publish their works on-line; www.itsonlywords.com.

- ✔ **Jingle University:** Online course in the world of commercial jingles, great for songwriters, musicians, and singers; www.jingleuniversity.com.

- ✔ **The Muse's Muse:** An organization connecting songwriters around the world and supplying them with tips, tools, and interactivities; www.musesmuse.com.

- ✔ **Music Business Registry:** The frequently updated guides listing contact details for companies that are actively signing talent, including A&R Registry, Music Publisher Registry, Music Business Attorney Registry, and the Film and Television Music Guide; www.musicregistry.com.

- ✔ **Music Yellow Pages:** A guide directing you to the facets of the music and entertainment industries, listing many manufacturers, wholesalers, and distributors; www.musicyellowpages.com.

✔ **National Association of Music Merchandisers (NAMM):** The host to the giant yearly NAMM convention which displays the latest in musical instruments and technology associated with making and recording music; www.namm.com.

✔ **Singer Songwriter:** Resource for the creation of contracts associated with the business of songwriting; www.singersongwriter.ws.

✔ **The Songwriters Guild of America:** A songwriters association run by and for songwriters that provides information, contracts, services, and activities to maximize their chances of succeeding in the music business; www.songwriters.org.

✔ **Songwriters Resource Network:** An organization dedicated to helping songwriters develop their craft and market their songs. Sponsor of the annual Great American Song Contest; www.songwritersresourcenetwork.com.

✔ **Taxi:** An independent A&R vehicle connecting unsigned artists, bands, and songwriters with major record labels, publishers, and film and TV music supervisors; www.taxi.com.

✔ **Harry Fox Agency, Inc. (HFA):** The mechanical rights organization that provides an information source, clearinghouse, and monitoring service for licensing musical copyrights and pays out mechanical royalties to writers and publishers. www.nmpa.org/hfa.html.

✔ **Songwriters Directory:** A directory of resources for songwriters, musicians, and music industry professionals providing information on songwriting contests, scholarships, camps, cruises, and other avenues of development. www.songwritersdirectory.com/index.htm.

Songwriting Magazines

✔ *Billboard Magazine:* published by the Billboard Music Group — the standard of the American record business listing producers, writers and labels of all the songs on their sales charts in all genres of popular music.

✔ *Billboard Musician's Guide to Touring And Promotion:* published by the Billboard Music Group — a complete guide to all types of music industry contacts.

✔ *The Musician's Atlas:* published by Music Resource Group — a comprehensive guide to managers, publishers, record companies, and live venues for the working songwriter.

✔ *Performing Songwriter:* published by Desktop Communications — interviews, equipment profiles, and insider information for the songwriter who performs his own tunes.

Books Used As Songwriting Tools

- ✔ *Bartlett's Familiar Quotations* **(16th edition):** by John Bartlett and Justin Kaplan, published by Little, Brown and Company — great quotes from the ancient Egyptians to the latest movie, that can create a springboard for ideas that you can incorporate into your lyrics.

- ✔ *The Highly Selective Thesaurus for the Extraordinarily Literate:* by Eugene Ehrlich, published by Harper Collins — unusual synonyms to spice up your songs.

- ✔ *Random House Historical Dictionary of American Slang:* by J. E. Lighter, published by Random House — gives the meaning of many slang terms and street phrases through the years and up to the present.

- ✔ *Tunesmith — Inside the Art of Songwriting:* by Jimmy Webb, published by Hyperion — anecdotes, insider tips, and instruction on the art of constructing a song from multi-Grammy-winning songwriter, Jimmy Webb.

- ✔ *Random House Rhyming Dictionary:* published by Random House — rhymes for 30,000 words and syllables with a glossary of poetic terms.

- ✔ *Roget's International Thesaurus:* published by Harper and Row — the definitive book of synonyms (alternate words that have the same meaning) for the words in the English language.

- ✔ *The Songwriter's Rhyming Dictionary:* by Sammy Cahn, published by New American Library — more than 50,000 rhyme words for songs by the Academy Award–winning lyricist. Also contains explanations of poetic devices and song forms.

- ✔ *The Writer's Quotation Book — A Literary Companion* **(Third Edition):** published by Penguin Books — Quotes from Walt Disney to Woodrow Wilson — words that can supply a writer with "food for thought" for a new song.

Reference Resources for the Business and Craft of Songwriting

- ✔ *The Craft Of Lyric Writing:* by Sheila Davis, published by Writer's Digest Books — sound advice and examples to aid you in the process of writing words for songs written by an expert in the field.

- ✔ *All You Need To Know About The Music Business:* by Donald S. Passman, published by Simon and Schuster — a detailed primer, written by one of the industry's top entertainment attorneys, on the legal end of the entire music business including a wealth of valuable information for the songwriter.

- ✔ *The Craft and Business Of Songwriting:* by John Braheny, published by Writer's Digest Books — a practical guide to creating and marketing your song written by a songwriting expert.

- ✔ *How To Make Big Money Scoring Soundtracks:* by Jeffrey Fisher, published by Fisher Creative Group/Mix Bookshelf — everything you need to know about the art and business of writing music for motion pictures.

- ✔ *The Mix Bookshelf:* A comprehensive mail order source for books, tapes, videos, music software programs, and sound effects libraries for the ambitious songwriter. (Phone number: 800-233-9604.)

- ✔ *Music, Money and Success:* by Jeffrey Brabec and Todd Brabec, published by Schirmer Books — an insider's guide to the music industry covering the business/legal side to show you the many ways your song makes money and how you can make sure you're getting it. Written by two award-winning entertainment attorneys.

- ✔ *Notes On Broadway, Conversations With the Great Composers On Theater:* by Al Kasha and Joel Hirschhorn, published by Contemporary Books Inc. — a must for songwriters who would like to write for the Broadway stage with valuable insights from the pros.

- ✔ *The Soul Of A Writer:* by Susan Tucker with Linda Lee Strother, published by Journey Publishing — roundtable discussion involving some of the industries top songwriters with many insights into the creative process. Includes many road-tested tips on subjects such as writer's block, co-writing, and where to find inspiration.

- ✔ *6 Steps to Songwriting Success:* by Jason Blume, published by Billboard Books — a plain English, step-by-step guide to developing the creative and business skills needed to write and market songs.

- ✔ *Songwriter's Market:* edited by Ian Bessler, published by Writer's Digest Books — the songwriter's networking companion, this book which is updated yearly lists over 1,200 places to market your song. It also includes insights by songwriting pros and listings of agencies, organizations, contests, and events that can help you "get into the game" of songwriting.

Appendix C

Glossary

● ●

a cappella: A performance by a solo voice or voices without instruments.

A&R (Artist and Repertoire): The person who finds talent and songs for a record company.

AAA song form: A song form that consists of verses only.

AABA song form: A song form where there are two verse sections followed by a second section (generally a chorus or bridge) and then back to a third verse.

aabb **rhyming pattern:** A rhyme pattern where the first and second lines end in similar sounding words, and the third and forth lines end in a different set of similar sounding words.

abab **rhyming pattern:** A rhyme pattern when the words are rhymed at the ends of alternating lines.

advance: Money lent to the artist by a record label or publishing company when a contract is signed. A record label typically advances the artists money to pay for recording an album, to buy equipment, and to support themselves. In rare circumstances, some portion of an advance may be non-recoupable (not needing to be paid back to the record company by an artist).

alliteration: The repetition of the same sound — usually a consonant — at the beginning of two or more words immediately succeeding each other.

anaphora: The lyric technique where the same word or words are repeated at the beginning of succeeding verses or lines.

arrangement: The musical shape a song takes in terms of instrumentation, orchestration and all forms of musical accompaniment.

arranger: The person who puts all the musical pieces in the right place and adds sonic color where it's needed.

ASCAP: The American Society of Composers, Authors, and Publishers, one of the "big two" nonprofit performing rights organizations (the other being BMI) who monitors the performances of your songs through various radio and television sampling techniques that scan for use of ASCAP affiliated songs. See also *performing rights organization.*

assonance: Two or more syllables or single-syllable words that have the same vowel sound. The word *hope* is an assonant rhyme with *own* because they have the *o* vowel sound in common.

augmented and diminished rhymes: A class of rhymes where one of two rhymes has an extra consonant (for example, *plunder* and *wondered*). Augmented describes the situation in which the syllable *without* the added consonant appears first; diminished is the other way around.

author: The creator of a work, whether it's artistic, literary, dramatic, or musical.

ballad: Formerly used to describe a song, often in the AAA form, that related a story. Today, the term is usually used to describe a slow tempo (usually love) song.

bar: A unit of musical time. A song consists of a particular number of bars, and each bar contains a certain number of beats. In written music, bars are defined by vertical lines that appear after a set number of beats.

beat: The consistent rhythmic pulse of a song or piece of music.

blanket license: A license issued by a performing rights society authorizing the public performance of all the songs in the society's catalog. See also *performing rights license.*

BMI: Broadcast Music, Inc., one of the "big two" nonprofit performance rights organizations (the other being ASCAP). BMI has elaborate computerized methods of monitoring the performances of your songs, and also collects monies on the songwriter's behalf. See also *performing rights organization.*

blues: A form of music that originated in the African-American community, often focusing on the harsh realities of life, consisting of repeating 12-bar sections, each section containing a standard three chord "blues" progression.

bridge: A contrasting section of words and/or music that is usually after the second chorus.

business manager: A person who manages the income, expenses, taxes, and investments of a performer or artist.

chord: A set of three or more musical notes sung or played at the same time.

chord chart: The musical map used in a rehearsal or recording session where the chords of a song are broken down in bars and assigned a note or number in accordance with the tonic note of the chord.

chord progression: A series of chords that defines the harmonic pattern of a section of a song.

chorus: The section of a song that is sung between verses in a song in verse-chorus form often containing the title. Formerly, a chorus was called the *refrain*.

clichés: Lyric phrases or words that have become trite due to their overuse.

coda: An ending section, also called an *outro,* or a *tag,* that can be optionally added to the end of a song.

commercial use: Any use of a song or part of a song to sell a product for which a songwriter and his representative receive a negotiated fee.

common time: A unit of rhythmic measurement that is identified by having four beats to a bar and often eight bars to a section.

composer: A term for someone who specializes in composing instrumental music, such as movie scores or symphonies, or who collaborates with a lyricist to write songs or other vocal works.

compulsory mechanical license: An exception to the copyright holder's exclusive rights of reproduction and distribution that allows anyone to record and distribute any previously commercially-released song as long as the mechanical license rates established by copyright law are paid to the copyright owner of the song.

consonance: A near rhyme where the final consonant sounds are the same but the vowels are different as in *song* and *young* or *think* and *sank.*

copyright: Exclusive rights and protection granted to authors of songs, allowing the author to have control over that work and how it is used.

copyright infringement: When someone uses some part or all of someone else's copyrighted works (song or composition) without authorization.

copyright notice: The copyright owner's name, year, and the symbol ©, printed on a published work to give notice that a copyright owner is claiming possession.

couplet: Two adjacent lines of lyric that have the same end rhyme.

cover: A song performed by artist(s) other than the original artist.

cut: The term used when a publisher or writer convinces an artist to record (or "cut") his song.

demo: A recording that demonstrates a particular song or displays the musical talents of particular artist.

derivative work: This term, which you will find on a PA copyright form, refers to a song that is derived from one or more preexisting songs (such as a parody song that is based on a well-known hit).

dummy lyric: The temporary lyrics that are used as placeholders when writing song lyrics.

eighth note: A musical note having a length of one-half of a beat. There can be at most eight of these in a measure of common time.

engineer: The technician who sets up and operates the recording equipment to capture the sound during a recording session.

exclusive publishing agreement: A written contract that allows a specific music publisher to publish all works by a songwriter for a certain period of time.

external rhymes: Also known as *end rhymes,* these are rhymes that come at the end of lines.

feminine rhyme: Two-syllable end rhymes. The stressed syllable is always the first one.

genre: A type of musical style such as country, pop, rock 'n' roll, urban, rap, gospel, blues, and so on.

gospel music: Defined today mainly by its Christian lyrical content, and subject matter, this genre now encompasses practically all of the musical styles.

half note: A music note that has a length of two beats (one-half of a measure in common time).

Harry Fox Agency: A mechanical rights organization that provides an information source, clearinghouse and monitoring service for thousands of compositions, as well as payments of mechanical royalties to writers and publishers and licensing recorded work to others.

hook: The hook is the most memorable and most immediately catchy part of a song. It can be the title itself, a musical phrase, a riff, or even a sound effect. In some musical circles this term is synonymous with the title.

imagery: Those magic words and phrases in a lyric that impress images into your mind, the descriptive words that help drive home lasting impressions. Imagery is the indelible stamp of a truly great phrase.

internal rhymes: Sometimes referred to as *inner rhymes,* these are rhymes that occur within the lines of the song.

jingle: The term for the catchy succession of repetitious sounds usually rhyming, light, or humorous that has become synonymous with music for commercials.

lead: A section where a particular instrument takes a solo in a designated section to offer contrast to the lead vocal.

lead sheet: The most basic kind of sheet music where only the bars are written out with chord indications, a sketch of the melody line, some simple cues, and in some cases, lyrics.

license: An authorization (usually granted by a songwriter's publisher or administrator) to record, perform, or otherwise use a copyrighted song.

lick: A throwback phrase from the be-bop days, a lick is a phrase of generally improvised music that a musician uses as a part of his or her style.

lyricist: A person who writes words for songs.

lyrics: The words of a song, as distinguished from the music.

major key: A musical key that is based on a major scale.

manager: The person who helps the artist develop his career. The manager advises the artist on business decisions and helps promote the artist through all available means.

masculine rhyme: Where the lyrics have two end syllables that rhyme. They can be either one-syllable words or words that end in a stressed syllable.

measure: See *bar.*

mechanical license: The license that is required when someone wants to record someone else's song. Mechanical licensees are granted by song administration companies and mechanical rights organizations such as the Harry Fox Agency. Based on this license, the songwriter will then be paid for every piece of product sold, based on the prevailing statutory rate.

mechanical rights: An agreement made between an author or songwriter (usually a performer), or a publisher and a record company, giving the rights to reproduce songs in recordings.

mechanical royalties: Monetary fees that are earned from product sales and not from airplay; all the money paid to copyright owners for the manufacturing and distribution of records, CDs, DVDs, and tapes.

melody: An identifiable tune or set of notes.

metaphor: A figure of speech where one thing is likened to another thing, as if it were that other thing, for instance, "The Moon Is a Harsh Mistress" by Jimmy Webb.

meter: The flow of beats in a song defined by particular accentual patterns.

minor key: A musical key that is based on a minor scale.

music attorney: An attorney who specializes in the law relating to music.

music supervisor: The right-hand man of the director and the producer of a film when it comes to finding the right music to go with the action on the screen.

near rhyme: Also called *slant rhyme,* near rhyme is like perfect rhyme except that it's not a true rhyme — either the vowel or the last consonant will rhyme, but not both, as in perfect rhyme.

noodling: The creative experimentation at an instrument until something of substance emerges from the rubble.

octave: A standard music scale has seven notes (not including the sharps and flats) before it reaches the same note higher up — the next octave (of another seven notes).

para rhyme: Like consonance, except both of the consonants that surround the vowel are the same and the vowel is different, as in *love* and *live* or *ham* and *home.* A feminine para rhyme occurs when two-syllables are used (for example, *liver* and *lover* or *snifter* and *swifter*).

parody lyrics: A comical reinterpretation of someone else's more serious lyric.

perfect rhymes: Where rhymes consist of two or more syllables that each contains the same final vowel and consonant sound, but begin with differing consonant sounds.

performance royalties: The sums of money calculated for the songwriter (and publisher if the publisher shares ownership of the song's copyright) by the performing rights organization that he is affiliated with — ASCAP, BMI, or SESAC, every time his songs are played, on radio, television, in movie theaters, clubs or restaurants, or anywhere else in public. Payments are distributed quarterly and arrive about one year after the quarter that they were generated.

performing rights license: A contract that authorizes someone (usually radio and TV stations and networks) for the public performance of a song frequently granted by a performing rights society through a blanket license. With venues like clubs and concert halls, license fees are based factors such as maximum room occupancy, seating capacity, ticket prices, and annual entertainment expenses.

performing rights organization: An organization that monitors (and collects license fees for) all the music that is performed in public (primarily radio, television, and music venues) and makes sure that the copyright owner gets paid all royalties that are due. There are three organizations in the U.S. (and many others worldwide) that do this: BMI, ASCAP and SESAC.

personal manager: A person who guides and assists the musician or songwriter in the development and management of his music and entertainment career. See also *business manager.*

personification: When a poet or lyricist refers to a thing, quality, or idea as if it were a person.

phonorecord: Any material object used to hold sound recordings of copyrighted songs, including cassette tapes, vinyl records, and compact discs, but not audiovisual devices (such as VHS tapes or DVDs).

platinum hit: When the album, tape, and CD sells 1,000,000 copies. (Gold is 500,000 copies.)

poetry: The expressing in words of thoughts and feelings in a manner that the sounds of the words themselves create a kind of music.

pop: The most popular of all genres (hence its name). Pop(ular) music ranges from Johnny Mathis to Billy Joel to Christina Aguilera.

pre-chorus: A mini-bridge that follows the verse and sets the stage for an upcoming chorus.

progression: See *chord progression.*

prologue: An introduction written for many popular songs for the stage and screen. The prologue helped introduce the song in the context of the motion picture or play. Today, the prologue (which used to be called the *verse*, not to be confused with the other verse in this glossary) has become nearly obsolete.

public domain: A recording or composition that is free of copyright protection (due to the expiration of the song's term of copyright) and available for unrestricted use by anyone.

publisher/publishing company: Music publishing is the business of acquiring and exploiting rights in musical compositions. Music publishers often handle registration of copyrights, issue licenses, and collect royalties on behalf of the copyright owner of a song, usually the author(s).

quarter note: A note that has a length of one beat. There can be at most four of these in a measure of common time.

R&B: With initials that stand for "rhythm and blues" this ever-evolving segment of the music charts (sometimes referred to as "soul" music) started life in the African-American community during the 1940s and has adapted and updated its sound with every generation.

recording engineer: See *engineer.*

refrain: See *chorus.*

reprise: A repeat of a section.

rhyme: A regular recurrence of corresponding sounds, especially at the end of lines.

rhyme scheme: A regular sequence of rhyming that occurs at the ends of the lines of a stanza.

rhythm: A pattern of sound created by the repetition and accentuation of beats.

RIAA: The Recording Industry Association of America, an organization that represents the interests of the U.S. recording industry. The RIAA is also responsible for certifying album sales awards such as Gold and Platinum.

riff: A repeated musical phrase that is positioned throughout the song. Often a riff can serve as a "hook" in a song.

rock: A broad spectrum of styles that ranges from hard to soft (and all stops in between) that has been around since the mid-1950s. It's typified by a heavy snare drum back beat and electric guitars.

royalty: The income earned by a song and paid to the copyright owner(s). There are three principle kinds of royalties: mechanical, performance, and synchronization.

scale: A set of notes used in the creation of melodies and chords.

SESAC: The Society of European Stage Authors and Composers, the smallest of the three performing rights organizations, which operates on a for profit basis. See also *performing rights organization.*

session: The event of recording in a professional studio. Session musicians are artists that are hired to play on records, jingles, and other recordings. In musician union's parlance, a session is a unit of recording time, three hours in length.

session musician: See *sideman.*

sharp/flat: The changing of a note of music by altering its pitch. Sharpening makes the sound higher, flattening lower.

sideman: A professional musician hired to perform or record with a group of which he is not formally a member.

simile: The figure of speech used in poetry and lyrics where one thing is compared to a dissimilar thing by the use of *like* or *as.* "Love Is Like An Itching in My Heart" by the Supremes is a good example, as is "Your Love Is Like Oxygen" by Sweet.

singer/songwriter: A singer who also writes some, if not all, of the songs he sings.

sixteenth note: A music note that has a length of one-quarter of a beat. There can be at most four of these in a beat of common time.

slant rhyme: See *near rhyme.*

song form: The manner in which a song is divided into sections.

song plugger: Someone hired to find artists to record your songs that usually get paid on a monthly basis or on a percentage of publishing based on songs they get cut.

songwriter: Someone instrumental in the creation of a song, whether she specializes in words, music, or a combination of the two.

standards: The great songs that refuse to die especially associated with the classics written in the first half of the twentieth century.

stanza: See *verse.*

synch rights: The right granted by copyright owners allowing a song to be recorded on a soundtrack (or to be used as background music) for television or a motion pictures production. The onscreen images are often synchronized with the song, thus the phrase synchronization (or synch) rights.

synchronization license: When authorization is granted by a music publisher or songwriter to use a song with visual images (as in a motion picture or television program).

term of copyright: The amount of time for which a copyright is in effect. The current term for songs written after 1978 is the life of the longest-living songwriting partner, plus 70 years.

triple rhyme: Lines with three-syllable end rhymes.

unstressed rhyme: A feminine rhyme with a non-rhyming first syllable, and a second, unstressed, syllable that is the same in both words (for example, "Boy you know your love's my one true *weakness*/When it comes to you I'm *helpless*").

venue: A place where live music is performed, including coffee shops, taverns, nightclubs, theaters, major arenas, and so on.

verse: A set of lines of lyric, also called a *stanza.* The verse in a song is a single section of that song that is usually repeated using the same, or nearly the same, melody throughout the song, but with different words. In songs from the heyday of Broadway musicals, the verse describes the introductory section of a song.

verse-chorus form: A type of song form that is very popular today where verses alternate with a chorus.

vocal: The singing part of a song. There are lead vocals, in which the singer sings the melody and background vocals, which refer to the accompanying harmony.

whole note: A music note that has a length of four beats. It lasts for a whole measure in common time, hence its name.

writers' nights: An intimate club-type gathering where you can interact with songwriting associates, watch or perform new songs live, pick up industry tips, and network with new friends.

Index

Notes

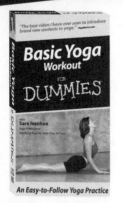

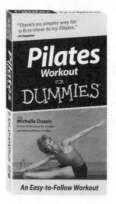
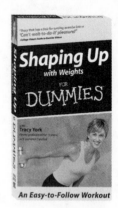

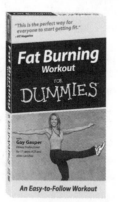
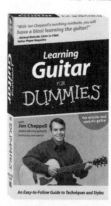

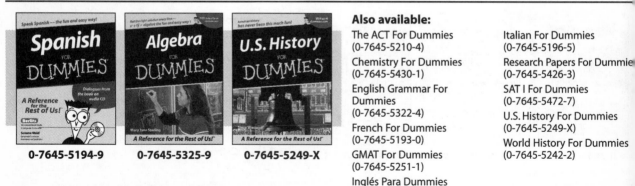

FOR DUMMIES®

Plain-English solutions for everyday challenges

HOME & BUSINESS COMPUTER BASICS

0-7645-0838-5

0-7645-1663-9

0-7645-1548-9

INTERNET & DIGITAL MEDIA

0-7645-0894-6

0-7645-1642-6

0-7645-1664-7

Get smart! Visit www.dummies.com

- **Find listings of even more Dummies titles**
- **Browse online articles, excerpts, and how-to's**
- **Sign up for daily or weekly e-mail tips**
- **Check out Dummies fitness videos and other products**
- **Order from our online bookstore**